The Holiest of All

The Holiest of All

*An Exposition of the Epistle
to the Hebrews*

Andrew Murray

ABRIDGED EDITION

Foreword by Gloria Copeland

Kenneth Copeland Ministries
Fort Worth, Texas 76192

Retypeset edition © 1993
by Baker Book House Company

Abridgement of retypeset edition
published by Kenneth Copeland Ministries
Fort Worth, TX 76192
Product no.: 30–0811

Published through special arrangement with Baker Books
a division of Baker Book House Company
P.O. Box 6287, Grand Rapids, MI 49516-6287

Second printing, September 1997

Printed in the United States of America

ISBN: 0-8010-5763-9

Foreword

The *Holiest of All* has added a wonderful dimension to my life. It has so stirred me to go on with God. It has increased my desire and determination to enter into His holy presence in a greater measure than ever before.

Though this is an old book that I've had a long time, I've just discovered it! It ministered to me so much, that as soon as I finished the final chapter, I began to read it again.

Andrew Murray has been a blessing to me for many years. His consecration and dedication to God inspire me. I have received so much from *The Holiest of All,* that I want to share it with as many people as possible. I recommend that as you read this powerful book, you go slowly and thoroughly, allowing it to settle in your heart. Even if you can read only a chapter a day without hurrying through it, take your time (the chapters are only three or four pages.)

As you do, *The Holiest of All* will inspire you with the same hunger and desire that it has me—to go on with God and lay aside every weight that would hold me back from enjoying God's very best for me. God wants us to enjoy our full salvation! Jesus said, I have come that you might have and enjoy life (John 10:10b, *The Amplified Bible*).

As we prepared this abridged edition of *The Holiest of All,* I requested to delete three chapters and one paragraph from the original text, because they centered on suffering being the will of God. (There are still a few references to this, but not many.) This was the prevalent thinking when Andrew Murray first published the book in 1894. Even today many are still held captive by this belief. One of the most effective strategies of Satan within the Church is to convince people that God causes bad things to come into their lives.

If Satan can make you believe that God is your problem, then there is no way you can go to God in faith for your deliverance. It puts you in a state of non-resistance and therefore allows Satan to continue to steal, kill and destroy (John 10:10a). Thank God, Jesus came that we might have life and that we might have it more abundantly. As though to make sure we get it, in the next verse Jesus says, "I am the good shepherd."

Light has come to the Church through the years, and we have more understanding from God's Word concerning the events and circumstances of life. We recognize that we have an enemy and his name is Satan. Our adversary is still trying to stop God from executing His great and wonderful plan of salvation[a] for man—His family.

The Bible teaches us that we are to resist Satan and give him no place (James 4:7). We also understand that we open the door to evil by disobedience, ignorance and failure to believe and act on God's Word.

The revelation that Andrew Murray's generation walked in, that the Church lacks today, is holiness and consecration. We can receive so much from this great man of God and increase our understanding and desire of absolute dedication to the Father.

I believe Jesus is coming soon. We must separate ourselves unto God for this mighty end time move of God (2 Timothy 2:19–22). I believe that *The Holiest of All* will energize you with great desire to go forward.

Gloria Copeland

The following Scripture verses expose the truth of God's Word regarding His will for our good, and for our well-being:

---

a. Salvation: denotes deliverance, preservation; material and temporal deliverance from danger and apprehension (fear); pardon, protection, liberty, health, restoration, soundness, wholeness.

Psalm 145:8–9: *The Lord is gracious, and full of compassion; slow to anger, and of great mercy. The Lord is good to all: and his tender mercies are over all his works.*

James 1:16–17: *Do not err, my beloved brethren. Every good gift and every perfect gift is from above, and cometh down from the Father of lights, with whom is no variableness, neither shadow of turning.*

Acts 10:38: *How God anointed Jesus of Nazareth with the Holy Ghost and with power: who went about doing good, and healing all that were oppressed of the devil; for God was with him.*

Galatians 1:3–4: *Grace be to you and peace from God the Father, and from our Lord Jesus Christ, Who gave himself for our sins, that he might deliver us from this present evil world, according to the will of God and our Father.*

Galatians 3:13: *Christ hath redeemed us from the curse of the law, being made a curse for us: for it is written, Cursed is every one that hangeth on a tree.* (Read the blessing and the curse in Deuteronomy 28.)

Editors' Foreword

When you think of Andrew Murray, you think of his outstanding books on prayer and the deeper life. His *With Christ in the School of Prayer* and *Abide in Christ* have become Christian classics.

Murray, a Dutch Reformed pastor who ministered a hundred years ago in South Africa, was also popular as a conference speaker in the United States, Canada, and the British Isles.

Whatever he wrote glowed with the radiance of the Lord and reflected his close walk with God. This is just as true in this exposition of the Epistle to the Hebrews as it is in any of his other writings.

Originally prepared in Dutch for Christian people of South Africa, *The Holiest of All* has gone through numerous editions since its first publication in 1894. It is both a commentary of this important New Testament Epistle and a devotional book. These pages present an intimate and insightful study of every chapter of the epistle. Throughout the book, Murray reveals Jesus Christ as the fulfillment of Old Testament symbol and prophecy.

Andrew Murray was born to Scottish parents in South Africa in 1828. Sent to Scotland for his education, he and his brother graduated from Marischal College, Aberdeen. He continued his theological studies at Utrecht University in Holland, before being ordained and returning to South Africa when barely twenty years old.

He served as a missionary to the Transvaal and the Orange Free State before an attack of malaria weakened his health. Later he was part of the revival movement that swept the United States, Great Britain, and South Africa and began writing those gems of devotional literature through which he became beloved around the world.

The Editors of Fleming H. Revell

Preface

When first I undertook the preparation of this exposition in Dutch for the Christian people among whom I labour, it was under a deep conviction that the Epistle just contained the instruction they needed. In reproducing it in English, this impression has been confirmed, and it is as if nothing could be written more exactly suited to the state of the whole Church of Christ in the present day. The great complaint of all who have the care of souls is the lack of whole-heartedness, of stedfastness, of perseverance and progress in the Christian life. Many, of whom one cannot but hope that they are true Christians, come to a stand-still, and do not advance beyond the rudiments of Christian life and practice. And many more do not even remain stationary, but turn back to a life of worldliness, of formality, of indifference. And the question is continually being asked, What is the want in our religion that, in so many cases, it gives no power to stand, to advance, to press on unto perfection? And what is the teaching that is needed to give that health and vigour to the Christian life that, through all adverse circumstances, it may be able to hold fast the beginning firm to the end.

The teaching of the Epistle is the divine answer to these questions. In every possible way it sets before us the truth that it is only the full and perfect knowledge of what Christ is and does for us that can bring us to a full and perfect Christian life. The knowledge of Christ Jesus that we need for conversion does not suffice for growth, for progress, for sanctification, for maturity. Just as there are two dispensations, the Old Testament and the New, and the saints of the Old, with all their faith and fear of God, could not obtain the more perfect life of the New, so with the two stages in the Christian life of which the Epistle speaks. Those who, through sloth, remain babes in Christ, and do not press on to maturity, are ever in danger of hardening their heart, of coming short and falling away. Only those who hold fast the beginning firm to the end, who give diligence to enter the rest, who press on unto perfection, do in very deed inherit and enjoy the wonderful new covenant blessings secured to us in Christ. And the great object of the Epistle is to show us that if we will but follow the Lord fully, and yield ourselves wholly to what God in Christ is ready to do, we shall find in the gospel and in Christ everything that we need for a life of joy and strength and final victory.

The cure the Epistle has for all our failures and feebleness, the one preservative from all danger and disease, is—the knowledge of the higher truth concerning Jesus, the knowledge of Him in His heavenly priesthood. In connection with this truth, the writer has three great mysteries he seeks to unfold. The one is that the heavenly sanctuary has been opened to us, so that we may now come and take our place there, with Jesus in the very presence of God. The second, that the new and living way by which Jesus has entered, the way of self-sacrifice and perfect obedience to God, is the way in which we now may and must draw nigh. The third, that Jesus, as our heavenly High Priest, is the minister of the heavenly sanctuary, and dispenses to us its blessings, the spirit and the power of the heavenly life, in such a way that we can live in the world as those who are come to the heavenly Jerusalem, and in whom the spirit of heaven is the spirit of all their life and conduct; the heavenly priesthood of Jesus, heaven opened to us day by day, our entering it by the new and living way, and heaven entering us by the Holy Spirit. Such is the gospel to the Hebrews the Epistle brings, such is the life to which it reveals the way and the strength. The knowledge of the heavenly character of Christ's person and work is what alone can make heavenly Christians, who, amid all the difficulties and temptations of life on earth, can live as those whom the superior power of the upper world has possessed, and in whom it can always give the victory.

In offering these meditations now to a wider circle of readers, I do so with the prayer that it may please God to use them to inspire some of His children with new confidence in their blessed Lord, as they learn to know Him better and give themselves up to expect and experience all that He is able to do for them. I have not been afraid of continually repeating the one thought: *Our one need is to know Jesus better;* the one cure for all our feebleness, to look to Him on the throne of heaven, and really claim the heavenly life He waits to impart.

Just as I was about the write the Preface to the Dutch issue, in the first week of last year, I received from my beloved colleague as a New Year's text, with the wish that it might be my experience, the words: "Jesus taketh *with Him* Peter and James and John, and bringeth them into a *high mountain, apart by themselves,* and *He was transfigured* before them." I at once passed the word on to my readers, and I do so again. May the blessed Master take us *with Himself* into the *high mountain,* even the Mount Sion, where He sits as Priest-King upon the throne in power, each of us *apart by himself,* and prepare us for the blessed vision of seeing Him *transfigured before us,* seeing Him in His heavenly glory. He will then still be to us the same Jesus we know now. And yet not the same; but His whole Being, bright with the glory and the power of the heavenly life which He holds for us, and waits to impart day by day to them who forsake all to follow Him.

In humble trust and prayer that it may be so, I commend all my readers to His blessed teaching and guidance.

Andrew Murray

13th September 1894

Contents

Contents

14

Contents

15

Contents

16

The Epistle to the Hebrews

The Knowledge of the Son of God the Strength of the Christian Life

FIRST HALF—DOCTRINAL—Chap. i.–x. 18
The Son of God the Mediator of the Better Covenant
Chapter I.
THE THEME—i. 1–3
The Glory of the Son in His Person and Work

God, having of old time spoken unto the fathers in the prophets by divers portions and in divers manners,

2 Hath at the end of these days spoken unto us in *his* Son, whom he appointed heir of all things, through whom also he made the worlds;

3 Who being the effulgence of his glory, and the very image of his substance, and upholding all things by the word of his power, when he had made purification of sins, sat down on the right hand of the Majesty on high;[a]

FIRST SECTION—i. 4–14
The Son of God More Than the Angels

The Son—a More Excellent Name

4 Having become by so much better[b] than the angels, as he hath inherited a more excellent name than they.

The Son—the Only Begotten

5 For unto which of the angels said he at any time, Thou art my Son, this day have I begotten thee? And again, I will be to him a Father, and he shall be to me a Son?

6 And when he again bringeth in the firstborn[c] into the world he saith, And let all the angels of God worship him.

7 And of the angels he saith, Who maketh his angels winds, and his ministers a flame of fire:

---

a. Ch. 2. 9; 4. 14; 6. 20; 7. 16, 25, 28; 8. 1; 9. 12, 24; 10. 12; 12. 3, 24, 25.
b. Ch. 1. 4; 6. 9; 7. 7, 19, 22; 8. 6; 9. 23; 10. 34; 11. 16, 35, 40; 12. 24.
c. Rom. 8. 29; Col. 1. 18; Rev. 1. 5.

17

The Son Himself God

8 But of the Son *he saith,* Thy throne, O God, is for ever and ever; and the sceptre of uprightness is the sceptre of thy kingdom.

9 Thou hast loved righteousness, and hated iniquity; therefore God, thy God, hath anointed thee with the oil of gladness above thy fellows.

The Son—the Everlasting Creator

10 And, Thou, Lord, in the beginning hast laid the foundation of the earth, and the heavens are the works of thy hands:

11 They shall perish; but thou continuest: and they all shall wax old as doth a garment;

12 And as a mantle shalt thou roll them up, as a garment, and they shall be changed: but thou art the same, and thy years shall not fail.

The Son—on the Right Hand of God

13 But of which of the angels hath he said at any time, Sit thou on my right hand, till I make thine enemies the footstool of thy feet?

14 Are they not all ministering spirits, sent forth to do service for the sake of them that shall inherit salvation?

Chapter II.

THE FIRST WARNING

Chap. ii. 1–4

To Take Heed to What the Son Speaks (1–4)

Therefore we ought to give the more earnest heed to the things that were heard,[a] lest haply we drift away *from them.*

2 For if the word spoken through angels proved stedfast, and every transgression and disobedience received a just recompense of reward;

3 How shall we escape if we neglect so great salvation? which having at the first been spoken through the Lord, was confirmed unto us by them that heard;

4 God also bearing witness with them, both by signs and wonders, and by manifold powers, and by gifts of the Holy Ghost, according to his own will.

SECOND SECTION—ii. 5–18

Jesus as Man More Than the Angels
The Reason of His Humiliation

All Things Made Subject to Man, Not to Angels

5 For not unto angels did he subject the world to come, whereof we speak.

a. Ch. 1. 1, 2; 3. 7, 19; 4. 2, 11; 5. 11; 6. 5; 10. 26, 39; 12. 25.

6 But one hath somewhere testified, saying, What is man, that thou art mindful of him? or the son of man, that thou visitest him?

7 Thou madest him a little lower than the angels; thou crownedst him with glory and honour, and didst set him over the works of thy hands:

8 Thou didst put all things in subjection under his feet. For in that he subjected all things unto him, he left nothing that is not subject to him. But now we see not yet all things subjected to him.

Man's Destiny Fulfilled in Jesus

9 But we behold him who hath been made a little lower than the angels, *even* Jesus, because of the suffering of death **crowned with glory and honour,** that by the grace of God he should taste death for every *man*.

The Reasons for the Humiliation of Jesus—

10 For it became him, for whom are all things, and through whom are all things, in bringing many sons unto glory, to make the author[a] of their salvation perfect through sufferings.

1. His Being Made Perfect as Our Leader

11 For both he that sanctifieth[b] and they that are sanctified are all of one; for which cause he is not ashamed to call them brethren,

12 Saying, I will declare thy name unto my brethren, in the midst of the congregation will I sing thy praise.

13 And again, I will put my trust in him. And again, Behold, I and the children which God hath given me.

2. Our Deliverance from the Power of the Devil

14 Since then the children are sharers in flesh and blood, he also himself in like manner partook of the same; that through death he might bring to nought him that had the power of death, that is, the devil;

15 And might deliver all them who through fear of death were all their lifetime subject to bondage.

3. That He Might Become a Merciful High Priest

16 For verily not of angels doth he take hold, but he taketh hold of the seed of Abraham.

17 Wherefore it behoved him in all things to be made like unto his brethren[c] that he might be a merciful and faithful high priest in things pertaining to God, to make propitiation for the sins of the people.

18 For in that he himself hath suffered being tempted, he is able to succour them that are tempted.

a. Ch. 6. 19; 12. 2; 13. 13.
b. Ch. 3. 1; 6. 10; 8. 2; 9. 8, 12, 13; 10. 10, 14, 19, 29; 12. 10, 14, 16; 13. 12.
c. Ch 2.14; 4.15; 5.2, 3; 10.5, 7; 12.2; 13.13.

Chapter III.
THIRD SECTION—iii. 1–6
Christ Jesus More Than Moses

Christ Faithful As Moses

Wherefore, holy brethren, partakers of a heavenly calling,[a] consider the Apostle and High Priest of our confession,[b] *even* Jesus;

2 Who was faithful to him that appointed him, as also was Moses in all his house.

Christ the Son, More Than Moses, the Servant

3 For he hath been counted worthy of more glory than Moses, by so much as he that built the house hath more honour than the house.

4 For every house is builded by some one; but he that built all things is God.

5 And Moses indeed was faithful in all his house as a servant, for a testimony of those things which were afterward to be spoken;

6 But Christ as a son, over his house; whose house are we, if we hold fast our boldness[c] and the glorying of our hope[d] firm unto the end.[e]

THE SECOND WARNING
Chap. iii. 7–iv. 13
Not to Come Short of the Promised Rest

How Israel Failed

7 Wherefore, even as the Holy Ghost saith, Today if ye shall hear his voice,

8 Harden not your hearts, as in the provocation, like as in the day of the temptation in the wilderness,

9 Wherewith your fathers tempted *me* by proving *me,* and saw my works forty years.

10 Wherefore I was displeased with this generation, and said, They do alway err in their heart: but they did not know my ways;

11 As I sware in my wrath, They shall not enter into my rest.

The Need of Perseverance

12 Take heed, brethren, lest haply there shall be in any one of you an evil heart[f] of unbelief, in falling away from the living God:[g]

a. Ch. 1. 3; 8. 1.
b. Ch. 4. 14; 10. 23; 11. 13; 13. 15.
c. Ch. 4. 16; 6. 18; 10. 19, 35; 13. 6.
d. Ch. 6. 11, 18; 7. 19; 10. 23; 11. 1.
e. Ch. 3. 14; 4. 14; 5. 12, 14; 6. 18, 19; 9. 17; 10. 23; 11. 27; 12. 28.
f. Ch. 3. 12.
g. Ch. 9. 14; 10. 31; 12. 22.

13 But exhort one another day by day, so long as it is called Today; lest any one of you be hardened by the deceitfulness of sin:

14 For we are become partakers of Christ, if we hold fast the beginning of our confidence firm unto the end:

15 While it is said, Today if ye shall hear his voice, harden not your hearts, as in the provocation.

Israel's Unbelief and Disobedience

16 For who, when they heard, did provoke? nay, did not all they that came out of Egypt by Moses?

17 And with whom was he displeased forty years? was it not with them that sinned, whose carcases fell in the wilderness?

18 And to whom sware he that they should not enter into his rest, but to them that were disobedient?

19 And we see that they were not able to enter in because of unbelief.

Chapter IV.

By Faith We Enter the Rest

Let us fear therefore, lest haply, a promise being left of entering into his rest, any one of you should seem to have come short of it.

2 For indeed we have had good tidings preached unto us, even as also they: but the word of hearing did not profit them, because they were not united by faith with them that heard.

3 For we which have believed do enter into that rest; even as he hath said, As I sware in my wrath, they shall not enter into my rest: although the works were finished from the foundation of the world.

Joshua Did Not Bring the People into the Rest of God

4 For he hath said somewhere of the seventh *day* on this wise, And God rested on the seventh day from all his works;

5 And in this *place* again, They shall not enter into my rest.

6 Seeing therefore it remaineth that some should enter thereinto, and they to whom the good tidings were before preached failed to enter in because of disobedience,

7 He again defineth a certain day, saying in David, after so long a time, To-day, as it hath been before said, Today if ye shall hear his voice, Harden not your hearts.

8 For if Joshua had given them rest, he would not have spoken afterward of another day.

9 There remaineth therefore a Sabbath rest for the people of God.

Let Us Enter into the Rest

10 For he that is entered into his rest hath himself also rested from his works, as God did from his.

11 Let us therefore give diligence to enter into that rest, that no man fall after the same example of disobedience.

The Power of God's Word to Judge Us

12 For the word of God[a] is living, and active, and sharper than any two-edged sword, and piercing even to the dividing of soul and spirit, of both joints and marrow, and quick to discern the thoughts and intents of the heart.

13 And there is no creature that is not manifest in his sight: but all things are naked and laid open before the eyes of him with whom we have to do.

FOURTH SECTION—iv. 14–v. 10

Jesus Our High Priest More Than Aaron

Jesus the Great and Sympathising High Priest

14 Having then a great high priest, who hath passed through the heavens, Jesus the Son of God, let us hold fast our confession.

15 For we have not a high priest that cannot be touched with the feeling of our infirmities; but one that hath been in all points tempted like as *we are, yet* without sin.

16 Let us therefore draw near with boldness unto the throne of grace, that we may receive mercy and may find grace to help *us* in time of need.

Chapter V.

A High Priest Must Have Compassion

For every high priest, being taken from among men, is appointed for men in things pertaining to God, that he may offer[b] both gifts and sacrifices for sins:

2 Who can bear gently with the ignorant and erring, for that he himself also is compassed with infirmity;

3 And by reason thereof is bound, as for the people, as also for himself, to offer for sins.

A High Priest Must Be Appointed of God

4 And no man taketh the honour unto himself, but when he is called of God, even as was Aaron.

5 So Christ also glorified not himself to be made a high priest, but he that spake unto him, Thou art my Son, This day have I begotten thee:

a. Ch. 2. 2; 3. 18, 19; 4. 11; 5. 11; 6. 5, 6; 11. 26, 28, 38, 39; 12. 25.
b. Ch. 5. 7; 8. 3; 9. 7, 9, 14, 23, 25, 26, 28; 10. 1, 2, 5, 6, 8, 10, 12, 14, 18, 26.

6 As he saith also in another *place,* Thou art a priest for ever after the order of Melchizedek.

Jesus Our High Priest Perfected Through Obedience

7 Who in the days of his flesh, having offered up prayers and supplications with strong crying and tears unto him that was able to save him from death, and having been heard for his godly fear,

8 Though he was a Son, yet learned obedience by the things which he suffered;

9 And having been made perfect, he became unto all them that obey him the author of eternal salvation;

10 Named of God a high priest after the order of Melchizedek.

The Third Warning
Chap. v. 11–vi. 20
Against Sloth and Apostasy

The Difference Between the Slothful and the Perfect

11 Of whom we have many things to say, and hard of interpretation, seeing ye are become dull of hearing.[a]

12 For when by reason of the time ye ought to be teachers, ye have need again that some one teach you the rudiments of the first principles of the oracles of God; and are become such as have need of milk, and not of solid food.

13 For every one that partaketh of milk is without experience of the word of righteousness; for he is a babe.

14 But solid food is for full-grown[b] men, *even* those who by reason of use have their senses exercised to discern good and evil.

Chapter VI.

The Need of Pressing on to Perfection

Wherefore let us cease to speak of the first principles[c] of Christ, and press on unto perfection; not laying again a foundation of repentance from dead works,[d] and of faith toward God,

2 Of the teaching of baptisms, and of laying on of hands, and of resurrection of the dead, and of eternal judgment.

3 And this will we do, if God permit.

---

a. Ch. 6. 12; 12. 12.
b. Ch. 2. 10; 5. 9, 14; 6. 1; 7. 28; 9. 9; 10. 1, 9, 14; 11. 40; 12. 23; 13. 21.
c. Ch. 3. 14; 5. 12.
d. Ch. 9. 14.

No Hope for the Apostate

4 For as touching those who were once enlightened and tasted of the heavenly gift, and were made partakers of the Holy Ghost,

5 And tasted the good word of God, and the powers of the age to come,

6 And *then* fell away, it is impossible to renew them again unto repentance; seeing they crucify to themselves the Son of God afresh, and put him to an open shame.[a]

7 For the land which hath drunk the rain that cometh oft upon it, and bringeth forth herbs meet for them for whose sake it is also tilled, receiveth blessing from God:

8 But if it beareth thorns and thistles, it is rejected and nigh unto a curse; whose end is to be burned.

Encouragement to Perseverance

9 But, beloved, we are persuaded better things of you, and things that accompany salvation, though we thus speak:

10 For God is not unrighteous to forget your work and the love which ye showed toward his name, in that ye ministered unto the saints, and still do minister.

11 And we desire that each one of you may shew the same diligence unto the fulness[b] of hope even to the end:

12 That ye be not sluggish, but imitators of them who through faith and patience inherit the promises.[c]

Our Hope in the Faithfulness of God

13 For when God made promise to Abraham, since he could swear by none greater, he sware by himself,

14 Saying, Surely blessing I will bless thee, and multiplying I will multiply thee.

15 And thus, having patiently endured, he obtained the promise.[d]

16 For men swear[e] by the greater: and in every dispute of theirs the oath is final for confirmation.

17 Wherein God, being minded to shew more abundantly unto the heirs of the promise the immutability of his counsel, interposed with an oath:

18 That by two immutable things, in which it is impossible for God to lie, we may have a strong encouragement, who have fled for refuge to lay hold of the hope set before us;

a. Ch. 10. 26, 29, 39; 12. 17.
b. Ch. 10. 22.
c. Ch. 6. 17; 9. 15; 11. 7, 8; 12. 17.
d. Ch. 11. 13, 33, 39.
e. Ch. 3. 11; 7. 21.

19 Which we have as an anchor of the soul, *a hope* both sure and stedfast and entering into that which is within the veil;

20 Whither as a fore-runner Jesus entered for us, having become a high priest for ever after the order of Melchizedek.

Chapter VII.

FIFTH SECTION

The New Priesthood after the Order of Melchizedek

Melchizedek Made Like to the Son of God

For this Melchizedek, king of Salem, priest of God Most High, who met Abraham returning from the slaughter of the kings, and blessed him,

2 To whom also Abraham divided a tenth part of all (being first, by interpretation, King of righteousness, and then also King of Salem, which is, King of peace;

3 Without father, without mother, without genealogy, having neither beginning of days nor end of life, but made like unto the Son of God), abideth a priest continually.

Melchizedek More Than Abraham

4 Now consider how great this man was, unto whom Abraham, the patriarch, gave a tenth out of the chief spoils.

5 And they indeed of the sons of Levi that receive the priest's office have commandment to take tithes of the people according to the law, that is, of their brethren, though these have come out of the loins of Abraham:

6 But he whose genealogy is not counted from them hath taken tithes of Abraham, and hath blessed him that hath the promises.

7 But without any dispute the less is blessed of the better.

Melchizedek More Than Levi

8 And here men that die receive tithes; but there one, of whom it is witnessed that he liveth.

9 And, so to say, through Abraham even Levi, who receiveth tithes, hath paid tithes;

10 For he was yet in the loins of his father, when Melchizedek met him.

The New Priesthood Sets Aside the Order of Aaron

11 Now if there was perfection through the Levitical priesthood (for under it hath the people received the law), what further need *was there* that another priest should arise after the order of Melchizedek, and not be reckoned after the order of Aaron?

12 For the priesthood being changed, there is made of necessity a change also of the law.

13 For he of whom these things are said belongeth to another tribe, from which no man hath given attendance at the altar.

14 For it is evident that our Lord hath sprung out of Judah; as to which tribe Moses spake nothing concerning priests.

The New Priesthood after the Power of the Endless Life

15 And *what we say* is yet more abundantly evident, if after the likeness of Melchizedek there ariseth another priest,

16 Who hath been made, not after the law of a carnal commandment, but after the power of an endless life:

17 For it is witnessed *of him,* Thou art a priest for ever after the order of Melchizedek.

18 For there is a disannulling of a foregoing commandment because of its weakness and unprofitableness.[a]

19 (For the law made nothing perfect), and a bringing in thereupon of a better hope, through which we draw nigh unto God.[b]

The New Priesthood Appointed by the Oath of God

20 And inasmuch as *it is* not without the taking of an oath.

21 (For they indeed have been made priests without an oath; but he with an oath by him that saith of him, The Lord sware and will not repent himself, Thou art a priest for ever);

22 By so much also hath Jesus become the surety of a better covenant.

As an Eternal Priesthood It Brings a Complete Salvation

23 And they indeed have been made priests many in number, because that by death they are hindered from continuing:

24 But he, because he abideth for ever, hath his priesthood unchangeable.[c]

25 Wherefore also he is able to save to the uttermost them that draw near unto God through him, seeing he ever liveth to make intercession for them.

Our High Priest the Son Perfected for Ever

26 For such a high priest became us, holy, guileless, undefiled, separated from sinners, and made higher than the heavens;

27 Who needeth not daily, like those high priests, to offer up sacrifices, first for his own sins, and then for the *sins* of the people: for this he did once[d] for all, when he offered up himself.

28 For the law appointeth men high priests, having infirmity; but the word of the oath, which was after the law, *appointeth* a Son, perfected for evermore.

a. Ch. 8. 13; 10. 9; 12. 18.
b. Ch. 4. 16; 7. 25; 9. 8, 14; 10. 1, 19; 12. 22.
c. Ch. 1. 8; 5. 6, 9; 6. 20; 7. 17, 21, 24, 25, 28; 9. 12, 14, 15; 10. 14, 15; 13. 8, 21.
d. Ch. 9. 12, 26, 28; 10. 10, 12, 14.

Chapter VIII.

SIXTH SECTION—viii. 1–13

The New Sanctuary and the New Covenant

The High Priest on the Throne

Now in the things which we are saying the chief point is this: We have such a high priest, who sat down on the right hand of the throne of the Majesty in the heavens,[a]

A Minister of the True Sanctuary

2 A minister of the sanctuary, and of the true tabernacle, which the Lord pitched, not man.

3 For every high priest is appointed to offer both gifts and sacrifices: wherefore it is necessary that this *high priest* also have somewhat to offer.

4 Now if he were on earth, he would not be a priest at all, seeing there are those who offer the gifts according to the law;

5 Who serve *that which* is a copy and shadow of the heavenly things, even as Moses is warned *of God* when he is about to make the tabernacle: for, See, saith he, that thou make all things according to the pattern that was shewed thee in the mount.

The Mediator of the New Covenant

6 But now hath he obtained a ministry the more excellent, by how much also he is the mediator of a better covenant, which hath been enacted upon better promises.

7 For if that first *covenant* had been faultless, then would no place have been sought for a second.

8 For finding fault with them, he saith, Behold, the days come, saith the Lord, that I will make a new covenant with the house of Israel and with the house of Judah;

9 Not according to the covenant that I made with their fathers in the day that I took them by the hand to lead them forth out of the land of Egypt; for they continued not in my covenant, and I regarded them not, saith the Lord.

The Blessings of the New Covenant

10 For this is the covenant that I will make with the house of Israel after those days, saith the Lord; I will put my laws into their mind, and on their heart[b] also will I write them: and I will be to them a God, and they shall be to me a people:

---

a. Ch. 1. 3; 2. 9; 4. 14; 6. 20; 7. 16, 25, 26; 8. 5; 9. 12, 23, 24; 10. 12; 12. 3, 22, 24, 25.

b. Ch. 3. 8, 10, 12; 10. 22; 13. 9.

27

11 And they shall not teach every man his fellow-citizen, and every man his brother, saying, Know the Lord: for all shall know me, from the least to the greatest of them.

12 For I will be merciful to their iniquities, and their sins will I remember no more.

13 In that he saith, A new *covenant,* he hath made the first old. But that which is becoming old and waxeth aged is nigh unto vanishing away.

Chapter IX.

SEVENTH SECTION—ix. 1–28

The Power of Jesus's Blood to Inaugurate the New Sanctuary and the New Covenant

The Holy Place and the Most Holy

Now even the first *covenant* had ordinances of divine service, and its sanctuary, *a sanctuary* of this world.

2 For there was a tabernacle prepared, the first, wherein *were* the candlestick, and the table, and the shew-bread; which is called the Holy place.

3 And after the second veil, the tabernacle which is called the Holy of holies;

4 Having a golden censer, and the ark of the covenant overlaid round about with gold, wherein *was* a golden pot holding the manna, and Aaron's rod that budded, and the tables of the covenant;

5 And above it cherubim of glory overshadowing the mercy-seat; of which things we cannot now speak severally.

The Way into the Holiest Not Yet Opened

6 Now these things having been thus prepared, the priests go in continually into the first tabernacle, accomplishing the services;

7 But into the second the high priest alone, once in the year, not without blood, which he offereth for himself, and for the errors of the people:

8 The Holy Ghost this signifying, that the way into the holy place[a] hath not yet been made manifest, while as the first tabernacle is yet standing;

9 Which is a parable for the time *now* present; according to which are offered both gifts and sacrifices that cannot, as touching the conscience, make the worshipper perfect,

10 *Being* only (with meats and drinks and divers washings) carnal ordinances, imposed until a time of reformation.

a. Ch. 9. 12, 24; 10. 19, 22; 12. 22.

Christ, Through His Own Blood, Openeth the Holiest

11 But Christ having come a high priest of the good things to come, through the greater and more perfect tabernacle, not made with hands, that is to say, not of this creation,

12 Nor yet through the blood of goats and calves, but through his own blood,[a] entered in once for all into the holy place, having obtained eternal redemption.

The Blood Cleansing Our Conscience

13 For if the blood of goats and bulls, and the ashes of a heifer sprinkling them that have been defiled, sanctify unto the cleanness of the flesh:

14 How much more shall the blood of Christ, who through the eternal Spirit, offered himself without blemish unto God, cleanse your conscience from dead works to serve the living God?

The Death of the Mediator of the New Covenant

15 And for this cause he is the mediator of a new covenant, that a death having taken place for the redemption of the transgressions that were under the first covenant, they that have been called may receive the promise of the eternal inheritance.

16 For where a testament is, there must of necessity be the death of him that made it.

17 For a testament is of force where there hath been death: for doth it ever avail while he that made it liveth?

The Old Covenant Dedicated with Blood

18 Wherefore even the first *covenant* hath not been dedicated without blood.

19 For when every commandment had been spoken by Moses unto all the people according to the law, he took the blood of the calves and the goats, with water and scarlet wool and hyssop, and sprinkled both the book itself, and all the people,

20 Saying, This is the blood of the covenant which God commanded to you-ward.

21 Moreover the tabernacle and all the vessels of the ministry he sprinkled in like manner with the blood.

22 And according to the law, I may almost say, all things are cleansed with blood, and apart from shedding of blood there is no remission.

a. Ch. 9. 14, 20; 10. 19, 22, 29; 11. 28; 12. 24; 13. 12, 20.

The Better Sacrifice Has Opened Heaven Itself

23 It was necessary therefore that the copies of the things in the heavens should be cleansed with these; but the heavenly things themselves with better sacrifices than these.

24 For Christ entered not into a holy place made with hands, like in pattern to the true; but into heaven itself, now to appear before the face of God for us:

Christ Once Offered to Put Away Sin

25 Nor yet that he should offer himself often; as the high priest entereth into the holy place year by year with blood not his own;

26 Else must he often have suffered since the foundation of the world: but now once at the end of the ages hath he been manifested to put away sin by the sacrifice of himself.

27 And inasmuch as it is appointed unto men once to die, and after this *cometh* judgment;

28 So Christ also, having been once offered to bear the sins of many, shall appear a second time apart from sin, to them that wait for him, unto salvation.

Chapter X.

EIGHTH SECTION—x. 1–18

The Infinite Value of Christ's Sacrifice

The Law Only a Shadow of Good Things to Come

For the law having a shadow of the good *things* to come, not the very image of the things, they can never with the same sacrifices year by year, which they offer continually, make perfect them that draw nigh.

2 Else would they not have ceased to be offered, because the worshippers, having been once cleansed, would have had no more conscience of sins?

3 But in those *sacrifices* there is a remembrance made of sins year by year.

4 For it is impossible that the blood of bulls and goats should take away sins.

The Doing of God's Will, the Value of Christ's Sacrifice

5 Wherefore when he cometh into the world, he saith, Sacrifice and offering thou wouldest not, but a body didst thou prepare for me;

6 In whole burnt offerings and *sacrifices* for sin thou hadst no pleasure:

7 Then said I, Lo, I am come (in the roll of the book it is written of me) To do thy will, O God.

8 Saying above, Sacrifices and offerings and whole burnt offerings and *sacrifices* for sin thou wouldest not, neither hadst pleasure therein (the which are offered according to the law),

9 Then hath he said, Lo, I am come to do thy will. He taketh away the first, that he may establish the second.

10 By which will we have been sanctified through the offering of the body of Jesus Christ once for all.

The One Sacrifice Perfects for Ever

11 And every priest indeed standeth day by day ministering and offering oftentimes the same sacrifices, the which can never take away sins:

12 But he, when he had offered one sacrifice for sins for ever, sat down on the right hand of God;

13 From henceforth expecting till his enemies be made the footstool of his feet.

14 For by one offering he hath perfected for ever them that are sanctified.

15 And the Holy Ghost also beareth witness to us: for after he hath said,

16 This is the covenant that I will make with them after those days, saith the Lord; I will put my laws on their heart, and upon their mind also will I write them; *then saith he,*

17 And their sins and their iniquities will I remember no more.

18 Now where remission of these is, there is no more offering for sin.

Second Half—Practical—

Chap. x. 19–xiii. 25

Of a Life in the Power of the Great Salvation

NINTH SECTION—x. 19–25

The New Worship

Of Entering the Holiest

19 Having therefore, brethren, boldness to enter into the holy place by the blood of Jesus,

20 By the way which he dedicated for us, a new and living way,[a] through the veil, that is to say, his flesh;

21 And *having* a great priest over the house of God;

22 Let us draw near with a true heart in fulness of faith, having our hearts sprinkled from an evil conscience, and our body washed with pure water;

Of Our Life in the Holiest

23 Let us hold fast the confession of our hope that it waver not; for he is faithful that promised:

24 And let us consider one another to provoke unto love and good works;

a. Ch. 2. 10; 6. 20; 10. 10; 12. 1; 13. 13.

25 Not forsaking the assembling of ourselves together, as the custom of some is, but exhorting *one another;* and so much the more, as ye see the day drawing nigh.

The Fourth Warning
Chap. x. 26–39
Against Sinning Wilfully and Drawing Back

The Terrible Danger of Sinning Wilfully

26 For if we sin wilfully after that we have received the knowledge of the truth, there remaineth no more a sacrifice for sins,

27 But a certain fearful expectation of judgement, and a fierceness of fire which shall devour the adversaries.

28 A man that hath set at nought Moses' law dieth without compassion on *the word of* two or three witnesses:

29 Of how much sorer punishment, think ye, shall he be judged worthy, who hath trodden under foot the Son of God, and hath counted the blood of the covenant, wherewith he was sanctified, an unholy thing, and hath done despite unto the Spirit of grace?

30 For we know him that said, Vengeance belongeth unto me, I will recompense. And again, The Lord shall judge his people.

31 It is a fearful thing to fall into hands of the living God.

Exhortation to Boldness and Patience

32 But call to remembrance the former days, in which, after ye were enlightened, ye endured a great conflict of sufferings;

33 Partly, being made a gazingstock both by reproaches and afflictions; and partly, becoming partakers with them that were so used.

34 For ye both had compassion on them that were in bonds, and took joyfully the spoiling of your possessions, knowing that ye yourselves have a better possession and an abiding one.

35 Cast not away therefore your boldness, which hath great recompense of reward.

36 For ye have need of patience, that, having done the will of God, ye may receive the promise.[a]

Exhortation to Believe and Not Draw Back

37 For yet a very little while, he that cometh shall come, and shall not tarry.

38 But my righteous one shall live by faith: and if he shrink back my soul hath no pleasure in him.

a. Ch. 4. 1; 6. 12, 13, 17; 7. 6; 8. 6; 9. 15; 11. 9, 13, 17, 33, 39.

39 But we are not of them that shrink back unto perdition; but of them that have faith unto the saving of the soul.

Chapter XI.

TENTH SECTION—xi. 1–40

The Fulness of Faith

Faith, the Eye of the Unseen

Now faith is the assurance of *things* hoped for, the proving of things not seen.

2 For therein the elders had witness borne to them.[a]

3 By faith we understand that the worlds have been framed by the word of God, so that what is seen hath not been made out of things which do appear.

Of Faith Before the Deluge

4 By faith Abel offered unto God a more excellent sacrifice than Cain, through which he had witness borne to him that he was righteous, God bearing witness in respect of his gifts: and through it he being dead yet speaketh.

5 By faith Enoch was translated that he should not see death; and he was not found, because God translated him: for before his translation he hath had witness borne to him that he had been well-pleasing unto God.

6 And without faith it is impossible to be well-pleasing *unto him:* for he that cometh to God must believe that he is, and *that* he is a rewarder of them that seek after him.

7 By faith Noah, being warned *of God* concerning things not seen as yet, moved with godly fear, prepared an ark to the saving of his house; through which he condemned the world, and became heir of the righteousness which is according to faith.

Abraham and Sarah

8 By faith Abraham, when he was called, obeyed to go out unto a place which he was to receive for an inheritance; and he went out, not knowing whither he went.

9 By faith he became a sojourner in the land of promise, as in a *land* not his own, dwelling in tents, with Isaac and Jacob, the heirs with him of the same promise:

10 For he looked for the city which hath the foundations, whose builder and maker is God.

11 By faith even Sarah herself received power to conceive seed when she was past age, since she counted him faithful who had promised.

a. Ch. 11. 4, 5, 39; 12. 1.

12 Wherefore also there sprang of one, and him as good as dead, *so many* as the stars of heaven in multitude, and as the sand, which is by the sea shore, innumerable.

13 These all died in faith, not having received the promises, but having seen them and greeted them from afar, and having confessed that they were strangers and pilgrims on the earth.

14 For they that say such things make it manifest that they are seeking after a country of their own.

15 And if indeed they had been mindful of that *country* from which they went out, they would have had opportunity to return.

16 But now they desire a better *country,* that is, a heavenly: wherefore God is not ashamed of them, to be called their God: for he hath prepared for them a city.

17 By faith Abraham, being tried, offered up Isaac: yea, he that had gladly received the promises was offering up his only begotten *son;*

18 *Even he* to whom it was said, In Isaac shall thy seed be called:

19 Accounting that God *is* able to raise up, even from the dead; from whence he did also in a parable receive him back.

Isaac, Jacob, and Joseph

20 By faith Isaac blessed Jacob and Esau, even concerning things to come.

21 By faith Jacob, when he was a dying, blessed each of the sons of Joseph; and worshipped, *leaning* upon the top of his staff.

22 By faith Joseph, when his end was nigh, made mention of the departure of the children of Israel; and gave commandment concerning his bones.

Moses

23 By faith Moses, when he was born, was hid three months by his parents, because they saw he was a goodly child; and they were not afraid of the king's commandment.

24 By faith Moses, when he was grown up, refused to be called the son of Pharaoh's daughter;

25 Choosing rather to be evil entreated with the people of God, than to enjoy the pleasures of sin for a season:

26 Accounting the reproach of Christ greater riches than the treasures of Egypt: for he looked unto the recompense of reward.

Of the Deliverance of Israel by Faith

27 By faith he forsook Egypt, not fearing the wrath of the king: for he endured, as seeing him who is invisible.

28 By faith he kept the passover, and the sprinkling of the blood, that the destroyer of the firstborn should not touch them.

29 By faith they passed through the Red sea as by dry land: which the Egyptians assaying to do were swallowed up.

30 By faith the walls of Jericho fell down, after they had been compassed about for seven days.

31 By faith Rehab the harlot perished not with them that were disobedient, having received the spies with peace.

The Wonders Faith Has Wrought

32 And what shall I more say? for the time will fail me if I tell of Gideon, Barak, Samson, Jephthah; of David and Samuel and the prophets.

33 Who through faith subdued kingdoms, wrought righteousness, obtained promises, stopped the mouths of lions,

34 Quenched the power of fire, escaped the edge of the sword, from weakness were made strong, waxed mighty in war, turned to flight armies of aliens.

35 Women received their dead by a resurrection: and others were tortured, not accepting their deliverance; that they might obtain a better resurrection:

The Sufferings Faith Has Endured

36 And others had trial of mockings and scourgings, yea, moreover of bonds and imprisonment:

37 They were stoned, they were sawn asunder, they were tempted, they were slain with the sword: they went about in sheepskins, in goatskins; being destitute, afflicted, evil entreated.

38 (Of whom the world was not worthy), wandering in deserts and mountains and caves, and the holes of the earth.

Some Better Thing for Us

39 And these all, having had witness borne to them through their faith, received the promise,

40 God having provided some better thing concerning us, that apart from us they should not be made perfect.

Chapter XII.

ELEVENTH SECTION—xii. 1–13

The Patience of Hope

Jesus, the Leader in the Race

Therefore let us also, seeing we are compassed about with so great a cloud of witnesses, lay aside every weight, and the sin which doth so easily beset us, and let us run with patience the race[a] that is set before us,

a. Ch. 2. 10; 6. 20; 10. 20; 13. 13.

2 Looking unto Jesus the author and perfecter of *our* faith, who for the joy that was set before him endured the cross, despising shame, **and hath sat down at the right hand of the throne of God.**

3 For consider him that hath endured such gainsaying of sinners against themselves, that ye wax not weary, fainting in your souls.

Trial the Portion of God's Children

4 Ye have not yet resisted unto blood, striving against sin:

5 And ye have forgotten the exhortation, which reasoneth with you as with sons, My son, regard not lightly the chastening of the Lord, nor faint when thou art reproved of him;

6 For whom the Lord loveth he chasteneth, and scourgeth every son whom he receiveth.

7 It is for chastening that ye endure; God dealeth with you as with sons; for what son is there whom *his* father chasteneth not?

8 But if ye are without chastening, whereof all have been made partakers, then are ye bastards, and not sons.

The Blessing of Chastisement

9 Furthermore, we had the fathers of our flesh to chasten us, and we gave them reverence: shall we not much rather be in subjection unto the Father of spirits, and live?

10 For they verily for a few days chastened *us* as seemed good to them; but he for *our* profit, that *we* may be partakers of his holiness.

11 All chastening seemeth for the present to be not joyous, but grievous: yet afterward it yieldeth peaceable fruit unto them that have been exercised thereby, *even the fruit* of righteousness.

12 Wherefore lift up the hands that hang down, and the palsied knees;

13 And make straight paths for your feet, that that which is lame be not turned out of the way, but rather be healed.

The Fifth Warning
Chap. xii. 14–29
To Beware of Sin and Rejection of Jesus

Of Falling Short of the Grace of God

14 Follow after peace with all men, and the sanctification without which no man shall see the Lord:

15 Looking carefully lest *there be* any man that falleth short of the grace of God; lest any root of bitterness springing up trouble *you,* and thereby the many be defiled;

15 Lest *there be* any fornicator, or profane person, as Esau, who for one mess of meat sold his own birthright.

17 For ye know that even when he afterward desired to inherit the blessing, he was rejected (for he found no place of repentance), though he sought it diligently with tears.

Ye Are Not Come to Mount Sinai

18 For ye are not come unto *a mount* that might be touched, and that burned with fire, and unto blackness, and darkness, and tempest,

19 And the sound of a trumpet, and the voice of words; which *voice* they that heard intreated that no word more should be spoken unto them:

20 For they could not endure that which was enjoined, If even a beast touch the mountain, it shall be stoned;

21 And so fearful was the appearance, *that* Moses said, I exceedingly fear and quake:

Ye Are Come to Mount Sion

22 But ye are come unto mount Zion, and unto the city of the living God, the heavenly Jerusalem, and to innumerable hosts of angels,

23 To the general assembly and church of the firstborn who are enrolled in heaven, and to God the Judge of all, and to the spirits of just men made perfect,

24 And to Jesus the mediator of a new covenant, and to the blood of sprinkling that speaketh better than *that of* Abel.

Let Us Fear Him Who Is a Consuming Fire

25 See that ye refuse not him that speaketh. For if they escaped not, when they refused him that warned *them* on earth, much more *shall not* we *escape,* who turn away from him that *warneth* from heaven:

26 Whose voice then shook the earth: but now he hath promised, saying, Yet once more will I make to tremble not the earth only, but also the heaven.

27 And this *word,* Yet once more, signifieth the removing of those things that are shaken, as of things that have been made, that those things which are not shaken may remain.

28 Wherefore, receiving a kingdom that cannot be shaken, let us have grace, whereby we may offer service well-pleasing to God with reverence and awe:

29 For our God is a consuming fire.

Chapter XIII.

TWELFTH SECTION—xiii. 1–25

Love and Good Works

Of Love

Let love of the brethren continue.

2 Forget not to show love unto strangers: for thereby some have entertained angels unawares.

3 Remember them that are in bonds, as bound with them; them that are evil entreated, as being yourselves also in the body.

4 *Let* marriage *be* had in honour among all, and *let* the bed *be* undefiled: for fornicators and adulterers God will judge.

Of Contentment

5 Be ye free from the love of money; content with such things as ye have: for himself hath said, I will in no wise fail thee, neither will I in any wise forsake thee.

6 So that with good courage we say, The Lord is my helper; I will not fear: What shall man do unto me?

Jesus Always the Same—Our Comfort and Safety

7 Remember them that had the rule over you, which spake unto you the word of God; and considering the issue of their life, imitate their faith.

8 Jesus Christ is the same yesterday and today, *yea* and for ever.

9 Be not carried away by divers and strange teachings: for it is good that the heart be stablished by grace; not by meats, wherein they that occupied themselves were not profited.

Our Fellowship in the Sacrifice of Jesus without the Camp

10 We have an altar, whereof they have no right to eat which serve the tabernacle.

11 For the bodies of those beasts, whose blood is brought into the holy place by the high priest *as an offering* for sin, are burned without the camp.

12 Wherefore Jesus also, that he might sanctify the people through his own blood, suffered without the gate.

13 Let us therefore go forth unto him without the camp, bearing his reproach.

14 For we have not here an abiding city, but we seek after *the city* which is to come.

Of the Sacrifices We Are to Bring

15 Through him then let us offer up a sacrifice of praise to God continually, that is, the fruit of lips which make confession to his name.

16 But to do good and to communicate forget not: for with such sacrifices God is well pleased.

Submission to Our Rulers and Prayer for Them

17 Obey them that have the rule over you, and submit *to them,* for they watch in behalf of your souls, as they that shall give account; that they may do this with joy, and not with grief: for this *were* unprofitable for you.

18 Pray for us: for we are persuaded that we have a good conscience, desiring to live honestly in all things.

19 And I exhort *you* the more exceedingly to do this, that I may be restored to you the sooner.

The Farewell Prayer

20 Now the God of peace, who brought again from the dead the great shepherd of the sheep with the blood of the eternal covenant,

21 *Even* our Lord Jesus, make you perfect in every good thing to do his will, working in us that which is well-pleasing in his sight, through Jesus Christ; to whom *be* the glory for ever and ever. Amen.

Last Words

22 But I exhort you, brethren, bear with the word of exhortation: for I have written unto you in few words.

23 Know ye that our brother Timothy hath been set at liberty; with whom, if he come shortly, I will see you.

24 Salute all them that have the rule over you, and all the saints. They of Italy salute you.

25 Grace be with you all. Amen.

Introduction

Ere we enter upon the study of our Epistle, there are some questions on which it is desirable to have some light. It is well to know what can be told as to its author, the Church to which it was addressed, the object the author had in view, and the plan he adopts to attain that object. The reader then knows something of what he is to expect, and has a point of view suggested from which to overlook the whole.

The Author of the Epistle

From the very earliest times there have been some among the Church Fathers who maintained that the Epistle was not written by Paul, while those who held the opposite view have admitted that they had no decisive evidence to offer to prove that authorship. All admit that the literary style is not that found in Paul's writings. And some say that the substance of the teaching differs too, and that the great truth which he had been set apart to announce, that the Gentiles are fellow-heirs, and of the same body, is entirely wanting. The Epistle speaks as if salvation was for the Jew only: it is absolutely silent as to the existence of a heathen or Christian world outside the Church it addresses.

On the other hand, it may be said that the Epistle contains so much of what had been specially revealed to Paul more than to others concerning the fulfilment of the law in Christ and its passing away, concerning the glory of Christ seated on the throne of heaven and the alone power of faith, that it is almost impossible not to recognise his spirit in its teaching. What adds special weight to this view is that, while from the style it is certain that it cannot be the work of any other of our Bible writers, it appears strange that the history of the Church does not even mention the name of a man who had been favoured with such special revelations from God as the Epistle bears witness to.

The difficulty has led from the earliest times to the supposition that Paul either wrote the letter to the Hebrews in their tongue, and that we only have it in the Greek translation, or that he gave the substance of its contents to someone who gave expression to them in his own peculiar style. The names have been suggested of Barnabas, of Luke (to whose style in the Acts there is considerable resemblance), of Aquila, of Apollos the Alexandrian (eloquent and mighty in the Scriptures), and Clement of Rome. There is such an entire absence of material for forming a decision that we are compelled to rest in the certainty that the name of the author cannot be known. All the more we praise God that we know for certain that the Holy Spirit spake in him who wrote, and that it is He who has given us in the Epistle one of the deepest and fullest revelations which the Bible contains of the counsel of redemption, and the glory of the Son who makes us partakers of it.

To Whom the Epistle Was Written

The Jews had the name of Hebrews from Abraham, who, in Gen. xiv. 13, is spoken of as "the Hebrew." It was counted a title of honour, as we see in Paul's, "an Hebrew of the Hebrews." Some have thought that, because no special place or church is mentioned, it was meant for all Christians among the Jews. But expressions as, "Pray that I may be restored to you the sooner," "With Timothy, if he come shortly, I will see you," compel us to think of some special community. The most probable view is that it was addressed, in the first place, to the Christians in Jerusalem. From Acts xxi. 20, we know that there were many thousands of them, who, while believing in Christ, yet clung to the temple and its worship. Nowhere were they in greater danger of yielding to the temptation of conformity to the spirit of the world around them, and losing the boldness and the brightness of their Christian life; and nowhere would there be better opportunity of securing for the letter the widest possible circulation through all the scattered Christian churches among the Jews.

The Object of the Epistle

What was it that led the writer to take his pen? The Epistle itself gives us the answer. The religious state of those to whom it was addressed was far from right or satisfactory. Some had grown "slothful," were "not giving earnest heed," were "neglecting the great salvation." They were no longer "holding fast their profession" or "their confidence." The Christian life was feeble and ready to die. Others had "gone back," were in danger of "coming short of the promises," and, yielding to "wilful sin," "drawing back to perdition." Still others were in danger of "refusing Him who speaks from heaven," of giving up their faith in Jesus. Expressions such as we have quoted, and others, indicate clearly that there had been much backsliding, and that the Church was in a state that needed most solemn and pointed warning.

Great stress has been laid upon the difficulties that arose in the mind of the Hebrews from the circumstances in which they were placed. They had hoped that their countrymen would speedily accept the Messiah: they had been signally disappointed. They still clung to the old worship; but felt more and more that, suspected and despised as they were, they could no longer be at home there. The prophecies appeared to fail them, both in regard to the power with which Christ should reign, and the blessing He would bestow. To meet these difficulties, it is said, the Epistle seeks to open up the true glory of the religion of Christ, and to show that all that they lost in the old worship was a hundredfold restored in the "something better" God had now provided. It seeks to solve the problem that troubled them in the light of the gospel.

There is doubtless a measure of truth in this view. And yet, the more I study the Epistle, the more confident I feel that this was not the chief trouble; the main difficulty lay in the want of religious earnestness. Their case was very much what has been the story of almost every Church, and what marks the state of the greater part of Christendom at the present day.

It was to meet this spirit of backsliding, to warn against the disease and its danger, and to make known the infallible cure, that our author takes up his pen. He saw that the one cause of all the feebleness and faithlessness was this: the want of the knowledge and the faith of what Christ and His salvation truly are. He sets himself to show them how wonderfully, how divinely, all the prophecies and types of the Old Testament have their fulfilment in the salvation the Son of God has wrought for us. He unceasingly places their weakness and Christ's person side by side: he is sure that, if they but know Christ, all will be well.

The Plan of the Epistle

In what way does the writer propose to attain his object? In the opening verses we find the substance of his whole argument. God, who spoke to the fathers in the prophets, hath now spoken to us in the Son. There have been two revelations of God to man. The first was through men; the second through the Son. As much more glorious as God's Son is than His servants, has the new revelation more of life and of glory than the old. He not only writes to prove the superiority of the new above the old, but specially to show what that intrinsic excellence is which gives it that superiority. In the knowledge of this its excellence, both faith and experience will find their strength. The contents of the Epistle, taking its doctrinal and practical aspect together, may be summarised—the knowledge of the Son of God, the power of the Christian life.

The Epistle is divided into two parts. In the first, the doctrinal half (i. 1–x. 18), we have the glory of the person and work of Christ set forth. In the second, or practical half (x. 19–xiii. 25), the life is described which the knowledge of Christ and His salvation will enable us to live.

I have had the Epistle printed at the beginning of the book with headings showing the contents of the different parts, with the view of inviting and helping the reader to make himself master of the writing as a whole. It is of great consequence that the student of God's word should not only seek his edification from individual texts or passages, but that each book should be to him a living and connected organism, all alive with the Spirit that dwells in it. The more we thus take time and trouble to accept the great thoughts of God, the more will our life be brought to that unity and breadth, in which the purpose of God will be perfectly fulfilled.

The first three verses give us the summary of the doctrinal part.

Then follow twelve sections.

1. Christ, as Son of God, is more than the angels (i. 4–14).
2. Jesus, as Son of Man, is more than the angels too. Reasons for His being made lower than the angels (ii. 5–18).
3. Christ Jesus more than Moses (iii. 1–6).
4. Jesus, our High Priest, more than Aaron (iv. 14–v. 10).
5. The New Priesthood after the order of Melchizedek (vii.).
6. The New Sanctuary and the New Covenant (viii.).
7. The power of Christ's blood to inaugurate the New Sanctuary and the New Covenant (ix.).
8. The New Way into the Holiest (x. 1–18).

Here commences the second, the practical, half, with its call to a life corresponding to our privileges.

9. Of entering the Holiest and dwelling there (x. 19–25).
10. Of the Fulness of Faith (xi. 1–40).
11. Of the Patience of Hope (xii. 1–13).
12. Of Love and Good Works (xiii. 1–25).

In this summary of contents I have not taken up the passages containing the solemn warnings by which the Epistle is characterised. They are so inserted that they could in each case be left out, without the argument suffering. In some cases, the connection would in fact be clearer. I have had this indicated in the printing, because I am sure that it is of importance, if we would thoroughly master the lesson given us, that we should fully apprehend the danger which threatened, and in some right measure see how the only deliverance for Christians from all that weakness and hinders them, is the full knowledge of the person and work of Jesus.

The Warnings

1. After the proof of Christ being more than the angels—*Not to neglect so great salvation* (ii. 1–4).
2. After the proof of Christ being more than Moses—*Not like Israel in the wilderness to come short of the promised rest* (iii. 7–iv. 13).
3. After the mention of Christ being more than Aaron—*Against the danger of sloth, standing still, and falling away* (v. 11–vi. 21).
4. After the call to enter the opened Holiest—*Against sinning wilfully, and drawing back to perdition* (x. 26–39).
5. After the exhortation to patience—*Against falling short of the grace of God and refusing Him who speaks* (xii. 15–29).

The deeper our impression is of the danger that existed, the clearer will be our insight into the truth that the only source of health and strength to the Church is the knowledge of Christ Jesus.

The Epistle and the Church of Our Days

There is one more point in which an Introduction can help the reader. It is to suggest the relation in which a book stands to the special needs of our present times.

In the Christian Church of our day the number of members is very large, whose experience corresponds exactly with that which the Epistle pictures and seeks to meet. How many Christians are there yet who, after the profession of faith in Christ, come to a standstill. "Taking more abundant heed to what they hear"; "giving diligence to enter into the rest of God"; "pressing on to perfection"; "running with patience the race"—just these are the things which are so little found. So many rest contented with the thought that their sins are pardoned, and that they are in the path of life, but know nothing of a personal attachment to Christ as their Leader, or of a faith that lives in the invisible and walks with God. With many this is the consequence of the hopelessness that came from the failure of their utmost efforts to live as they desired. They struggled in their own strength; they knew not Christ as the secret of strength; they lost heart, and went back. The profession of faith is not cast away; religious habits are kept up; but there is nothing to show that they have entered or are seeking to enter the Holiest to dwell there. The power of the world, the spirit of its literature, the temptations of business and pleasure, all unite to make up a religion in which it is sought to combine a comfortable hope for the future with the least possible amount of sacrifice in the present. The Epistle, with its warnings, is indeed a glass in which the Church of the present day may see itself.

But it is a glass too, thank God, in which we can also see the glory of Jesus on the throne of heaven, in the power that can make our heart and life heavenly too. What the Hebrews needed is what we need. Not in ourselves or our efforts is salvation, but in Christ Jesus. To see Him, to consider Him, to look to Him, *as He lives in heaven,* that will bring the healing. As little as the Hebrews with the Old Testament, its God-given law, its temple service, and its prophecy, could withstand the temptation to "wax weary and grow faint," can the New Testament, with a sound Church and Church doctrine, and its religious services, give us the true life and power of godliness. It is Jesus Christ we must know better. It is He who lives today in heaven, who can lead us into the heavenly sanctuary, and keep us there, who can give heaven into our heart and life. *The knowledge of Jesus in His heavenly glory and His saving power;* it is this our Churches and our Christians need. It is this the Epistle will bring us, if we yield to that Spirit who speaks in it, to reveal it in us.

It is, therefore, with great confidence that I invite all who long for the rest of God, for a life in the holiest of God's love, for the fulness of faith and hope and love, to take up the study of the Epistle, with the confident assurance of finding in its revelation of what Christ and His salvation are, the deliverance from sin and sloth, the joy and the strength of a new life.

First Half—Doctrinal—Chap. i.-x. 18.

The Son of God the Mediator of the Better Covenant

The Theme—i. 1-3
The Glory of the Son in His Person and Work

I.

The Son in Whom God Hath Spoken

I.–1. God, having of old time spoken unto the fathers in the prophets by divers portions and in divers manners,

2. Hath at the end of these days spoken unto us in his Son.

God hath spoken! The magnificent portal by which we enter into the temple in which God is to reveal His glory to us! We are at once brought into the presence of God himself. The one object of the Epistle is to lead us to God, to reveal God, to bring us into contact with Himself. Man was created for God. Sin separated from God. Man feels his need, and seeks for God. This Epistle comes with the gospel message of redemption, to teach us where and how to find God. Let all who thirst for God, for the living God, draw nigh and listen.

God hath spoken! Speaking is the vehicle of fellowship. It is a proof that the speaker considers him he addresses as capable of fellowship with himself; a token that he longs for that fellowship. Man was created for fellowship with God. Sin interrupted it. Nature speaks of God and His work, but of Himself, His heart, and His thoughts of love towards us as sinners, nature cannot tell. In his deepest misery man seeks for God—but how often, to all appearance, in vain. But, God be praised, not for al-

51

ways. The silence has been broken. God calls man back to fellowship with Himself. God hath spoken!

God hath spoken! For a time, imperfectly and provisionally in the prophets, in preparation for the more perfect revelation of Himself. But now at length the joyful tidings are heard—**God hath spoken in His Son!** God, the infinite, incomprehensible, unseen One, hath spoken! And that in His Son! Oh the joy and the glory! who can measure it? "Hear! O heavens, and give ear! O earth, for the Lord hath spoken."

God hath spoken! When man speaks it is the revelation of himself, to make known the otherwise hidden thoughts and dispositions of his heart. When God, who dwells in light that is inaccessible, speaks out of the heights of His glory, it is that He may reveal Himself. He would have us know how He loves us and longs for us, how He wants to save and to bless, how He would have us draw nigh and live in fellowship with Himself.

God hath spoken in His Son! The ministry of angels and prophets was only to prepare the way; it never could satisfy the heart either of God or man; the real power of the life of God, the full experience of His nearness, the true deliverance from sin, the shedding abroad of the love in the heart—this could not be communicated by the ministry of creatures. The Son Himself had to come as the Word of God to us, the bearer of the life and love of the Father. The Son Himself had to come to bring us into living contact with the divine Being, to dwell in our heart, as He dwells in God's heart, to be in us God's word as He is in God, and so to give us the living experience of what it means that God speaks to us.

God hath spoken! The words of a man carry weight according to the idea I have of his wisdom, his veracity, his power, his love. The words of God! Oh, who can express what they ought to be worth to us! Each word carries with it all the life of God, all His saving power and love. God speaking in His Son! Surely they who have begun to know Him will be ready to cast aside everything for the sake of hearing Him.

God hath spoken! The words of men have often exerted a wonderful and a mighty influence. But the words of God—they are creative deeds, they give what they speak. "He spake, and it was done." When God speaks in His Son, He gives Him to us, not only for us and with us, but in us. He speaks the Son out of the depth of His heart into the depths of our heart. Men's words appeal to the mind or the will, the feelings or the passions. God speaks to that which is deeper than all, to the heart, that central depth within us whence are the issues of life. Let us believe the mighty, quickening power God's word will have.

God hath spoken! Speaking claims hearing. God asks but one thing; it is so simple and right; that we should listen. Shall we not hearken, in holy reverence and worship, with whole-hearted attention and surrender, to what He would say to us in this Epistle too? We too shall know what the power and the joy is of God speaking to us in His Son. God is a Spirit. As such He has no other way of communicating to us His life or His love, but by entering our spirit and dwelling and working there. There He causes Christ to dwell, and there He speaks to us in Christ these words of redeeming love and power which bring life to us. The words of Christ can bring us no profit, except as they unfold to us what God is working in us, and direct us to what is to be revealed in our heart. It is the heart God wants; let us open the whole heart to listen and to long.

God hath spoken in His Son! The living Jesus, come forth from the fiery furnace of God's holiness, from the burning glow of everlasting love, He Himself is the living Word. Let us seek in the study of this Epistle, in which His glory is so wondrously re-vealed, to come into contact with Him to receive Him into our hearts, to take Him as our life, that He may bring us to the Fa-ther. In the beginning God spake: "Let there be light! and there was light." Even so now He speaks with creative power in His

Son, and the presence and the light of Christ become the life and the light of the soul.

1. *What trouble people take to learn a foreign language, to have access to its writers. Let no trouble be too great to understand the language of God, His Word, His Son. To learn a foreign language I get someone who knows it to teach me. The language of God is heavenly, spiritual, supernatural—altogether divine; only the Holy Spirit can teach me to understand it, to think God's own thoughts. Let me take Him as my teacher.*

2. *"And Abram fell on his face: and God talked with him." As personally and directly, even more wonderfully and effectually, will God speak to me in His Son; but deep, holy reverence, and an intense desire to know what God says, must be the spirit in which I study the Epistle and hearken to the blessed Son.*

3. *"Heavenly truth is nowhere spoken but by the voice of Christ, nor heard but by the power of Christ, living in the hearer." "He that is of God heareth God's words." It is only he who yields himself to the new nature who can truly know what God's speaking in Christ is.*

4. *During Christ's life the word of God was thrice heard. Each time it was: "This is My beloved Son: hear Him." "I have glorified Him." Let us allow God to speak this one word into our hearts—My beloved Son. O my God! speak to me in Thy Son. Oh, speak that one word out of the depth of Thy heart into the depth of my heart.*

II.

The Son—More Than the Prophets

I.–1. God, having of old time spoken unto the fathers in the
prophets by divers portions and in divers manners,
2. Hath at the end of these days spoken unto us in his Son.

We all know that there are two Testaments—the Old and the
New. These represent two dispensations, two modes of worship,
two sorts of religions, two ways in which God has intercourse
with man, and man draws nigh to God. The one was provision-
al, preparatory, and intended to pass away. What it gave and
wrought was not meant to satisfy, but only to awaken the expectation of something better that was to come. The other was the
fulfilment of what had been promised, and destined to last for
ever, because it was itself a complete revelation of an everlasting
redemption, of a salvation in the power of an endless life.

In both Old and New Testament it was God who spake. The
prophets in the Old, and the Son in the New, were equally God's
messengers. God spake in the prophets no less truly than in the
Son. But in the Old everything was external and through the
mediation of men. God Himself could not yet enter and take
possession of man and dwell in him. In the New all is more directly and immediately divine—in an inward power and reality
and life, of which the Old had only the shadow and hope. The
Son, who is God, brings us into the very presence of God.

And wherefore was it that God did not, could not, from the
very beginning, reveal Himself in the Son? What need was there
of these two ways of worshipping and serving Him? The answer

55

is twofold—If man were indeed intelligently and voluntarily to appropriate God's love and redemption, he needed to be prepared for it. He needed first of all to know his own utter impotence and hopeless wretchedness. And so his heart had to be wakened up in true desire and expectancy to welcome and value what God had to give.

When God speaks to us in Christ it is as the Father *dwelling in the Son.* "The words that I say unto you, I speak not from Myself, but *the Father abideth in Me* doeth the works." Just as God's speaking in Christ was an inward thing. So God can still speak to us in no other way. The external words of Christ, just like the words of the prophets, are to prepare us for, and point us to, that inner speaking in the heart by the Holy Spirit, which alone is life and power. This is God's true speaking in His Son.

It is of the utmost consequence for our spiritual life that we should rightly understand these two stages in God's dealing with man. In two ways, not in one; not in more than two; in two ways has God spoken.

They indicate what, in substance, is God's way with every Christian.[1] There is, after his conversion, a time of preparation and testing, to see whether he willingly and heartily sacrifices all for the full blessing. If in this stage he perseveres in earnest effort and striving, he will be brought to learn the two lessons the Old Testament was meant to teach. He will become more deeply conscious of his own impotence, and the strong desire will be wakened after a better life, to be found in the full revelation of Christ as able to save completely. When these two lessons are learned—the lesson of despair of self and hope in God alone—the soul is prepared, if it will yield itself in faith to the leading of the Holy Spirit, to enter truly into the New Testament life within the veil, in the very Holiest of All, as it is set forth in this Epistle.

---

1. "The characteristics which before marked the revelation itself, now mark the human apprehension of the final revelation."—Westcott.

Where Christians, through defective instruction, or through neglect and sloth, do not understand God's way for leading them on unto perfection, the Christian life will always remain full of feebleness and failure. It was thus with the Hebrew Christians. They belonged to the New Testament, but their life was anything but the exhibition of the power and joy Christ came to reveal. They were far behind what many of the Old Testament saints had been; and the reason was this—they knew not the heavenly character of the redemption Christ had brought. They knew not the heavenly place in which He ministers, nor the heavenly blessing He dispenses, nor the heavenly power in which He secures our enjoyment of these blessings. They knew not the difference between the prophets and the Son; what it means that God has now spoken to us in His Son. The one object of the Epistle is to set before us the heavenly priesthood of Christ and the heavenly life to which He in His divine power gives us access. It is this gives the Epistle its inestimable value for all time, that it teaches us the way out of the elementary stage of the Christian life to that of full and perfect access to God.

Let us grasp and hold firmly the difference between the two stages. In the one, the action of man is more prominent: God speaks in the prophets. In the other, the divine presence and power are more fully revealed: God speaks in the Son, who bears and brings the very life of God, and brings us into living contact with God Himself. In the one, it is the human words that occupy and influence and help us to seek God; in the other, the divine indwelling Word reveals its power within. In the one, it is multiplicity of thoughts and truths, of ordinances and efforts; in the other, the simplicity and the unity of the one Son of God, and faith in Him alone.

How many have sought by study and meditation and acceptance of the words of the Bible to find God, and yet have failed. They knew not that these were but the finger-posts pointing to living Son—words coming indeed from God, most needful and profitable, and yet not sufficient; only yielding us their true blessing when they have brought us to hear God Himself speaking in His Son.

1. *Let none of us rest content with the lower stage. Let us see that personal fellowship with God, through the Holy Spirit, is what Christ gives. God calls us to it: Christ lives in heaven to work it, through the Spirit He gives from heaven.*

2. *One may know much of the Bible and the words of God, and yet remain feeble. What one needs is to know the living Word, in whom God speaks within, in life and power.*

3. *All the prophets point to the Son, as the true Prophet. Let us take them very definitely as our teachers, to reveal God in us.*

4. *When I speak a word, I desire all its meaning and force to enter into him whom I address. God has in these last days but one Word. He desires to have all that Word is and means enter in and live in us. Let us open our hearts, and God will speak into it that one Word, This is My Son, in such a way that He will indeed be all our own.*

III.

The Son—the Glory of His Person

I.–2. God hath spoken unto us in his Son, whom he appointed heir of all things, through whom also he made the worlds;
3. Who being the effulgence[2] of his glory, and the very image of his substance, and upholding all things by the word of his power.

We know that whatever a man sets his heart on exercises a mighty influence on the life, and leaves its stamp upon his character. He that follows after vanity becomes vain. He that trusts in a god of his own fancy will find his religion an illusion. He that sets his heart upon the living God will find the living God take possession and fill the heart. It is this that makes it of such infinite consequence that we should not only have a general idea of the Christ through whom God speaks to us, but should know Him aright and have our heart filled with all that God has revealed of Him. Our knowledge of Him will be the food of our faith, and as our faith is will be our experience of His saving power, and of the fellowship with God to which He leads. Let us listen to what we are taught of the Son in whom God speaks to us.

Whom He appointed Heir of all things. The great object and aim of God in creation was to have an inheritance for His Son, in which He might show forth His glory and find His blessedness. The Son is the Final Cause, the End of all things.

He is the Beginning too. **Through whom He also made the worlds.** He is the origin and Efficient Cause of all that exists.

2. Outshining.

"Without Him nothing was made that was made." The place the Son had in the divine Being was such that God's relation to all that was outside of Himself was only through the Son. Of all that exists the end and the beginning meet in Him.

And He is the Middle, too. **Upholding all things by the word of His power.** He bears all things, "all things consist in Him." As little as they were created without Him, can they exist without Him? He *upholds* them *every moment* by the word of His power, even as by His word they were created. This is the Son through whom God speaks to us.

And what is it that makes Him worthy of taking this high place between the Creator and the creature? Because, as the Son, it is He alone in whom the unapproachable and utterly incomprehensible glory of God is made manifest, through whom as Mediator the uncreated God, and the works of His hand, can come into contact and fellowship. His relation to creation rests on His relation to the Father. **He is the outshining of God's glory, and the express image of His substance.** As we only know the sun by the light that shines from it, so is Christ **the outshining,** the revelation **of God's glory.** As the light that shines from the sun is of the same nature with it, so the Son is of one nature with the Father—God of God. And as a son bears the likeness of his father, because he has his life and nature from him, so the Son of God is **the express image of His substance.** He is of one substance with the Father—its express image—and hath therefore life in Himself, even as the Father hath life in Himself.

Someone may be tempted to think that these are theological mysteries too deep for the ordinary Christian, and not needful for our Christian faith and life. And they are inclined to ask, of what importance it can be to a simple believer to know all this? My brother, think not thus. It is all important that we know the glory of Jesus. The more the soul is filled with that glory, and worships Him in it, the more it will see with what confidence it can count upon Him to do a divine and supernatural work in us, and to lead us to an actual living fellowship with God as our Father. Oh, let us not be so selfish and mean as to be content with the hope that Jesus saves us, while we are careless of having intimate personal acquaintance with Him. If not for our sake, then for God's sake, for the sake of His infinite love and grace, let us seek to know aright this blessed Son whom the Father has given us. Let us turn away from earth, let us meditate and gaze and worship, until He, who is the outshining of the divine glory, *shines into* our very heart, and He, to whom the Father hath given such a place as Creator and Upholder and Heir of all, take that place with us too, and be to us the beginning and the centre and the end of all.

It is through this Son God speaks to us. Not through the words of the Son only, for they too are human words, and may, just like the inspired words of the prophets, bring in but little profit. It is through the Son—the living, mighty, divine Son, direct—that God speaks: it is only in direct living contact with the Son that the words can profit. And the Son, not as we superficially think of Him, but the real divine Son as God has revealed Him, known and worshipped and waited on as the outshining of the divine glory—it is this Son of God, entering into our heart and dwelling there, in whom God will speak to us, and in whom we shall be brought nigh to God. When Christ reveals the Father, it is not to the mind, to give us new thoughts about Him, but in the heart and life, so that we know and experience the power in which God can dwell and work in man, restoring him to the enjoyment of that blessed fellowship for which he was created, and which he lost by the fall. The great work of God in heaven, the chief thought and longing of His heart is, in His Son, to reach your heart and speak to you. Oh, let it be the great work of your life, and the great longing of your heart, to know this Jesus; as a humble, meek disciple to bow at His feet, and let Him teach you of God and eternal life. Yes, even now, let us bow before Him in the fourfold glory in which the word has set Him before us. He is the Heir of all that God has. He is its Creator. He is the Upholder too. He is the Outshining of God's glory, and the perfect Image of His substance. O my Saviour! anything to know Thee better, and in Thee to have my God speak to me!

1. *"No man knoweth the Son, save the Father, neither doth any know the Father save the Son, and he to whomsoever the Son willeth to reveal him." How dependent we are on the Father to know the Son; on the Son to know the Father. Let us acknowledge this dependence in deep humility, and believe and wait in meekness of soul for the divine revealing.*

2. *There are times when there arises in the soul a deep longing to know God. External teaching does not satisfy. Treasure such longing as God's loving drawing. Turn from the world in stillness of soul, and exercise faith in the secret power that Jesus can exert in the heart.* Become a disciple of Jesus, *one who follows Him and learns of Him.*

3. *O Thou who art Heir, Creator, Upholder of all, the brightness of the Father's glory, the express image of His substance—O my Lord Jesus, reveal the Father to me, that I may know that God speaks to me.*

IV.

The Son—the Glory of His Work

I.–3. Who, when he had made purification[3] of sins, sat down on the right hand of the Majesty on high.

The description of the glory of Christ's person is followed by that of the work of this Son in whom God speaks to us. God's words are deeds. It is in what Christ is and works that God speaks to us. In His divinity and incarnation we see what God has given us. In His life and death and ascension we see how the gift of God enters and acts in all our human life, how complete our salvation is, and what God now asks of us. All Christ's work is God's word to us.

That work consists in two parts: the one on earth, the other in heaven. Of the former it is said, **When He had effected the cleansing of sins**; of the latter, **He sat down on the right hand of the Majesty on high.** In a healthy Christian life we must know and hold fast both parts of Christ's work. The work He did upon earth was but a beginning of the work He was to do in heaven; in the latter the work on earth finds its perfection and its glory. As Priest He effected the cleansing of sins here below; as Priest-King He sits on the right hand of the throne to apply His work, in heavenly power to dispense its blessings, and maintain within us the heavenly life.

When He had effected the cleansing of sins. The cleansing of sins, as something effected by Christ ere He went to heaven,

3. Effected the cleansing.

63

is the foundation of all His work. Let us learn, at the very outset, that what God has to speak to us in Christ begins here: *sin* must be cleansed away. This is the root-thought of redemption. As long as we seek salvation chiefly from the desire of personal safety, or approach the study of Christ's person and work as the revelation of what is true and beautiful and good, we cannot enter fully into its power. It is the cleansing of *sin* God insists on; in a desire so intense that He gave His Son to die for it! It is in the intense desire after the cleansing of sins, that, all the way through the Christian life, the spiritual capacity to approach and enter into the salvation of Christ will be found. It lies at the root of all. It is the secret of Christian perfection. It was only when He had effected this that heaven opened to Him. The full acceptance of the cleansing of sins, as the meaning of the word will be unfolded later on, will be to us, too, the entrance into the heavenly life.

When He had effected the cleansing of sins, **He sat down on the right hand of the Majesty on high.** *There* He lives, opening up and keeping open the blessed access to God's presence and fellowship for us; lifting us up into and maintaining us in its enjoyment; and in the power that prevails there, making the kingdom of heaven a reality within the heart. It is the great object of the Epistle to bring home to us the *heavenly glory of Christ* as the ground of our confidence, the measure of our expectation, and the character of that inward salvation He imparts. That Christ as our Leader and Forerunner has rent asunder the veil, and in the power of His blood has taken possession and secured access into the Holiest of All, does *not* mean only that we are to enter heaven when we die. The whole practical teaching of the Epistle is summed up and applied in the one word: "We have boldness for entering in: let us draw nigh: let us enter in." Christ seated on the throne in heaven means our being actually brought, in the supernatural power which the coming down of the Holy Spirit supplies, into God's holy presence, and living there our daily life. It was because the Hebrews did not know this, because they had rested content with elementary truths about faith and conversion, and then the life in heaven after death, that they had so signally failed. Truly to know Jesus at the right hand of God would be the healing of their diseases, the restoration to the joy and the strength of a life in accordance with their heavenly calling.

The Church of our days is suffering from the same cause, and needs the same cure. It is so much easier to appropriate the work of Christ on earth than that in heaven. It is so much easier to take in the doctrine of a Substitute and an atonement, of repentance and pardon, than of a High Priest bringing us into God's presence, and keeping us in loving communion with Him. It is not the blood-shedding upon earth only, *it is the blood-sprinkling in heaven, and the blood-sprinkling from heaven on heart and conscience,* that brings the power of the heavenly life unto us. And it is this alone that makes us Christians, who not only seek to enter the gate, but who daily press on in the living way that leads ever deeper into the Holiest.

Let no one think that I speak of what is too high. I speak of what is your heritage and destiny. The same share you have in Jesus on the cross, you have in Jesus on the throne. Be ready to sacrifice the earthly life for the heavenly; to follow Christ fully in His separation from the world and His surrender to God's will; and Christ in heaven will prove in you the reality and the power of His heavenly priesthood. Let the cleansing of sins be to you, as it was to Christ, the entrance to the Holiest. He who effected the cleansing on earth, and applies it in person from heaven, will assuredly lead you into all the fulness of blessing it has opened up for Him and for you.

1. *Faith has in its foundation four great corner-stones on which the building rests—the* Divinity of Christ, *the* Incarnation, *the* Atonement on the Cross, *the* Ascension to the Throne. *The last is the most wonderful, the crown of all the rest, the perfect revelation of what God has made Christ for us.* And so in the Christian life it is the most important, *the glorious fruit of all that goes before.*

2. The Holy Spirit was sent down after the ascension. Why? That He might witness to us of a heavenly Christ, *and bring the kingdom of heaven into our hearts and lives.*

3. "Cleansing of sins." Some one says: "At this time I saw plainly that whatever the Lord would communicate and make known of Himself and the mystery of His kingdom, He would do it in a way of purity and holiness." There are two sides from which we can approach the higher truth of God's word as to holiness and likeness to Jesus. The one is the desire to know all Scripture truth fully, and to have our system of doctrine complete and perfect. The other is the deep, intense longing to be made free from sin, as free as God can make us in this life. It is only from this side that real access will be given into the heavenly life of Christ.

First Section—i. 4.-14
The Son of God More Than the Angels

V.

The Son—a More Excellent Name

I.–4. Having become so much better than the angels, as he hath
inherited a more excellent name than they.

5. For unto which of the angels said he at any time,
Thou art my Son,
This day have I begotten thee? and again,
I will be to him a Father,
And he shall be to me a Son?

The superior excellence of the New Testament above the Old
consists in this, that God has spoken to us, and wrought salvation for us, in His Son. Our whole Epistle is the unfolding of the
glory of the person and work of the Son. The more completely
we apprehend this, and have our heart permeated by it, the better we shall apprehend the completeness of the salvation God
hath now provided for us. To know Jesus Christ in His glory is
the great need, the only safeguard, the sure growth of the Christian life.

There is often no better way of knowing a thing than by placing it in contrast with what is less perfect. Our Epistle would
teach us the glory of the New Testament by placing it in contrast
with the Old, especially with those who were its great mediators
and representatives. It will show us the superiority of Christ

over the angels, over Moses, over Joshua, over Abraham and Levi and Aaron.

It begins with the angels. **Having become so much better[4] than the angels, as He hath inherited a more excellent name than they.** Though these words belong grammatically to the preceding verses, they are in reality the heading of what follows. They form the transition from the theme to the first part of the argument—the excellence of Christ as Son of God above the angels. The Jews counted it one of their great privileges that the law was given by the ministration of angels (ch. ii. 2; Acts vii. 38, 53; Gal. iii. 19), heavenly spirits, who came direct from the throne of God. The manifestation of God had frequently been in the form of an angel: "the angel of the Lord" had been Israel's leader. And yet great as was the privilege, it was as nothing to that of the new revelation. Angels were but creatures; they might show signs of heavenly power, and speak words of heavenly truth; as creatures, they could not bring down the life of God itself, nor truly reach into the life of man. They had indeed as a title of honour been called "sons of God" (Ps. xxix. I, lxxix. 6); there is but One to whom it was said, *Thou art my Son; this day I have begotten Thee.* He alone, making us partakers of the very life of God, could indeed bring God nigh to us, and us nigh to God.

It is the superiority of the Son to the angels the writer is going to prove in this first chapter by a series of quotations from Old Testament Scripture. We must not, however, only regard these as so many proof-texts for the divinity of our Saviour, but as a divine revelation of the glory of that divinity in its various aspects. At the very commencement of his argument he will prove how the Old Testament had all along borne witness to the glory of God's Son, as the great thought that in God's revelation to man ever had the first place in God's heart.

4. The word "better" is one of the key words of the Epistle. It occurs thirteen times. See References.

Ere we proceed to study the texts themselves, it is of importance that we notice how the writer uses them. When our Lord on earth, or Paul, cites the Old Testament, they say: Moses says, or David says, or the prophets say. Our Epistle mostly quotes the words as coming from the lips of God Himself. In the seven quotations in our chapter it always is, *"He saith."* Farther on we find more than once, "The Holy Ghost saith." Scripture has two sides, the human and the divine. The knowledge of all that can illustrate the Scriptures as human compositions has its very great value. But it is of still more importance never to forget the divine side, and to be full of the conviction that Scripture is indeed God's word; that God Himself, through His Spirit, spoke in the prophets, and that it has the power of God dwelling in it.

This conviction will teach us two things, absolutely necessary to the profitable study of the Epistle. The one, that we recognise that these words of God contain a divine depth of meaning which the human mind never could have grasped or expounded. The wonderful exposition of Ps. ii. and the Son of God; of Ps. viii. and the human nature of Jesus; of Ps. xcv. and the rest of God; of Ps. cx. and the priesthood of Melchizedek; all prove to us how they were inbreathed by that Spirit of Christ who knew what was to come, and how it was that same Spirit who alone could have taught our writer to apprehend and unfold their divine meaning.

The other lesson is this, that the divine thoughts, thus deposited in the Old Testament as a seed by the Holy Spirit and unfolded by that same Spirit in the New, still need the teaching of the Spirit to make them life and truth to us. It is God who must shine in our hearts to give the knowledge of His glory in the face of Jesus Christ. Christ is the Word, "that was God," that speaks to us as coming out of the depth of God's heart, a living person; it is only the heart that yields to be led by the Holy Spirit that can expect to profit by the teaching of the word, and truly to know Christ in His divine saving power. The truths of Christ's sonship and divinity and priesthood and redemption *were given in charge to the Holy Spirit;* He revealed them from time to time; *He alone can reveal them to us.* To the written words all have free access; our mind can see their purport; but their life and power and blessing, the glory of the Son of God as a power of salvation—this is given to none but those who wait humbly on God's Spirit to teach them.

1. *The angels brought wonderful messages from God of old: but God is now drawing far nearer to thee, and waiting to speak in a far more wonderful and blessed way, by revealing the eternal Word in thy heart.*

2. *Words and wonders, these angels could bring. But to bring the life and the love of God, and give it in the heart—this the Son alone can do. But He does it. Christ is the divine nature manifesting and communicating itself; I have no contact with Christ or God in Him, but as I receive Him, as the divine nature imparting itself, as manifested in His human life, and will, and character.*

3. *If I were favoured this day with the visit of an angel—what a privilege I would count it. But Christ, the Son at the right hand, will not only visit, but will dwell in me. O my soul, rise to thy privileges: God speaks to thee in His Son.*

VI.

The Son—the Only Begotten

I.–5. For unto which of the angels said he at any time,
Thou art my Son,
This day have I begotten thee? (Ps. ii. 7). and again,
I will be to him a Father,
And he shall be to me a Son? (2 Sam. vii. 14).
6. And when he again bringeth in the firstborn into the world,
he saith, And let all the angels of God worship him (Ps. xcvii. 7).

It is because Christ is the Son of God that He is higher than the angels, and that the New Testament is so much higher than the Old. If we would grasp the teaching, and get the blessing of our Epistle, and indeed become partakers of the inner power and glory of the redemption Christ hath brought, we must tarry here in deep humility until God reveals to us what it means, that *His only Son* has become our Saviour. The infinite excellence of the Son above the angels is the measure of the excellence of that heavenly life He brings and gives within us. The angels could tell of God and of life. The Son has, the Son is, that life of God, and gives it. He that hath the Son, hath life.

Thou art My Son, this day have I begotten Thee. The words are used in Acts xiii. 33, of the resurrection of Christ. So the word **firstborn** in the next verse also has reference to the resurrection (Col. i. 18; Rev. i. 5). The Son was not only begotten of the Father in eternity, but begotten again in the resurrection. In the incarnation the union between the divine and the human nature was only begun: it had to be perfected by Christ, in His human will, yielding Himself to God's will even unto the

71

death. In the resurrection (Rom. i. 4), "He was declared to be the Son of God with power"; the full outbirth of humanity into the perfected fellowship and equality with Deity was completed; the Son of Man was begotten into all the likeness and glory of the Son of God. Thus Paul applies it (Acts xiii. 33): "God raised up Jesus, as also it is written in the second Psalm, Thou art My Son, this day have I begotten Thee." He then became the first begotten from the dead.

And again, I will be to Him a Father, and He shall be to me a Son. The words were spoken to David of a son God should give to him, but with the clear indication that their meaning reached far beyond what any mere man could be. In the Son of Man, who in the resurrection was raised up in power, and declared to be the Son of God, they find their complete fulfilment.

And when He again bringeth in the firstborn into the world, He saith, And let all the angels of God worship Him. The Psalm speaks of Jehovah coming to redeem His people: the Son is so one with the Father, that as the Father works only through Him, and can only be known in Him, the worship can only arise to God through Him too. The angels worship the deliverer as Jehovah.

Christ is the Son of God! What does this mean to us, and what is the blessing it brings our faith? It points us first to the great mystery that God has a Son. This is the mystery of divine love; and that in a double sense. Because God is love He begets a Son, to whom He gives all He is and has Himself, in whose fellowship He finds His life and delight, through whom He can reveal Himself, with whom He shares the worship of all His creatures. And because God is love, this Son of God becomes the Son of Man, and the Son of Man, having been perfected for evermore, enters through death and resurrection into all the glory that belonged to the Son of God. And now this Son of God is to us the revelation, the bearer, of the love of the divine Being. In Him the love of God dwells in us; in Him we enter and rest in it. When God speaks to us in this His Son, it is the infinite love imparting itself to us, becoming the inward life of our life.

And if we ask how this can be done, our answer is the second great lesson taught us by the truth that Christ is the Son of God! It was by being begotten of God, by a divine birth, that Christ became the Son. In eternity it was a birth; in the resurrection it was a birth from the dead. And so it is only by a divine birth that the Son, that the love of God, can enter and possess us. It is by an eternal generation that the Son is God. In eternity there is no past; what God is and does is all in the infinite power of an ever-present now. And so it is in the power of that eternal generation that the Father begetteth us in His Son (1 John v. 1–18), and be-getteth His Son in us; that the Father speaks the eternal Word to us and in us. *The Word of God is the Son,* coming from the heart of the Father, spoken into our hearts, and dwelling there. The Son is the Love of God; as the Son, so the Love of God is begotten within us, making us, by a new birth, partakers of its own nature and blessedness.

If we would learn the lesson of the Epistle, and experience in our Christian life the full power of the everlasting redemption, we must above all learn to know Jesus better. The general knowledge we had of Him before and at conversion is not enough for a strong and healthy growth. God desires that we come to a close friendship, to an intimate acquaintance, with His beloved Son, that we should be the loving, happy witnesses of how completely He can save. Let us do so. Remembering that angels and prophets could only point to Him who was to come, that the words of Scripture, and even of Christ Himself, only profit as they waken the expectancy of something higher, let us wait on God to speak in His Son to us. God's speaking in us will be a mighty act of creative power, a birth of His love within us.

O God! teach us that the blessed secret of a full salvation is this—Christ, our Saviour, is *the Son of God.*

1. *Christ, the Son of God's love: in His heart and in mine.*

2. *"Let all the angels of God worship Him."* All the servants around His throne point to Him: it is to Him we must look. And that in worship. It is worship, worship, worship, the Son must have. It is to the heart that worships Him He will make Himself known. Let our study of the glory of Christ in the Epistle be all in the spirit of worship, all tend to make us fall down in adoring worship.

3. The Son is a Son only in the power of a divine birth. And that not only in eternity, and in the resurrection, but in our heart too. This is the mystery of the divine life: let us bow in deep impotence and ignorance, and wait on God Almighty to reveal the Son to us.

4. The Son is the Word, because the divine speaking is but another aspect of the divine begetting. Speaking to us in His Son is all in the power of a divine life. The speaking, just as the begetting, is love imparting and communicating itself in divine power as an inward life. It is by God speaking to us in the First Begotten that we are begotten of God.

VII.

The Son Himself God

1.–7. And of the angels he saith,
   Who maketh his angels spirits,
   And his ministers a flame of fire: (Ps. civ. 4).
   8. But of the Son he saith,
   Thy throne, O God, is for ever and ever;
   And the sceptre of uprightness is the sceptre of thy
   kingdom.
   9. Thou hast loved righteousness, and hated iniquity;
   Therefore God, thy God, hath anointed thee
   With the oil of gladness above thy fellows (Ps. xiv. 7, 8).

In contrast to what is said of the angels as servants, the Holy Spirit hath said of the Son, **Thy throne, O God, is for ever and ever.** Christ is not only the Son, but is God. He is one with the Father: as Son He is partaker of the Father's own nature and being.

Christ is God: to many Christians this has been a dead article of faith, held fast and proved out of Scripture, but without any living influence on the soul. To the true believer it is one of the deepest and most precious truths for the nourishment of the inner life. *Christ is God:* the soul worships Him as the Almighty One, able to do a divine work in the power of divine omnipotence. *Christ is God:* even as God works in all nature from within, and in secret, so the soul trusts Christ as the everywhere present and the Indwelling One, doing His saving work in the hidden depths of its being. *Christ is God:* in Him we come into living contact with the person and life of God Himself. The truth lies at the foundation of our Epistle, and the Christian life it would build up: *Christ is God.*

Thy throne, O God, is for ever and ever. *As God, Christ is King:* the throne of heaven belongs to Him. When an earthly father has begotten a son, they may be separated from each other by great distance, both in place and character, and know each other no more. In the divine Being it is not so. The Father and the Son are inseparable, one in life and love; all that the Father is and has, the Son is and has too. The Father is ever in the Son, and the Son in the Father. God is on the throne and Christ in Him: the throne and the kingdom are Christ's too.

For ever and ever. *Christ is the King eternal.* His dominion is an everlasting dominion. The full meaning of the word eternal will become clear to us later on. Eternal is that which each moment and always exists in its full strength, immovable, unchangeable. "We receive a kingdom that cannot be moved," because our King is God, and His Kingdom for ever and ever. The rule of Christ our Priest-King, even now, in our souls, is in the power of an endless, an imperishable life: the faith that receives this will experience it.

And the sceptre of uprightness is the sceptre of Thy kingdom. *Christ is a righteous King:* He is Melchizedek, the King of Righteousness. In His kingdom all is righteousness and holiness. There "grace reigns through righteousness." It is the kingdom of heaven: in it the will of God is done on earth as in heaven. And when it is farther said, **Thou hast loved righteousness and hated iniquity,** we are reminded that the righteousness is not only His as a divine attribute, but His too as the fruit of His life on earth. There He was tested, and tried, and perfected, and found worthy as man to sit upon the throne of God. The throne which belonged to Him, as Son of God and heir of all things, He had as Son of Man to win. And now He reigns over His people, teaching them by His own example, enabling them by His own Spirit to fulfil all righteousness. As the King of Righteousness He rules over a righteous people.

Therefore God, Thy God, hath anointed Thee with the oil of joy above Thy fellows. *He is an anointed King. Therefore,* because He loved righteousness and hated iniquity, *therefore* God anointed Him. When He ascended to heaven, and sat down on the right hand of the throne, He received from the Father anew and in fullest measure, as the Son of Man, the gift of the Holy Ghost to bestow on His people (Acts ii. 33). That Spirit was to Him the oil of joy, **the joy that had been set before him,** the joy of His crowning day when He saw of the travail of His soul. An anointing **above His fellows,** for there was none like Him; God gave Him the Spirit without measure. And yet for His fellows, His redeemed, whom, as Head, He had made members of His body. They become partakers of His anointing and His joy. As He said, "The Lord hath anointed Me to give the oil of joy." Christ, our King, our God, is anointed with the oil of joy, anointed, too, *to give* the oil of joy: His kingdom is one of everlasting gladness, of joy unspeakable and full of glory.

O ye souls, redeemed by Christ, behold your God! the Son in whom the Father speaks. Let this be the chief thing you live for—to know, to honour, to serve your God and King. This is the Son in whom God speaks to you in all the divine mystery, but also in all the divine power and blessing, which marks all God's speaking. Let our hearts open wide to receive the King God hath given us.

And as often as we are tempted with the Hebrews to sloth or fear or unbelief, let this be our watchword and our strength: *My Redeemer is God!* In this faith let me worship Him. *My Redeemer is God!* let my whole heart be opened up to Him, to receive, as a flower does the light of the sun, His secret, mighty, divine working in me. *My Redeemer is God!* let me trust this omnipotent Lord to work out in me His every promise, and to set up His throne of righteousness in my soul in a power that is above all we ask or think. *My Redeemer is God!* let me wait for Him, let me count upon Him, to reveal Himself in the love that passeth knowledge. Blessed be the name of God for ever and ever: *My Redeemer is God!*

1. *Who is God? And what is God to us? "He in whom we live and move and have our being." He is the life of the universe. And how wonderfully perfect all that life is in nature. When we know this God as our Redeemer, "in whom we live and move and have our being" in a higher sense, what an assurance that He will make His new life in us as wonderful and perfect.*

2. *"Thou hast loved righteousness and hated iniquity, therefore" . . . This was His way to the throne; this is the only way for us, living and doing right, and hating everything that is sin.*

VIII.

The Son—the Everlasting Creator

I. 10. And,
>Thou, Lord, in the beginning hast laid the foundation of the earth,
>And the heavens are the work of thy hands:

11. They shall perish; but thou continuest:
>And they all shall wax old as doth a garment

12. And as a mantle shalt thou roll them up,
>As a garment, and they shall be changed:
>But thou art the same,
>And thy years shall not fail (Ps. cii. 26, 27).

Come and hearken once more to what the divine message has to tell us of the glory of the Son, in whom the Father speaks to us. Come and see how truly He is one with God, and shares with Him all His glory. The deeper our insight into the true Godhead of our Lord Jesus Christ, His perfect oneness with God, the more confident shall we be that He will, in a divine power, make us partakers of His work, His life, His indwelling.

We find Christ here set before us as the Creator, to whom all owes its existence, as the everlasting and unchangeable One, to whom alone, when all waxeth old and perisheth, can be said, **Thou continuest; Thou art the same; Thy years shall not fail.** In Isaiah God speaks of Himself: "Hast thou not heard, the everlasting God, the Lord, the Creator of the ends of the earth fainteth not, neither is weary." In our text we see the Son as the Almighty Creator, the everlastingly unchangeable One, that we may know who it is through whom God speaks to us, and to whom He has entrusted the work of our salvation.

The words are taken from Ps. cii. The ordinary reader would not think that the Messiah or the Son was here spoken of. But, taught by the Holy Spirit, our writer sees how all redemption is wrought only through the Son, and how, therefore, the building up of Zion and the appearing in His glory (ver. 16), the looking down from the sanctuary and the loosing those who are appointed unto death (ver. 20), all points to the Son as Redeemer. And then what follows is true of Him too. It is: "Thou hast laid the foundations of the earth, and the heavens are the work of Thy hands: they shall perish, but Thou shalt endure." God is the Almighty and everlasting: these are the attributes of Him to whom our salvation is entrusted.

Listen, believer! Christ, thy Redeemer, is the Almighty One. God saw that none but His Son could meet thy need: hast thou so seen it, too, that this, His almighty power, has been claimed and appropriated for thy daily life? Hast thou learnt never to think of Him otherwise than as the One who calleth the things that are not as though they were, and creates what otherwise could not be?

Christ, thy Redeemer, is the everlasting and unchangeable One: hast thou heard Him speak? "I, Jehovah, change not; therefore ye are not consumed," and learnt to trust Him as the One who is each moment to thee all that He can be, and who will, without variation or shadow of turning, maintain in neverceasing power His life within thee? Oh learn that God saw it needful to speak to thee through none other than such a One as could reach the heart and fill it with the power of His eternal Word. The Almighty Son, through whom God hath created all things, who upholdeth and filleth all things by the word of His power; this is He who will even so, in the power of His Godhead, uphold and fill thy whole life and being. Thy Creator is thy Redeemer! One great cause of feebleness and backsliding in the Christian life is the power of circumstances. We often say that temptations that come to us from our position in life, from the struggle to live, from the conduct of our fellow-men, draw us away from God, and are the cause of our falling into sin. If we but believed that our Redeemer is our Creator! He knows us; He appoints and orders our lot; nothing that comes to us but what He has in His hands. He has the power to make our circumstances, however difficult, a heavenly discipline, a gain and a blessing. He has taken them all up into the life-plan He has for us as Redeemer. Did we but believe this, how we should gladly meet every event with the worship of an adoring faith. My Creator, who orders all, is my Redeemer, who blesses all.

And now let me once again urge my reader to mark well the lesson this chapter is teaching us and the object it has in view. Let no one think, as I myself long thought, that, because we firmly believe in the divinity of our Saviour, this chapter, with its proof-texts, has no special message for our spiritual life, and that we may therefore hasten on to what the Epistle has to teach farther on. No, let us remember that this is the foundation chapter. The divinity of Christ is the rock on which we rest. It is in virtue of His divinity that He effected a real cleansing and putting away of sin, that He can actually communicate and maintain the divine life in us, that He can enter into our inmost being, and dwell there. If we open our hearts and give them time to receive the full impression of the truth, we shall see that all that we are to learn of the person and work of Christ has its value and its power from this—that He is God. Our Creator, from whom we have our life—it is He who alone can enter into us to give the new life; it is He, blessed be His name, who will do it now. As God, He is the hidden ground of all existence, and has the power to enter all and fill it with Himself. Every part of His work has the character and the power of a divine work. If we would but believe that Christ the Son is God, is Jehovah, the

Eternal, the Creator, how He would make our inner life the proof of His Almighty power!

Paul said: "I count all things but loss for the excellency of the knowledge of Christ Jesus my Lord." Let us do so, too. In the Christian life the chief thing, the one thing needful, is the knowledge of Christ. Not the intellectual apprehension of the truth, but the living experimental heart knowledge that comes from faith and fellowship with Him, from love and obedience. May it be ours!

1. *God is the incomprehensible One. In all thy thoughts of Him, in all thy efforts to know Him as revealed in Christ, remember the true knowledge of God is something above sense and reason. As the light reveals itself to the open eye that has been created for it, God reveals Himself to the longing heart. All the teaching of angels and prophets, of the words and the truths of the Bible, can but point the way: let God in Christ speak in thy heart. Then shalt thou know Him. Bow in adoring awe, and worship Christ. "Let all His saints worship Him. It is worship, not study, will prepare us to know."*

2. They shall perish: they all shall wax old: *this is what the creature is, even though created by God, with every experience, even though coming from God.* Thou continuest; thou art the same: *this is our security and our joy. Christ my Redeemer is the unchangeable—every moment the same, my Keeper and my Life.*

IX.

The Son—on the Right Hand of God

13. But of which of the angels hath he said at any time,
    Sit thou on my right hand,
    Till I make thy enemies the footstool of thy feet (Ps. cx.).
14. Are they not all ministering spirits, sent forth to do service
for the sake of them that shall inherit salvation?

Sit thou on My right hand, till I make Thy enemies the footstool of Thy feet. These words we have from Psalm cx. Luther called it the chief of all the Psalms. The first verse, and the fourth about Melchizedek, contain the hidden mysteries, which we never should have understood without the exegesis of the Holy Spirit. It is from this Psalm that the expression, which is become one of the great articles of our faith, **Sitting on the right hand of God,** has been taken into the New Testament. Our Lord quoted the words when he taught (Matt. xxii. 41) how David, when he said, "Jehovah said unto *my Lord*," had acknowledged that the Messiah who was to be His Son, would also be his Lord. Before Caiaphas (Matt. xxvi. 64) Christ spoke of Himself as "the Son of Man, sitting at the right hand of power." Mark (xvi. 19) in the narrative of the ascension, uses the words, "The Lord Jesus was received up into heaven, and sat down at the right hand of God." At Pentecost (Acts ii. 35) Peter proved from this text that David had prophesied of the Messiah. Paul (1 Cor. xv. 25) applies the words to the final conquest of all the enemies of the Lord Jesus. And to the Ephesians (chap. i. 20–22) he speaks of the "working of the strength of God's might, which He wrought in Christ when He raised Him from the dead, and made Him to sit at His right hand in the heavenlies." Our Epistle uses the expression five times (*see* Ref.). The words of David spoken through the Holy Spirit of what he could but very little have apprehended, became, through Jesus and the apostles, the revelation of what is the highest glory of Christ, and the greatest strength of our faith and hope.

The word suggests two thoughts. The one, that as Son of Man He is admitted to the perfect fellowship and equality with God; the other, that He is now possessor of divine, of universal authority and power. We are so familiar with the truth, that its infinite magnificence hardly strikes us. God is a God who is, and must be, infinitely jealous of His honour: His glory He will not give to another. When Jesus, the crucified Son of Man, takes His place at the right hand of the Majesty on high, it can only be because He is also the Son of God, because He is God. And it assures us that now the power and dominion of God Himself are in His hands, to carry out the work of redemption to its full consummation, until all His enemies have been put under His feet, and He shall deliver up the kingdom to the Father.

When the writer quotes the words, it is with the question: **Of which of the angels hath He said at any time?** And He gives the answer: **Are they not all ministering spirits sent forth to do service for them who shall be heirs to salvation?** He would impress deep upon us the thought that angels, though they come from God's throne, and are the instruments of His power, are still infinitely distinct from the Son. The redemption from sin, the true fellowship with God, the life and the love of God they cannot communicate. It is the Son, sitting at the right hand of God, acting in the power of God, to whom we must look for the everlasting redemption, for the true inward deliverance from sin, for a complete salvation. The angels, by contrast, all point us to the Son, seated as Man on the throne, in proof of, and to impart, that perfect restoration to the fellowship of the Most High in the Most Holy Place.

This is the Son in whom God speaks to us. The word, **Sit thou on My right hand,** is spoken in our hearing and in our behoof. In that word we have concentrated all God's speaking. See, He says, how I have exalted Him, your Brother, your Surety, your Head, to My right hand, in token of My perfect acceptance of His work; your perfect admittance to My presence and the enjoyment of all the power of the heavenly life; your full participation, in your inmost being, of what the kingdom of heaven is. **Sit thou on My right hand:** let the word enter and master all our heart and life. I have said that it occurs five times in the Epistle. Compare these passages, and the others having reference to Christ's place in heaven (*see* Ref. i. 3), and observe how the great truth we are to learn is this: the knowledge of Jesus as having entered heaven for us, and taken us in union with Himself into a heavenly life, is what will deliver the Christian from all that is low and feeble, and lift him to a life of joy and strength. To gaze upon the heavenly Christ in the Father's presence, to whom all things are subject, will transform us into heavenly Christians, dwelling all the day in God's presence, and overcoming every enemy. Yes, my Redeemer, *seated at God's right hand*—if I only know Him aright and trust Him as able to save completely—He will make me more than conqueror.

If we would obtain this blessed knowledge of our Lord, and the blessed life in the experience of His power, Scripture has a prayer for us (Eph. i. 17–22), that we will do well to pray often: "That the God of our Lord Jesus would give us the spirit of wisdom and revelation, that we may know what is *the exceeding greatness of His power to us-ward who believe,* according to *that working of the strength of His might* which He wrought in Christ, when *He made Him to sit at His right hand in the heavenlies.*" Let us pray for this spirit of divine illumination; let us study and adore the strength of God's might that lifted Him to the throne;

and let us believe joyfully, that that power works in us every day to lift us up and enable us to live as those who are set with Him in the heavenlies. And let us sing without ceasing: Praised be God for such a Saviour!

1. *"Now the chief point is this: We have such an High Priest who sat down on the right hand of the throne of the Majesty on high" (viii. 1). Yes, this is the chief point: Jesus in heaven, keeping it open for me, drawing me to enter into the Holiest, and keeping me in it: sending down heaven into my heart.*

2. *"He that descended is the same also that ascended far above all the heavens, that He might fill all things." On earth everything is limited by space and matter, in heaven all is in a divine, all-pervading power. As the light of the sun pervades all the air, the light and spirit of heaven can fill all our heart. The heavenly Christ fills all things.*

3. *See how they worship Him who sits on the throne in heaven (Rev. v. 8–14, vii. 9–12), and let every thought of Jesus on the throne lead to worship. It was as, during ten days, the disciples worshipped Him that had just sat down on the right hand of God, that they were filled with the Holy Ghost. The Pentecostal gift is ours: here is the place and the posture in which we shall enter into its full experience.*

The First Warning

Chap. ii. 1-4

To Take Heed to What the Son Speaks (1–4)

X.

The Danger of Neglecting So Great Salvation

II.–1. Therefore we ought to give more earnest[5] heed to the things that were heard lest haply we drift away.

2. For if the word spoken through angels proved stedfast, and every transgression and disobedience received a just recompense of reward;

3. How shall we escape, if we neglect so great salvation? which having at the first been spoken through the Lord, was confirmed unto us by them that heard;

4. God also bearing witness with them, both by signs and wonders, and by manifold powers, and by gifts[6] of the Holy Ghost, according to his own will.

The first chapter has set before us the divine glory of Christ the Son, in whom God hath spoken to us in these days. In the second the humanity and the humiliation of Jesus are to be unfolded. Ere the writer proceeds to this, he pauses to sound a note of warning. He reminds his readers of the greater responsibility

5. Abundant.
6. *Marg.*, Distributions.

and greater danger in case of neglect, which greater privileges bring, and to urge them to take more earnest, more abundant heed to what God is speaking in His Son.

Therefore, this is the link between the teaching of chapter i. with regard to the Godhead and glory of the Son, and the warning that now comes. The everlasting God speaks to us in His Son; we surely ought to **give more abundant heed.**

More abundant heed: it is the same word as is used in chapter vi. 17. "God being minded to shew *more abundantly* unto the heirs of the promise, the immutability of His counsel." In what God speaks and does, it is all with the desire to show to us *more abundantly,* in full and overflowing measure, what the purpose of His heart is. It is for this He speaks in none less than His own Son. He has a right to claim that we meet Him with a corresponding whole-heartedness, and give *more abundant* heed to what He speaks. Nothing less will satisfy Him; nothing less, in the very nature of things, will satisfy us, because nothing less than man's more abundant heed is capable of receiving God's more abundant grace. It is the lack of this taking more earnest heed, the lack of intense earnestness, giving God and religion the first place and the best powers of our life, which is at the root of the feebleness and sickliness of the Christian life. *God is speaking to us in His Son,* therefore we *ought* to take more abundant heed.

Lest haply we drift away—and perish more surely and more terribly than those who sinned under the Old Testament. There the word spoken, with its threatening, was stedfast, and every transgression was punished. **How shall we escape, if we neglect so great salvation?** The gospel does not, as so many think, lessen—it increases our danger. It does not diminish, but will terribly intensify, the soreness of the punishment in those who neglect it. Oh, let us sound out the warning: it is not only positive enmity or open sin that will be punished. No, simply "not taking earnest heed," just "drifting away" unconsciously with the current of worldliness and half-hearted religion, "neglecting" to give the great salvation that supremacy, that entire devotion which it claims—it is this which will render escape impossible.

And why? How can we show men that it is right and meet that it should be so? And what is the motive that will stir men to take heed? The answer is in the one word: **So great salvation.** The insight into the more abundant glory, the divine, the all-surpassing greatness of this salvation, is what will compel men willingly and joyfully to give up all and buy this pearl of great price.

And wherein does the greatness of this salvation consist? In this that it comes to us from and through the Triune God; the Holy Trinity is revealed as combining to work out this salvation for us. Listen. "**So great salvation,** *which having at the first been spoken by the Lord,* was confirmed unto us by them that heard." Christ the Son, the brightness of the Father's glory, and the express image of His substance, it was He in whom God spoke to us; it was He, the Redeemer, God and King, who Himself first preached the kingdom which He established when He effected the cleansing of our sins, and sat down on the right hand of the throne.

So great salvation! First spoken by the Lord, *God also bearing witness* both by signs and wonders, and by manifold powers. God the Father himself set His seal from heaven on the preaching of the word. The existence of His church is His standing sign and wonder, the proof of His divine power. Not to take heed, to neglect the great salvation, is nothing less than despising God Himself.

God also bearing witness, *by distributions of the Holy Ghost,* according to His own will. Not only did God bear witness to the great salvation by signs and wonders and powers, but above all by the Holy Ghost sent down from heaven. The Holy Spirit is God come to dwell on earth, to strive and plead and testify in the hearts of men. There is no fellowship with the Father but through the Son, and *no fellowship with the Son and His salvation,* but through the Holy Spirit in us. Let us enter the study of Christ's person and work in the Epistle in this faith. Yes, this is the greatness of the great salvation—in its offer the Three-One God comes to us. The Lord preached, the Father bore witness, the Holy Spirit came as the power of God to work. What a salvation! What sin to neglect it! May God reveal to us, as we study this Epistle, the glory of the so great salvation, that we may indeed more abundantly take heed to it.

1. *To know the Son who speaks and reveals the Father; to know the Father to whom, and whose love, the Son brings us in; to know the Holy Spirit with His wonderful gifts of grace and power; to be restored to the image and fellowship of the Holy Trinity: this is* salvation.

2. *Let every thought of the glory of Christ, and of God, and of the Spirit, and of the great salvation leave this one impression: Take more abundant heed to what you hear! Meet God's abounding grace with abounding desire to listen and believe.*

3. *To the preaching of Christ and the apostles God bore witness. If this was needful then, how much more now, at this long distance from those days of heavenly joy and power. Ask, for the study of the Word in the Epistle, that God bear witness of the Holy Ghost. Claim and expect it. Without this, even the teaching of the apostles by Christ Himself availed little.*

4. *Once again. This is the greatness of salvation; the everlasting Father in His love speaks to me Himself in the Son. The Son shows and brings and gives me all the Father speaks; and I have the Holy Spirit in me, fitting me to hear and know and possess and enjoy all that the Father in the Son speaks and gives. Let us, above all, hold this fast that there is no divine witness, or assurance, or experience of the salvation Christ effected, except as the Holy Spirit, which came from heaven, communicates and maintains it within us. Let us, therefore, take more abundant heed to the Holy Spirit in us, in whom the Father and the Son come to us.*

Second Section—ii. 5-18

Jesus, Even in His Humiliation As Man, More Than the Angels

The Reason of His Humiliation

XI.

The World Made Subject to Man, Not to Angels

II.–5. For not unto angels did he subject the world to come, whereof we speak.

6. But one hath testified somewhere, saying (Ps. viii. 5),
    What is man, that thou art mindful of him?
    Or the Son of man, that thou visitest him?

7. Thou madest him a little lower than the angels;
    Thou crownedst him with glory and honour,
    And didst set him over the works of thy hands:

8. Thou didst put all things in subjection under his feet.
For in that he subjected all things to him, he left nothing that is not subject to him. But now we see not yet all things subjected to him.

9. But we behold Jesus crowned with glory and honour.

As the Son of God Christ is more than the angels. As the Son of Man Jesus is more than the angels too. He was indeed, as man, made a little lower than the angels, and yet, because to man the world to come, of which the Spirit of Christ in the prophets spake, had been made subject, he had a place of honour and dominion greatly excelling them. Not only the divinity but the humanity of Christ will prove how infinitely superior the new dispensation is to that which was given by the ministry of angels.

For not unto angels did He subject the world to come, that world to which the Psalm looks forward, the kingdom of the Messiah, the kingdom of heaven upon earth. The Psalm does not speak directly of the Messiah, but of man and his destiny. But it is applied more justly to the Messiah, because in Him the Psalm and man find the fulfilment of what is promised.

The Psalmist first speaks of man's littleness and the wonder that God should notice him. **What is man that Thou art mindful of him? or the son of man that Thou visitest him?** He then points out how high the place is which man occupies. His nature is little less than divine. **Thou madest him a little lower than the angels; Thou crownedst him with glory and honour.** And universal dominion is assigned to him. **Thou didst set him over the works of thy hands. Thou didst put all things in subjection under his feet.** Our Epistle points out how this promise, though not yet true of man, has received its fulfilment in Jesus. **Now we see not yet all things subjected to man, but we see Jesus crowned with glory and honour.** What was true of man in promise, we see fulfilled in Jesus: what we see in Jesus, will be made true of man. What wonderful thoughts the Psalm suggests.

How glorious is the destiny of man! Created in the image of God, he was to bear God's likeness in this too, that as king he was to be ruler of all. The whole world to come was made subject to him. Man has received from God a life, a nature, a spirit, capable of partaking of His own life and spirit. His will and His holiness, capable of likeness to and fellowship with Himself, even to the sitting on His throne, and sharing with Him the dominion over all creation. What a destiny!

How gloriously we see that destiny fulfilled in Jesus! It was because man had been created with a nature capable of such a destiny, that the Son of God could become man, and not count it
unworthy of His divine glory Himself to work out that destiny.
He came and proved what the life of man was meant to be—
how humility and subjection to God were the sure path to glory
and honour. He came and glorified a life of humiliation as the
training-school for the exaltation to the right hand of God; fulfilling man's destiny in Himself as Son of Man. He, as Son of
God, fulfilled it for us too.

How gloriously and certainly man's destiny will yet be realised!
Jesus, the Son of Man, came as the Second Adam. He stands to
us in a relation as close, as real, as intimate, as Adam did. As
complete as was Adam's communication of a sinful nature will
be His impartation of a new, of His own nature. As Son of God,
Creator and Upholder of all, in whom all things consist, He has
a divine power of living within us with all that He was in Himself. His humanity is the revelation of what we can be; His divinity the pledge that we can be it. **We see not yet all things
subject to man, but,** and that is enough, **we see Jesus crowned
with glory and honour.**

It was by His union with us in our life in the flesh, by His
identifying Himself with our nature, that Jesus was able to claim
and to work out and enter into possession of the glory God had
promised to man. It is by our receiving His nature, and identifying ourselves with Him in this life on earth and in heaven, that
what He has achieved for us can really become ours. Let us here,
at the very outset of our Epistle, get well hold of the truth that
what Christ does for as our Leader, our Priest, our Redeemer, is
not anything external. All that God works in nature in heaven
or on earth, in the stars or in the trees, He does from within, by
laws that pervade their whole existence. All that Adam wrought
in us is from within, by a power that rules our inmost life. And
all that Christ does for us, whether as Son of God or Son of Man,

is equally and entirely a work done within us. It is when we know that He is one with us and we with Him, even as was the case with Adam, that we shall know how truly our destiny will be realised in Him. His oneness with us is the pledge, our oneness with Him the power, of our redemption.

1. *Thy destiny, O man, is to sit with Jesus on His throne. Live as one preparing for it. Cultivate a royal spirit. Abide in Him: He will abide in thee.*

2. The world made subject to man. *How terrible the ruin of sin, by which man was made subject to the world. Its king became its slave, and is so just when he appears most to master it. Christ teaches us to conquer the world by denying it; to hold it in subjection by not being of it. It is in the path of humiliation and self-denial alone that man's destiny can be realised.*

3. *The Epistle has two things to show us in Jesus, as inseparably connected: the place of glory where He is now; the path of humiliation that brought Him there. Make it thy care to follow Christ in His humility; He will make it His care to bring thee to His glory.*

4. *Study to see the intimate connection, the real unity between the two. It is the spirit that is subject to God on earth, to which God makes all things subject in heaven. The soul that in the humiliation of earth makes God all is fit for the heavens, when God is manifested in glory as the All in All.*

XII.

We See Jesus Crowned with Glory and Honour

II.–8. But now we see not yet all things subjected to him.
9. But we behold Him who hath been made a little lower than the angels, even Jesus, because of the suffering of death crowned with glory and honour.

What a glorious contrast! We see not yet all things subjected to him, that is, to man: **but**—what is far better—**we see Jesus crowned with glory and honour.** When we look round upon this world, with all its sin and misery, it does indeed not appear as if man was destined to be higher than the angels, and to have dominion over all the works of God's hands. But when we remember that Jesus became Man, that He might taste death for all men, and that He, a Man upon the throne, now lives as our Surety, our Redeemer, and our Head, it is enough if we see *Him* crowned with glory and honour. In that we have the pledge that He will one day bring man to that glory and honour too. In that we have the assurance that He is using all that glory and honour even now on our behalf. We see not yet all things subjected to man, **but—we see Jesus crowned with honour and glory.** Blessed contrast!

The right knowledge and use of this antithesis is the secret of the life of faith. **We see not yet all things subjected to Him**—how exactly this expresses the disappointment and failure which is often the experience of the believer when his first joy and hope begin to pass away. He finds that sin is stronger than he knew; that the power of the world and the flesh and self are not yet made subject to him as he had hoped. At times it is as if he feels that the promises of God, and the expectations they raised in his heart, are vain. Or else, if he acknowledge that God is indeed faithful to fulfil them, the way for one who is as weak as he is, and in his circumstances, to obtain these promises is too hard. The promises of God, to put all things in subjection to us and make us more than conquerors, are indeed most precious, but, alas, ever again the bitter experience comes—man sees not yet all things subjected to him.

Blessed the man who knows, then, in living faith to say: **But we see Jesus crowned with glory and honour.** Blessed the man who knows to look away from all that he finds in himself of imperfection and failure, to look up and behold all the perfection and glory he finds in Jesus! Yes, blessed the man who finds his delight and his life in meeting every disappointment and every difficulty with the blessed: **But—we see Jesus crowned with glory and honour.** This is all I need! this satisfies the soul, and gives it peace and joy and strength.

The Epistle is about to expound to us the great mystery, why the Son of God was made a little lower than the angels. It was that, by the grace of God, He might taste death for every man, and so open up again the entrance into God's presence and favour. The necessity and meaning of His sufferings and death it will present to us in three different aspects. The first (v. 10), that in suffering and death Christ Himself must needs be made perfect, so that as our Leader He might open up to us the path of perfection, and prepare that new nature, that new way of living, in which we are to be led to glory. The second (14, 15), that through death, making propitiation for sin, He might destroy the devil, with his power of death, and give us a perfect deliverance from all fear of it. And the third (16–18), that in what He suffered, He might be made a merciful and faithful High Priest, able to secure our perfect confidence, and to give us the succour we need. But before the writer thus unfolds the meaning of Christ's humiliation, he first points to His glory. It is this which constitutes the excellency of the New Testament, which gives our faith its power of endurance and victory; we see Jesus now at the right hand of the Majesty of God. Let us hold this fast as the chief thought of the Epistle, as the one great lesson the Hebrews, and all feeble backsliding Christians, need: Jesus, who suffered for us; Jesus who in His suffering as our Leader, opened a way to God for us; Jesus who sympathises with us—this Jesus is crowned with honour and glory. To see Him is to know that we have all we can need.

Would you, my reader, give more abundant heed to the great salvation? would you experience how completely Jesus is able to save? do you long for just as much of the love and the presence, the holiness and the joy and the power of God in you as there is in Jesus for you? here you have the secret of it all! Amid all sin and weakness, all darkness and doubt, all failure and perplexity, hold fast this one truth, engage in this one exercise of faith: **We see not yet all things subjected to man, but we see Jesus crowned with honour and glory.** This gives peace, and victory, and joy unspeakable.

And if you would know how thus ever to have the heart turned to Jesus, remember, He came to save His people *from their sins.* It is the heart that is weary of itself and its sins, that fully accepts the fact of the utter corruption and the utter helplessness of all that is of the old nature and of self, that will find itself attracted with strong desire to this mighty Redeemer. In such a heart Jesus, the crowned One, will not only be a distant object, but, by the Holy Spirit, an indwelling presence. The coming of the Holy Spirit is inseparably connected with, is our only proof of, the glorifying of Jesus (John vii. 38, 39; xvi. 14; xvii. 10), is our only real participation in the blessings that flow from it. Let all our worship of Him, crowned with glory and honour, be in the faith that the Pentecostal Spirit glorifies Him in us, so that our whole inner being is filled with His presence.

1. *Jesus,* made a little lower than the angels. *Jesus,* because of the suffering of death, *crowned with glory and honour. Look not only at the glory, but look well at the place of its birth, at the way in which it was gained. It is in the way in which you are walking now. Learn to welcome humiliation and suffering as the seed, the power out of which the glory is brought forth, as the way in which Jesus in glory is preparing you for the glory.*

2. *We see Jesus crowned with glory and honour. Let every experience of the contrast—we see not yet all things subject to man—become a call and a motive and a help to turn to Jesus. Let us take time and gaze and worship until our whole soul is filled with the faith: this life of humiliation is the bud of the glory everlasting: Jesus in glory is proof that it is so, the pledge that it will be so with us. Be this our life: We see Jesus, because of the suffering of death, crowned with glory and honour.*

XIII.

Jesus Tasting Death for Every Man

II.–9. We behold him who hath been made a little lower than the angels, even Jesus, because of the suffering of death crowned with glory and honour, that by the grace of God He should taste death for every man.

Here we have the one great reason why it was meet that Jesus should be made a little lower than the angels. It was that He might taste death for every man. In the counsel of divine grace, and in the great plan of redemption, this was one of the first objects of the incarnation—the birth was for the sake of the death. Without that wonderful birth—the Word, that was God, made flesh—the death would not have profited us. Without that wonderful birth the death would have availed us little. What God hath joined together let no man put asunder. Let us beware of exalting the one at the expense of the other. The birth and the death are two inseparable parts of the one process by which He was perfected as the Firstborn from the dead, and became our Deliverer and King. The humanity and humiliation of Jesus was needful for His death for or on behalf of every man.

And what was the meaning of this death? And wherein lies its efficacy? In Scripture there is a twofold aspect in which the death of Christ, as our Head, is set before us. The one is that *He died for sin,* bearing its curse, and suffering death as God's righteous judgment on account of it. His death opened up the way to God for us. It did for us what we cannot and need not do; it wrought out a finished salvation, which we have but to accept and repose upon. According to the other aspect, *He died to sin.* His death was a proof of His resistance to sin and its temptation, of His readiness rather to give up life than yield to sin; a proof that there is no way of being entirely free from the flesh and its connection with sin, but by yielding the old life to death, in order to receive afresh and direct from God a life entirely new. In this view His death was an act of infinite moral and spiritual value—the consummation of the work God wrought when He perfected Him through suffering.

The former aspect, the death for sin on our behalf, has its value from the second, which reveals what constitutes its true nature and power. And, even so, the faith in the death for sin, must lead us into the death to sin. The one view is that of substitution: Christ doing what I cannot do. The other that of fellowship: Christ working in me what I see in Himself. The former is a finished work, and gives me boldness at once and for ever to trust God. The latter is the power of sanctification, as the death and the life of Christ work in me.

Both views are found in the Epistle in perfect harmony. See how clearly the former comes out in this chapter. It is **because of the suffering of death**, that He has been crowned with glory and honour. "He was made a little lower than the angels **that He might taste death for every man**," might drink the cup of death, as the fruit of sin, for all. Some men die without tasting the bitterness of death; Jesus tasted its bitterness, as the curse of sin, in full measure. Then we read, ver. 14, that He became man, **that through death He might bring to nought Him that had the power of death, that is, the devil, and deliver them who were subject to bondage.** His death accomplished for us what we never could, what we now need not do. And ver. 17 tells us that His being made Man was that He might be a High Priest in things pertaining to God; *to make reconciliation for the sins of the people.* All these expressions—suffering death, tasting death for all, bringing to nought the devil, making reconciliation for the sins of the people—refer to the finished work which Christ wrought, the sure and everlasting foundation on which our faith and hope can rest.

In its subsequent teaching the Epistle will show us what the building is that rests on that foundation, what the heavenly power and life, the blessed nearness and service of God, to which the High Priest, our Forerunner and Leader, brings us in fellowship with Himself in the way He opened up. But it would have us begin here and strike the roots of our faith deep in the work which Christ, as our Substitute, wrought on Calvary. Let us study the words carefully, and remember them well, and believe them fully: Christ hath tasted death for all, and emptied the cup; Christ hath brought to nought the devil; Christ hath made reconciliation for sin. Death and the devil and sin: these have been put away, have been brought to nought. A complete deliverance has been effected. The sufferings and death of Christ have such an infinite worth and preciousness in God's sight that no soul, who is resolved to have nothing more to do with sin, need any longer fear, but may with boldness meets its God. The death of Christ hath wrought with mighty power in heaven and earth and hell. It has satisfied, and delighted God; it has conquered death and sin and hell; it has redeemed and delivered mankind. Let that death live in thy heart; it will work there its mighty wonders too. And thou shalt find Jesus in thine heart, for the suffering of death crowned with glory and honour.

1. *The first Adam tasted the forbidden fruit, and won death for all. The Second Adam tasted this death, and brought life for all. To all who accept Him, the power, the indwelling, the energy of the life is no less true and real than that of sin and death has been. "We see Jesus for the suffering of death crowned with glory and honour."*

2. *Jesus tasted the bitterness of thy sin and death, O my soul; that thou mightest taste the sweetness of His life and love. O taste and see that the Lord is good.*

3. *"By the grace of God taste death for every man." "Where sin abounded, grace did abound more exceedingly, that, as sin reigned in death, even so might grace reign through righteousness unto eternal life."*

XIV.

The Leader of Our Salvation

II.–10. For it became Him, for whom are all things, and through whom are all things, in bringing[1] many sons unto glory, to make the author[2] of their salvation perfect through sufferings.

We have seen that there is more than one reason for the humiliation of the Lord Jesus, even unto the suffering of death. Here we have the first: that as the Leader of our salvation, through whom God leads His sons to glory, He might open up the path, the way of life, in which we were to go. For this He needed to be made perfect through suffering and death. So only could He become a Leader,[3] in the true and full sense of the word. In suffering, His will was perfected, His character fashioned, His dependence on God and delight in His will was confirmed and made manifest. In suffering, His obedience unto death opened up the living way in which alone the creature can reach the Creator—the deepest humility and entire surrender. As Leader He opened up the path of life, a mode of living and acting, in which we are to follow.

1. Leading.
2. Leader.
3. The Dutch version has: "The Leader-in-Chief." The translation "Leader" makes more clear the connection with what precedes: "God leading (agagon) makes the *Leader*-in-Chief (Archēgos) perfect." Of *Captain* in A.V. and *Author,* R.V., Westcott says: "Neither word gives the fulness of sense. The *Archēgos* Himself first takes part in that which He establishes." In xii. 1 he adopts the word "Leader" in his translation—Jesus the Leader and Finisher of faith.

It is this that we also spoke of as the second aspect of Christ's death. That death is not only atonement but fellowship. It is only in suffering, in being crucified and dead with Christ, that we know Christ and His salvation. Christ was made perfect through suffering that He might be a Leader, that in conformity to Him, and in partaking of His Spirit and likeness, we might find the path to God and to glory.

The work of a leader supposes three things. The first: He must Himself lead the way, passing through all its difficulties and dangers, knowing and showing it to those who follow. The second: those who follow must yield themselves wholly to His guidance, walking even as He walked. The third: He must take charge of His followers, seeing that all hindrances are removed, and providing for all their needs. Let us see how blessedly all this is fulfilled in Jesus, and what a comfort it brings us to know that Jesus bears this name too: the Leader of our salvation.

The leader must walk in the very path his followers have to go.— The path we sought in vain was one that could bring us out from under the dominion of sin, both in its guilt as transgression against God, and its power as death to all that is holy and good. There was no possible way out of this state of sin and guilt and death, but by the submission to the judgment of God, and by giving proof, in bearing that judgment, of entire and willing surrender to God's will. There was no way to come out of fallen nature, with the power of self and selfwill ruling it, but by entirely dying to it; suffering anything rather than let it have its way. This was the way in which Jesus would have to lead us. And He had to walk in it Himself. **It became God, in leading many sons unto glory, to make the Leader of their salvation perfect through suffering.** Christ was perfect from His birth; every wish and inclination was as it should be; but only as a disposition, as a power, that needed to be tested and developed and strengthened by trial. What the suffering and the death effected in Christ personally, in perfecting His character, is the groundwork of what it effected on our behalf. It was needful that God should make Him perfect through suffering; the perfectness that comes through suffering is meekness and gentleness, patience and perfect resignation to God's will. It was because of the humility and meekness and lowliness of heart, which the Lamb of God showed here upon earth, that He is now the Lamb on the throne. Through suffering He was made perfect, and found worthy to be our High Priest.

A leader must be followed.—His followers must walk in the very path in which he walks. Jesus came and was made like us: we must come and be made like Him. His suffering and death is not only substitution and atonement. It is that, thank God! but it is much more too. It calls to fellowship and conformity. The substitution rests on identification: out of that conformity has its growth and strength. The Lamb of God has no salvation and no perfection to give us but His own meek spirit of entire dependence and absolute submission to God. The meekness and humility that it was needful God should perfect in Him are as needful for us. We must suffer and be crucified and die with Him. Death to self and the world, at the cost of any suffering or self-denial, this is the only path to glory the Leader of our salvation has opened up to us.

A leader cares for his followers.—He does not say, Follow me, who can. He watches over everyone, the very feeblest. Remember what care Stanley took in darkest Africa to gather in the stragglers—to leave the feeble ones provided in camp, and then to wait for their coming up. Jesus is a Leader, compassionate and sympathetic, and most faithful: with all the faithfulness and steadfastness with which He walked that path Himself on earth, will He help everyone, who will only in meekness trust and obey Him, to walk in that way to the end.

My brethren! do you understand what it means that the Father, in leading you to glory, has made Jesus **the Leader of our salvation.** Jesus is responsible for you. Take Him and trust Him as your Leader. The great need in one who follows a leader is a tender, teachable spirit. Rejoice that you have such a Leader, Himself made perfect in meekness and submission through suffering, that He might lead you in the blessed path that brought Him, and will bring you as surely, to the glory of the Father.

And remember who this Leader is—the Son of God, the divine Maker and Upholder of all things. Not only the Son of Man as a Leader outside of us, influencing us by example and instruction, by authority and kindness does He guide us. No, but as the Son of God who works in us by His Spirit, yea who Himself dwells within us. Even as it was God who worked in Him and perfected Him, will He, as God, now work in us and perfect us.

1. Christ came to give us an entirely new conception of what true life is, to show us a new way of thinking and living, to teach us that a heavenly life consists in giving up everything that has the slightest connection with sin for the sake of pleasing the Father perfectly. This is the new and living way He opened up through the rent veil of the flesh.

2. "It became God to perfect Him." All that Christ wrought, and all that was wrought in Him, was wrought by God. He yielded Himself to God: He did nothing of Himself: He allowed God to do all in Him. This is the path of perfection, the path to glory, in which Jesus leads. His divinity is inexpressibly precious to us for what He can be and do in us. But as inexpressibly precious His humanity, showing us how He was perfected, how God worked in Him, what we must be, what through Him we can most surely be.

3. Seek to get very clear hold of the truth that He is only a Saviour as He is a Leader. Salvation is being led by Him.

XV.

For Whom and Through Whom Are All Things

II.–10. For it became Him, for whom are all things, and through whom are all things, in bringing[4] many sons unto glory, to make the author[5] of their salvation perfect through sufferings.

For whom are all things. God is the final Cause of all that is. It exists with the one purpose of showing forth His glory. Every object in nature has its only reason of existence in this that the wondrous goodness and power of God may shine out through it. Above all, man was created that the adorable Being, whose very nature is love, might have the opportunity of proving in Him how freely and how fully he would make him partaker of the riches of His grace and glory.

For whom are all things, that in them His glory and goodness may be made known. "Worthy art thou, O our Lord and our God, to receive the glory and the honour and the power, for thou didst create all things; and because of Thy will they are and were created."

Through whom are all things. God is the efficient cause of all that is. God is the end and aim of all things, because He is their beginning and origin. All must return to Him because all came from Him and exist only through Him. There is no life or goodness or beauty, which does not rise up to Him again, its

4. Leading.
5. Leader.

only fountain and source. "There is one God, the Father, *of whom* are all things, and we *unto Him.*" "One God and Father of all, who is over all, and through all and in all."

The apostle might have written: "It became God to make the Leader of our salvation perfect through suffering." Not without good reason does he introduce here the character in which God acted in perfecting the Son as Leader of our salvation. When man sinned and fell from God, he lost together the two blessed truths in which his relation to God had stood. His holy allegiance to God, having all things *for Him,* his blessed dependence on God, having all things *through Him;* instead of these came the reign of self, with its life for self and through self.

It was from this life of self Jesus came to redeem us, to bring us back to God, to know and honour Him as the God and Father, **for whom are all things and through whom are all things.** In doing this he opened again the only way which could lead to glory. He did it first by showing us in His life, as Man, how men ought to live for God and through God. And then by delivering us through His death from the dominion of sin, and winning for us the power of the heavenly life.

For whom are all things, and through whom are all things. It was in this character that God perfected Christ through sufferings. It was in this character that Christ revealed and honoured God in His sufferings. It is to win and bring us to know and love and serve God in this character that Jesus is Saviour.

For whom are all things. Throughout His whole life there is nothing that Jesus sought to impress more distinctly on His disciples than this, that He was the Father's messenger and servant; that there was no thought of doing His own will or seeking His own honour; that He only sought and did what would be for the Father's pleasure and glory. He gave us the example of a man on earth living absolutely and entirely for God in heaven. His life on earth was the exhibition here in the flesh, the translation into human language, of the divine claim—"*All things for God.*" His allegiance to God was absolute. He proved to us that man's destiny and blessedness and everlasting glory are to be found in this: Living wholly for God.

Through whom are all things. Of this too Christ's life was the exposition. He was not ashamed continually to say that He could do nothing of Himself, and that only as the Father showed Him or spake to Him, could He work and speak. He counted this His blessedness and His strength—not to be able to do anything of Himself, but in continual dependence to wait on God and His working in Him. He knew and taught us that the man who has said in whole-hearted devotion to God, "All things for God," may confidently say too, "All things through God."

"*All for God,*" "*All through God.*" Jesus Christ has made it possible for us to make these our watchwords. In all aspirations after a closer walk with God, in all efforts after a purer, truer, higher life, they are the two poles between which the soul ought to move. They are the sure marks of that true scriptural mysticism, which has such attractions for all hungry souls, who long to know and please God perfectly.

All for God! absolutely, without a moment, a thought, a word, a person, a possession, excepted; wholly for God, this becomes the soul's one desire. It has seen that God is worthy of this, that He claims it, and that in the very nature of things, nothing less can satisfy the heart God made to be filled with Himself.

All through God! The clearer the aim becomes to be all for God, and the deeper the soul sinks into its own emptiness and impotence, under the conviction that with man it is impossible, the sooner does faith rise to see that we can not only say, but that we do dare to say, *All for God!* because we may also say, *All through God!* God Himself will work it in us.

This is the God who has revealed Himself to us in His Son. **It became Him, for whom all things and through whom are all things, to make the Leader of our salvation perfect through**

sufferings. Let us worship Him! Let us adore Him! Let us offer Him the sacrifice of full allegiance and childlike dependence, as the words ring through heart and life—All for God! All through God! God is all.

1. *The practice of the presence of God is a most needful and most blessed spiritual exercise. As the soul bows in stillness and lowliness, and worships in silence, it gets into the right spirit for recognising its own nothingness, and realising that God is all—that all is for Him, and all through Him.*

2. *All for God: that is consecration. All through God: that is faith. This was the spirit in which Christ yielded Himself to God: consecration and faith.*

3. *This was the God who perfected Christ. To know and honour God in this character is the secret of perfection, for in such He can do His work. This is the God who is leading many sons to glory; to know and honour Him is the path to glory. To reveal this God and His claims, to show how to give up everything to Him—this was what Christ came for. This is the life He brought us, the path He opened, the salvation He gives.*

XVI.

Jesus Calls Us Brethren

II.–11. For both He that sanctifieth and they that are sanctified
are all of[6] One: for which cause he is not ashamed to call them
brethren, saying (Ps. xxii. 23),
12. I will declare thy name unto my brethren,
   In the midst of the congregation will I sing thy praise.
13. And again, I will put my trust in him (Isa. viii. 17). And
again, Behold, I and the children which God hath given me (Isa.
viii. 18).

We have here the reason of what precedes. Why was it that it
was needful for God, in leading many sons unto glory, to make
the Leader of their salvation perfect through suffering? Or, how
was it, that making Him perfect could perfect them, and bring
salvation to them? The answer is, He that sanctifieth, that is,
Jesus, and they who are sanctified, God's sons, are all out of
One, that is, of God. In proof of this three texts are quoted, in
which Jesus calls us brethren, takes His place with us in trusting
God, and speaks of us as the children God hath given Him. It is
because Jesus, the firstborn Son, and the sons He leads to glory,
are one in their being begotten of God, that His perfection secures their salvation. It is the oneness of Jesus with us that fits
Him to be the Leader of salvation.

This oneness has its root in the truth of the divine life. **Both
He that sanctifieth, and they that are sanctified are all out of
One.** Jesus is the only begotten, the eternal Son, one with the Fa-

6. Out of.

111

ther in His divine Being and Majesty. We are sons of God, as we partake of the divine life through and in Him. Nothwithstanding the difference between His Sonship and ours, His being original and ours derived, they are at root one; the life of both has its origin in the life of God. It is this oneness of Christ with us in origin, that made it possible for Him to become one with us in our humanity, and so to be the Leader of our salvation. It is this oneness that makes it possible for Him to communicate to us that perfection, that perfect meekness and delight in God's will, which was wrought out in His human nature through suffering, that holiness of His with which we must be made holy.

For both He that sanctifieth, and they that are sanctified are all of One. Jesus is the sanctifier, we are the sanctified. The object for which Christ became the Leader of our salvation, the great work He has to do for us, the bond of union between the Son and the sons of God, the proof of their bearing His image and likeness, and the mark of their real oneness, is *Holiness*.

The word Holy is one of the deepest in Scripture. It means a great deal more than separated or consecrated to God. The Triune God is the Thrice-Holy One: Holiness is the deepest mystery of His Being, the wondrous union of His righteousness and His love. To be holy is to be in fellowship with God, possessed of Him. Therefore the Spirit specially bears the name of Holy, because He is the bearer to us of the love of God, and the maintenance of the divine fellowship is His special work. Jesus is the Holy One of God, who makes us holy in filling us with His Holy Spirit.[7] The difference between Jesus and us is great—the oneness is greater. He and we are of one, together partakers of God's life and God's holiness. Let us give abundant heed to so great salvation.

7. Here and throughout the Epistle the word holy and sanctify includes much more than is ordinarily meant by the doctrine of sanctification. "Sanctify here includes all that God does for our restoration, as He calls, justifies, and glorifies." Rieger in Lange on x. 10 (comp. ix. 13, 14; x. 10, 14, 29; xiii. 12).

This oneness finds its manifestation in the Brother-name which Jesus gives us. **For which cause He is not ashamed to call them Brethren, saying, I will declare Thy name unto My brethren.** The writer had spoken of our inner oneness with Jesus. But oh, what a difference in actual life, such a terrible difference that He might well be ashamed of us! Yes! before angels as well as before the world, how often His saints have put Him to shame, have given Him reason to be ashamed of His relationship! But—blessed be His name—His becoming man was an act of condescension, which had its root in the sense of His oneness with us as being one with Him out of God, which had its strength in the love as of an elder Brother.

Three texts are now quoted; the one from Ps. xxii. 23, in which the suffering Messiah promises to make known the Father's name to His brethren; the second and third from Isa. viii. 17, 18, in which, in prophetic types, His fellowship with all His people in the life of faith and trust, and His place at the head of those whom God has given Him as children, find expression.

What wonderful thoughts! We, as truly as Jesus, are of God! It is in the light of this truth that Jesus looks on us, and loves us, and deals with us! It is in the light of this truth we must look on Jesus, and love Him, and deal with Him. And in the light of this truth let us look on ourselves too. This is the life of faith—to see Jesus and ourselves as He sees us, to think as He thinks, to live in His heart. Then will the promise be fulfilled to us, "I will declare thy name unto my brethren," "that the love wherewith thou hast loved me may be in them." As we bow in lowly, waiting silence before Him, the soul will hear Him say: My Brother! let me reveal to thee the Father. And the name and the love and the nearness of the Father will have new meaning when I can say, Jesus calls me His brother! God has spoken to me in His Son! And I shall understand that, to faith, the incomprehensible reality of oneness with Jesus becomes the blessed, conscious experience of the soul in its daily life.

1. *Union with Jesus in being born of God, in being holy, in being acknowledged by Him as a brother! What a blessed life! what a full salvation!*

2. *"He that doeth the will of God, the same is My brother." Wouldst thou know the holy joy of Jesus saying to thee, Brother!—let thy life be what His was—the doing of the will of God! It was in this He was perfected in suffering. It is in this that His Spirit and life in thee will manifest itself, and the Brother-name will be the index not only of His compassion but of the oneness in Spirit and the likeness in conduct which prove thee a son of God.*

3. *Sanctification, holiness, is nothing more than a life in union with Jesus. Nothing more, and nothing less. He that sanctifieth, and they who are sanctified, are all of One. To live in that oneness, to have Jesus living in us, is the way to be holy.*

4. *"And again, I will put my trust in Him." Jesus lived by faith in God. He is the Leader and Perfecter of faith. He opened up to us the path of faith and leads us in it.*

XVII.

That He Might Bring to Nought the Devil

II.–14. Since then the children are sharers in flesh and blood, he
also himself in like manner partook of the same; that through
death he might bring to nought him that had the power of death,
that is, the devil;
15. And might deliver all of them who through fear of death
were all their lifetime subject to bondage.

The previous verses spoke of the oneness of Jesus and His brethren from the divine side: they are all of One. Here we have it put
before us from its human side: **Since the children are sharers
in flesh and blood, He Himself in like manner partook of the
same.** We have already said that for this, Christ becoming man,
there was more than one reason. The first, that, as our Leader,
He might Himself be perfected, and so prepare a way—a way or
state of living, a nature, a life, in which we might draw nigh to
God. The second, that He might deliver us from the power of
death and the devil. The third, that in all His work for us and in
us, He might be a merciful High Priest in things pertaining to
God, able to understand and sympathise with us, and ready to
bear and to succour. Here it is the second of these three aspects
of Christ's incarnation that is brought out: He became man that
He might meet and conquer and destroy the power of death and
the devil.

**Since the children are sharers in flesh and blood, He also
Himself likewise partook of the same.** However familiar the
thought of the incarnation is, let us again seek to realise fully all

that it means. As Adam never could have brought us under the power of sin and death, if he had not been our father, communicating to us his own nature, so Christ never could save us, except by taking our nature upon Him, doing in that nature all that we would need to do, had it been possible for us to deliver ourselves, and then communicating the fruit of what He effected as a nature within us to be the power of a new, an eternal life. As a divine necessity, without which there could be no salvation, as an act of infinite love and condescension, the Son of God became a partaker of flesh and blood. So alone could He be the Second Adam, the Father of a new race.

That through death He might bring to nought him that had the power of death, that is, the devil. Death is a power that has its sanction from God Himself. In the very nature of things it could not be otherwise than that man, when he turned from God, the fountain of life, to Satan and to self, fell under the power of death. He had yielded himself to Satan, and Satan had power over him. As the jailor keeps the prisoner under the authority of the king, Satan holds the sinner in the power of death so long as no true legal release is given. The only way for us to come from under the power of Satan and death was, to lay off that fallen nature over which they had power, to come out of that sinful life by dying to it, and, in dying, to be entirely freed from it. We had no power to do this. Jesus entered into all the conditions of our fallen humanity. He entered into our death, and endured it as the penalty of sin, and, enduring it, satisfied the law of God. And so, because the law had been the strength of sin, He took from sin and the devil the power of death over us. He endured death as the end of the life of the flesh, in full acknowledgment of God's righteous judgment, yielding up His spirit to the Father. Death, as the penalty of the law, death as the end of the life of nature, death as the power of Satan over man, was destroyed, and he that had the power of death was brought to nought. And now, as little claim or power as death has on

Him, has it on those who are in Him, on those in whom the power of His life now works. **He also Himself partook of flesh and blood, that through death He might destroy him that had the power of death, that is, the devil.**

And might deliver all them who, through fear of death were all their lifetime subject to bondage. The power of death and the devil has been so completely broken that there is now perfect deliverance from that fear of death which keeps so many in bondage. Under the Old Testament, life and immortality had not yet been fully brought to light. No wonder the older saints often lived and spoke as those subject to bondage. But how sad that the redeemed of Jesus Christ, His brethren, so often prove that they know but little of the reality and power of His deliverance, or of the song of joy: "Death is swallowed up in victory. Thanks be to God who giveth us the victory, through Jesus Christ our Lord."

My brother! art thou living in the full experience of this blessed truth? Because thou sharest in flesh and blood, Christ came and likewise partook of the same, that there might be perfect oneness between Him and thee. Livest thou in this oneness? By His death He destroyed the devil, that thou mightest be entirely freed from out of his power. Is thy life in this liberty? He delivers from the fear of death and the bondage it brings, changing it into the joy of the hope of glory. Is this joy thy portion? Let us believe that he, who is now crowned with glory and honour, is indeed able to make all a reality to us, so that, as those who are one with Him by the double bond of the birth from God, and the birth in flesh and blood, we may be His ransomed, His sanctified ones, His beloved brethren. He gave Himself to be wholly like us and for us—shall we not give ourselves to be wholly like Him and for Him?

1. *"Through death destroyed him that had the power of death." Death had its power from the law. There was no way of conquering it but by fulfilling its claim. Through death He destroyed death. This is the way for us too.*

As I give myself up to death, as I give up the sinful life, and die to self in the power of Christ's death, the power of His deliverance will work in me. 2. Through death to life. *This is the law of nature, as seen in every corn of wheat. This is the law of the life of Christ, as seen in His resurrection. This is the law of the life of faith, to be felt and experienced every day, as the power of the New Death which Christ died, and the New Life He lives, works in us.*

3. *The first chapter revealed to us the divinity of Christ, as the foundation of the gospel, that we might know that all that He accomplished in His humanity has been effected in divine reality, and works in us in divine creative power.*

XVIII.

A High Priest Able to Succour

II.–16. For verily not of angels doth he take hold, but he taketh hold of the seed of Abraham.

17. Wherefore it behoved him in all things to be made like unto his brethren, that he might be[8] a merciful and faithful high priest in things pertaining to God, to make propitiation for the sins of the people.

18. For in that he himself hath suffered being tempted, he is able to succour them that are tempted.

In the first chapter we saw the writer quoting text after text from the Old Testament, in order that he might bring us to the full apprehension of the truth and the meaning of our Lord's divinity. In this chapter we see him in the same way, time after time, reiterate the fact of our Lord's humanity, lest we should not fully realise all that it means. So it is here. He had just said, **Since the children were sharers of flesh and blood, He also Himself in like manner partook of the same.** It is as if He feels the insufficiency of the words, and therefore once again repeats and confirms his statement: **For verily not of angels doth He take hold, but He taketh hold of the seed of Abraham.** Man may have been made lower than the angels, but this honour have they not, that He took hold of them—**He taketh hold of the seed of Abraham.**

And how doth He take hold? There is no way in which God can take hold of a creature other than by entering into him with

8. Become.

His life and spirit, so imparting His own goodness and power, and bringing him into union with Himself. So did Jesus take hold of man. He entered into humanity and became one with it. And so he takes hold of individual souls by entering with each into personal union and fellowship.

Wherefore, being thus minded to take hold of man, **it behoved Him,** it was divinely right and proper, and, in the nature of things, an absolute necessity, as a consequence of His purpose, **it behoved Him in all things to be made like unto His brethren.** The laying hold implied His identifying Himself with them, and this again was impossible without being made like them in all things. So only could He save them. It was indeed needful, **that so He might become a merciful and a faithful High Priest in things pertaining to God, to make propitiation for the sins of the people.**

Here we have, for the first time, the word High Priest—a word which is used in no other book of the New Testament of our Lord Jesus, but in this Epistle is its central thought. We shall see later (chap. v.) how inseparably His divine sonship and His priesthood are linked. Here we are taught that His real humanity is just as much essential to it. It is one of the remarkable things in the Epistle that it unfolds so wonderfully the value of the personal development in our Lord's life. It ever connects the person and the work as inseparable.

See it here. The work He had to do was—**to make propitiation for the sins of the people.** Sin had incurred the wrath of God, and His love could not flow forth towards men till the sin had been covered up, atoned for, taken away. In fulfillment of all that had been taught us in the Old Testament sacrifices, Christ came to do this. He put away sin by the sacrifice of Himself, and obtained everlasting redemption. Of this the Epistle will speak later on. What it here seeks to press, is that Christ became Man, not merely to die and atone, but that in doing this, He might be a faithful and merciful High Priest. His relation to us was to be a personal one. He must Himself minister to us the salvation He worked out. Everything would depend upon His winning our confidence, getting possession of our heart and love, and as a living Leader guiding us into the path to God. It is this which makes His human life on earth so precious to us. It proved Him faithful: we dare fully trust Him. It found Him merciful: we need not fear coming to Him. He was made in all things like unto His brethren, that He might become a merciful and faithful High Priest.

For in that He Himself hath suffered being tempted, He is able to succour them that are tempted. The work of our High Priest does not only consist in His atonement, nor even in the advocacy and intercession which is the fruit of that atonement. But above all, as the result of all these, in that personal charge of our spiritual life which He takes, in that never-ceasing succour which He is able to give in every temptation. This is the greatest and most blessed part of His work in bringing us to God, that, as the Leader in the path of suffering and perfection, He inspires us with His own dispositions, and, by the mighty operation of His Spirit within us, gives us His help in every time of need. The one thing we need is, to know and trust Him fully. To know Him as High Priest who not only has opened a way to God for us to walk in, and not only in heaven prays for us, but who undertakes to keep us so in fellowship with Himself, and under the covering of His power, and in the experience of His full redemption, that temptation can never conquer us. His divinity secures to us His unfailing and never-ceasing presence. His humanity assures us of His sympathy and compassion. More ever-present and more mighty than the temptation, His unfailing love is always near to give the victory. He can and will do it. Our High Priest is a living, faithful helper: let us trust Him. Salvation is not a thing He gives us apart from Himself. Full salvation is nothing but Jesus Himself, most compassionately and most faithfully watching over us in daily life, most really and fully giving and living His life in us. The abiding, indwelling presence of Jesus, *able to succour*, is the true secret of the Christian life. Faith will lead us into the experience that Jesus is and does all that is said of Him.

1. *What a chapter! Jesus crowned with glory and honour. Our Leader, our Sanctifier, our Brother, made like to us, our merciful and faithful High Priest, tempted as we are, our helper in temptation. What a Saviour!*

2. *No member of my body can be hurt without my feeling it and seeking to guard it. No temptation can touch me without Jesus feeling it at once, and giving succour. Is not the one thing we need to know Him better, in faith to realise His ever-present nearness, and to count on His help?*

3. *The knowledge of Jesus that sufficed for conversion will not suffice for sanctification. For the growth of the spiritual life it is essential that we enter more deeply into the knowledge of all that Jesus is. Jesus is the bread of heaven, the food of our spiritual life; knowing Him better is the only way to feed upon Him.*

4. *Learn to regard every temptation as the blessed opportunity for trusting and realising the succour of your ever-present High Priest.*

Third Section—iii. 1-6
Christ Jesus More Than Moses

XIX.

Consider Jesus

III.–1. Wherefore, holy brethren, partakers of a heavenly calling, consider the Apostle and High Priest of our confession, even Jesus.

Consider Jesus! This is the central thought of the verse, and of the passage of which it is a part, as it is indeed of the whole Epistle. It is the one aim of the writer to persuade the Hebrews that, if they but knew aright the Lord Jesus as the faithful, compassionate, and almighty High Priest in heaven, they would find in Him all they needed for a life such as God would have them lead. Their life would be in harmony with their faith, in harmony with the life of Him whom their faith would apprehend. The words might have been taken as the title of my book: **Consider Jesus!** is indeed the keynote of the Epistle.

The word *consider,* from the root of the Latin word for Star, originally means to contemplate the stars. It suggests the idea of the astronomer, and the quiet, patient, persevering, concentrated gaze with which he seeks to discover all that can be possibly known of the stars which the object of his study are. And Jesus, who is God, who became man, and perfected our human nature in His wonderful life of suffering and obedience, and now dwells in heaven to communicate to us its life and blessedness—oh, what reason there is for saying, **Consider Jesus.** Gaze upon Him, contemplate Him. For some increased knowledge of the stars what devotion, what enthusiasm, what sacrifices are ofttimes witnessed. Oh, let the study and possession of the Son of God waken our devotion and our enthusiasm, that we may be able to tell men what beauty and what glory there is in Jesus.

Holy brethren! Thus the Hebrews are now addressed. In the previous chapter the word *brethren* had been used twice. **He is not ashamed to call them brethren. It behoved Him to be made like unto His brethren.** The sacred name is now applied personally: Christ's brethren are brethren in Christ. And the heart of the writer warms to them personally, as he seeks to urge them to what with him is indeed the one aim of the Epistle— **Consider Jesus.**

Holy brethren! The word *holy* had also been just used. He that sanctifieth, maketh holy, and they who are sanctified, made holy, are all of one. We saw how holiness is the common mark of Christ and His people: their bond of union, and the great object they both aim at. One of the great mysteries the Epistle is to reveal to us is that our great High Priest has opened the way for us into the Most Holy Place or the Holiest of All. In Hebrew it is the Holiness of Holinesses. There we have boldness of access, there we are to have our dwelling encircled by the holiness of God. We must know that we are holy in Christ; this will give us courage to enter into the Holiness of Holinesses, to have God's holiness take complete possession, and fill our whole being. It is Jesus who makes holy: it is we who are to be made holy: what more natural than that the thoughts should be coupled together: holy brethren, consider Jesus.

Holy brethren! partakers of a heavenly calling, consider Jesus! What is elsewhere spoken of as a holy calling is here named a *heavenly* calling. That does not only mean a calling from heaven, or a calling to the heaven, whence the call proceeds. No, there is much more in it. Heaven is not only a place, but a state, a mode of existence, the life in which the presence of God is revealed and experienced in its unhindered power. And the heavenly calling is that in which the power of the heavenly life works to make our life heavenly. When Jesus was upon earth the kingdom of heaven was nigh at hand; after He had ascended and received the kingdom from the Father, the kingdom of heaven came to this earth in power, through the descent of the Holy Spirit. Christians, at Pentecost, were people who by the new birth entered into the heavenly kingdom or state of life. And the kingdom entered into them. And they were partakers of a heavenly calling, because the spirit and the life and the power of heaven was within them.

It is to such men the invitation comes. **Holy brethren! partakers of the heavenly calling! consider Jesus!** If you would know what it is to be holy and to live holy, consider Jesus who makes holy! If you would know the privileges and powers that belong to you as partakers **of a heavenly calling, consider Jesus!** He is God, the King of heaven! He is Man who has ascended to heaven as your Priest and Saviour, has opened it for you, and can communicate its life and blessedness. Oh, **consider Jesus!** set your heart on Him; He will make you holy and heavenly.

There is more than one of my readers who mourns that he knows so little what it is to live a holy and a heavenly life. Listen, God's word speaks to you—Holy brethren, partakers of a heavenly calling! **consider Jesus!** This is your weakness: you have looked at yourself and your own strength; you have not studied Jesus! This will be your cure: each day, each hour, **consider Jesus,** and in Him you will find all the holiness and the heavenliness you need.

1. In the latter part of the Epistle all the glory of Jesus as He entered heaven, and opened it for us, as He became a minister of the heavenly sanctuary, and leads us to dwell in the Father's presence, will be opened to us. But let us even now, from the commencement, hold fast the truth that the knowledge of Jesus seated in heaven *is the power of* the heavenly calling *and* the heavenly life.

2. *Do not think that you know all that can be told about Jesus. Believe that there are wonders of heavenly joy to be revealed to you if you know Him better: His divine nearness and oneness with you, His ever-present indwelling to succour and lead you, His power to bring you into the Holiest of All, into the Father's presence and love, and to keep you there, will be revealed.*

XX.

Christ and Moses

III.–1. Wherefore, holy brethren, partakers of a heavenly calling, consider the Apostle and High Priest of our confession, Jesus.

2. Who was faithful to him that appointed him, as also was Moses in all his house.

3. For he hath been counted worthy of more glory than Moses, by so much as he that built the house hath more honour than the house.

4. For every house is builded by some one; but he that built all things is God.

5. And Moses indeed was faithful in all his house, for a testimony of those things which were afterward to be spoken:

6. But Christ as a Son, over his house; whose house are we, if we hold fast our boldness and the glorying of our hope firm unto the end.

The writer had just spoken (ii. 17) of Christ as a *merciful* and *faithful* High Priest. Later (iv. 14–v. 7), he will speak again of Him as merciful. Here he wishes first to set before us His faithfulness. To this end he compares Him to Moses, of whom God Himself had spoken (Num. xii. 7): "My servant Moses, who is faithful in all My house." But he goes on at the same time to prove that Christ the Son is more than Moses the servant. We have seen that Christ is more than the angels through whom the law was given; we shall yet see that He is more than Aaron, through whom the law was ministered; He is more than Moses too, the mediator of the law, the servant in the house of God. In every aspect the New Testament has more glory than the Old.

127

Moses and Aaron together represented God in Israel; the one as apostle or messenger, the other as high priest. In the person of Jesus the two offices are united. As High Priest He is merciful as Aaron; as Apostle of our profession He is faithful as Moses. Moses was the great apostle or messenger of God, the Old Testament type of Christ as prophet. He had access to God, and brought the word of God to the people. Christ is the great Apostle or Prophet of the New Covenant. He ever spake of Himself as the one whom the Father had sent; in Him, the Son, God speaks to us. As Apostle He is God's Representative with us, making God known to us; as High Priest, our Representative with God, bringing us into His presence. As High Priest He stands linked to us by His mercy and compassion, as He now, having died for us, helps us in our temptation and weakness; as Apostle He pleads for God with us, and proves Himself entirely faithful to Him. We need to consider Christ Jesus, not only as a High Priest in His mercy, but as the Apostle of our profession **who was faithful to Him that appointed Him, as also was Moses in all his house.** Faithfulness is trustworthiness. As we see Jesus faithful to Him who appointed Him, our faith and trust will rise into perfect and joyful assurance that He will indeed most faithfully fulfil all God's promises in us, that in us too He will be faithful as a Son over His own house. Nothing gives such strength to faith as resting on the faithfulness of Jesus. The glory of Jesus is the glory of Christianity; is the strength and glory of the Christian life.

Moses was in every respect a type of Christ. In what he suffered from his very brethren; in his rejection by his brethren; in his zeal and his sacrifice of all for God; in his willingness to die for his people; in his fellowship with God; we see the marks of an apostle, as they were to be perfectly revealed in Christ Jesus. And yet it was all only a shadow and a prophecy, a testimony of things to come. **For He hath been counted worthy of more glory than Moses, by so much as he that built the house hath** more honour than the house. **For every house is builded by some one; but He that built all things is God. And Moses verily was faithful in all his house as a servant, for a testimony of those things which were afterwards to be spoken; but Christ, as a Son over His house.** Moses was himself but a part of the house: Jesus Christ is the builder. Moses was a servant in the house; Jesus was a Son over His own house.

Whose house we are. The true house, the true dwelling of God, is His people. In Christ we are builded together for a habitation of God in the Spirit. Of the Church, as His body, of the individual soul, Christ says: "We will come and make our abode." It is the characteristic of spiritual things that each part is also a living whole. Collectively and individually we are Christ's house: he that would know the faithfulness of Christ in His house, must yield himself to be His house, must allow Christ as Son over His house to be Master, to have the keys alone, to hold undisturbed possession and rule.

Whose house we are. Later on we shall see how the great work of Christ, as the great High Priest over the house of God, is to open the way into the holiest of God's dwelling, His living, loving presence. The word we have here today tells us beforehand that the Holiest is not only with God, and that we must enter into it; it is also with us, and God will come in to us too. God's heart is our habitation; our heart is God's habitation. When Jesus spake, "Abide in me, and I in you," He taught us that mutual relationship. The more my heart goes out to Jesus and lives in Him, the more He comes to live in me.

Whose house we are. Would you have the full experience of all that means and brings? Holy brethren, partakers of the heavenly calling, *consider Jesus,* who is faithful to Him that appointed Him, as a Son over His house. Yield yourself to Him as His house, and trust His faithfulness to do His work. And, remember, as the Epistle teaches us the spiritual meaning of the external symbols of the Old Testament, that we must not seek their fulfilment again in other external things, however much we conceive of them as infinitely higher and greater, but in that inward spiritual experience which comes when Jesus dwells in us as His house. It is as the Indwelling Saviour that He does His work, whether it be Prophet, Priest, or King. *Whose house we are.*

1. Faithful to God. *This is the spirit of God's house, the mark of being of His household. It was so with Moses the servant. It was so with Christ the Son. It must be so through the whole household. Be it so with us:* Faithful to God.

2. Whose house we are. *Not like a house of stone and wood, in which the indweller has no living connection with it. No, Christ dwells in us as a life within a life, inspiring us with His own temper and disposition. Our moral and spiritual being, our power of willing and living and acting, within these He comes and dwells in us a divine, hidden, but mighty power and operation.*

3. Faithful as Son over His house. *But He must be Master in His own house. Not only an honoured guest, while thou hast the keys and the care. So it is with many Christians. So it may not be. No, give Him the keys; give Him entire control over the whole being: as Son over His house. He will blessedly prove how faithful He is to God and to thee.*

4. *Consider well the faithfulness of Christ: this will work in thee the fulness of faith.*

XXI.

If We Hold Fast Our Boldness
Firm to the End

III.–6. Whose house we are, if we hold fast our boldness and the glorying of our hope firm unto the end.

Among the Hebrews there were not a few who had gone back and were in danger of falling away. They had given way to sloth, and had lost the joy and confidence of their first faith. The writer is about (iii. 7–iv. 13) to sound a note of solemn warning, to call them to beware of that evil heart of unbelief, which departs from the living God. As the transition he writes, making the words as it were the text for what follows, Whose house we are, **if we hold fast our boldness, and the glorying of our hope firm to the end.**

Holding fast firm to the end. Steadfastness, perseverance this is indeed the great need of the Christian life. There is no question that exercises the earnest minister of the gospel in our days, as in early times, more deeply than what may be the reason that so many converts grow cold and fall away, and what can be done that we may have Christians who can stand and conquer. How often does it not happen, both after times of revival and special effort, and also in the ordinary work of the Church, that those who for a time ran well, got so entangled in the business or the pleasure of life, the literature, or the politics, or the friendships of the world, that all the life and the power of their profession is lost. They lack steadfastness; they miss the crowning grace of perseverance.

The words of our text teach us what the cause of backsliding is, and whence the want of power to stand comes, even in those who strive after it. They show us at the same time what the secret is of restoration, as well as of strength to endure unto the end. Whose house we are, he says, **If we hold fast our boldness and the glorying of our hope firm to the end.** Or, as it is expressed a few verses further on (ver. 14) **If we hold fast the beginning of our confidence firm unto the end.** A boldness and confidence that make us abound in hope, that make us glory in hope of the glory of God, and glory in tribulation too—this it is that makes us strong to resist and overcome. Nothing can make us conquerors but the bold and joyful spirit that day by day glories in the hope of what God will do.

It is in this that so many fail. When first they found peace they learnt that they were saved by faith. They understood that pardon and acceptance and peace and life all come by faith alone. But they did not understand that we can only stand by faith; that we must always walk by faith; that ever and increasingly we must live by faith; and that every day and every hour nothing can help us but a clear, definite, habitual faith in God's power and working, as the only possibility of growth and progress. They sought to hold fast the light and blessing and the joy they had found; they knew not that it was their boldness of faith, the glorying of their hope, the beginning of their confidence—that this it was they needed to hold fast firm to the end. And even when they learnt something of the need of faith and hope, they did not know how indispensable **the boldness** of faith and **the glorying** of hope were. No one can conquer without the spirit of a conqueror. The powers of sin and Satan, of the world and the flesh, are so great, only he who is bold and glories in his hope upon what God will do will have strength to resist them. And he only can be bold to face the enemy who has learnt to be bold with God, and to glory in Him. It is when faith becomes a joy, and hope is a glorying in God, that we can be more than conquerors.

The lesson is one of the most important the Christian has to learn. We shall see later on how our whole Epistle has been written to teach us that boldness is the only root of steadfastness and perseverance, and therefore the true strength of the Christian life; and how, too, its one object is to show what abundant ground for the boldness we have in the work and person and glory of our Lord Jesus.

Whose house we are, if we hold fast our boldness and the glorying of our hope firm unto the end. Would you know the blessedness of all it means, **Whose house we are, Christ as a Son is faithful in His house,** see here the open gate. In spite of all the enemies that surround you, yield yourself boldly to Jesus Christ as His—your heart a home for Him to dwell in. Glory in the hope of all that He has promised to perfect in you. **Hold fast the beginning of your confidence firm to the end.** Was not that beginning this, that you confessed yourself to be nothing, and Christ to be all? Did you not just cast yourself on His mighty saving power? Hold fast this beginning with the greatest confidence. He will each moment guard and keep His house, and maintain His work within it. Claim boldly and expect confidently that Christ the Son will be faithful over His house as Moses the servant was over his. And when the difficulty arises: But how always to maintain this boldness and glorying of hope, just remember the answer the Epistle gives, **Consider Jesus, who was faithful.** Yes, just consider Jesus! How faithful, even unto death, He was to God in all that He had given Him to do for us. Let that be to us the assurance that He, who is still the same Lord, will be no less faithful in all the blessed work He can now do in us, **if we hold fast our boldness and the glorying of our hope firm to the end.**

1. Faith is the mother of hope. How often a daughter can be a help and a strength to her mother. So, as our hope reaches out to the future and glories in it, our faith will grow into the boldness that can conquer all.

2. Hold fast together what this passage has joined: the faithfulness of Jesus and the boldness or confidence of our faith. His faithfulness is our security.

3. The glorying of our hope. Joy is not a luxury or a mere accessory in the Christian life. It is the sign that we are really living in God's wonderful love, and that that love satisfies us. "The God of hope fill you with all joy in believing, that ye may abound in hope through the power of the Holy Ghost."

4. Christ is faithful as a Son over His house: how confidently I may trust Him to keep charge and rule in it.

The Second Warning

Chap. iii. 7–iv. 13

Not to Come Short of the Promised Rest

XXII.

On Hearing the Voice of God

III.–7. Wherefore, even as the Holy Ghost saith,
  Today, if ye shall hear his voice,
8. Harden not your hearts, as in the provocation,
  Like as in the day of temptation in the wilderness,
9. Wherewith your fathers tempted me by proving me,
  And saw my works forty years.
10. Wherefore I was displeased with this generation,
  And said, They do always err in their heart:
  But they did not know my ways;
11. As I sware in my wrath,
  They shall not enter into my rest.

The writer has such a deep impression of the low and dangerous state into which the Hebrews had sunk, that, having mentioned the name of Moses, he makes a long digression to warn them against being like their fathers and hardening themselves against Him who is so much more than Moses. From Ps. xcv. he quotes what God says of Israel in the wilderness, hardening its heart against Him, so that He sware that they should not enter into His rest. The words of the quotation first point us to what is the great privilege of God's people; they hear His voice; then, to their great danger, hardening the heart against that voice. Not to the unbelieving Jews, but to the Christian Hebrews are these words of warning directed. Christians in our day have no less need of them. Let us take more abundant heed to the word: **Even as the Holy Ghost saith, Today, if ye will hear His voice, harden not your hearts.**

When God spake to Israel, the first thing He asked of them was a heart that did not harden itself, but that in meekness and gentleness, in tenderness and docility turned itself to listen to His voice. How much more may He claim this, now that He speaks to us in His Son. As the soil must be *broken up by the plough* and softened by the rain, so a broken, tender spirit is the first requisite for receiving blessing from God's word, or being in truth made partakers of God's grace. As we read in Isaiah, "To this man will I look, even to him that is poor and of a contrite heart, and trembleth at My word." When this disposition exists, and the thirsty heart truly waits for divine teaching, and the circumcised ear opens to receive it, God's voice will bring real life and blessing, and be the power of living fellowship with Himself. Where it is wanting, the word remains unfruitful, and we go backward, however much head and mouth be filled with Bible truth. **Wherefore, even as the Holy Ghost saith, If ye hear His voice, harden not your hearts.**

It is not difficult to say what it is that hardens the hearts. The seed sown by the wayside could not enter the soil, because it had been trodden down by the passers-by. When the world, with its business and its interests, has at all times a free passage, the heart loses its tenderness. When we trust too much to the intellect in religion, and very great care is not taken to take each word as from God into the heart, into its life and love, the heart gets closed to the living voice of God. The mind is satisfied with beautiful thoughts and pleasant feelings; but the heart does not hear God. When we are secretly content with our religion, our sound doctrine and Christian life, unconsciously but surely the heart gets hardened. When our life does not seek to keep pace with our knowledge, and we have more pleasure in hearing and knowing than obeying and doing, we utterly lose the meekness to which the promise is given, and, amidst all the pleasing forms of godliness, the heart is too hard to discern the voice of the Spirit. More than all, when unbelief, that walks by sight, and looks at itself and all around in the light of this world, is allowed to have its way, and the soul does not seek in childlike faith to live in the invisible, as revealed in the word, the heart gets so hardened that God's word never enters. Yes, it is an unspeakably solemn thought, that with a mind occupied with religious truth, and feelings stirred at times by the voice and words of men, and a life apparently given to religious works, the heart may be closed to the humble, direct intercourse with God, and a stranger to all the blessing the living word can bring. **Wherefore, even as the Holy Ghost saith, If ye hear His voice, harden not your heart.**

Let all who would seek the blessing to be found in this Epistle, beware of studying it simply as an inspired treatise on divine things. Let it be to us a personal message, the voice of God speaking to us in His Son. Let us, under a sense of the spiritual mystery there is in all divine truth, and the impotence of the human mind rightly to apprehend spiritual things, open our heart in great meekness and docility to wait on God. The whole of religion, and the whole of salvation, consists in the state of the heart. God can do nothing for us, in the way of imparting the blessings of redemption, but as He does it in the heart. Our knowledge of the words of God will profit nothing but as the heart is opened to receive Himself to fulfil His words in us. Let our first care be a meek and lowly heart that waits on Him. God speaks *in His Son, to the heart, and in the heart.* It is in the heart that the voice and the Son of God must be received. The voice and the word have weight according as we esteem the speaker. As we realise the glory and the majesty of God, His holiness and perfection, His love and tenderness, we shall be ready to sacrifice everything to hear what He speaks, and receive what He gives. We shall bid all the world around us, all the world within us, be silent that we may hear aright the voice of the divine Being speaking to us in the Son of His love.

1. *Salvation will be found in these two things—God speaking to me in His Son, and my heart opening to hear His voice. It is not only in order to salvation, as a means to an end that is something different and higher, that He speaks. No, His speaking gives and is salvation, the revelation of Himself to my soul. Let the work of my life be to hearken with a meek and tender spirit.*

2. *The Lord opened the heart of Lydia to give heed to the things which were spoken. This is what we need. God Himself will draw our heart away from all else, and open it to take heed. Let us ask this very earnestly.*

3. *Nothing so effectually hinders hearing God's voice as opening the heart too much to other voices. A heart too deeply interested in the news, the literature, the society of this world, cannot hear the divine voice. It needs stillness, retirement, concentration, to give God the heed He claims.*

XXIII.

Even As the Holy Ghost Saith

III.–7. Wherefore, even as the Holy Ghost saith, Today if ye shall hear his voice.

In quoting the words of the 95th Psalm the writer uses the expression, **Even as the Holy Ghost saith.** He regards that Psalm as simply the language of the Holy Spirit. He looks upon the Scriptures as truly inspired by God, God-breathed, because men spake from God, being moved by the Holy Ghost (2 Tim. iii. 16, 2 Pet. i. 21). He regards them as the very voice of God, and attaches to the words all the weight of divine authority, and all the fulness of meaning they have in the divine mind. It is on this ground that he sees in them a deeper meaning than we would have looked for, and teaches us to find in the words, *enter into my rest,* the revelation of a deep spiritual mystery and a prophecy of what Christ should bring. As it was the Holy Spirit who of old first gave the word, so it was the same Spirit who taught the apostle to set forth to us its spiritual meaning and lessons, as we have them in the fourth chapter. And even now it is that same spirit alone who can reveal the truth spiritually within us, and make it life and power in our experience. Let us wait on Him as we meditate on these words, **Even as the Holy Ghost saith.** The words of the Holy Ghost need the Holy Ghost as their interpreter. And the Holy Ghost interprets only to those in whom He dwells and rules.

In the opening words of the Epistle we were told that it was the same God, who had spoken to the fathers in the prophets, who has now spoken to us in His Son. The inferiority of the Old Testament did not consist in this that the words were less the words of God than in the New. They are equally the words of the Holy Spirit. But the superior excellence of the new dispensation lies in this that, in virtue of the mighty redemption wrought out by Christ, taking away the veil between God and us, and the veil from our eyes and heart (Heb. x. 20, Is. xxv. 7, 2 Cor. iii. 16), the word can enter more fully into us with its life-giving power. The Son of God, as the living Word, dwelling in us through the Holy Spirit, brings the truth and the power of the word as a divine reality into our living experience. The Old Testament was as the bud; in the New the bud has opened and the flower is seen. **Even as the Holy Ghost saith.** This word assures us that the Holy Spirit will Himself unfold in the New what He had hidden in the words of the Old.

This brings us to a lesson of the very deepest importance in our spiritual life: that what the Holy Ghost hath spoken, He alone can make plain. He uses human words and thoughts, and, as regarded from the human side, human reason can understand and expound them. But even in one who may be a true Christian, this does not bring him farther than the Old Testament, the preliminary stage: "The prophets sought and searched diligently what manner of time the Spirit of Christ which was in them did point unto" (1 Pet. i. 11). Beyond this, to the real possession and experience of the redemption they proclaimed, they did not come. It was only when Christ was glorified, and the Spirit was given as an indwelling fountain of light and life, that the divine meaning and power could be known. And so it is with ourselves; *to understand the words of the Holy Spirit I must have yielded myself to be led by the Spirit, I must be living in the Spirit.* It is only one who knows Hebrew who can expound a Hebrew writing; it is only the Spirit of God who knows the mind of God and can reveal it to us. Take, for instance, what is said of entering into the rest of God; anyone who will take trouble, and study it carefully, will be able to form some conception of what it means. But truly to know the rest of God, to enter into it, to enjoy it in living power—none but the Holy Spirit can teach us this.

Wherefore, even as the Holy Ghost saith, Today if ye shall hear His voice, harden not your heart. Here is the first lesson the Holy Spirit teacheth. He calls us not to harden or close the heart, but to hearken to the voice of God there; *the Holy Spirit cannot possibly lead us into the power and the blessing of God's word unless with our whole heart we hearken to the voice.* The Holy Spirit can teach in no way but in a heart that is given up to hearken and obey. When the Son came into the world he spake: **Lo, I am come to do Thy will, O God.** The proof of the Spirit's presence in Him, the sacrifice in the power of the Eternal Spirit, the way to the outpouring of the Spirit, was that of hearkening and obedience. The first message of the Holy Spirit, and the condition of all further teaching is ever, **If ye hear His voice, harden not your heart.** God has sent the Spirit of His Son into our heart; God asks us to yield our whole heart to His leading; it is as the indwelling Spirit that He will call us and fit us to listen to God's voice.

We are commencing the study of an Epistle of which the key-note is, God speaks to us now in His son. The wonderful truths of the heavenly priesthood of our Lord Jesus, and of our access into the Holiest of All by the blood, to dwell and worship there, and there in God's presence to be made partaker of the full union with Christ, are to be unfolded. Let us seek a deeper sense of the need, and also the certainty, of the teaching of the Spirit within us: Let us pray "that the Father give us the Spirit of wisdom and revelation in the knowledge of Christ." Let us hear God's voice in meekness and tenderness of heart. Let us in deep humility yield ourselves to the Spirit's guidance. We can count upon it that the same Spirit who first of old inspired the words of the Psalm, who then in this Epistle revealed their fulness of meaning, will reveal to us in power all the light and truth they are meant to bring into the believing heart.

1. *God speaking to us in His word, and in His Son, is all by the Holy Spirit. Everything depends upon our right relation to the Spirit. Let the word be as a seed in which the life of God dwells. Let us receive the word, in the faith that the Holy Spirit will open it, and make it work mightily, in us who believe.*

2. *And as we wait on the Spirit to open the word, we shall through the word be led to and receive the spirit of heaven, as the divine seal of our faith in the word.*

3. *So shall we learn to speak the word in the power of the Spirit. The disciples, however much they knew of Jesus through His intercourse and teaching, and as the witnesses of His death and resurrection, were not allowed to go and preach Him, until they received the Spirit from on high. The Spirit-breathed word, the Spirit-opened word, must also be a Spirit-spoken word; we, too, must speak out of a living communication of the Spirit from the throne of the glorified Christ. From beginning to end, everything connected with God's word must be in the power of the Holy Spirit.*

XXIV.

Today

III.–7. Wherefore, even as the Holy Ghost saith, Today, if ye shall hear His voice, harden not your hearts.

These words are generally applied to the unconverted; the Psalm in which they occur, and the context in which they stand in this Epistle, both prove that they are meant for God's people. In all the dealings of the Holy Ghost with believers, be they weak and erring, or strong and glad, His great word to them is, Today.

The Holy Ghost saith, Today. What does this mean? God is the Eternal One. With Him there is no yesterday or tomorrow; what we call past and future are with Him an ever-present Now; His life is an ever-blessed, never-ending Today. One of the great words of this Epistle in regard to Christ and His salvation is the word Eternal, For ever. He has become the author of eternal salvation—that is, a salvation which bears the character of eternity; its chief mark is that it is an ever-present Now—that there is not a moment in which Christ, who ever lives to pray for us, is not able to maintain us in it in the power of an endless life.

Man is the creature of a moment; the past has gone from him, and over the future he has no control; it is only the present moment that is his. Therefore it is that, when he is made partaker of Christ, a High Priest for ever, and the eternal salvation He imparts, God's great word to him is Today. In Christ all the blessedness of the great eternity is gathered up in an ever-present Now: the one need of the believer is to know it, to respond to it, and to meet the Today, the Now, my child! of God's grace with the Today, the Even now, my Father! of his faith.

If you would understand the meaning of this divine Today, look at it in its wondrous setting. **Even as the Holy Ghost saith, Today.** Satan's word is ever Tomorrow, man's favourite word, too, Tomorrow. Even with the child of God the word of unbelief is too often Tomorrow; God's demand is too great for today; God's promise too high; we hope it will come easier later on. **The Holy Ghost saith, Today.** That means that He who is the mighty power of God is Himself ready to work in us all that God wills and asks; it is He who is each moment pleading for immediate surrender, for a present trust, because He bears with Him the power of a present salvation.

Today! it is a word of wonderful promise. It tells that Today, this very moment, the wondrous love of God is for thee—it is even now waiting to be poured out into thy heart; that Today, all that Christ has done, and is now doing in heaven, and is able to do within thee—this very day, it is within thy reach. Today the Holy Ghost, in whom there is the power to know and claim and enjoy all that the Father and the Son are waiting to bestow, today the Holy Ghost is within thee, sufficient for every need, equal to every emergency. With every call we find in our Bible to full and entire surrender; with every promise we read of grace for the supply of temporal and spiritual need; with every prayer we breathe, and every longing that rules in our heart, there is the Spirit of promise whispering, Today. **Even as the Holy Ghost saith, Today.**

Today! it is a word of solemn command. It is not here a question of some higher privilege which you are free to accept or reject. It is not left to your choice, O believer, whether you will receive the fulness of blessing the Holy Spirit offers. That Today of the Holy Ghost brings you under the most solemn obligation to respond to God's call, and to say, Yes, Today, Lord, complete and immediate submission to all Thy will; Today, the surrender of a present and a perfect trust in all Thy grace. **Even as the Holy Ghost saith, Today.**

Today! a word, too, of earnest warning. **Even as the Holy Ghost saith, Today, if ye shall hear His voice, harden not your hearts.** *They shall not enter into My rest.* There is nothing so hardening as delay. When God speaks to us, He asks for a tender heart, open to the whispers of His voice of love. The believer who answers the Today of the Holy Ghost with the Tomorrow of some more convenient season, knows not how he is hardening his heart; the delay, instead of making the surrender and obedience and faith easy, makes it more difficult. It closes the heart for today against the Comforter, and cuts off all hope and power of growth. O believer, **Even as the Holy Ghost saith, Today,** so when you hear His voice, open the heart in great tenderness to listen and obey; obedience to the Spirit's Today is your only certainty of power and of blessing.

To all Christians whose life has been one of feebleness and of failure, who have not yet entered into the rest of faith, into God's own rest, this word Today is the key to all their disappointments and to all their failures. You waited for strength, to make obedience easier; for feeling, to make the sacrifice less painful. You did not listen to the voice of God breathing through every word. He speaks that wondrous note, even through the living word, Jesus Christ, that wondrous note of hope, Today. You thought it meant for the sinner a call to immediate repentance; you did not know that it means for the believer, each time he hears the voice, immediate, wholehearted submission to all God says, immediate trustful acceptance of all He gives. And yet just this is what it does mean.

In the Epistle to the Hebrews we have a very wonderful exhibition of what Christ, as a High Priest at the right hand of God, can do for us in the power of an endless life. The entering into the rest of God, the perfect cleansing of the conscience in the blood through which He entered into the presence of God, our access within the veil into the presence of God, the being brought close to the very heart of God, the being taken up and kept in Christ in the love of God—these blessings are all ours. And over each of them is written the words, Now is the accepted time. **Even as the Holy Ghost saith, Today.**

1. Brother, let you and me bow in great stillness before God to hear this wonderful message: the Holy Ghost whispering, Today, Today. Let our whole heart open up to take it in. Let all fear and unbelief pass away as we remember: it is the Holy Ghost Himself, the giver of strength, the dispenser of grace, the revealer of Jesus, who says Today.

2. Let our faith simply listen to God's voice, until it rings through our soul day by day, and all the day. We shall take God's word Today, and make it our own. We shall meet this wonderful Today of God's love with the confident Today of our faith. And it will become to us a foretaste of that eternal Today in which He dwells.

3. The Holy Spirit's Today, accepted and lived in, will be within us the power of an endless life, the experience of an eternal salvation, as an ever-present, never-ceasing reality. "Even as the Holy Ghost saith, Today."

4. Just yesterday I heard a servant of God testify that at his conversion he was led to say: I am going to do the will of God today, without thinking of tomorrow; and he had found the unspeakable blessing of it. Let anyone begin to live a whole-hearted life, by the grace of God, for one day; for tomorrow will be as today, and still better.

XXV.

An Evil Heart of Unbelief

III.–12. Take heed, brethren, lest haply there shall be in any one of you an evil heart of unbelief, in falling away from the living God.

The great practical aim of the Epistle is to call us to faith. It is with this view that it will show us what a sure ground we have for it in the word and oath of God, in the person and power of our heavenly High Priest. It will remind us how unbelief has been the cause of all falling away from God, and all failing of entrance into the enjoyment of His promise and His rest, as faith has in all ages been the one power in which God's saints have lived and worked. It has already spoken of "holding fast our boldness and the glorying of our hope firm to the end"; it here uses the word "believe" for the first time in the call to beware of an evil heart of unbelief.

An evil heart of unbelief. Think a moment of what the expression means. And note first the place the heart takes in religion. We have heard the warning (ver. 7), **Harden not your hearts.** It is in the heart God speaks, and where He longs to give His blessing. On that there followed God's complaint, "They do alway err in their *heart;* they did not *know* my ways." It is a heart that goes wrong that cannot know God's ways. And so here again, it is the evil heart that cannot believe, that falls away from the living God. Do let us, in our study of the Epistle and in our whole religious life, beware of rejoicing in beautiful thoughts and happy feelings, while the heart, with its desire and will and love, is not wholly given up to God. In our intercourse with God, everything depends on the heart. It is with the heart man believeth and receiveth the salvation of God.

An evil heart of unbelief. Many think and speak of unbelief as a frailty; they wish to believe, but do not feel able; their faith, they say, is too weak. And of course they have no sense of guilt or shame connected with it: not being able to do a thing is counted a sufficient excuse for not doing it. God thinks differently. The Holy Ghost speaks of the **evil heart** of unbelief. The heart is the organ God created in man for holding fellowship with Himself. Faith is its first natural function; by faith and love it lives in God. It is the ear that hears the voice of God, the eye that can ever see Him and the unseen world; the capacity for knowing and receiving all that God can communicate. It begins as trust in the word spoken; it grows into fellowship with the Person who speaks; its fruit is the reception of all God has to bestow. Sin turned the heart from the unseen to the seen, from God to self, and faith in God lost the place it was meant to have, and became a faith in the visible world and its good. And now unbelief, whether avowed and definite, or more secret and unconscious, is the great mark of the evil heart, the great proof of sin, the great cause of everlasting darkness and damnation. There is no warning the professing Christian Church needs to have sounded more loudly than this one to the Hebrews: **Take heed lest there be in any one of you an evil heart of unbelief in falling away from the living God.**

In falling away from the living God. This is the terrible evil of unbelief; it incapacitates a man for holding fellowship with God as the living One. The expression, *the living God,* occurs four times in the Epistle. In the Old Testament it contrasted God with the dead idols, who could not hear or speak or help. Alas, how often professing Christians have, instead of a graven image, the more dangerous idol of a thought-image—a conception of the mind to which they bring their worship. *The living God,* speaking in His Son, hearing them when they speak, working out in them His mighty salvation—the living God who loves and is loved—Him they know not. With all their Christian profession and religious exercises there is an evil heart of unbelief, in falling away from the living God.

Let us take the warning. Ere we come to the deeper truth the Epistle has to teach us, let us learn well our first lesson: the one thing God looks to, the one thing we need to receive, the fulness of blessing our great High Priest has for us and waits to bestow, is a heart of faith—a true heart drawing nigh to God in fulness of faith (x. 23). *Take heed*—we ought to give more abundant heed—lest there be in any of us, even for a moment, an evil heart of unbelief. Let us cast out everything that can cause or can strengthen it, whether it be worldliness or formality, too little knowledge, or too much head-knowledge of God's word, too little looking to the state of our heart or too much occupation with self; let us take heed lest there be at any time in us an evil heart of unbelief. Let a tender heart, hearkening to His voice, listening to and trusting His word, ever be the sacrifice we bring Him.

With the heart man believeth, whether in God or the world. As our heart is, so is our faith, and so our life. Our enjoyment of Christ, our spiritual strength and fruitfulness, our nearness to God, and our experience of His working in us, all depend, not upon single, isolated acts of faith, but upon the state of the heart. Therefore God breathes into us the Spirit of faith, to keep our heart ever tender and open towards Him. Oh, let us above everything beware of an evil heart of unbelief.

And if we would know how true living faith is to be obtained and increased, note the connection. As unbelief falls away from the living God, so faith draws nigh to Him and is fed and nourished in His presence. Practise the presence of God in deep humility and stillness of heart. Thirst for God, the living God. "My soul, be thou silent unto God: for my expectation is from Him." He is the living God. He sees and hears and feels and loves. He speaks and gives and works, and reveals Himself. His presence wakens and strengthens and satisfies faith. Bow in lowly meditation and worship before the living God, and faith will waken up and grow into boldness and the glorying of hope. He is the living God, *who makes alive, out of whom life comes into them that draw near to Him:* tarry in His presence—that, and nothing else, but that, most surely, will free thee from the evil heart of unbelief.

1. *Unbelief and falling away from the living God: remember with holy fear the close connection. They act and react on each other.*

2. *The faithfulness of Jesus fills the heart with the fulness of faith. You remember the lesson? Here it is the same again: drawing nigh to the living God will fill the heart with living faith. And the Epistle is going to teach us how God draws nigh to us in Jesus, and how in Jesus we draw nigh to God.*

3. *Never speak or think of unbelief as a weakness, but always as the sin of sins, the fruitful mother of all sin.*

4. *The living God in heaven, and the believing heart on earth: these are the two powers that meet and satisfy each other. Let thy faith know of no other measure or limit than the living God. Let it be living faith in a living God.*

XXVI.

Exhort One Another Day by Day

III.–13. But exhort one another day by day, so long as it is called today, lest any one of you be hardened by the deceitfulness of sin.

In the previous verse we read, "Take heed lest there be *in any one of you* an evil heart of unbelief." That is not only, let each one look to himself, but let all look to it that there be not *in any one of you* the evil unbelieving heart. The Church is one body; the sickness of one member is a danger to the whole body. Each one must live to care for those around him. Each member is entrusted by Christ to the love and care of his brethren, and is dependent on their help. Believers who are joined together in one house, in a neighbourhood, in a church, are responsible for one another; they must take heed that there be not in anyone the unbelief that falls away from God. They are called to help and encourage each other so that all may at all times continue steadfast in the faith.

In our meditation on ver. 6 we spoke of the painful fact that in so many cases the first boldness and joy of hope is not held fast firm to the end. Here is one cause. There is not the care and help for each other which the Lord intended. In caring only for ourselves, our brother not only suffers, but we lose much ourselves. The healthy life of the individual member is dependent on the life around him, and on the part he takes in maintaining that life. The warning has a deeper significance than we think: "Take heed lest there be *in any one of you* an evil heart of unbelief."

It is this thought our text seeks to enforce: **But exhort one another day by day, lest any one of you be hardened by the deceitfulness of sin.** Christians are bound to exhort one another; it is their duty and their right. It is implied in the whole constitution of the body of Christ, that the members care for one another. Its life is entirely dependent on the Spirit of Christ, who pleased not Himself, and that Spirit is a love that seeketh not its own, but has its very being in loving and blessing others. As each member humbly yields himself to be helped and to help, the safety and vigour of all will be secured. The communion of saints in all our Church circles must be proved in the cultivation of a practical ministering love and care for each other.

Exhort one another day by day, so long as it is called Today. We saw what solemn meaning there was in the Holy Spirit's call, **Today, if ye hear His voice.** We sought to apply that personally. Here we are taught that all the urgency that call implies must by each one of us be applied to our neighbour as well as ourselves. We must think of the danger of delay, of the time when it will be no longer *Today* for those around us, who are forgetting it, and exhort them *day by day. Today!* The work is urgent and must be done immediately. It may be difficult—He who commands will enable. Our conscious unfitness must drive us to Him who can fill us with the love and the boldness, and the wisdom we need. *Day by day.* The work is slow, and must be done unceasingly, "*so long* as it is called Today." The Spirit of Jesus can give us grace and patience and faith to persevere. "In due time we shall reap if we faint not."

Day by day. This word of the Holy Spirit is the complement of that other *Today.* The *Today* of the Holy Spirit must day by day be afresh accepted and obeyed. It is only as we are ready, every day without one exception, to live fully in the obedience to the voice of God and the faith of Jesus, that our life can grow. What has once, or for a time, been done, will not avail; day by day, our fellowship with Jesus, our consecration to Him, our service for Him, must be renewed. So shall we in our care for others, as much as in our personal walk, hold fast our boldness firm to the end.

"Exhort one another, **lest any one of you be hardened by the deceitfulness of sin.**" We heard the warning, **Harden not your hearts.** Here is its exposition, **Hardened by the deceitfulness of sin.** All sin is deceit, its promised pleasures are all a lie. But there are some sins that are open and unmistakable. There are others that are specially deceptive. Where the sanction of the Christian world, or the force of habit and custom, or the apparent insignificance of what we do, makes us think little of the sin, it has a terrible power to deceive the professing Christian. And through this deceitfulness of sin, be it worldliness, or unlovingness, or pride, or want of integrity, hearts are hardened, and become incapable of hearing the voice of God. What a call to all who are awake to their own danger to listen, "Exhort one another day by day, lest **any one of you be hardened through the deceitfulness of sin.**"

Let me press upon everyone who would study this Epistle, the solemn obligation resting upon him to care for those around him—not only the outcast, but those with whom he is associated in church fellowship, very specially any who are in danger of being hardened through the deceitfulness of sin. The Christ unto whom we are to grow up in all things is the Christ "from whom all the body, fitly framed and knit together, through that which every joint supplieth, according to the working in its measure of each several part, maketh the increase of the body unto the building up of itself in love." Our connection with the head, the power of our growth unto Him in all things, must be maintained in our love to the members of His body around, however feeble or backward.

And if we would know where the grace for this work is to be found, the answer is not far to seek. It is in Jesus Christ our Head and in His love shed abroad in our hearts. As in this Epistle we study the compassion of Jesus, as our High Priest and Leader, let us believe that He makes us partakers of His Spirit. He forms us in His own likeness, He leads us in His footsteps, He makes each of us what He was, a Priest with a priestly heart ready to live and die for those around us. **Therefore, brethren, exhort one another day by day.**

1. *This work is most difficult. But strength for it will come as for any other work. First of all, accept the command; get the heart filled with the sense of obligation; yield yourself to your Master in willing obedience, even though you see not the slightest prospect of doing it. Then wait on Him for His light and strength—for wisdom to know how to begin, for boldness to speak the truth in love. Present yourself unto God as one alive from the dead, and your members as instruments of righteousness in His hands. Let the fire within the heart be kept burning: the grace of obedience will not be withheld.*

2. *This Epistle is an exposition of the inner life, the life of faith. But with this, work is considered as a matter of course that needs no vindication. Let every Christian give himself to his Lord to watch over others: let all the fresh grace and the deeper knowledge of Jesus we seek be for the service of those around us. Exhort one another daily.*

XXVII.

Partakers of Christ

III.–14. For we are become partakers of Christ, if we hold fast the beginning of our confidence firm unto the end; while it is said,
15. Today, if ye shall hear his voice,
Harden not your hearts, as in the provocation.

In the second chapter the twofold oneness of our Lord Jesus and His believing people was set before us. On the divine side they are one, **for both He that sanctifieth, and they that are sanctified are all of one,** that is, of God. Therefore He calls them brethren. On the other, the human side, they are one, because He became man, and took our nature upon Him. **Since the children are sharers of flesh and blood, He also Himself in like manner partook of the same.** There we have the same word as here. Just as truly as Christ became *partaker of flesh and blood* we become *partakers of Christ.* In partaking with us of flesh and blood, Christ entered into perfect fellowship with us in all we were, our life and our death became His. When we become partakers of Christ, we enter into perfect fellowship with Him in all He was and is; His death and His life become ours.

We are become partakers of Christ! What a mystery! What a treasure! What a blessedness! The whole object of the Epistle is to show what there is in the Christ of whom we are become partakers, and what He can do for us. But here at the outset, amid needful words of remonstrance against giving way to sloth or unbelief, believers are reminded of what their portion and possession is; they are **become partakers of Christ.** There is often danger, as we listen to the teaching of Scripture about Christ as our High Priest, of regarding Him as an outward person, and His work as something that is done outwardly for us in heaven. This precious word reminds us that our salvation consists in the possession of Himself, in the being one life with Him, in having Himself as our own. Christ can do nothing for us but as an inward Saviour. Himself being our life, personally dwelling and working in us. As truly and fully as Christ, when He became partaker of flesh and blood, was entirely and eternally identified with man and His nature, so that He and it were inseparably united in one life, so surely, when we become partakers of Christ, do we become indissolubly identified with Him. Since Christ became partaker of flesh and blood, He is known, and will be to all eternity, even upon the throne, as the Son of Man. No less will we, when we truly become partakers of Christ, be known, even now and to all eternity, as one with Christ on the throne of glory. Oh, let us know ourselves as God knows us—partakers of Christ.

It is the one thing God desires. When God set forth His only begotten Son as the only possible way of access to Himself, it meant that He can delight in or have fellowship with nothing in which the likeness of His Son is not to be seen. We can have no farther entrance into God's favour or good pleasure than He can see Christ in us. If God has called us to the fellowship of His Son, and made us participators of all there is in Christ, the sonship, and the love, and the Spirit of the Father, let us live worthy of our privilege—let us live as men who are—oh the riches of the grace!—are become *partakers of Christ!*

And how can we know in full assurance that it is so, and ever rejoice in the blessed consciousness of all it implies. Just as it was said before, where our blessed relation to Christ was set forth in another aspect, we are His house, **if we hold fast our boldness and the glorying of our hope firm unto the end,** so we have the answer here again: "We are become partakers of Christ, **if we hold fast the beginning of our confidence firm unto the end.**" The beginning of our confidence must be held fast. We must not, as many think, begin with faith, and continue with works. No, the confidence with which we began must be held fast firm to the end. We must see that when we are made partakers of Christ, that includes all, and that as at first, so all the way unto the end, we can receive out of Christ only by faith and according to our faith. Apart from faith receiving Christ's strength, our works avail not. God works nothing but through Christ, and it is as by faith we live in our riches in Christ that God can work into us all there is in Him for us. It is this faith through which God can work all our works for us and in us.

For we are become—note, not we shall become—we are become, **partakers of Christ, if we hold fast to the end.** Our perseverance will be the seal of our being partaker of Christ. The faith by which, at conversion, we know at once that we have Christ, grows clearer and brighter, and more mightily effectual in opening up the treasures of Christ, as we hold it fast firm unto the end. Persevering faith is the witness that we have Christ, because through it Christ exercises His keeping and perfecting power.

Believer! would you enjoy the full assurance and the full experience that you are partaker of Christ? *It is alone to be found each day in the living fellowship with Christ.* Christ is a living person, He can be known and enjoyed only in a living personal intercourse. Christ is my Leader; I must cling to Him, I must follow Him, in His leading. Christ is my High Priest; I must let Him lift me into God's presence. Christ is the living Son of God, our life; I must live Him. I am His house; I can only know Him as Son in His house as I yield myself to His indwelling.

But, all and only through faith, we are become partakers of Christ, **if we hold fast the beginning of our confidence firm unto the end.** Begin each day, meet each difficulty, with the renewal of the confidence you reposed in Jesus, when first you came to Him; with a brightness that shines unto the perfect day you will know what boundless blessing it is to be a *partaker of Christ.*

1. *When Christ became partaker of human nature, how entirely He identified Himself with it, that all could see and know it. I am become partaker of Christ: let me be so identified with Him that my whole life may be marked by it. So may all see and know that I am partaker of Jesus Christ.*

2. *How did Christ become partaker of our nature? He left His own state of life, forsook all, and entered into our state of life. How do I become partaker of Christ? By coming out from my state of life, forsaking all, giving myself wholly to be possessed of Him and to live His life.*

3. *If we hold fast the beginning. Christ maintained His surrender to be Man firm to the end, even unto death. Let me maintain my surrender to Christ, live one life with Christ, at any cost.*

4. *Partaker of Christ, of His life, His dispositions as man, His meekness and lowliness of heart; partaker of a living Christ—who will live His life out in me.*

XXVIII.

The Rest in Canaan

III.–16. For who, when they heard, did provoke? nay, did not all they that came out of Egypt by Moses?
17. And with whom was he displeased forty years? was it not with them that sinned, whose carcases fell in the wilderness?
18. And to whom sware he that they should not enter into his rest, but to them that were disobedient?
19. And we see that they were not able to enter in because of unbelief.

In the opening verses of the Epistle we saw that God has two dispensations, or ways of dealing with man, and that these find their counterpart in the Christian life. There are believers who always walk in the twilight and bondage of the Old Testament; there are others, who truly know the joy and the power of the New Testament, and have fellowship with God, not as through the prophets, but truly and directly in the Son Himself.

In the words we are now to meditate on we have the same truth in another aspect. The writer had spoken of Christ as more than Moses. This gives him occasion to speak, in the tone of solemn warning, of the people of Israel who came out of Egypt. They did not all enter Canaan. There came a separation among those that God had redeemed out of Egypt; some perished in the wilderness; others did indeed enter and possess the promised land. The cause of this failure to enter Canaan was, we are told, disobedience, arising out of unbelief. When God commanded them to go up and possess the land, they gave way to fear. They believed not God's promise, and were disobedient. Unbelief is ever the cause of disobedience; they could not enter in because of unbelief and disobedience.

The story has a deep spiritual significance, and teaches a lesson of great solemnity. In our chapter we have twice heard already that it is not enough to begin well; we must hold fast *unto the end.* Of the people of Israel we read—"By faith they kept the Passover and the sprinkling of the blood; by faith they passed through the Red Sea." There was the initial faith to go up out of Egypt. But when they were tested to see if they would **hold fast the beginning of their confidence firm unto the end,** the great majority failed. Their faith was but for a time: they had faith to leave Egypt; they had not faith to enter Canaan.

Among the Hebrews there were Christians who were in the same state. They had begun well, but had been hindered. Some were standing still; some had already turned back. And even so there are many Christians in our churches who never come farther than the initial faith of conversion. They say they know God has saved them from Egypt. They rest content with the thought of having been converted. There is no hearty desire, no earnest purpose to press on to a life of holiness, no readiness at any sacrifice to go up into the promised land of rest and of victory.

When Israel was about to enter the land of Canaan, Moses used the words: "He *brought us out* from thence, that He *might bring us in* to give us the land." It is to be feared that there are many Christians who put asunder what God hath joined together. They would fain be brought out from the land of bondage; they are not ready to go all the length with God, to enter the land and conquer every enemy. They would fain be made happy in being delivered from bondage; they long not to be made holy in a life of separation and service. To the voice that calls to enter into God's rest they hearken not, but harden their hearts. It was not in Egypt—let us note this well—it was on the very borders of Canaan that the men God had begun to save hardened their hearts. It is among Christians who profess conversion, who have not only begun the Christian life, but even made some progress in it, that the hardening of the heart is now still found. The call to holiness, the call to cease from the life of wandering and murmuring, and enter into the rest of God, the call to the life of victory over every enemy and to the service of God in the land of promise, is not obeyed. They say it is too high and too hard. They do not believe with Caleb, "We are well able to possess the land"; they fear the sacrifice and cling to the carnal life; in not hearkening to God's voice their heart is hardened. God has sworn, they shall not enter into His rest.

I cannot with too much earnestness urge every Christian reader to learn well the two stages of the Christian. There are the carnal, and there are the spiritual; there are those who remain babes, and those who are full-grown men. There are those who come up out of Egypt, but then remain in the wilderness of a worldly life; there are those who follow the Lord fully, and enter the life of rest and victory. Let each of us find out where we stand, and taking earnest heed to God's warnings, with our whole heart press on to go all the length in following Jesus, in seeking to stand perfect and complete in all the will of God.

What mean all the warnings in our Epistle, specially dedicated to the unfolding of the heavenly life and power, the complete salvation of our great High Priest? It means this, that no teaching of what Christ is can profit, unless our hearts *are longing and ready to follow Him fully.* The Epistle will sum up all its teachings in its call to enter into the Holiest of All, into the rest of God. But it wants us to feel deeply that there can be no entering in, except in the path of faith and full obedience, except with a heart that is ready to forsake all its own will, to follow Him who bore the cross, a heart that will be content with nothing less than all that God is willing to give.

1. They were not able to enter in because of unbelief. Take heed, lest there be in any of you an evil heart of unbelief. Everything depends upon faith. At each step in the teaching of our Epistle, let faith be exercised. Faith in the God who speaks to us; faith in the blessed Son, in the divine power and all-pervading nearness in which He works, in His true humanity, and the heavenly life He perfected for us and imparts from heaven; faith in the Holy Spirit who dwells within us, and is God's power working in us—let faith be the habit of our soul, the every breath of our life.

2. *Because of unbelief.* Just what Jesus says: Because of your unbelief, in answer to our Why? Let us cultivate the deep conviction that the root of all disobedience and failure, of all weakness and trouble in the spiritual life, is unbelief. Let us not think that there is some inexplicable mystery about our prayers not being heard; it is simply unbelief that will not trust God, will not yield itself wholly to God, will not allow God to do what He promises. God save us from unbelief!

XXIX.

The Rest of Faith

IV.–1. Let us fear therefore, lest haply a promise being left us of entering into his rest, any of you should seem to have come short of it.

2. For indeed we have had good tidings preached unto us, even as also they: but the word of hearing did not profit them, because they were[1] not united by faith with them that heard.

3. For we which have believed do enter into that rest: even as he hath said,

As I sware in my wrath,
They shall not enter into my rest: although the works were finished from the foundation of the world.

We have seen that with Israel, after its deliverance from Egypt, there were two stages. The one, the life in the wilderness, with its wanderings and its wants, its unbelief and its murmurings, its provocation of God and its exclusion from the promised rest. The other, the land of promise, with rest instead of the desert wanderings, with abundance instead of want, and the victory over every enemy instead of defeat: symbols of the two stages in the Christian life. The one in which we only know the Lord as the Saviour from Egypt, in His work on the cross for atonement and pardon. The other, where He is known and welcomed as the glorified Priest-King in heaven, who, in the power of the endless life, sanctifies and saves completely, writes God's laws in the heart, and leads us to find our home in the holiest of

1. It was.

God's presence. The aim of the writer in this whole section is to warn us not to rest content with the former, the preparatory stage, but to show all diligence to reach the second, and enter the promised rest of complete deliverance. **Let us fear therefore, lest haply, a promise being left of entering into His rest, any of you should come short of it.**

Some think that the rest of Canaan is the type of heaven. This cannot be, because the great mark of the Canaan life was that the land had to be conquered and that God gave such glorious victory over enemies. The rest of Canaan was for victory and through victory. And so it is in the life of faith, when a soul learns to trust God for victory over sin, and yields itself entirely, as to its circumstances and duties, to live just where and how He wills, that it enters the rest. It lives in the promise, in the will, in the power of God. This is the rest into which it enters, not through death, but through faith, or rather, not through the death of the body, but the death to self in the death of Christ through faith. For indeed we have **had good tidings preached unto us, even as also they: but the word of hearing did not profit them, because it was not united by faith with those that heard.** The one reason why they did not enter Canaan was their unbelief. The land was waiting: the rest was provided; God Himself would bring them in and give them rest. One thing was lacking; they did not believe, and so did not yield themselves to God to do it for them what He had promised. Unbelief closes the heart against God, withdraws the life from God's power; in the very nature of things unbelief renders the word of promise of none effect. A gospel of rest is preached to us as it was to them. We have in Scripture the most precious assurances of a rest for the soul to be found under the yoke of Jesus, of a peace of God which passeth all understanding, of a peace and a joy in the soul which nothing can take away. But when they are not believed they cannot be enjoyed: faith is in its very nature a resting in the promise and the promiser until

He fulfil it in us. Only faith can enter into rest. The fulness of faith enters into the full rest.

For we which have believed do enter into rest. It is not, shall enter. No. Today, even as the Holy Ghost saith, "Today," now and here, we which have believed do enter into rest. It is with the rest of faith here as with what we heard of being partakers of Christ—the blessing is enjoyed, **if we hold fast the beginning of our confidence firm unto the end.** The initial faith, that passes out of Egypt through the Red Sea, must be held fast firm, then it comes to the fulness of faith that passes through Jordan into the land.

Let every student of this Epistle realise how intensely personal its tone is, and with what urgency it appeals to us for faith, as the one thing needful in our dealings with the word of God. Without this the word cannot profit us. We may seek by thought and study to enter into the meaning of the promise— God has sworn that we never shall enter into its possession, or into His rest, but by faith. The one thing God asks in our intercourse with Him and His word is the habit of faith, that ever keeps the heart open towards God, and longs to enter in and abide in His rest. It is the soul that thirsts for God, for the living God, that will have the spiritual capacity for receiving the revelation of how Jesus, the High Priest, brings us into God's presence. What is to be taught us later on of our entering into the Holiest of All is nothing but the clearer unfolding of what is here called entering into rest. Let us in studying the Epistle above everything have faith.

Would you enter into the rest? Remember what has been taught us of the two stages. They are represented by Moses and Joshua. Moses the leader, Joshua the perfecter or finisher of the faith of Israel. Moses brought the people out: Joshua brought them in. Accept Jesus as your Joshua. Let past failure and wandering and sin not cause either despair or contentment with what you are. Trust Jesus who, through the sprinkling of the blood, brought you out of Egypt, to bring you as definitely into the rest. Faith is always repose in what another will do for me. Faith ceases to seek help in itself or its efforts, to be troubled with its need or its weakness; it rests in the sufficiency of the all-sufficient One who has undertaken all. Trust Jesus. Give up and forsake the wilderness. Follow Him fully: He is the rest.

1. *Let no one imagine that this life in the rest of faith is something that is meant only for a favoured few. I cannot too earnestly press it upon every reader: God calls you—yes you, to enter the rest. He calls you to a life of entire consecration. If you rest content with the thought of having been converted, it may be at the peril of your soul: with Israel you may perish in the wilderness. "I have sworn in my wrath: they shall not enter into my rest."*

2. *If God be indeed the fountain of all goodness and blessedness, it follows that the nearer we are to Him, and the more we have of Him, the deeper and the fuller our joy will be. Has not the soul, who is not willing at all costs to yield to Christ when He offers to bring us into the rest of God, reason to fear that all its religion is simply the selfishness that seeks escape from punishment, and is content with as little of God here as may suffice to secure heaven hereafter.*

XXX.

The Rest of God

IV.–4. For he hath said somewhere of the seventh day on this wise, And God rested on the seventh day from all his works;
5. And in this place again,
  They shall not enter into my rest.
6. Seeing therefore it remaineth that some should enter thereinto, and they to whom the good tidings were before preached failed to enter in because of disobedience,
7. He again defineth a certain day, saying in David, after so long a time
  Today, as it hath been before said,
  Today if ye shall hear his voice,
  Harden not your hearts.
8. For if Joshua had given them rest, he would not have spoken afterward of another day.

We speak, with Scripture, of the rest of faith. Faith, however, only gives rest because it rests in God; it rests because it allows God to do all; the rest is in God Himself. It is His own divine rest into which we enter by faith. When the Holy Ghost says, *My rest, His rest, God rested,* it teaches us that it is God's own rest into which we enter, and which we partake of. It is as faith sees that the creature was destined to find its rest nowhere but in the Creator, and that in the entire surrender to Him, to His will and His working, it may have perfect rest, that it dares to cast itself upon God, and have no care. It sees that God, the cause of all movement and change, is Himself the immovable and unchangeable One, and that His blessed rest can never be disturbed by what is done either by Himself or by others. Hearkening to the loving offer, it forsakes all to find its dwelling-place in God and His love. Faith sees what the rest of God is; faith believes that it may come and share in it; faith enters in and rests, it yields itself to Jesus to lead it in and make it partaker. Because it honours God and counts Him all, God honours it; He opens the door, and the soul is brought in to rest in Him.

This faith is faith in Jesus. It is the insight into His finished work, the complete salvation He bestows, the perfection which was wrought in Him personally, and in which we share as **partakers of Christ.** The connection between the finishing of a work and the rest that follows is clearly seen in what is said of creation. **God rested on the seventh day from all His works. He that is entered into His rest, hath himself also rested from his work, as God did from His.** The rest of God was His glad complacency in what He had finished in Creation, the beginning of His blessed work of Providence to care for and bring on to perfection what He had wrought. And so it is the finished work of Jesus that is ever set before us in the Epistle as the ground of our faith, the call for us in fulness of faith to draw nigh and enter in and rest. Because Christ hath put away sin, hath rent the veil, and is set down on the right hand of the throne—because all is finished and perfected, and we have received the Holy Spirit from heaven in our hearts to make us the partakers of that glorified Christ, we may with confidence, with boldness, rest in Him to maintain and perfect His work in us. And, resting in Him, He becomes our Joshua, perfecting our faith, bringing us in, and giving us a home in the rest of God with Himself, now to go no more out for ever.

And if you would know why so few Christians enjoy this rest, *it is because they do not know Jesus as their Joshua.* We shall see later how Aaron was only a type of Christ in His work on earth. Melchizedek is needed as a type of His work in heaven, in the power and joy of the heavenly life. Moses and Aaron both shadow forth the beginning of Christ's work—His work on earth; Melchizedek and Joshua His work in heaven. They show us clearly how, as in the type God ordained, so in reality there are two stages in Christian knowledge and experience. All the feebleness of our Christian life is owing to one thing: we do not know Jesus in heaven; we do not know that Jesus has *entered in* for us (vi. 20, ix. 12, 14), and that this secures to us *boldness and the power of entrance* into a heavenly state of life; that He there *sits* upon the throne as our High Priest in power, maintaining in us His own heavenly life; keeping us in personal fellowship with the living Father, so that in Him we too enter the rest of God. It is because we do not know Jesus in His heavenly life and power that our life is feeble; if we learn to know Him as He is to be revealed in this Epistle, as our heavenly Joshua, actually bringing us and our inmost nature into the rest of God, we cannot but enter into that rest. When Joshua went before, the people followed at once in fellowship with him. Entering the rest of God is a personal practical experience of the soul that receives the word in living faith, because in it it receives Jesus on the throne.

Let us do what Israel did in crossing Jordan; they allowed Joshua to bring them in; they followed him. Let us follow Jesus in the path He trod. In heaven God's will is all. On earth Jesus made that will all. He lived in the will of God, in suffering and doing, in meeting trial, in waiting for the Father's guidance; in giving up everything to it, He proved that God's will was His path. Follow Him. Yield thyself, in the death to self, to the will of God; have faith in Jesus on the throne, as thy Head and life, that He has brought thee in and will make it true in thy experience; trust Jesus, as being partaker of His nature and life, to work all in thee that the Father seeks; and thou shalt know how blessed it is to enter the rest of God.

1. Deep restfulness, even amid outward activity, is one of the most beautiful marks and aids of the life of faith. Cultivate that holy stillness that seeks to abide in God's presence, and does not yield too much to things around.

2. *This rest is God's rest: it is found in His fellowship.* Think of all He sees, of all He feels, and has to bear; think of the divine peace and patience with which He guides all; and learn to be patient and trustful, and to rest in Him. Believe in Him, as the one God who worketh all in all, and works in thee that which is well-pleasing in His sight, and thou shalt have perfect rest in letting Him do all for thee and in thee.

3. *God is a supernatural, incomprehensible Being; we must learn to know Him in a way that is above reason and sense.* That way is the adoration of faith, and the deep humility of obedience. Through these the Holy Spirit will work the work of God in us.

4. *All entering in means a coming out from the place we were in before.* Forsake all, and follow Jesus into God's presence.

5. O my soul, listen to this word of the great God, and let His unspeakable love draw thee—Today, enter into My rest.

XXXI.

Rest from Works

IV.–9. There remaineth therefore a sabbath rest for the people of
God.
10. For he that is entered into his rest hath himself also rested
from his works, as God did from his.

**There remaineth therefore a sabbath rest for the people of
God:** taken in connection with what precedes about the seventh
day or Sabbath, the rest is here called a sabbatism or sabbath
rest. It is spoken of as *remaining,* with reference to the rest in
Canaan. That was but a shadow and symbol: the real sabbath
rest remained, waiting its time, till Christ the true Joshua should
come, and open it to us by Himself entering it.

In ver. 10 we have here another proof that the rest does not
refer to heaven. How needless it would be in that case to say to
those who have died, **For he that hath entered into his rest,
hath himself also rested from his works, as God did from
His.** The remark would have no point. But what force it has in
connection with the rest of faith in this life, pointing us to what
is the great secret of this entrance into rest—the ceasing from
works, as God did from His.

In God we see, as it were, two distinct stages in His relation
to His work. The first was that of creation—until He had finished all His work which He created and made. The second, His
rest when creation was finished, and He rejoiced in what He had
made, now to begin the higher work of watching the development of the life He had entrusted the creature with, and secur-

171

ing its sanctification and perfection. It is a rest from work which is now finished, for higher work now to be carried on. Even so there are the two stages in the Christian life. The one in which, after conversion, a believer seeks to work what God would have him do. The second, in which, after many a painful failure, he ceases from his works, and enters the rest of God, there to find the power for work in allowing God to work in him.

It is this resting from their own work which many Christians cannot understand. They think of it as a state of passive and self-ish enjoyment, of still contemplation which leads to the neglect of the duties of life, and unfits for that watchfulness and warfare to which Scripture calls. What an entire misunderstanding of God's call to rest. As the Almighty, God is the only source of power. In nature He works all. In grace He waits to work all too, if man will but consent and allow. Truly to rest in God is to yield oneself up to the highest activity. We work, because He worketh in us to will and to do. As Paul says of himself, "I labour, striving according to His working who worketh in me with might" (lit. "agonising according to His energy who energises in me with might"). Entering the rest of God is the ceasing from self-effort, and the yielding up oneself in the full surrender of faith to God's working.

How many Christians are there who need nothing so much as rightly to apprehend this word. Their life is one of earnest ef-fort and ceaseless struggling. They do long to do God's will, and to live to His glory. Continued failure and bitter disappointment is their too frequent experience. Very often as the result they give themselves up to a feeling of hopelessness: it never will be otherwise. Theirs is truly the wilderness life—they have not en-tered into God's rest. Would that God might open their eyes, and show them Jesus as our Joshua, who has entered into God's presence, who sits upon the throne as High Priest, bringing us in living union with Himself into that place of rest and of love, and, by His Spirit within us, making that life of heaven a reality and an experience.

He that is entered into rest, hath himself also rested from his works, as God did from His. And how does one rest and cease from his works? It is by ceasing from self. It is the old self life that always insists upon proving its goodness and its strength, and presses forward to do the works of God. It is only in death that we rest from our works. Jesus entered His rest through death; each one whom He leads into it must pass through death. "Reckon yourself to be indeed dead unto sin, and alive unto God in Christ Jesus our Lord." Believe that the death of Christ, as an accomplished fact, with all that it means and has effected, is working in you in all its power. You are dead with Him and in Him. Consent to this, and cease from dead works. "Blessed are the dead that die in the Lord. Yea, saith the Spirit, for they do rest from their labours." That is as true of spiritual dying with Christ as of the death in the body. To sinful nature there is no rest from work but through death.

He that is entered into rest hath rested from his works. The ceasing from our works and the entering the rest of God go together. Read the first chapter of Joshua, and hear God's words of strength and encouragement to everyone who would enter. Exchange the wilderness life with your own works for the rest-life in which God works. Fear not to believe that Jesus came to give it, and that it is for you.

1. *Not I, but Christ. This is the rest of faith in which a man rests from his works. With the unconverted man it is,* Not Christ, but I. *With the feeble and slothful Christian,* I and Christ: *I first, and Christ to fill up what is wanting. With increasing earnestness it becomes,* Christ and I: *Christ first, but still I second. With the man who dies with Christ it is,* Not I, but Christ: *Christ alone and Christ all. He has ceased from his work: Christ liveth in him. This is the rest of faith.*

2. *God saith of His dwelling among His people,* "This is My rest; here will I dwell." *Fear not to say this too. It is the rest of God in His delight and*

pleasure in the work of His Son, in His love to Jesus and all who belong to Him. It is the rest of Jesus in His finished work, sitting on the throne, resting in the Father's love. It is the rest of our faith and love in Jesus, in God, in His love.

XXXII.

Give Diligence to Enter into the Rest

IV.–11. Let us, therefore, give diligence to enter into that rest, that no man fall after the same example of disobedience.

Our Epistle is intensely practical. How it detains and holds us fast in hope of persuading us not to be content with the knowledge or the admiration of its teaching, but personally to listen to the message it brings from God by the Holy Ghost, and indeed do the thing God would have us do—enter into His rest. **Let us give diligence to enter into that rest.**

Let us give diligence. The word means, Make haste—be in earnest, put your whole heart into it, see that you do it; enter into the rest. **That no man fall after the same example of disobedience.** The danger is imminent—the loss will be terrible. God has sworn in His wrath that unless we hearken and obey, we shall not enter His rest. Let us give diligence to enter in. All the wonderful teaching the Epistle contains farther on, as to the Holiest that is opened for us as the place where God wants to receive us into His rest and live, as to the great High Priest who has opened the way and entered in and lives as our Joshua to bring us in, will profit us nothing, unless there be the earnest desire, the willing readiness, the firm resolve, *to enter in.* It is this disposition alone that can fit a man spiritually to apprehend the heavenly mysteries the Epistle opens up.

And surely it ought not to be needful to press the motives that should urge us to obedience. Ought not the one motive to suffice?—the unspeakable privilege God offers me in opening to me the entrance into His own rest. No words can express the inconceivable greatness of the gift. God speaks to me in His Son as one who was created in His image, capable of fellowship with Himself; as one whom He has redeemed out of the awful captivity of sin and death, because He longs to have me living with Him in His love. As one for whom He has made it possible to live the outer life in the flesh, with the inner life in Christ, lifted up, kept safe in the Holiest of All, in God's own rest—oh, can it be that anyone believes this and does not respond? No, let each heart say, Blessed be God, into this rest would I enter, here would I dwell.

We are so accustomed to the wilderness life of stumbling and sinning, we have so learnt to take the words God speaks of that life (iii. 10), "They do alway err in their heart," as descriptive of what must be daily Christian experience, that we hardly count it a practical possibility to enter into the rest. And even when the desire has been awakened, the path appears so dark and unknown. Let me for the sake of such once again gather up what has been said as to the way to enter in: it may be God, of His great mercy, may help some to take the step. The instructions need be very simple.

First, settle it in your mind, *believe with your whole heart that there is such a rest, and that Today.* It is God's rest, in which He lives; into which Jesus, as your Joshua, has entered. It is your rest, prepared for you; your land of promise; the spiritual state of life which is as surely yours as Jesus is; into which Jesus will bring you, and where He will keep you. It is the rest in which you can live every hour, free from care and anxiety, free from weariness and wanderings, always resting in the rest that trusts God for all. Believe this.

Then *cease from your own works.* Not as if you had to attain this perfectly before entering into God's rest. No, but consent, yield, be willing that all self-working should come to an end. Cease from self. Where there is life there is action; the self-life will seek to work, except you give up self into the death of Christ; with Him you are buried, in Him you live. As Christ said, Hate your own life, lose it. Cease from your own works, and bow in deep humility and helplessness of all good, as nothing before God.

Trust Jesus as your Joshua, who brings you in, even now. Israel had simply to trust and obey and follow Joshua. Set your heart on Him who has entered the heavens to appear before God for us. Claim Jesus as yours, not only in His cross and death and resurrection, but above all in His heavenliness, in His possession of the rest of heaven. Claim Him, and leave Him to do His blessed work. You need not understand all. Your feelings may not be what you would wish. Trust Him, who has done all for you in earth and heaven, to do all in your heart too.

And then be *a follower of them who through faith and patience have inherited the promises.* Israel passed in one day through Jordan into Canaan, but did not in one day come to the perfect rest. It is at the end of the life of Joshua we read, "The Lord gave them rest round about." Enter today into the rest. Though all may not be bright at once, look to Jesus, your Joshua, and leave all in His hands. Come away out of self, and live in Him. Rest in God whatever happen. Think of His Rest, and Jesus who has entered it in your name, and out of it fills you with its Spirit, and fear not. *Today,* if you hear His voice, enter in.

1. *Jesus said, "Take My yoke upon you, and learn of Me, for I am meek and lowly in heart, and ye shall find rest unto your souls." It was through meekness and lowliness of heart that Jesus found His rest in God: He allowed God to be all, trusted God for all—the rest of God was His abode. He invites us to share His rest, and tells us the secret. In the meekness and lowliness of Jesus is the way to the rest.*

2. *Israel did not enter Canaan. And why? It is twice said because of disobedience, and thrice because of unbelief. The two things always go together. Yield yourself in everything to obey. This will strengthen you to trust for everything He has promised to do.*

3. *The rest includes victory: "The Lord will give thee rest from all thy enemies round about, and thou shalt dwell in safety." "And the Lord gave them rest round about, all their enemies gave He into their hand."*

XXXIII.

The Heart-Searching Word of God

IV.–12. For the word of God is living, and active, and sharper than any two-edged sword, and piercing even to the dividing asunder of soul and spirit, of both joints and marrow, and quick to discern the thoughts and intents of the heart.

13. And there is no creature that is not manifest in his sight: but all things are naked and laid open before the eyes of him with whom we have to do.

They have been earnest words with which the writer has been warning the Hebrews against unbelief and disobedience, hardening the heart and departing from God, and coming short of the promised rest. The solemn words of God's oath in Ps. xcv., *I have sworn in My wrath, they shall not enter into My rest,* have been repeated more than once to urge all to give diligence lest any man fall after the same example of unbelief. He is about to close his warning. He does so by reminding them of the power of the word of God as the word of the omniscient One, of Him with whom we have to do, before whose eyes all things, our hearts and lives too, are naked and open. Let each student of the Epistle make a very personal application of the words. Let us take the oath of God concerning His rest, and the command to labour that we may enter in, home to our heart, and say whether we have indeed entered in. And if not, let us all the more yield ourselves to the word to search and try us: it will without fail do its blessed work in us, and prepare us for following with profit the further teaching concerning our Lord Jesus.

179

For the word of God is living and active. At times it may appear as if the word effects so little. The word is like seed: everything depends on the treatment it receives. Some receive the word with the understanding: there it cannot be quickened. The word is meant for the heart, the will, the affections. The word must be submitted to, must be lived, must be acted out. When this is done it will manifest its living, quickening power. It is not we who have to make the word alive. When, in faith in the life and power there is in the word, the heart yields itself in humble submission and honest desire to its action, it will prove itself to be life and power.

And sharper than any two-edged sword, and piercing even to the dividing of soul and spirit, of both joints and marrow. The first action of God's word is to wound, to cut, to divide. In the soul the natural life has its seat; in the spirit the spiritual and divine. Sin has brought confusion and disorder; the spirit is under the mastery of the soul, the natural life. God's word divides and separates; wakens the spirit to a sense of its destiny as the faculty for the unseen and eternal; brings the soul to a knowledge of itself as a captive to the power of sin. It cuts deep and sure, discovering the deep corruption of sin. As the knife of the surgeon, who seeks to heal, pierces even to the dividing of the joints and marrow, where it is needed, so the word penetrates all; there is no part of the inner being to which it does not pass.

And quick to discern the thoughts and intents of the heart. It is specially with the heart that God's word deals. In chapter iii. we read of the hardened heart, the evil heart of unbelief, the erring heart. When the word heart occurs later in the Epistle we shall find everything changed; we shall read of a heart in which God's law is written, of a true heart, a heart sprinkled with the blood, a heart stablished by grace (viii. 10, x. 22, xiii. 9). We have here the transition from the one to the other. God's appeal was, **Today, if ye hear His voice, harden**

not your heart. The heart that will but yield itself to be searched by God's word, to have its secret thoughts and intents discerned and judged by it, will be freed from its erring and unbelief, and quickened and cleansed, and made a living table on which the word is written by God Himself. Oh, to know how needful it is, but also how blessed, to yield our hearts to the judgment of the word.

And there is no creature that is not manifest in His sight. God's word bears the character of God Himself. He is the all-knowing and all-pervading: nothing can hide itself from the judgment of His word. If we will not have it judge us now, it will condemn us hereafter. **For all things are naked and laid open before the eyes of Him with whom we have to do.** Yes, the God with whom we have to do is He of whom we later read: "It is a fearful thing to fall into the hands of the living God." And again: "Our God is a consuming fire." It is this God who now pleads with us to enter into His rest.

Let each of us gladly yield ourselves to have to do with Him. If perhaps there be a secret consciousness that all is not right, that we are not giving diligence to enter into the rest, oh, let us beware of setting such thoughts aside. It is the first swelling of the living seed of the word within us. Do not regard that thought as coming from thyself, or from man who brings thee God's word; it is God waking thee out of sleep. Have to do with Him. Be willing that the word should show thee what is wrong. Be not afraid of its discovering to thee thy sin and wretchedness. The knife of the physician wounds to heal. *The light that shows thee thy sin and wrong will surely lead thee out.* The word is living and will give thee life.

1. God has spoken to us in His Son. This is the keynote of the Epistle. To-day, if ye hear His voice, harden not your heart: this is the keynote of this long and solemn warning. Let us hearken, let us yield to the word. As we deal with the word, so we deal with God. And so will God deal with us.

2. Judge of thy life not by what thy heart says, or the Church, or the so-called Christian world—but by what the word says. Let it have its way with thee: it will greatly bless thee.

3. All things are naked before the eyes of Him with whom we have to do. Why, then, through indifference or discouragement, shut thine eyes to them? Oh, lay everything open before God, the God with whom we have to do, whether we will or not.

4. The word is living and active. Have great faith in its power. Be sure that the Holy Spirit, that the living Word, that God Himself works in it. The word ever points to the living God, who is present in it, and makes it a living word, in the heart that is seeking for life and for God.

XXXIV.

A Great High Priest

IV.–14. Having, then,[1] a great High Priest, who hath passed through the heavens, Jesus the Son of God, let us hold fast our confession.

After his digression, in the warning to the Hebrews not like their fathers with Moses, to harden their hearts through unbelief, our writer returns to his argument. He had already twice used the words High Priest (ii. 16, iii. 1), and is preparing the way for what is the great object of the Epistle—the exposition of the heavenly priesthood of the Lord Jesus, and the work He has by it accomplished for us (vii.–x. 18). In this section (iv. 14–v. 10) he first gives the general characteristics of that priesthood, as typified by Aaron, and exhibited in our Lord's life here on earth. In chaps. i. and ii. he had laid the foundation of his structure in the divinity and the humanity of our Saviour: he here first speaks of Him in His greatness as a High Priest passed through the heavens, then in His sympathy and compassion, as having been tempted like as we are.

Having, therefore, a great High Priest. The therefore refers to the previous argument, in which Christ's greatness had been

1. Therefore.

183

set forth, and in view of the dangers against which he had been warning, the readers had been urged to steadfastness in holding fast their confession. The force of the appeal lies in the word **Having.** We know the meaning of that word so well in earthly things. There is nothing that touches men so nearly as the sense of ownership of property. I *have* a father, I *have* money, I *have* a home—what a world of interest is awakened in connection with such thoughts. And God's word comes here and says: You *have*—O best and most wonderful of all possessions—You *have* a great High Priest. You own Him; He is yours, your very own, wholly yours. You may use Him with all He is and has. You can trust Him for all you need, know and claim Him as indeed your great High Priest, to bring you to God. Let your whole walk be the proof that you live as one, *having a great High Priest.*

A great High Priest who hath passed through the heavens. We have said more than once, and shall not weary of repeating it again, that one of the great lessons of our Epistle has been to teach us this: *The knowledge of the greatness and glory of Jesus is the secret of a strong and holy life.* Its opening chapter was nothing but a revelation of His divine nature and glory. At the root of all it has to teach us of Christ's priesthood and work, it wants us to see the adorable omnipotent divinity of Christ. In that our faith is to find its strength, and the measure of its expectation. By that our conduct is to be guided. That is to be the mark of our life— that we have a Saviour who is God. **A great High Priest, who hath passed through the heavens.** Later on we read (vii. 26): **Such an High Priest became us, made higher than the heavens.** It is difficult for us to form any conception of what heaven is, so high, and bright, and full of glory. But all the heavens we can think of were only the vestibule through which he passed into that which is behind, and above and beyond them all—the light that is inaccessible, the very life and presence of God Himself. And the word calls us to follow our great High Priest in thought, and when thought fails, in faith and worship and love, into this glory beyond and above all heavens, and, *having* Him as ours, to be sure that our life can be the counterpart of His, the proof of what a complete redemption He has wrought, the living experience of what he has effected there.

A great High Priest, Jesus the Son of God. The name **Jesus** speaks of His humanity, and of His work as a Saviour from sin. This is the first work of the priest—the cleansing, the putting away of sin. The name **Son of God** speaks of His divinity, and His power as High Priest, really to bring us to God, into the very life and fellowship of the Holy One. It is in His Son God speaks to us; it is to the perfect fellowship and blessedness of the ever-blessed One that our great High Priest that is passed through the heavens can, and does indeed, bring us.

Having, therefore, a great High Priest, let us hold fast our confession! He is (iii. 1) the Apostle and **High Priest of our confession.** The knowledge of what He is is our strength to **hold fast our confession.** Twice the Hebrews had been told how much would depend on this (iii. 6, 14). "We are His house, *if we hold fast.*" "We are become partakers of Christ, *if we hold fast.*" Our faith in Christ must be confessed. If we *have* Him as our great High Priest, He is worthy of it; our souls will delight in rendering Him this homage; without it, failure will speedily come; without it, the grace of steadfastness, perseverance, cannot be maintained.

O brethren, having a great High Priest, who is passed through the heavens, let us hold fast our confession. Let every thought of Jesus, *in heaven for us,* urge us to live wholly for Him; in everything to confess Him as our Lord.

1. Ought it not to fill our hearts with worship and trust, and love without end, this wondrous mystery: the Son of God, become Man; the Son of Man, now God on the throne; that we might be helped.

2. Who hath passed through the heavens! beyond all thought of space and place, into the mystery of the divine glory and power. And why? That He might in divine power breathe that heavenly life into our hearts. His whole priesthood has, as its one great characteristic, heavenliness. He communicates the purity, the power, the life of heaven to us. We live in heaven with Him; He lives with heaven in us. With Him in our hearts we have the kingdom of heaven within us, in which God's will is done, as in heaven, so on earth. Let us believe it can most surely be.

3. After all the solemn warning about falling in the wilderness, coming short of the rest, see here your safety and strength—Wherefore, holy brethren, partakers of a heavenly calling, consider the Apostle and High Priest of our confession, Jesus. Having Jesus, *let us hold fast.*

XXXV.

A High Priest, Able to Sympathise

IV.–15. For we have not a high priest that cannot be touched
with the feeling[2] of our infirmities;[3] but one that hath been
tempted in all things like as we are, yet without sin.

May God in His mercy give us a true insight into the glory of
what is offered us in these words—even this, that our High
Priest, whom we have in heaven, is one who is able to sympathise with us, because He knows, from personal experience, exactly what we feel. Yes, that God might give us courage to draw
nigh to Him, He has placed upon the throne of heaven one out
of our own midst, of whom we can be certain that, because He
Himself lived on earth as man, He understands us perfectly, is
prepared to have patience with our weakness, and to give us just
the help we need. It was to effect this that God sent His Son to
become man, and as Man perfected Him through suffering. That
not one single feeble soul should be afraid to draw nigh to the
great God, or in drawing nigh should doubt as to whether God
is not too great and holy fully to understand, or to bear with his
weakness. Jesus, the tried and tempted One, has been placed
upon the throne as our High Priest. God gives us a glimpse into
the heart of our compassionate, sympathising High Priest!

**For we have not a high priest who is not able to sympa-
thise with our weaknesses.** The writer uses the two negatives
to indicate how common the thought is which he wishes to

2. Who is not able to sympathise with.
3. Weaknesses.

combat. A rich king, who lives every day in luxury, can he, even though he hear of it—can he fully realise what it means for the poor sick man, from year to year, never to know where his daily bread is to come from? Hardly. And God, the glorious and ever-blessed, can He truly feel what a poor sinner experiences in his daily struggle with the weakness and temptations of the flesh? God be praised! Jesus knows, and is **able to sympathise, He is one who hath been in all things tempted like as we are, yet without sin.**

In all things! The thought of Jesus as a sympathising High Priest, is ordinarily applied to those who are in circumstances of trial and suffering. But the truth has a far deeper meaning and application. It has special reference to the temptation which meets the soul in the desire to live wholly for God. **Jesus suffered, being tempted:** it was the temptation to refuse the Father's will that caused His deepest suffering. As the believer, who seeks in all things to do the will of God, understands this, the truth of the sympathising High Priest becomes doubly precious.

What is the ordinary experience of those who set themselves with their whole heart to live for God? It happens very often that it is only then they begin to find out how sinful they are. They are continually disappointed in their purpose to obey God's will. They feel deeply ashamed at the thought of how often, even in things that appear little and easy, they fail entirely in keeping a good conscience and in pleasing God. At times it is as if the more they hear of the rest of God and the life of faith, the fainter the hope of attaining it becomes. At times they are ready to give up all in despair: a life in the rest of God is not for them.

What comfort and strength comes at such a time to a soul, when it sees that Jesus is able to sympathise and to succour, because He has Himself been thus tempted. Or did it not become so dark in His soul, that He had to wrestle and to cry, "*If* it be possible?" and "*Why* hast thou forsaken Me?" He, too, had to trust God in the dark. He, too, in the hour of death had to let go

His spirit, and commit it, in the darkness of death, into God's keeping. He knew what it was to walk in darkness and see no light. And when a man feels utterly helpless and in despair, Jesus can sympathise with him; He was tempted in all things like as we are. If we would but rest in the assurance that He understands it all, that He feels for us with a sympathy, in which the infinite love of God and the tenderness of a fellow-sufferer are combined, and is able to succour him, we should soon reach the rest of God. Trusting Jesus would bring us into it.

Holy brethren! partakers of a heavenly calling! would you be strong to hold fast your confession, and know in full the power of your Redeemer God to save; listen to-day to the voice of the Holy Spirit: **Jesus was in all things tempted just as you are.** And why? that He might be able to help you. His being *able to sympathise* has no other purpose than that He should be *able to succour.* Let the one word be the food of your faith; the other will be its fruit, your blessed experience. Just think of God giving His Son to come and pass through all the temptations that come to you, that He might be **able to sympathise,** and then lifting Him up to the throne of omnipotence that He might be **able to succour,** and say if you have not reason to trust Him fully. And let the faith of the blessed High Priest in His infinite and tender sympathy be the foundation of a friendship and a fellowship in which we are sure to experience that He is able to save completely.

1. *Some time ago I asked a young lady who had come from Keswick, and spoke of her having been a happy Christian for years before, and having found such a wonderful change in her experience, how she would describe the difference between what she had known before and now enjoyed. Her answer was ready at once: "Oh, it is the personal friendship of Jesus!" And here is one of the gates that lead into this blessed friendship: He became a Man just that I might learn to trust His gentle, sympathising kindness.*

2. *Study well the three ables of this Epistle. Jesus able to sympathise, able to succour, able to save completely. And claim all.*

3. *Tempted like as we are. He was made like to us in temptation, that we might become like Him in victory. This He will accomplish in us. Oh, let us*

consider Jesus, who suffered being tempted, who experienced what temptation is, who resisted and overcame it, and brought to nought the tempter,
who now lives as High Priest to succour the tempted and give the victory—
let us consider Jesus, the ever-present Deliverer: He will lead us in triumph
through every foe.

XXXVI.

Let Us Draw Near with Boldness

IV.–16. Let us therefore draw near with boldness unto the throne of grace that we may receive mercy, and may find grace to help us in time of need.[4]

In the first two chapters the true divinity and the real humanity of our Saviour were set before us, as the very foundation of our faith and life. In the two verses we have just been considering these two truths are applied to the priesthood of Christ. Having a great High Priest who hath passed through the heavens; having an High Priest who is able to sympathise; let us draw near. The one work of the High Priest is to bring us near to God. The one object of revealing to us His person and work is to give us perfect confidence in drawing near. The measure of our nearness of access to God is the index of our knowledge of Jesus.

Let us therefore, with such an High Priest, **draw near with boldness to the throne of grace.** The word, *draw near,* is that used of the priests in the Old Testament. It is this one truth the Epistle seeks to enforce, that we can actually, in spiritual reality, draw near to God, and live in that nearness, in living fellowship with Him, all the day. The work of Christ, as our High Priest, is so perfect, and His power in heaven so divine, that He not only gives us the right and liberty to draw nigh, but by His priestly action He does in very deed and truth, so take possession of our

4. For timely help.

191

inmost being and inward life, and draw and bring us nigh, that our life can be lived in God's presence.

Let us draw near. The expression occurs twice; here and x. 21. The repetition is significant. In the second passage, after the deeper truths of the true sanctuary, and the rent veil, and the opening of the Holiest have been expounded, it refers to the believer's entrance into the full blessing of a life spent in the power of Christ's heavenly priesthood, in the presence of God. Here, where all this teaching has not yet been given, it is applied more simply to prayer, to the drawing nigh to the throne of grace, in a sense which the feeblest believer can understand it. It is as we are faithful in the lesser, the tarrying before the throne of grace in prayer, that we shall find access to the greater—the life within the veil, in the full power of the Forerunner who hath entered there for us.

Let us draw near, that we may receive mercy. This has reference to that compassion which we need when the sense of sin and guilt and unworthiness depress us. In drawing nigh to the throne of grace, to the mercy-seat, in prayer, we first receive mercy, we experience that God pardons and accepts and loves. **And we find grace for timely help.** This refers to that strengthening of the inner life by which He, who was tempted in all things like as we, meets us and enables us to conquer temptation. Grace is the divine strength working in us. "My *grace* is sufficient for thee; my power is made perfect in weakness." The Holy Spirit is "the Spirit of grace." The believing supplicant at the throne of grace not only receives mercy, the consciousness of acceptance and favour, but finds grace, in that Spirit whose operation the Father always delights to bestow. And that grace is **for timely help,** *lit.* "well-timed help," just the special help we need at each moment. The infinite mercy of God's love resting on us, and the almighty grace of His Spirit working in us, will ever be found at a throne of grace, if we but come boldly, trusting in Jesus alone.

And now comes the chief word, "Let us therefore draw near **with boldness.**" We have already been taught to **hold fast our boldness.** We shall later on be warned, **cast not away your boldness.** And the summing up of the Epistle will tell us that the great fruit of Christ's redemption is that we have **boldness to enter in.** It is the expression of the highest form of confidence, in the unhesitating assurance that there is nothing that can hinder, and in a conduct that corresponds to this conviction. It suggests the thought of our drawing nigh to God's throne without fear, without doubt, with no other feeling but that of the childlike liberty which a child feels in speaking to its father.

This boldness is what the blood of Christ, in its infinite worth, has secured for us, and what His heavenly priesthood works and maintains in us. This boldness is the natural and necessary result of the adoring and believing gaze fixed on our great High Priest upon the throne. This boldness is what the Holy Spirit works in us as the inward participation in Christ's entrance into the Father's presence. This boldness is of the essence of a healthy Christian life. If there is one thing the Christian should care for and aim at, it is to maintain unbroken and unclouded the living conviction and practice of this *drawing near with boldness.*

Let us, **therefore,** draw near with boldness! Jesus the Son of God is our High Priest. Our boldness of access is not a state we produce in ourselves by meditation or effort. No, the living, loving High Priest, who is able to sympathise and gives grace for timely help, He breathes and works this boldness in the soul that is willing to lose itself in Him. Jesus, found and felt within our heart by faith, is our boldness. As the Son, whose house we are, He will dwell within us, and by His Spirit's working, Himself be our boldness and our entrance to the Father. **Let us, therefore, draw near with boldness!**

1. Do take hold of the thought that the whole teaching of the Epistle centres in this, that we should so be partakers of Christ and all He is, should so have *Him as our High Priest, that we may with perfect boldness, with the most undoubting confidence enter into, and dwell in, and enjoy the Father's presence. It is in the heart that we partake of and have Christ; it is Christ, known as dwelling in the heart, that will make our boldness perfect.*

2. Each time you pray, exercise this boldness. Let the measure of Jesus' merit, yea more, let the measure of Jesus' power to work in you and lead you on to God, be the measure of your boldness.

3. What tenderness of conscience, what care, what jealousy, what humility, this boldness will work, lest we allow anything for which our heart can condemn us, and we so lose our liberty before God. Then it will truly be our experience—

So near, so very near to God,
More near I cannot be.

XXXVII.

The High Priest Bearing Gently with the Ignorant

V.–1. For every high priest, being taken from among men, is appointed for men in things pertaining to God, that he may offer both gifts and sacrifices for sins:
2. Who can bear gently with the ignorant and erring, for that he himself also is compassed with infirmity;[5]
3. And by reason thereof is bound, as for the people, so also for himself, to offer for sins.

We know how much the Epistle has already said of the true humanity and sympathy of the Lord Jesus. In chapter ii. we read: **It became God to perfect Him through suffering; since the children are sharers of flesh and blood, He also in like manner partook of the same. It behooved Him in all things to be made like unto His brethren. In that He Himself hath suffered, being tempted, He is able to succour them that are tempted.** And in chapter iv. we have just heard, **We have not a high priest who is not able to sympathise with our weaknesses, but one who hath in all things been tempted like as we are.** And yet the truth is counted of such importance, that once again our attention is directed to it. It is not enough that we have a general conviction of its truth, but we need to have it taken up into our heart and life, until every thought of Jesus is interpenetrated by such a feeling of His sympathy, that all sense

5. Weakness.

195

of weakness shall at once be met by the joyful consciousness that all is well, because Jesus is so very kind, and cares so lovingly for all our feebleness and all our ignorance.

Let us listen once again to what the word teaches. **Every high priest being taken from among men, is appointed for men in things pertaining to God, that He may offer both gifts and sacrifices for sins.** Here we have the work of a high priest, and the first essential requisite for that work. His work is *in things pertaining to God:* he has charge of all that concerns the access to God, His worship and service, and has, for this, to offer gifts and sacrifices. And the requisite is, he must be a man, because he is to act for men. And that for this great reason that he may be one **who can bear gently with the ignorant and erring, for that he himself also is compassed with weakness; and who by reason thereof is bound, as for the people, so also for himself to offer for sins.** At the root of the priestly office there is to be the sense of perfect oneness in weakness and need of help. In priestly action this is to manifest itself in sacrificing, as for the people, so for himself. And all this, that the priestly spirit may ever be kept alive for the comfort and confidence of all the needy and weary—he must be one **who can bear gently with the ignorant and erring.**

Glory be to God for the wondrous picture of what our Lord Jesus is. A priest must be God's representative with men. But he cannot be this, without being himself a man himself encompassed with weaknesses, and so identified with and representing men with God. This was why Jesus was made a little lower than the angels. The high priest is to offer as for the people, so for himself. Offering for himself was to be the bond of union with the people. Even so our blessed Lord Jesus offered (*see* ver. 7), prayers and supplications with strong crying and tears, yea, in all that, offered Himself unto God. And all this, that He might win our hearts and confidence as one **who can bear gently with the ignorant and erring.** God has indeed done everything to assure us that, with such an High Priest, no ignorance or error need make us afraid of not finding the way to Him and His love. Jesus will care for us—He bears gently with the ignorant and erring.

Have we not, in our faith in the priesthood of Christ, been too much in the habit of looking more at His work than at His heart? Have we not too exclusively put the thought of our sins in the foreground, and not sufficiently realised that our weaknesses, our ignorance and errors—that for these too a special provision has been made in Him who was made like us, and Himself encompassed with weaknesses, that He might be a merciful and faithful High Priest, who can bear gently with the ignorant and erring. Oh, let us take in and avail ourselves to the full of the wondrous message: Jesus could not ascend the throne as Priest, until He had first, in the school of personal experience, learnt to sympathise and to bear gently with the feeblest. And let our weakness and ignorance henceforth, instead of discouraging and keeping us back, be the motive and the plea which lead us to come boldly to Him for help, **who can bear gently with the ignorant and erring.** In the pursuit of holiness our ignorance is often our greatest source of failure. We cannot fully understand what is taught of the rest of God, and the power of faith, of dwelling within the veil or of Christ dwelling in our heart. Things appear too high for us, utterly beyond our reach. If we but knew to trust Jesus, not only as He who made propitiation for our sins, but as one who has been specially chosen and trained and prepared, and then elevated to the throne of God, to be the Leader of the ignorant and erring, bearing gently with their every weakness! Let us this day afresh accept this Saviour, as God has here revealed Him to us, and rejoice that all our ignorance need not be a barrier in the way to God, because Jesus takes it into His care.

1. Oh the trouble God has taken to win our poor hearts to trust and confidence. Let us accept the revelation, and have our hearts so filled with the sympathy and gentleness of Jesus, that in every perplexity our first thought shall always be the certainty and the blessedness of His compassion and help.

2. How many souls there are who mourn over their sins, and do not think that they are making their sins more and stronger by not going with all their ignorance and weakness boldly to Jesus.

3. Do learn the lesson: the whole priesthood of Jesus has but this one object, to lead thee boldly and joyfully to draw near to God, and live in fellowship with Him. With this view trust Jesus as definitely with thy ignorance and weakness as with thy sins.

XXXVIII.

The High Priest, Called of God

V.–4. And no man taketh the honour unto himself, but when he is called of God, even as was Aaron.

5. So Christ also glorified not Himself to be made a high priest, but he that spake unto him,

Thou art my Son,
This day have I begotten thee:

6. As he saith also in another place,

Thou art a priest for ever
After the order of Melchizedek.

A priest sustains a twofold relationship—to God and to man. Every high priest is appointed *for men* in things *pertaining to God*. We have just seen what the great characteristic is of his relation to men: he must himself be a man, like them and one with them, with a heart full of gentleness and sympathy for the very weakest. In his relation to God, our Epistle now proceeds to say, the chief requirement is that he should have his appointment from God. He must not take the honour to himself: he must be called of God. All this is proved to be true of Jesus.

The truth that Jesus had His appointment from God was not only of importance to the Hebrews to convince them of the divine and supreme right of Christianity; it is of equal interest to us, to give us an insight into that which constitutes the real glory and power of our religion. Our faith needs to be fed and strengthened, and this can only be as we enter more deeply into the divine origin and nature of redemption.

No man taketh the honour unto himself, but when he is called of God. It is God against whom we have sinned, in separation from whom we are fallen into the power of death. It is God we need; it is to Him and His love the way must be opened. It is God alone, who can say what that way is, who is able to have it opened up. And this now is what gives the gospel, and our faith in Christ, its security and sufficiency—that it is all of God. Christ has been called of God to be High Priest. The very God who created us, against whom we sinned, gives His Son as our Redeemer.

So Christ also glorified not Himself to be made a High Priest, but He that spake unto Him, Thou art My Son, this day I have begotten thee. As He saith also in another place, Thou art a Priest for ever after the order of Melchizedek. Here it is not merely the fact that Christ was called of God to be High Priest, but the ground upon which He was chosen, that we must specially notice. The two passages quoted teach us that it was as Son of God that He was appointed High Priest. This opens up to us the true nature and character of the priesthood. It shows us that the priesthood is rooted in the sonship: the work of the priesthood is to reveal and communicate the blessed life of sonship.

As Son, Christ alone was heir of all that God had. All the life of the Father was in Him. God could have no union or fellowship with any creature but through His beloved Son, or as far as the life and spirit and image of the Son was seen in it. Therefore no one could be our High Priest but the Son of God. If our salvation was not to be a merely legal one—external and, I may say, artificial—but an entrance anew into the very life of God, with the restoration of the divine nature we had lost in paradise, it was the Son of God alone who could impart this to us. He had the life of God to give; He was able to give it; He could only give it by taking us into living fellowship with Himself. The priesthood of Christ is the God-devised channel through which the ever-blessed Son could make us partakers of Himself, and with Himself of all the life and glory He hath from and in the Father.

And this now is our confidence and safety—that it was the Father who appointed the Son High Priest. It is the love of the God against whom we had sinned that gave the Son. It is the will and the power of this God that ordained and worked out the great salvation. It is in God Himself our salvation has its origin, its life, its power. It is God drawing nigh to communicate Himself to us in His Son.

Christ glorified not Himself to be made a High Priest: it was God gave Him this glory. Just think what this means. God counts it an honour for His Son to be the Priest of poor sinners. Jesus gave up His everlasting glory for the sake of this new, which He now counts His highest, glory—the honour of leading guilty men to God. Every cry of a penitent for mercy, every prayer of a ransomed soul for more grace and nearer access to God, He counts these His highest honour, the proofs of a glory He has received from His Father above the glory of sonship, or rather the opening up of the fulness of glory which His sonship contained.

O thou doubting troubled soul! Wilt thou not now believe this: that Jesus counts it His highest honour to do His work in any needy one that turns to Him? The Son of God in His glory counts His priesthood His highest glory, as the power of making us partake as brethren with Him in the life and love of the Father. Do let Jesus now become thy confidence. Be assured that nothing delights Jesus more than to do His work. Do thou what God hath done; glorify Him as thy High Priest; and, as thou learnest to turn from thyself and all human help, to trust the Son of God, He will prove to thee what a great High Priest He is; He will, as Son, lead thee into the life and love of the Father.

1. Could God have bestowed a more wondrous grace upon us than this, to give His own Son as our High Priest? Could He have given us a surer ground of faith and hope than this, that the Son is Priest? And shall we not trust Him? and give Him the honour God has given Him?

2. What is needed is that we occupy and exercise our faith in appropriating this blessed truth: Jesus is the eternal Son, appointed by the Father as our Priest to introduce us into His presence, and to keep us there. He was Himself so compassed with weaknesses and tried with temptations, that no ignorance or weakness on our part can weary Him, or prevent Him doing His blessed work—if we will only trust Him. Oh, let us worship and honour Him. Let us trust Him. Let our faith claim all He is able and willing to do—our God-appointed High Priest.

3. Faith opens the heart—through faith this divine Being fills, pervades, the whole heart, dwells in it. He cannot bring thee nigh to God except as He brings thy heart nigh. He cannot bring thy heart nigh except as He dwells in it. He cannot dwell in it except as thou believest. Oh, consider Jesus, until thy whole heart is faith in Him and what He is in thee.

XXXIX.

The High Priest Learning Obedience

V.-7. Who in the days of his flesh, having offered up prayers and supplications, with strong crying and tears, unto him that was able to save him out of death, and having been heard for his godly fear,

8. Though he was a Son, yet learned obedience by the things which he suffered.

We have already noticed with what persistence the writer has sought to impress upon us the intense reality of Christ's humanity—His being *made like* unto His brethren, His partaking of flesh and blood *in like manner* as ourselves, His being tempted in all things *like as we are.* In the opening verses of our chapter he has again set before us the true High Priest—Himself compassed with weaknesses. He now once more returns to the subject. In verse 6 he has already quoted the promise in regard to the order of Melchizedek, as the text of his farther teaching, but feels himself urged to interpose, and before repeating the quotation in verse 11, still more fully to unfold what the full meaning is of the blessed humiliation of the Son of God. He leads us in spirit down into Gethsemane, and speaks of the wondrous mystery of the agony there, as the last stage in the preparation and the perfecting of our High Priest for the work He came to do. Let us enter this holy place with hearts bowed under a consciousness of our ignorance, but thirsting to know something more of the great mystery of godliness, the Son of God become flesh for us.

Who in the days of His flesh. The word "flesh" points to human nature in the weakness which is the mark of its fallen state. When Jesus said to His disciples in that dark night, "Watch and pray; the spirit is willing, but the flesh is weak," He spoke from personal experience. He had felt that it was not enough to have a right purpose, but that, unless the weakness of the flesh were upheld, or rather overcome, by power received in prayer from above, that weakness would so easily enter into temptation, and become sin. The days of His flesh, encompassed with its weaknesses, were to Him a terrible reality. It was not to yield to this that He watched and prayed.

Who in the days of His flesh, having offered up prayers and supplications with strong crying and tears unto Him that was able to save Him out of death, and having been heard for His godly fear, having gained the strength to surrender His will and fully accept the Father's will, and the renewed assurance that He would be saved and raised out of it, **though He was a Son**—the form of the expression implies that no one would have expected from the Son of God what is now to be said—**yet learned obedience by the things which He suffered.** Gethsemane was the training-school where our High Priest, made like to us in all things, learnt His last and most difficult lesson of obedience through what He suffered.

Though He was a Son. As the Son of God, come from heaven, one would say that there could be no thought of His learning obedience. But so real was His emptying Himself of His life in glory, and so complete His entrance into all the conditions and likeness of our nature, that He did indeed need to learn obedience. This is of the very essence of the life of a reasonable creature, of man, that the life and the will he has received from God cannot be developed without the exercise of a self-determining power, without the voluntary giving up to God in all that He asks, even where it appears a sacrifice. The creature can only attain his perfection under a law of growth, of trial, and of development, in the overcoming of what is contrary to God's will, and the assimilating of what that will reveals.

Of Jesus it is written: *The child grew, and waxed strong, becoming full of wisdom.* What is true of His childhood is true of His maturer years. At each stage of life He had to meet temptation, and overcome it; out of each victory He came with His will strengthened, and His power over the weakness of the flesh, and the danger of yielding to its desire for earthly good, or its fear of temporal evil, increased. In Gethsemane His trial and His obedience reached their consummation.

He learned obedience by the things which He suffered. Suffering is something unnatural, the fruit of sin. God has made us for joy. He created us not only with the capacity, but the power of happiness, so that every breath and every healthy movement should be enjoyment. It is natural to us, it was so to the Son of God, to fear and flee suffering. In this desire there is nothing sinful. It only becomes sinful where God would have us submit and suffer, and we refuse. This was the temptation of the power of darkness in Gethsemane—for Jesus to refuse the cup. In His prayers and supplications, with strong crying and tears, Jesus maintained His allegiance to God's will: in wrestlings and bloody sweat He became obedient unto death, even the death of the cross. The deepest suffering taught Him the highest lesson of obedience: when He had yielded His will and His life, His obedience was complete, and He Himself was perfected for evermore.

This is our High Priest. He knows what the weakness of the flesh is. He knows what it costs to conquer it, and how little we are able to do it. He lives in heaven, able to succour us; sympathising with our weaknesses; bearing gently with the ignorant and erring; a High Priest on the throne, that we may boldly draw nigh to find grace for timely help. He lives in heaven and in our heart, to impart to us His own spirit of obedience, so that His priesthood may bring us into the full enjoyment of all He Himself has and is.

1. Heard for His godly fear. *How it becomes me then to pray in humble, holy reverence, that I may pray in His spirit, and be heard too for His godly fear. This was the very spirit of His prayer and obedience.*

2. He learned obedience through suffering. *Learn to look upon and to welcome all suffering as God's message to teach obedience.*

3. He learned obedience: *This was the path in which Christ was trained for His priesthood. This is the spirit and the power that filled Him for the throne of glory; the spirit and the power which alone can lift us there; the spirit and the power which our great High Priest can impart to us. Obedience is of the very essence of salvation. Whether we look at Christ being perfected personally, or at the merit that gave His death its value and saving power, or at the work wrought in us—obedience, the entrance into the will of God, is the very essence of salvation.*

4. He learned obedience. *Jesus was obedience embodied, obedience incarnate. I have only as much of Jesus in me as I have of the spirit of obedience.*

XL.

The High Priest,
Perfected Through Obedience

V.–8. Though he was a Son, yet learned obedience by the things
which he suffered;
9. And having been made perfect, he became unto all them that
obey him, the cause of eternal salvation.

Our Lord Jesus **learned obedience by the things which He
suffered.** Through this obedience **He was made perfect, and
became the cause of eternal salvation to all that obey Him.**
So he entered heaven as our **High Priest, a Son, perfected for
evermore.**

The word *perfect* is one of the keywords of the Epistle. It occurs thirteen times. Four times in regard to the Old Testament,
which could make nothing perfect. **The law made nothing perfect** (vii. 19). **Sacrifices that cannot, as touching the conscience, make the worshipper perfect** (ix. 9). **The law can
never make perfect them that draw nigh** (x. 1). **That apart
from us they should not be made perfect** (xi. 40). As great as
is the difference between a promise and its fulfilment, or hope
and the thing hoped for, between the shadow and substance, is
the difference between the Old and New Testament. The law
made nothing perfect: it was only meant to point to something
better, to the perfection Jesus Christ was to bring. With the New
Testament perfection would come. Thrice the word is used of
our Lord Jesus, who in Himself prepared and wrought out the
perfection He came to impart. **It became God to make the**

Leader of our salvation perfect through suffering (ii. 11). **He learned obedience, and being made perfect, became the cause of salvation** (v. 9). **Appointed High Priest; a Son perfected for evermore** (vii. 28). The perfection brought by Christ was that which was revealed in His own personal life. He came to restore to us the life of God we had lost—a life in the will and love of God. This alone is salvation. God perfected Him through suffering—wrought out in Him a perfect human character, in which the divine life was fully united with the human will. He learned obedience through suffering, and manifested perfectly the humility and submission and surrender to God, which is man's duty and blessedness. So, when He had been perfected, He became the author of eternal salvation to all who obey Him, because He now had that perfected human nature which He could communicate to them. And so He was appointed High Priest—a Son, perfected for evermore. As Son of God, He was to take us up into the very life of God; as High Priest, He was to lift us, in actual spiritual reality, into God's fellowship and will and presence; the way in which He was perfected through obedience was the living way in which He was to lead us—as the Son, perfected through obedience, who had found and opened and walked the path of obedience as the path to God, and would animate us with His own Spirit to do it too, He, the perfected One, can alone be our salvation.

Then twice we have the word of what Christ has done for us. **By one offering He hath perfected for ever them that are sanctified** (x. 14); **the Leader and Perfecter of our faith** (xii. 2). Christ's perfecting us for ever is nothing but His redeeming us by His one sacrifice into the perfect possession of Himself, the perfected One, as our life. His death is our death to sin, His resurrection as the perfected One is our life, His righteousness is ours, His life ours; we are put in possession of all the perfection which the Father wrought out in Him through suffering and obedience. And once of the spiritual sanctuary opened by

Christ: **The greater and more perfect tabernacle not made with hands** (ix. 11). And three times it is used in regard to Christian character: **Solid food is for the perfect** (v. 14); **Let us press on to perfection** (vi. 1); **The God of peace perfect**[6] **you in every good thing** (xiii. 21). The perfect for whom the solid food is, are those who are not content with the mere beginnings of the Christian life, but have given themselves wholly to accept and follow the perfected Master. These are they who press on to perfection—nothing else than the perfection which Christ revealed, as God's claim on men, and as what He has won and made possible for them.

He learned obedience, **and being perfected,** became the cause of eternal salvation. The perfection of God is His will. There is no perfection for man but in union with that will. And there is no way for attaining and proving the union with that will but by obedience. Obedience to the good and perfect will of God transforms the whole nature, and makes it capable of union with Him in glory. Obedience to God's will on earth is the way to the glory of God's will in heaven. The everlasting perfection of heaven is nothing but the obedience of earth transfigured and glorified. Obedience is the seed, the power, the life of Christ's perfection and ours.

We are approaching the threshold of the Holiest of All, as this Epistle is to open it up to us as the sphere of the heavenly priesthood of Him who was made after the order of Melchizedek. Ere we proceed thither let us learn this lesson well: The distinguishing mark of the earthly life of our High Priest; the source of His heavenly glory and His eternal salvation; the power of His atonement of our disobedience; the opening of the living way in which we are to follow Him our Leader; the inner disposition and spirit of the life He bestows—*of all this, the secret is obedience.* Through obedience He was per-

6. In the Greek here the word used is not the same as in the other passages.

fected, His sacrifice was perfect, He perfected us for ever, He carries us on to perfection.

1. *When the perfect heavenly life of the Lord Jesus comes down from heaven into our hearts, it can assume no form but that which it had in Him—obedience.*

2. God must be obeyed: *in that one word you have the key to the life and death of Jesus, His sitting at God's right hand, His priesthood, His dwelling in our hearts, as well as to the whole of the gospel message—God must be obeyed.*

3. *Christ, the obedient One, who inaugurated for us the new way of obedience unto death as the way to God. Is this the Christ thou lovest and trusteth? Is this thy delight in Him, that He now has delivered thee from thy disobedience, and makes thee strong to live only to obey God and Him? Is Christ precious to thee because the salvation He gives is a restoration to obedience?*

XLI.

The High Priest Saving the Obedient

V.–8. Though he was a Son, yet learned obedience by the things which he suffered;
9. And having been made perfect, he became unto all them that obey him, the cause of eternal salvation.

The death of Jesus has its value and efficacy in obedience, ours as well as His. With Him obedience was God's great object in His suffering; the root and power of His perfection and His glory; the real efficient cause of our eternal salvation. And with us, the necessity of obedience is no less absolute. With God and with Christ our restoration to obedience was the great aim of redemption. It is the only way to that union with God in which our happiness consists. Through it alone God can reveal His life and power within us. Again I say: The death of Jesus has its value and efficacy in nothing but obedience, ours as well as His. **"He learned obedience,** and being perfected became **to all them that obey Him** the cause of eternal salvation." Our obedience is as indispensable as His. As little as He could work out salvation without obedience, can we enjoy it. In us as much as in Him, obedience is the very essence of salvation.

Let us try and grasp this. God is the blessedness of the creature. When God is all to the creature, when He is allowed in humility and dependence to work all, and when all returns to Him in thanksgiving and service, nothing can prevent the fulness of God's love and joy entering and filling the creature. It has but one thing to do—to turn its desire or will toward God, and give

Him free scope, and nothing in heaven or earth can prevent the light and the joy of God filling that soul. The living centre round which all the perfections of God cluster, the living energy through which they all do their work, is the will of God. The will of God is the life of the universe; it is what it is because God wills it; His will is the living energy which maintains it in existence. The creature can have no more of God than he has of God's will working in him. He that would meet and find God must seek Him in His will; union with God's will is union with Himself. Therefore it was that the Lord Jesus, when He came to this world, always spoke of His having come to do one thing—the will of His Father. This alone could work our salvation. Sin had broken us away from the will of God. In doing the will of God He was to break the power of sin. He was to prove wherein the service of God and true blessedness consist; He was to work out in Himself a new nature to be communicated, a new way of living to be followed; He was to show that the doing of God's will at any cost is blessedness and glory everlasting. It was because He did this, because He was obedient unto death, that God highly exalted Him. It was this disposition, His obedience, that made Him worthy and fit to sit with God on the throne of heaven. Union with the will of God is union with God Himself, and must—it cannot be otherwise—bring to the glory of God.

And this is as true of us as of Him. It is to be feared that there are many Christians who seek salvation, and have no conception in what salvation consists—a being saved from their own will, and being restored to do the will of God alone. They seek after Christ, and trust in Him; but it is not the true Christ, but a Christ of whom they have framed their own image. The true Christ is the incarnate will of God, the incarnate obedience, who works in us what God wrought in Him. Christ came as the Son, to impart to us the very same life and disposition as animated Him on earth. Christ came to be a High Priest, to bring us to God in that very same way of obedience and self-sacrifice in which He drew nigh to God. As Son and Priest, Christ is our Leader and Forerunner; it is only as we follow Him in His path on earth that we can hope to share His glory in heaven. *"He learned obedience and became the cause of eternal salvation to them that obey Him."*

Let us beware that no wrong or one-sided views of what salvation by faith means lead us astray. There are some who think that salvation by faith is all, and obedience not so essential. This is a terrible mistake. In our justification there is indeed no thought of obedience in the past. God justifieth the ungodly. But repentance is a return to obedience. And without repentance there can be no true faith. Justification, and the faith by which it comes, are only for the sake of obedience, as means to an end. They point us to Christ, and the salvation which is to be found in union with Him. And He has no salvation but for *them that obey Him.* Obedience, as the acceptance of His will and life, is our only capacity for salvation. This is the reason there is so much complaining that we cannot find and do not enjoy a full salvation. We seek it in the wrong way. Jesus Himself said that the Father would give the Holy Spirit, that is, salvation as it is perfected in Christ in heaven, to them that obey Him. To such would He manifest Himself; with such would the Father and He dwell. The salvation of Christ was wrought out entirely by obedience; this is its very essence and nature; it cannot be possessed or enjoyed but by obedience. Christ, who was perfected by obedience, is the cause of salvation to none but *them that obey Him.*

God grant that the obedience of Jesus, with the humility in which it roots, may be seen of us to be the crowning beauty of His character, the true power of His redemption, the bond of union and likeness between Him and His followers, the true and real salvation, in the salvation He gives to them that obey Him.

1. Salvation to obedience. Let us draw off our eyes and desires from the too exclusive thought of salvation as happiness, and fix them more upon that which is its reality—obedience. *Christ will see to it that a full salvation comes to the obedient.*

2. *Let no wrong thoughts of our sinfulness and inability secretly keep us back from the surrender to entire obedience.* We are made partakers of Christ, *of Himself, with the very life and spirit of obedience which constitutes Him the Saviour. The Son of God came not only to teach and to claim, but to give and work obedience. Faith in this Lord Jesus may claim and will receive the grace of obedience, will receive Himself.*

3. *Jesus* personally *learned and exercised obedience; personally He communicates it in fellowship with Himself; it becomes a personal link with Himself to those* who obey Him.

The Third Warning

Chap. v. II-vi. 20

Against Sloth, Standing Still, and Apostasy

XLII.

Of the Sin of Not Making Progress in the Christian Life

V.–10. Named of God a High Priest after the order of Melchizedek.

11. Of whom we have many things to say, and hard of interpretation, seeing ye are become dull of hearing.

12. For when by reason of the time ye ought to be teachers, ye have need again that some one teach you the rudiments of the first principles[1] of the oracles of God; and are become such as have need of milk, and not of solid food.

13. For every one that partaketh of milk is without experience of the word of righteousness; for he is a babe.

We have here the commencement of the third of the five warnings to be found in the Epistle. The first was against indifference and neglect; the second against unbelief and disobedience; the third deals specially with the sloth that prevents all progress in the Christian life, renders the soul incapable of entering into the full meaning of gospel truth and blessing, and often leads to an entire falling away. In the previous part of the Epistle, the author

1. Beginning.

has been dealing with what he considers more elementary truths, the divinity and humanity of the Saviour, and His fitness as a merciful and faithful High Priest for the work He has to do for us. He is about to enter on the higher teaching he has to give us on the heavenly priesthood of Christ (vii.–x. 18), but feels that many of his readers are incapable of following or appreciating such spiritual truth. He feels it needful first to rouse them by words of earnest reproof and exhortation, because no teaching can profit where the heart is not wakened up to hunger for it as its necessary food.

In the Christian Church, there are, alas, too many, of whom we would fain hope that they are believers, who are living in this state. They are content with the thought of pardon and the hope of heaven; they rest in their orthodoxy, their attachment to the Church and its services, their correct deportment. But as to any strong desire for the deeper truths of God's word—they have no conception of what is meant, or why they should be needed. When our author speaks of the power of Jesus' blood in heaven, of the opening of the Holiest of All, of our entering in to dwell there, and then of our going out to Him without the camp, the words find no response, because they meet no need of the soul. Let every reader listen earnestly to what God says of this state.

We have many things to say, and hard of interpretation, because ye are become dull of hearing. The writer's complaint is not that they have not sufficient education or mental power to understand what he says. By no means. But spiritual things must be spiritually discerned. Spiritual truth can only be received by the spiritual mind, by a heart that thirsts for God, and sacrifices this world for the knowledge and enjoyment of the unseen One. They were content with their knowledge of the crucified Christ; the heavenly Christ, and His power to draw them up out of the world, and to give heaven into their hearts, had but little attraction.

He further says, **By reason of the time ye ought to be teachers.** In the Christian life every one who makes real progress feels himself constrained to teach others. Christ's love in the heart must overflow to those around. The Hebrews had been Christians so long that they ought to have been teachers. The very opposite of this, however, was the case. **Ye have need again that some one teach you the rudiments of the beginning of the oracles of God.** So there are numbers of Christians whose Christian life consists very much in always learning. Sermons and books are a delight, but they never get beyond the stage of being fed; they know not what it is to feed others. There is no effort so to appropriate God's word, as to be strong to impart it to others. Or there is no real longing for deliverance from the power of sin, and the great incentive to the fuller knowledge of Jesus and His heavenly power is wanting.

And ye are become such as have need of milk, and not of solid food. Where there is no hunger for the solid food (the higher truth of Christ's heavenly priesthood), or unwillingness to use what is received in helping others, the spiritual faculties are dwarfed and enfeebled, and the Christian never gets beyond the use of the milk meant for babes. In the Christian life, as in nature, there are two stages, the one of infancy or childhood, the other of manhood. In nature the growth out of the one into the other comes spontaneously. In grace this is not so. It is possible for a Christian to remain in a sickly infancy all his life, always needing help, instead of being a help. The cause of this is sloth, reluctance to make the sacrifice needed for progress, unwillingness to forsake all and follow Jesus. And this again is very much owing to the fatal mistake that in religion our only thought is to be of safety, that we may be content when some assurance of that is attained. Such a soul cares not for the heavenly blessedness of conformity to Jesus, of living fellowship with God, and the Godlike privilege of bringing life and blessing to men.

It is one of the great needs of the teachers in the Church in our day that they should have a clear insight into the feeble and sickly state in which most Christians live, as well as into what constitutes a healthy life that goes on to perfection. As they themselves enter into the full experience of the power of Christ's priesthood, as the Holy Spirit imparts it in the heart, they will be able to reprove with authority, and effectually to help all upright souls into the full salvation Christ has provided. God give His Church such teachers.

1. *Have we not here the reason there is so little earnest pursuit after holiness? so little true consecration to living to bless others? so little of the power of the Holy Spirit in the life of the Church? Let us plead with God to discover the evil and to visit His Church. Let us exhort one another daily, to rest content with nothing less than a whole-hearted enthusiastic devotion to Jesus.*

2. *In preparing to go on to the study of the inner sanctuary in what is to follow (vii.–x), do let us consider it a settled thing, that unless we are really hungering after righteousness, and longing for a very close fellowship with Jesus, our further study of the Epistle will do us very little good. Let us pray God to convince us of our sloth, our contentment with the beginnings of grace, and to stir in us a burning thirst after Himself.*

XLIII.

Solid Food for the Perfect

V.–13. For every one that partaketh of milk is without experience of the word of righteousness; for he is a babe.
14. But solid food is for perfect men, even those who by reason of use have their senses exercised to discern good and evil.

We have here the contrast between the two stages in the Christian life. Of the first we have already spoken. The second stage is that of manhood—the full-grown, mature, perfect man. This does not, as in nature, come with years, but consists in the whole-heartedness with which the believer yields himself to be all for God. It is the perfect heart makes the perfect man. The twenty years needed for a child to become a full-grown man are no rule in the kingdom of heaven. There is indeed a riper maturity and a mellowness which comes with the experience of years. But even a young Christian can be of the perfect of whom our Epistle speaks, with a heart all athirst for the deeper and more spiritual truth it is to teach, and a will that has indeed finally broken with sin, and counted all things loss for the perfect knowledge of Christ Jesus.

The contrast is expressed in the words: The babe is **without experience of the word of righteousness.** He has not yielded himself to the discipline which the word demands and brings; he has not, in the struggle of practical obedience, had experience of what the word can do to search and cleanse, to strengthen and bless. His religious life has been, as with a babe, the enjoyment of being fed. He is without real experience of the word of righteousness.

With the perfect, the full-grown men, it is the very opposite: **by reason of use they have their senses exercised to discern good and evil.** Just as in nature the use of the limbs, with plenty of exercise for every sense and organ, is one of the surest conditions of a healthy growth, so with the Christian too. It is when the faculties God gives us in the spiritual life are put to the use He meant them for, and our spiritual senses are kept in full exercise, that we pass from feeble infancy to maturity. This exercise of the senses has special reference to that which we have been saved to—a life of obedience and holiness; it is **to discern good and evil.** The eye is exercised to see and know God's way and Him who leads in it; the ear to hear His voice; the conscience to reject everything that is not well pleasing to God or even doubtful; the will to choose and do only what is His will.

It is of the utmost consequence that we should note this well. The capacity for entering into the deeper truths to be unfolded does not depend on talent or study, on sagacity or genius, but *on the tenderness with which the soul has exercised itself in daily life in discerning good and evil.* The redemption in Christ is to save us from sin, and bring us back to the perfect obedience and unhindered fellowship with God. It is as the desire not to sin becomes more intense; and the acceptance of Jesus as an indwelling deliverer from sin more entire; and the surrender to the operation of God in working His will in us more complete; that the spiritual teaching of our Epistle will be appreciated. *It is a holy sensitiveness to the least sin, arising from the faithful use and exercise of the senses as far as there was light, that is the spiritual sense or organ for spiritual truth, the mark of the perfect man.* In the things of God a tender conscience and a surrendered will are more than the highest intellect.

Such are the perfect. The word means here just what it meant when used of Jesus a few verses previously. His perfection came through obedience. Ours comes in no other way—the exercise of the senses to discern good and evil. In temptations Jesus Himself was exercised to discern between good and evil: in the wilderness and the garden He had to fast and watch and pray, lest the lawful desire of His human nature might lead to sin: thus He was perfected. And this is Christian perfection—the fellowship with Christ, through the indwelling Spirit, in His obedience.

Solid food is for the perfect. And what is this solid food? The context leaves no doubt as to the answer. It is the knowledge of Christ as Melchizedek, as it is now to be expounded. To know Christ as Aaron, to believe in His atonement on earth, and in pardon through His blood, this is often found with Christians who are content to remain mere babes, entirely slothful and stationary. But to know Christ as Melchizedek in His heavenly priesthood, working in us in the power of an endless life; as a Saviour able to save completely; as the minister of the sanctuary, who has opened the Holiest of All, and brings us in to dwell there; as the Mediator of the new covenant, who does actually fulfil its promise and write God's law in living power in our heart—this is **the solid food for the perfect.** The teaching in the word is open and free to all, but only those who have given themselves to be perfect, feel the need and hunger for it—only they are capable of receiving and assimilating it; because it is only they who have in very deed determined to rest content with nothing less than all Christ can do for them, and to count all things loss for the possession of this pearl of great price. All the outward teaching and knowledge of the words of the prophets and of Christ must give way to the inward speaking of Christ in the soul by the Holy Spirit. It is to souls who break through the husk, and hunger to feed on the kernel, on the very life of God in Christ, who will become perfect in Christ Jesus.

1. These Hebrew Christians are reproved for not being perfect. It is not left to their choice whether they are to be eminent Christians. God expects each child of His to be as eminent in grace and piety as it is possible for Christ to make him.

2. Till we all attain unto a perfect man, unto the measure of the stature of the fulness of Christ: *this ought to be our aim. The motive and the power to seek this we have in our Lord Jesus.*

3. *Let nothing satisfy us but living wholly for Christ; He is worthy.*

XLIV.

Let Us Press on to Perfection

VI.–1. Wherefore let us cease to speak of the first principles[2] of Christ, and press on unto perfection; not laying again a foundation of repentance from dead works, and of faith toward God. 2. Of the teaching of baptisms, and of laying on of hands, and of resurrection of the dead, and of eternal judgment. 3. And this will we do, if God permit.

We have seen how among the Hebrews there were two classes of Christians. They are to be found in every Christian Church—some who, instead of growing up to be teachers and helpers of others, always remain babes, and have need that some one again teach them the rudiments of the beginning of the oracles of God. Others who are perfect or fully-grown men, who have had their spiritual senses exercised in discerning good and evil, and are able to receive the solid food of the knowledge of the perfection of Christ and His work. Let us listen as the word calls us to come out of all sloth and feebleness, and to press on to the perfection Christ has come to reveal.

First we hear what it is we are to give up. **Let us leave the word of the beginning of Christ.** In chapter iii. 14 we were urged **to hold fast the beginning firm unto the end.** These two expressions are not at variance. The beginning is the seed or first principle out of which the farther life must grow and expand into perfection. This beginning, as the root of all that is to come, must be held fast to the very end. But the beginning, as being

2. Leave the word of the beginning.

223

only a commencement of something better, must be left. It is a terrible misunderstanding of the words, "Hold fast what thou hast," to imagine that we simply need to preserve what we already have. By no means. We must realise that the knowledge of Christ and the measure of grace we receive at conversion cannot suffice for our farther life. We need each day to learn more of Christ, to make new advances in obedience, to gain larger experience of the power of the heavenly life. There can be no healthy life without growth and progress. We must leave the word of the beginning of Christ.

Not laying again the foundation. A builder, when he has laid his foundation, leaves working at it any more, and builds upon it. There are Christians who never get beyond the foundation, who never know what the house is for the sake of which alone the foundation is; what it is to be an habitation of God through the Spirit, and to dwell in the love and the power of God. The writer mentions, in three pairs, six points which belong to the foundation truths, in which the young beginner has to be instructed. **Repentance from dead works and faith towards God:** these are in very deed only the rudiments of the word of Christ. Then follow two points that have reference to the public confession of faith and the connection with the Church: **the teaching of baptism and of the laying on of hands.** And then two more, that relate to the future life: **the resurrection of the dead and eternal judgment.** Without these elementary truths one could hardly be a Christian: but the man who rests content with them, and cares not to know more, cannot be a Christian as God would have him, has reason to doubt whether he be a Christian at all.

Wherefore, let us leave the word of the beginning of Christ, and press on unto perfection. It is not difficult to know what perfection here means. Perfect is that which corresponds to its ideal, which is as it should be, which answers to what its maker intended. No parent is content that his child should remain a babe; he educates it to be a full-grown man. God has set before us in His word the life He actually means us to live, and He calls every true child of His to leave the beginnings, and press on to perfection, to press on to be all that He has promised to make us. More God would not have us seek; with less, we dare not be content, lest we deceive ourselves.

In Christ Jesus, and His life on earth, we have the embodiment of that perfection, as it consists in a life given up to obedience to God's will; the proof that it is possible for a true man to live a life that is well-pleasing to the Father; the promise that from His throne in heaven He will now impart and work in us. In suffering He yielded Himself *to God to perfect Him.* In suffering He learned obedience, and *was made perfect,* thereby to be the cause of eternal salvation to us. He is now, as the **Son perfected for evermore,** our High Priest, in heaven working in us, in the power of the heavenly life, that perfection, through which as our Leader He opened the path to glory. Our perfection can be none other than Christ's: His perfection our model, His perfection our life and strength. God desires and can be satisfied with nothing in us but what He sees of His beloved Son, and His perfection through suffering and obedience.

Wherefore, let us leave the word of the beginning of Christ, and press on to perfection. And this will we do if God permit. As if he says, The following chapters are to be the teaching of Christian perfection. We will with you press on, and help you on, by giving the solid food which is the nourishment and strength of the perfect: *the heavenly priesthood of Christ, in* the power of an endless life. His glory and power as mediator of the new covenant, writing God's law into our very heart, the infinite efficacy of the blood as opening the Holiest of All to us, and cleansing us to enter in and serve the living God—these and such like truths, revealing the perfection that Christ attained in His human life, and into which He lifts us in His divine power, these constitute the solid food for the perfect. The perfection of

Christ, as truth revealed, becomes the perfection of the believer, as a life experienced, in those who count all things loss for the excellency of the knowledge of Him our Lord.

1. *Let us hold fast the distinction between foundation doctrine and perfection doctrine. There are truths of the beginning of Christ, which we have had in the first half of the Epistle—His divinity and humanity, His substitution, tasting death for all, and His entering into heaven, as far as that was typified by Aaron. In the second half we have what is needed for the completion of the Christian life; the power of the heavenly life as it is secured in the heavenly priesthood and the heavenly sanctuary.* Wherefore, let us press on to perfection.

2. Let us press on to perfection. *Do take this as a distinct injunction of the God who speaks to us in His Son. Hear His voice, rest not content with the beginnings—press on—unto perfection, unto the perfect man, unto the measure of the stature of the fulness of Christ.*

3. *Compare Paul (Phil. iii. 13–15):* I press on, *if so be I may apprehend that for which I also was apprehended of Christ Jesus. Forgetting the things which are behind,* I press on *toward the goal. Let us, therefore, as many as be* perfect, *be thus minded.* Let us press on to perfection.

XLV.

The Danger of Falling Away

VI.–4. For as touching those who were once enlightened, and tasted of the heavenly gift, and were made partakers of the Holy Ghost,

5. And tasted the good word of God, and the powers of the age to come, and then fell away,

6. It is impossible to renew them again unto repentance; seeing they crucify to themselves the Son of God afresh, and put him to an open shame.

7. For the land which hath drunk the rain that cometh oft upon it, and bringeth forth herbs meet for them for whose sake it is also tilled, receiveth blessing from God:

8. But if it beareth thorns and thistles, it is rejected and nigh unto a curse; whose end is to be burned.

Let us press on to perfection. For as touching those who were once enlightened, and fall away, it is impossible to renew them again. The argument is one of unspeakable solemnity. It is in the Christian life as with all progress amid difficulties. In commerce, in study, in war, it is so often said: there is no safety but in advance. To stand still is to go back. To cease effort is to lose ground. To slacken the pace, before the goal is reached, is to lose the race. The only sure mark of our being true Christians, of our really loving Christ, is the deep longing and the steady effort to know more of Him. Tens of thousands have proved that to be content with beginning well is but the first step on a backward course, that ends in losing all. The whole

point of the argument from the case of those who fall away is—
Let us press on to perfection.

To realise its force we must specially note two things with regard to those who fall away: the height which they may have attained, and the irrecoverable depth into which they sink. As to the former, five expressions are used. **They were once enlightened; tasted of the heavenly gift; were made partakers of the Holy Ghost; tasted the good word of God; and the powers of the age to come.** As to the latter, we are told: **Seeing they crucify to themselves the Son of God afresh, and put Him to an open shame: it is impossible to renew them again unto repentance.**

The question which always at once suggests itself here has reference to the Scripture truth of the perseverance of the saints, in which so many saints of God have found their strength and their joy. Our Lord Jesus spake of His sheep (John x. 28): "I give unto them eternal life; and they shall never perish, and no one shall snatch them out of my hand. My Father, which hath given them unto me, is greater than all; and no one is able to snatch them out of the Father's hand." Where He gives the eternal life to a soul, it is a life that cannot be lost.

This is the divine side of the truth. Every truth has two sides. The only way to apprehend the truth fully is to look at each side as if it were the whole, and yield ourselves to its full force. There is a human side too. Scripture speaks most solemn words of warning in regard to the possibility of receiving the grace of God in vain, of beginning well, and then falling away from grace (2 Cor. vi. 1, Gal. v. 4). Our Lord spoke more than once of the man who receives the word with joy, but had no root in himself: he only believes for a while. In a time of revival, of mighty spiritual influences, as in Corinth and Galatia, many were mightily affected and even manifestly changed, who in after times proved that they never had been truly born again; they had not received eternal life. It is of such our text speaks. It is possible to have the emotions touched and the will affected without the heart being truly renewed. The gifts of the Spirit may be received without His graces. The joy of light in the mind may be mistaken for life in the soul. And so some, who were counted true believers by man, may fall away beyond hope of renewal.

And how, then, are we to know who truly have received eternal life? and what is the mark of its being no mere superficial or temporary change? *There is no mark by which man can decide.* The only sure sign that the perseverance of the saints will be ours is—perseverance in sainthood, in sanctification and obedience. **We are His house, we are become partakers of Christ, if we hold fast, firm unto the end.** My assurance of salvation is not something I can carry with me as a railway ticket or a bank note, to be used, as occasion calls. No, God's seal to my soul is the Holy Spirit; it is in a life in the Spirit that my safety lies; it is when I am led by the Spirit that the Spirit bears witness with my spirit, and that I can cry Abba, Father (Rom. viii. 14–16). Jesus not only gives, but is Himself our life. *My assurance of salvation is alone to be found in the living fellowship with the living Jesus in love and obedience.*

This is what we see in verses 7 and 8. **The land which hath drunk the rain, and bringeth forth herbs, receiveth blessing from God: if it beareth thorns, it is rejected.** The soul that is content with drinking in the rain, and only seeks its own happiness, without bearing fruit, has every reason to fear. It is in growth and fruitfulness, in the exercising the senses to discern good and evil, in pressing on to perfection, in following our Forerunner in the path in which He was perfected, by obedience to God's will, that we know that we have eternal life.

The word of God is sharper than any two-edged sword. Let each one of us yield to its searching power. Anything like sloth, and resting content in our beginnings, is unspeakably dangerous. Nothing will do but to **give more abundant heed—**

to give diligence to enter into the rest, and with our whole heart **to press on unto perfection.**

1. *Self-deception is a solemn possibility. Our only safeguard is God, the surrender to His searching light, the trust in His faithfulness, the giving up to His will.* At the footstool of the throne no soul can perish.

2. To press on unto perfection *is a command not meant for a select few, but for all, and specially the backward and feeble ones. Beware of any suggestion that would make you evade the force of this command and immediate obedience to it. Let your only answer be—Yea, Lord. Open your eyes and heart to the state of all around you, who are slothful and at ease, lagging behind, and help them.* By reason of the time ye ought to be teachers.

XLVI.

Of Diligence and Perseverance

VI.–9. But, beloved, we are persuaded better things of you, and things that accompany salvation, though we thus speak:
10. For God is not unrighteous to forget your work, and the love which ye showed toward his name, in that ye ministered to the saints, and still do minister.
11. And we desire that each of you may show the same diligence unto the fulness of hope even to the end:
12. That ye be not sluggish, but imitators of them who through faith and patience[3] inherit the promises.

In every Christian community you have two classes. There are some who give themselves up with their whole heart to seek and serve God. There are others, too often the majority, who, like Israel, are content with deliverance from Egypt, and settle down in sloth, without striving for the full possession of the promise, the rest in the promised land. In speaking to such a Church, one might address the two classes separately. Or one might address the whole body now from one, then from the other of the two standpoints. This is what the Epistle does. In its warning it speaks to all as if all were in danger. In its exhortation and encouragement it speaks as if all shared the sentiments of the better half.

But, beloved, we are persuaded better things of you, and things that accompany salvation, though we thus speak of falling away, and the impossibility of renewal. We have the hope

3. Longsuffering.

that our word of warning will bear fruit, and that by the grace of God, which has already wrought in you, you will be stirred to rise up out of all sloth and unbelief and press forward. We look to God Himself to perfect His work in you.

For God is not unrighteous to forget your work and the love which ye showed toward His name, in that ye ministered to the saints, and still do minister. If there was much in the present state to make him anxious, the writer encourages himself and them by pointing to the past. When the gospel was preached among them they had received Christ's messengers with joy, and stood by them in sharing reproach and spoiling for His name. Even now still there was among them a love towards God's people. And God is not unrighteous to forget what has been done for His name and people; the reward of the cup of cold water may be remembered by God even when the giver has grown cold, and may come in the blessing that restores him again. God does not only remember sin; He much rather remembers the work of love.

And we desire that each one of you may show the same diligence unto the fulness of hope even unto the end. In all worldly business diligence is the secret of success. Without attention and trouble and hearty effort we cannot expect our work to prosper. And yet there are many Christians who imagine that in the Christian life things will come right of themselves. When they are told that Jesus undertakes to do all, they count this as a pass to a life of ease. Verily no. Jesus will indeed do all; but he undertakes it, just to inspire us with His own spirit of self-sacrifice and devotion to the Father's will, His own readiness to forsake all ease and comfort to please God and man, His own unwearying diligence in working while it was day. And so our writer urges his readers to show the same diligence they had formerly manifested, unto the fulness of the hope to the very end.

We have here the same three words we had in the second warning. There we read, "Let us **give diligence** to enter into that rest" (iv. 11). "If we hold fast the glorying **of our hope** firm **to the end** (iii. 6). "If we hold fast the beginning of our confidence firm **to the end.**" The great marks of Christian perseverance are here once again joined together. **Hope** looks forward and lives in the promises; it glories beforehand in the certainty of their fulfilment. Bright hopefulness is one of the elements of a healthy Christian life—one of the surest preservatives against backsliding. This hopefulness must be cultivated; **diligence** must be given unto the fulness of hope—a hope that embraces all the fulness of God's promises, and that fills all the heart. And all this **to the end,** with a patience and perseverance that knows no weariness, that waits God's time, and seeks in patience till the fulfilment has come.

That ye be not slothful. This is what had done so much harm—they had been slothful in hearing (v. 11). This is the danger that still threatens. **But be imitators of them who through faith and longsuffering inherit the promises.** The writer had spoken in warning of the example of the fathers in the wilderness; he here encourages them by reminding them of those who **through faith and longsuffering had inherited the promises.** Longsuffering is the perseverance of faith. Faith grasps at once all that God promises, but is in danger of relaxing its hold. Longsuffering comes to tell how faith needs daily to be renewed, and strengthens the soul, even when the promise tarries, still to hold fast firm unto the end. This is one of the great practical lessons of our Epistle, and one the young believer specially needs. Conversion is but a beginning, a step, an entrance on a path; day by day its surrender must be renewed; every day faith must afresh accept Christ, and find its strength in Him. Through faith and longsuffering we inherit, enter on the possession of the promises. Salvation consists in what Christ Jesus is to us and does in us. There must, each day, be personal intercourse with Him, distinct personal surrender to His teaching and working, if He is indeed to be our life. Let us beware, above everything, of unconsciously resting or trusting in what we have or enjoy of grace. It is alone by faith and longsuffering, by the never-ceasing daily renewal of our consecration and our faith in our quiet time with our Beloved Lord, that the heavenly life can be maintained in its freshness and power.

1. God is not unrighteous to forget your work. *How often God spoke to Israel of its first love. What an encouragement to any who have grown cold to return and trust Him to restore them. God cannot forget what has passed between thee and Him.*

2. That ye be not slothful, *not for a single day. We may lose in an hour by unwatchfulness what we have gained in a year. Christ and His service ask for your undivided, unceasing attention.*

3. *Let not God's way appear too slow or too difficult. Let patience have its perfect work. As the husbandman has long patience with the seed, God is patient with you. Be patient with Him. Just remember this simple lesson. Day by day renew your surrender to Jesus, and your faith in Him—your hope in God. Faith and patience must inherit the promises.*

XLVII.

Inheriting the Promise

VI.–13. For when God made promise to Abraham, since he could sware by none greater, he sware by himself,

14. Saying, Surely blessing I will bless thee, and multiplying I will multiply thee.

15. And thus, having patiently endured,[4] he obtained, the promise.

The Epistle is dealing with one of the greatest dangers in the spiritual life. All experience amply confirms what was seen in the first Christian churches, that many who began well stood still and then turned back. The Christian life is a race: to begin profits nothing unless we run to the end and reach the goal. Faith may accept; only longsuffering *inherits the promise.* Day by day, without intermission, rather with ever-growing zeal and diligence, our allegiance to Jesus our Leader must be maintained, or backsliding must inevitably ensue. And the Church of Christ is a very hospital of backsliding Christians, who meant honestly, in the joy of their first love, to live wholly for God, and who yet gradually sank down into a life of formality and feebleness. There is nothing the Church needs more than the preaching of daily diligence and perseverance as the indispensable condition of growth and strength. Let us learn from the Epistle how these virtues can be fostered in ourselves and others. It had spoken of those who through faith and longsuffering inherit the promises. It will now show us, from the example of Abraham, what this

4. Suffered long.

means. It first points us, as ever, to what God promises, and then to the disposition in man which this claims and works.

For when God made promise to Abraham, since He could swear by none greater, He sware by Himself, saying, Surely blessing I will bless thee, and multiplying I will multiply thee. The deeper our insight into the certainty and the fulness of the blessing of God, the more will our hearts be roused to believe and to persevere. The word of God is our assurance of what we are to expect. How much greater must our confidence be when that word is an oath? Of this the following verses are to speak. Here the fulness of God's blessing is set before us in the promise given to Abraham: as his seed we are his heirs, and what God promised him is for us too. We need to be content with nothing less; nothing less will stimulate us to a life like his in faith and patience.

Surely blessing I will bless thee, and multiplying I will multiply thee. In Hebrew the repetition of a verb is meant to give force to what is said, to express the certainty and the greatness of what is asserted. In the mouth of God the repetition, **Blessing I will bless, multiplying I will multiply,** was meant to waken in Abraham's heart the confidence that the blessing was indeed to be something very wonderful and worthy of God, blessing in divine power and fulness. What that blessing was to be, the second half of the sentence shows, **Multiplying I will multiply thee.** Scripture teaches us that the highest blessing which God can bestow, that which makes us truly Godlike, is the power of multiplying ourselves, of becoming, as God is, the source and the blessing of other lives. So the two words are connected in passages like Gen. i. 22, 28; ix. 1. Of the living creatures it is said: *God blessed them, saying, Be fruitful and multiply.* And of man: *And God blessed them, and God said unto them, Be fruitful and multiply.* So of Noah too: And *God blessed Noah and his sons, and said, Be fruitful and multiply.* It is the glory of God that He is the dispenser of life—that in His creatures He multiplies His own life and blessedness. And it is one of His highest blessings when He communicates this power of increase to those whom He chooses for His service. The power of His blessing to Adam is seen in the race that sprang from him, as of His blessing to Abraham in his seed, even in Jesus Christ Himself. And to each child of Abraham, to each true believer, the promise still comes in divine power: **Surely blessing I will bless thee, and multiplying I will multiply thee.** Every believer who will but claim, and give himself up to the blessing of God, will find that the blessing is a power of the divine life which will make him fruitful in blessing to others, and make it true of him too, **multiplying I will multiply thee.** Even we, like Christ, can become priests, bringing the blessing of God to those who know Him not.

It is when this fulness of blessing in its divine energy, when this **blessing I will bless thee** begins to be understood, and the soul sees that there is something beyond the mere being saved from wrath, that there is a becoming the recipient, and the channel, and the dispenser, of life and blessing to others, that it becomes willing to sacrifice everything, and in longsuffering to endure until it obtain the promise.

Christian! wouldest thou be an imitator of Abraham, and let the God who spake to him speak to thee? Remember it is not so easy to receive and claim this promise. Abraham received it in the way of faith and obedience and self-sacrifice, in the entire surrender to God's will and leading. It was when he had sacrificed Isaac, yea more, when in doing so he had sacrificed himself, that this promise was given him with an oath. God will speak to thee as truly as to Abraham. Learn with him to go out of thy country and thy home; give thyself to God's leading; be prepared to sacrifice all. God will meet thee too with His double blessing. And thy heart will become strong to hear His voice, "Blessing *I will* bless, multiplying *I will* multiply." And it will be true of thee as of Abraham: **And thus, having patiently en-**

dured, he obtained the promise. We shall not only be the heirs, but the actual inheritors of the promise.

1. It is after the most terrible warning this promise comes. Until the slothful Christian is roused the most precious promise finds no entrance. When he is roused, it is the preaching of the promise in its fulness will give him courage and strength.

2. Does your heart condemn you, and do you fear that there is but little hope of your becoming a bright, growing, holy child of God, blessed and made a blessing? Come and learn from Abraham the secret, God spake to him! *Listen to God. Let God speak to you, follow where He leads, obey what He commands. He will bring you to the place of blessing, the place of the revelation of Himself.*

3. And put at once into practice the lesson of today. Be not discouraged if you feel feeble and cold, and if there appears to be no progress. Listen to God's, Blessing I will bless you. Feed on what God says. And trust Him to work in you all you need.

4. Are you a worker in God's service? Wait upon God to speak this word to you too, Multiplying I will multiply you. *He can make even you a blessing to many. But such a promise needs an oath to find entrance to the heart. Accept and live on the oath of God.*

XLVIII.

The Oath of God

VI.–16. For men swear by the greater: and in every dispute of theirs the oath is final for confirmation.

17. Wherein God, being minded to shew more abundantly unto the heirs of the promise the immutability of his counsel, interposed[5] with an oath:

18. That by two immutable things, in which it is impossible for God to lie, we may have a strong encouragement, who have fled for refuge to lay hold of the hope set before us.

For any serious man it is always a solemn thing to take an oath, and appeal to the omniscient God for the truth of what He says. But there is something more solemn even than taking an oath before God, and that is, God's taking an oath before man. And this is what our writer proceeds now to speak of. He had already spoken of God's oath in His wrath, **They shall not enter into My rest.** He will in the next chapter point out the deep significance of Christ's appointment as High Priest being confirmed by an oath. Here he wishes to show believers what strong encouragement they have in God's oath to expect most confidently the fulfilment of the promise. It is this confidence alone that will enable the Christian to endure and conquer.

Let us once more consider this. The oath of God plainly proves that the thing He seeks above everything is—faith; He wishes to be trusted. Faith is nothing but depending on God to do for us what we cannot do—what He has undertaken to do.

5. Mediated.

God's purpose concerning us is something of infinite and inconceivable blessedness. He is ready, He longs, as God, Himself to work in us all that He has promised. He cannot do this except as we open our hearts to Him, and yield ourselves in stillness and surrender for Him to do His work. Until this faith takes possession of us, we are always seeking to do His work, and we hinder Him. Faith teaches us in deep humility and dependence, in meekness and patience, to place ourselves in God's hands, to make way for Him, and to wait His time. Faith opens the whole heart and life in expectation and hope. Then God is free to work; faith gives Him His place as God, and honours Him; and He fulfils the promise, *Him that honoureth Me, will I honour.* Oh, do learn the lesson, that the first and the last, the one thing God asks is that we trust Him, to do His work.

It is for this that He mediates, comes in between, with an oath. Just notice the expressions that are used: **God willing to show**—they had **shown** their love toward His name; they had been urged to **show** diligence unto the fulness of hope; here they are told what God will show them—willing to show **more abundantly to the heirs of salvation the immutability of His counsel.** God wills to show us how unchangeable His purpose to bless us is, if we will but let Him, if we will but trust Him, and by trusting let Him work. And He wills to show us this **more abundantly.** He wants us to have such more abundant proof of it, that we may, as we had it in chapter ii. 1, take more abundant heed, and see that there can be no possibility of a doubt: God will do it. It was for this He confirmed the promise with an oath.

That by two immutable things—His promise and His oath—**in which it is impossible for God to lie, we might have a strong encouragement.** Just notice the expression—*impossible for God to lie!* It is as if God asks, if we do not think His word enough, if we think it possible that He, the faithful and the unchangeable One, should lie. He knows how little our darkened hearts trust Him; His promises are so large, so divine, so heavenly, that we cannot take them in. And so, to waken and to shame us out of our unbelief, He comes, and as if it were *possible for God to lie,* calls us to listen as He takes an oath in our presence that He will do what He has said: **Blessing I will bless thee, and multiplying I will multiply thee.** And all, **that we, the heirs of salvation, might have a strong encouragement.** Surely every vestige of fear and doubt ought to pass away, and our whole soul fall down to worship and to cry out: O God! we do trust Thee. Never, never, will I doubt Thy word again.

God, since He could swear by none greater, sware by Himself. Yes. *By Himself!* in that lies the power of the oath, and the power of our faith in our oath. God points to Himself—His divine Being, His glory, His power, and *pledges Himself, gives Himself as security, as hostage,* that, as sure as He lives, He will fulfil His promise. Oh, if we would but take time to tarry in the presence of this God, and to listen to Him swearing to us that He will be faithful, surely we should fall down in confusion that we ever harboured for a moment the doubt, which thinks it possible that He may be untrue and not keep His word. Shall we not kneel and vow that by His grace we will rather die than again make such a God a liar?

And now let us pause and realise what all this argument about the blessing and the oath of God means. In the Christian life there is lack of steadfastness, of diligence, of perseverance. Of all the cause is simply—lack of faith. And of this again the cause is—the lack of the knowledge of what God wills and is, of His purpose and power to bless most wonderfully, and of His faithfulness to carry out His purpose. It is to cure these evils; it is to tell His people that He will do anything to win their trust, and will do anything for them if they will trust Him, that God had taken His oath of faithfulness. Oh, shall we not this day believe God and believe in the fulness of His blessing? And shall we not count it our most sacred duty, and our most blessed privilege, to honour God every day by a life of full and perfect trust?

1. "*The oath for* confirmation." *The same word as in Heb. iii. 7, 14, and vi. 19, firm. As we see how firm, how steadfast, God's promise and the hope He gives us, our confidence will grow more firm too. The fulness of my faith depends upon my being occupied with the faithfulness of God.*

2. By faith and long-suffering. Having suffered long. *God is often very slow. "He bears long with His elect." This is the patience of the saints: to let God take His time, and through all ever to trust Him.*

3. That ye be not slothful: *it is the faith that God will work all, that rouses to diligence both in waiting on Him and in doing His will.*

XLIX.

The Forerunner within the Veil

VI.–18. That we may have a strong encouragement, who have
fled for refuge to lay hold of the hope set before us;
19. Which we have as an anchor of the soul, a hope both sure
and stedfast[6] and entering into that which is within the veil;
20. Whither as a Forerunner Jesus entered for us, having become a High Priest for ever after the order of Melchizedek.

In chapter v., speaking of the priesthood of Jesus, the writer had
twice cited the words of Psalm cx., with its prophecy of a Priest
after the order of Melchizedek (v. 6, 10). But he feared that the
Hebrews were, by reason of sloth, too far back in the Christian
life to be able to receive this higher teaching. It was on this account he interposed his words of reproof and warning. From
these he had passed to exhortation and encouragement, and is
now ready to address himself to what is the central teaching of
the Epistle. There are specially two great heavenly mysteries he
is commissioned to unfold. The one, that of the heavenly priesthood of Christ; the other, that of the heavenly sanctuary in
which He ministers, and into which He gives us access. In the
last two verses of our sixth chapter we have the transition to the
new section, and in it these mysteries are both mentioned as the
hope set before us. Hope enters **within the veil;** it finds there
**the Forerunner, who has entered for us, Jesus a High Priest,
after the order of Melchizedek.**

6. Firm.

243

We who have fled for refuge to lay hold of the hope set before us. *The hope* sometimes means the object of hope, that which God sets before us; sometimes the subjective grace or disposition of hope in our hearts. Here it specially refers to the former. And what that hope is, is clear from the next chapter (vii. 19), where we read of the **bringing in of a better hope, through which we draw nigh to God.** This better hope is the access our High Priest in heaven gives us into God's very presence, into the enjoyment of His fellowship and blessedness, even while here on earth.

Which we have as an anchor of the soul, a hope both sure and firm, and entering into that which is within the veil. The hope is an anchor. A ship is held by the anchor cast into the unseen depth beneath. So the hope in the unseen within the veil, which God has given us, holds us fast. And as our heart is fixed upon it, hope as a subjective grace is stirred and drawn, and enters within the veil too. Where our hope lives there the heart lives. There we, our real selves, are living too.

Whither the Forerunner is for us entered. *The Forerunner.* Here we have another of the keywords of the Epistle, without the right understanding of which our view of the work of Jesus as High Priest must be defective. It points us to the work He did in opening up the way, by Himself walking in it; to our following Him in that way to the place into which He has entered, and into which we now have access. We have had His name as Leader. We shall yet have (x. 21) the new and living way He has opened up. We shall hear (xii. 1) of the race we have to run, looking to Jesus, who went on before, enduring the cross, and is now set down at the right hand of God. There is nothing will so much help us to understand the work Jesus does as Son and High Priest as the acceptance of Him as Leader and Forerunner, bringing us into the very presence of the Father.

Entered for us. We are so familiar with all the blessed meaning there is in the words *for us,* in reference to Christ on the cross. What He did there was all for us; by it and in it we live. No less is it true of Christ within the veil. It is all *for us;* all that He is and has there is for us; it is our present possession; by it and in it we live with Him and in Him. The veil was rent that the way through it might be opened *for us;* that we might have access to that which is *within the veil;* that we might enter into a new world, an entirely new way of living in close and intimate fellowship with God. A high priest must have a sanctuary in which he ministers. The mystery of the opened sanctuary is that we can enter too. The inner sanctuary, the Holiest of All, the presence of God, is the sphere of Christ's ministry and our life and service.

The Forerunner, even Jesus! It is as if the writer delights to repeat this name which our Saviour bears as Son of Man. Even in the glory of heaven He is still Jesus, our Brother.

Having become a High Priest for ever after the order of Melchizedek. We have yet to learn all that is contained in this Melchizedek priesthood. But this will be its chief glory—that He is a Priest for ever, a Priest in the power of an endless life, a Priest who opens to us the state of life to which He Himself has entered in, and brings us there to live here on earth with the life of eternity in our bosom.

Christian reader! knowest thou the power of this hope, entering into that which is within the veil, whither the Forerunner is for us entered. Jesus is in heaven *for thee,* to secure thee a life on earth in the power and joy of heaven, to maintain the kingdom of heaven within thee, by that Spirit, through whom God's will is done on earth as it is in heaven. All that Jesus is and has, is heavenly. All that He gives and does, is heavenly. As High Priest at God's right hand, He blesses with all heavenly blessings. Oh, prepare thyself, as the glory of His person and ministry in the heavenly places are now to be opened up to thee, to look upon it, and appropriate it all, as thy personal possession. And believe that His High Priesthood not only consists in His having secured certain heavenly blessings for thee, but in his fitting and enabling thee to enter into the full personal experience and enjoyment of them.

1. There is a sanctuary in which God dwells. There was a veil that separated man from God. Jesus came from within to live without the veil, and rend it, and open a way for us. He is now there for us as Forerunner. We may now enter in and dwell there, in the power of the Holy Ghost. This is the gospel according to the Epistle to the Hebrews.

2. Hope enters within the veil, rejoices in all there to be found, and counts upon the revelation in the heart of all that is there prepared for us.

3. Jesus the Forerunner, *follow Him. Even though thou canst not understand all, follow Him in His path of humility and meekness and obedience: He will bring thee in. This is the promise which, even in this life, thou shalt inherit, through patience and longsuffering.*

Fifth Section—vii. 1-28

The New Priesthood after the Order of Melchizedek

L.

Melchizedek Made Like unto the Son of God

VII.–1. For this Melchizedek, king of Salem, priest of God Most High, who met Abraham returning from the slaughter of the kings, and blessed him,

2. To whom also Abraham divided a tenth part of all (being first, by interpretation, King of righteousness, and then also King of Salem, which is, King of peace;

3. Without father, without mother, without genealogy, having neither beginning of days nor end of life, but made like unto the Son of God), abideth a priest continually.

In chapter v. we read that Jesus was called of God, even as was Aaron. In many points Aaron was a type of Christ. But there were other respects in which the priesthood of Aaron utterly failed even to prefigure that of Christ. By a special divine provision the name of another is found, in whom, what was wanting in Aaron as type, was foreshadowed. The difference between the priesthood of Aaron and Melchizedek is a radical one. In the right understanding of what that difference is, and in the knowledge of that in which Melchizedek has been made like unto the Son of God, lies the secret of this Epistle, and the secret of the

Christian life in its power and perfection. The secret may be expressed in one word—Priest for ever.

The whole place Melchizedek occupies in sacred history is one of the most remarkable proofs of the inspiration and the unity of Scripture, as written under the direct supernatural guidance of the Holy Spirit. In the Book of Genesis all we know of him is told in three short, very simple verses. A thousand years later we find a Psalm with just one single verse, in which God Himself is introduced, swearing to His Son that He is to be a High Priest after the order of Melchizedek. Another thousand years pass, and that single verse becomes the seed of the wondrous exposition, in this Epistle, of the whole work of redemption as revealed in Christ Jesus. All its most remarkable characteristics are found enveloped in the wondrous type. The more we study it the more we exclaim: *This is the Lord's doing; it is marvellous in our eyes.* We see in it nothing less than a miracle of divine wisdom, guiding Melchizedek and Abraham with a view to what was to take place with the Son of God two thousand years later; revealing to the Psalmist the secret purpose of the divine mind in the promise made to the Son in heaven; and then, by the same Holy Spirit, guiding the writer of our Epistle to his divinely-inspired exposition. To the believing mind no stronger proof of inspiration could possibly be given. It is indeed the Eternal Spirit, the Spirit of Christ Himself, through whom all was wrought and in due time recorded.

In the first three verses of our chapter we are reminded of the story of Melchizedek, and the exposition is given of his name and history. His name signifies—**King of righteousness.** He is also called, from the city where he reigned, Salem, meaning Peace—the **King of Peace.** The two titles thus combined proved how he was destined of God to be the figure of His Son. Righteousness and peace are mentioned together both in the Old Testament and in the New as characteristic blessings of the kingdom of Christ. Righteousness as the only foundation of peace: peace as its sure and blessed result. The kingdom of God is righteousness and peace, and, as the sure fruit of these, joy in the Holy Ghost.

Melchizedek was priest and king—a thing unknown in all the history of Israel. What was always kept asunder in God's people had, by the divine forethought, been united in Him who had been made like unto the Son of God. It is the glory of Christ as the Priest-King that our Epistle is specially to unfold.

The silence of Scripture as to his genealogy and birth and death is then interpreted as proof of how different his priesthood is from that of Aaron and the priests in Israel, where descent was everything. So had God prepared in Him a wondrous prophecy of His Son, whose right to the priesthood lay in no earthly birth, but in His being the Son of God from eternity to eternity. Made like unto the Son of God, Melchizedek abideth a priest continually.

A Priest for ever after the order of Melchizedek. This word of God is in the Psalm which forms the connecting link between Genesis and our Epistle. The Holy Spirit who first inspired it, and then expounded it, is waiting to lead us into the mystery of its glory, as a living experience. That word **for ever,** that we meet in the expressions, **Priest for ever, eternal salvation, eternal redemption, perfected for ever,** not only signifies without end, but infinitely more. God is the Eternal One; His life is eternal life. Eternal is that which is divine, in which there is no change or decay, but everlasting youth and strength, because God is in it. The everlasting priesthood of Christ means that He will do His work in us in the power of the eternal life, as that is lived in God and heaven. He lives for ever, therefore He can save completely.

May God teach us to know what it means that Christ is our Melchizedek, a Priest for ever. It is the spiritual apprehension of this everlasting priesthood, as communicating even here and maintaining an everlasting, unchangeable life in us, that lifts our inner experience out of the region of effort, and change, and failure, into the rest of God, so that the immutability of His counsel is the measure of that of our faith and hope.

1. In this chapter we have now the beginning of the things hard to be understood except by the perfect. It is only those who press on to perfection, who long to possess the very utmost of what God is able to work in them through Christ, who can inwardly appropriate the revelation of the eternal priesthood. Neither talent nor genius can suffice—it is the heart that thirsts for the living God that will understand this teaching about our being brought nigh to God.

2. The Holy Spirit, through whom the history was recorded, and the oath to the Son revealed, and the exposition inspired, can alone lead us into the spiritual power and blessing here revealed. And the Holy Spirit only leads as He is known as the indwelling One, is waited on in deep humility, and yielded to in meek resignation. What a solemn, holy, blessed thing to believe that the Spirit of God is leading us into this perfection-truth as a possession and experience.

3. He abideth continually: an unchanging, never-ending life, the characteristic of Melchizedek, who was made like to Christ, of Christ in His heavenly priesthood, and of the life of the believer who learns rightly to know and trust Him.

LI.

Melchizedek and Abraham

VII.–4. Now consider how great this man was, unto whom Abraham, the patriarch, gave a tenth out of the chief spoils.
5. And they indeed of the sons of Levi that receive the priest's office have commandment to take tithes of the people according to the law, that is, of their brethren, though these have come out of the loins of Abraham:
6. But he, whose genealogy is not counted from them, hath taken tithes of Abraham, and hath blessed him that hath the promises.
7. But without any dispute the less is blessed of the better.
8. And here men that die receive tithes; but there one, of whom it is witnessed that he liveth.
9. And, so to say, through Abraham even Levi, who received tithes hath paid tithes;
10. For he was yet in the loins of his father, when Melchizedek met him.

Now consider how great this man was. If we rightly apprehend the greatness of Melchizedek, it will help us to understand the greatness of Christ, our great High Priest. The Hebrews gloried in Abraham, as the father of the chosen people; in Aaron, who as high priest was the representative of God and His worship; in the law as given from heaven, in token of God's covenant with His people. In all these respects the superiority of Melchizedek is proved. He is more than Abraham (4–10), more than Aaron (11–14), more than the law (11–19).

Melchizedek is more than Abraham; of this a double proof is given. Abraham gave tithes to Melchizedek; Melchizedek blessed

Abraham. According to the law the priests received tithes from their brethren, but here a stranger receives them from the father of the whole people. There is more; in Israel men who die receive tithes; but here one of whom it is witnessed that **He liveth,** who **abideth continually.** And in Abraham, even Levi, who received tithes, paid tithes. All was so ordered of God as a hidden prophecy, to be unfolded in due time, of the greatness of Christ our High Priest. **Consider how great this man was.**

There is a second proof of his greatness; Melchizedek blessed Abraham. **But without any dispute the less is blessed of the better.** Abraham had already been blessed of God Himself (Gen. xii. 2). He here accepts a blessing from Melchizedek, acknowledging his own inferiority, unconsciously subordinating himself and the whole priesthood that was to come from him, to this priest of the Most High God.

The unfolding of this divinely-ordained type not only reveals the superiority of Christ to the Levitical priesthood, but sets before us most suggestively two of the characteristics of our relation to Christ as Priest. We receive blessing from Him; He receives tithes from us.

Christ comes to bring us God's blessing. We have seen in chapter vi. 14 what God's blessing is. It is in Christ that the blessing is confirmed and imparted. And if we would know fully what the blessing is Christ brings us, we have only to think of the priestly blessing in Israel.

On this wise ye shall bless the children of Israel, saying unto them,

> The Lord bless thee, and keep thee;
> The Lord make His face to shine upon thee,
>   and be gracious unto thee:
> The Lord lift up His countenance upon thee,
>   and give thee peace.

These are indeed the spiritual blessings in the heavenlies with which God hath blessed us in Christ and which, as High Priest,

Christ dispenses. He brings us to the Father, and we learn to know that He blesses and keeps us. In Him, the Son, God's face shines upon us, and the grace of our Lord Jesus Christ is our portion. In Him God lifts up His countenance upon us, and, by the Holy Spirit, gives His peace unto our hearts. Christ the High Priest makes every part of this blessing a divine reality, a living experience in the power of a life that abides continually.

Christ gives us the blessing, we give Him the tithes. The tithes to God are the acknowledgment of His right to all. Our High Priest has a right to the surrender of all we have, as belonging to Him, to the willing sacrifice of all He asks or needs for His service. The connection between the tithes and the blessing is closer than we know. The more unreservedly we place all that we have at His disposal, the more we in very deed forsake all for His sake, the richer will our experience be of the fulness and the power which our High Priest can bless.

Without dispute the less is blessed of the better. This is the true relation. The more we know of that better name which Jesus has received, and have our hearts filled with His glory, the lower we shall bow, the less we shall become in our own eyes; and thereby the fitter and the more willing to be blessed. And the more ready, too, to render Him not only the tithes, but the whole of all we are and possess. As in our spiritual life this two-fold relation to our great High Priest is maintained, and a deep faith and dependence on His divine fulness of blessing is cultivated, along with an absolute surrender to His disposal and service, the mighty power of His priesthood will be revealed in our hearts. And we shall see with ever-increasing clearness that the two dispositions, faith in Him who blesses and consecration to His service, have their root in the one cardinal virtue of humility, making us ever less and less in our own eyes, until we sink into that nothingness, which is the death to self, and makes room for Him to be All. Then the word will be fulfilled in us in a new meaning: *Without dispute the less is blessed of the better.*

1. Melchizedek blessed Abraham. *The work of thy High Priest, O my soul, is simply blessing. Learn to think this of Jesus, and seek to have a great confidence that He delights to bless. He is nothing but a fountain of blessing; rejoice greatly in this and trust Him for it.*

2. *Remember that the all-comprehensive blessing of thy Melchizedek in heaven is—the Holy Spirit from heaven in thy heart. As it is written: "Christ redeemed us, that the blessing of Abraham might come upon us, in Jesus Christ; that we might receive the promise of the Spirit through faith." The Holy Spirit "abiding continually" in the heart is the high-priestly blessing.*

3. *This day He comes to meet thee, as thou returnest from the battle weary and faint. Bow before Him, and let Him bless thee! "Even as the Holy Ghost saith, Today." Believe that Jesus is all to thee.*

LII.

Melchizedek More Than Aaron and the Law

VII.–11. Now if there was perfection through the Levitical priesthood (for under it hath the people received the law), what further need was there that another priest should arise after the order of Melchizedek, and not be reckoned after the order of Aaron?

12. For the priesthood being changed, there is made of necessity also a change of the law.

13. For he of whom these things are said belongeth to another tribe, from which no man hath given attendance at the altar.

14. For it is evident that our Lord hath sprung from Judah; as to which tribe Moses spake nothing concerning priests.

When God, in Psalm cx., spake with an oath of a priest after the order of Melchizedek, it was a prophecy of deep spiritual meaning. Why should the order of Aaron, whom God Himself had called, whose work took such a large place in the purpose of God and of Scripture, be passed over for the order of another, of whom we knew nothing save one single act? **What need was there that another priest should arise after the order of Melchizedek, and not be reckoned after the order of Aaron?** The answer is, Because the order of Aaron was only the figure of the work of Jesus upon earth; for His eternal and almighty priesthood in heaven something more was needed.

Let us see and grasp this. Aaron's work was the shadow of Christ's work upon earth, of sacrifice and blood-shedding, of atonement and reconciliation with God. Aaron entered indeed within the veil with the blood, in token of God's acceptance of the atonement and the people. But he might not tarry there; he had to come out again at once. His entering only once a year, and that only for a few moments, served mostly, as we see in chapter ix. 7, 8, to teach the people that the way into the Holiest was not yet opened; that for this they would have to wait till another dispensation came. Of a life in the Holiest of All, of a dwelling in God's presence, and fellowship with Him there, of a communication to the people of the power of a life within the veil—of all this there was no thought. The glory of Christ's priesthood consists in His rending the veil and entering in for us: of His sitting at the right hand of God to receive and impart the Spirit of God and the powers of the heavenly life; of His being able to bring us in, that we too may draw nigh to God; of His maintenance in us of the life of heaven by His unceasing intercession and ministry in the power of an endless life; of all this the ministry of Aaron could afford no promise.

It was in all this that Melchizedek was made like unto the Son of God. As priest of the Most High God, he was also king, clothed with honour and power. As such his blessing was in power. And as one, of whose death and the end of whose priesthood Scripture mentions nothing, and who **abideth continually, he is** the image of the eternal priesthood, which is ministered in heaven, in eternity, in the power of an endless life.

The revelation of the mystery and the glory of the Melchizedek priesthood of our Lord Jesus is the great object of the Epistle. And I cannot urge my reader too earnestly to see that he enters fully into the infinite difference between the two orders or ministries of Aaron and Melchizedek. The apparently simple question, **What need was there that another priest should arise after the order of Melchizedek?** has more to do with our spiritual life than we think.

In the opening verses of our Epistle we found the work of Christ divided into two parts. **When He had effected the cleansing of sins** (that was after the order of Aaron), **He sat**

down on the right hand of the Majesty on high (that was after the order of Melchizedek). There are too many Christians who see in Christ only the fulfilment of what Aaron typified. Christ's death and blood are very precious to them; they do seek to rest their faith upon them. And yet they wonder that they have so little of the peace and joy, of the purity and power which the Saviour gives, and which faith in Him ought to bring. The reason is simple, because Christ is only their Aaron, not their Melchizedek. They do indeed believe that He is ascended to heaven, and sits upon the throne of God; but they have not seen the direct connection of this with their daily spiritual life. They do not count upon Jesus working in them in the power of the heavenly life, and imparting it to them. They do not know their heavenly calling, with the all-sufficient provision for its fulfilment in them secured in the heavenly life of their Priest-King. And, as a consequence of this, they do not see the need for giving up the world, to have their life and walk in heaven.

The work of redemption was accomplished on earth in weakness (2 Cor. xiii. 4); it is communicated from heaven in resurrection and ascension power. The cross proclaims the pardon of sin; the throne gives the power over sin. The cross, with its blood-sprinkling, is the deliverance from Egypt; the throne, with its living Priest-King, brings into the rest of God and its victory. With Aaron there is nothing beyond atonement and acceptance; nothing of kingly rule and power; it is with Melchizedek that the fulness of power and blessing comes, the blessing that abideth continually. It is as the soul no longer ever again seeks the foundation, but resting on it and it alone, is built up into Christ Jesus, the perfected and exalted One, that it will be delivered from its feebleness, and know the power of the heavenly life. The more we consider and adore our blessed King-Priest, our Melchizedek, the stronger will our confidence become that from His throne in heaven He will, in divine power, Himself apply to us all the blessed fruits of His atonement, and make a life in God's presence and nearness our daily experience.

1. When He had effected the cleansing of our sins—*God be praised for our Aaron! Glory be to the Lamb that was slain!*—He sat down on the right hand of the Majesty on high! *God be praised for our Melchizedek! Glory to the Lamb in the midst of the throne! The Holiest is now opened, with our great High Priest to bring us in and keep us there.*

2. *The effecting the cleansing of sins by Jesus preceded the sitting on the throne. But the application in us in power follows. This is the reason why we are here first taught about the High Priest in heaven, then in chapter viii. about the heavenly sanctuary, and after that in chapter ix. about the power of the blood in heaven, and from heaven in us. It is only in the knowledge of Jesus in heaven we shall know the full power of the cleansing blood.*

3. *Wherefore, holy brethren, partakers of a heavenly calling, consider Jesus on the throne in heaven! The worship and the fellowship of a heavenly Christ makes heavenly Christians.*

LIII.

A Priest for Ever—in the Power of an Endless Life

VII.–15. And what we say is yet more abundantly evident, if after the likeness of Melchizedek there ariseth another priest,
16. Who hath been made, not after the law of a carnal commandment, but after the power of an endless life.
17. For it is witnessed of him,
> Thou art a priest for ever
> After the order of Melchizedek.

In the words of Psalm cx. each expression is full of meaning. We saw (v. 4–6) that the word, **Thou art Priest** is the proof that Christ did not glorify Himself to become Priest, but was appointed of God. We have seen the deep significance of the words, **after the order of Melchizedek.** We now come to what is implied in its being said, **Thou art a Priest for ever.**

The word **ever** or **eternal** is one of the most important in the Epistle. It is found seventeen times. It contains all that distinguishes the New Testament from the Old; the healthy Christian life of *the perfect,* from the stunted sickly growth of *the babes.* To understand what it means we must connect it with God, the eternal One. Eternity is an attribute of Deity and of the divine life, and has its true existence only in the fellowship of that life. In God there is no change, or aging, or fading; He is all that He is in an ever-fresh, never-changing, youth. As some one has said: "He is the Ancient of Days, and yet the youngest of all, for He lives ever in the freshness of the eternal strength that knows no past." The eternal life is that which always remains the same, because it is always in God. And when God speaks to His Son, **Thou art Priest for ever,** it not only means that the priesthood will never cease, but it points to what is the root and cause of this; it roots in the life and strength of God. Christ is become a Priest **after the power of an endless life.** Unceasingly, without one moment's cessation, in unbroken continuity, He lives and works in the power of the divine life.

The contrast will make the meaning clear. He is made Priest, **not after the law of a carnal commandment,** as Aaron, **but after the power of an endless life,** even as Melchizedek who abideth a priest continually. Law and life are the contrasts. Every creature naturally acts according to the life that is in it, without any law or compulsion from without. The bird needs no law to bid it fly, or the fish to make it swim: its life makes it a delight. A law is a proof that the life is wanting. The law that forbids stealing is a proof that the life of those for whom it is made is wrong. And a law is not only a proof that the right life is wanting, but it is helpless to produce it. It may check and restrain, but cannot inspire. It can demand, but cannot give; it has power to command, but not to create what it seeks. Aaron became priest after the law of a carnal commandment, a law that made nothing perfect, and was disannulled for the weakness and unprofitableness thereof; Christ, after the power of an endless life. Every act of His holy and blessed priesthood, every application of the fruits of His eternal redemption, is wrought in **the power of an endless life.**

These two principles mark two systems of religion, two ways of worshipping God, two experiences of the inner life. The one is that of the law, with atonement and acceptance with God, as typified in Aaron. The Christian trusts in Christ as his Redeemer, and seeks, by the great motive of gratitude, to compel himself to love and obedience. His life is one of unceasing effort. But he is painfully conscious of failure; obedience is not his life and delight. The New Testament offers a better life. Through unbelief and sloth the majority of Christians know little of it. But here it is, opened up by the Holy Spirit, as the mystery of Melchizedek. **Jesus Christ is become a Priest after the power of an endless life.** These precious words are the key to the higher life. Jesus lives in heaven as High Priest in **the power of an endless life.** And as He lives, so He works in that power. This is the meaning of His being **a Priest for ever.** His work does not consist, like that of Aaron, in a series of successive acts, that ever cease, and ever need to be renewed. No, each work He does for us He is able to do **in the power of an end-less life.** He works it within us *as a life,* as our own life, so that it is our very nature to delight in God and in His will. His priest-hood acts as an inner life within us, lifting us up, not in thought but in spirit and in truth, into a vital fellowship with God. He breathes His own life in us. And He works it in as *the power of life,* a life that is strong and healthy, because it is His own life from heaven. And He works it **in the power of an endless, an indissoluble life,** a life that never for a moment need know a break or an interruption, because it is the life of eternity, the life maintained in us by Him who is **a Priest for ever,** a Priest who abideth continually.

And why is it so many Christians experience and prove so lit-tle of this power of the endless, the unchanging life that abides continually? Some know nothing of it, they only know of Christ as Aaron. And some hear of it but are not willing to give up all to purchase this pearl of great price; to give up the world for this heavenly life. And some, who would fain give up all, cannot, dare not, will not, believe that Christ is indeed Melchizedek, a Priest for ever, a Priest who does everything in eternal life-power.

He abideth a Priest continually. The continuity of His priesthood is never interrupted or broken; as little the continu-ity of the action of His priesthood; as little experience of that ac-tion. Everything Christ as my High Priest in heaven does for me

He does in **the power of an endless life,** as **a Priest who abides continually;** what He works can abide continually too. Oh for faith to consider and know and trust Christ Jesus, **Priest for ever, Priest after the power of the endless life!**

1. The power of an endless life. *There is not a more significant or important expression in the whole Epistle. It is life we need, and a strong life, and a life that never gives way. Here we have it—the life more abundant.*

2. *We shall often have occasion to refer to these words. We are so accustomed to think of a priest as a man who does certain things on behalf of other men, separate from himself, that we apply this mode of thinking to the Lord Jesus. Christ is no outward Saviour, nor can He give us any salvation as an outward thing. All He does for us and to us He puts into our heart, makes it our life.* We need to know that all He does as High Priest for us in heaven, He also does within us as a life He gives. *He is Priest, and can save in no other way, than* after the power of an endless life. *It is only as a life within us that His priesthood can attain its object.*

3. *Jesus was crucified in weakness, but raised in the power of God. He won the power through the weakness, the sacrifice of all unto the death. Let all who would know Him in* the power of the endless life *enter into the fellowship of His death, walk in deep humility and meekness and dependence upon God, in the path in which He trod to reach the throne.*

LIV.

A Better Hope,
Through Which We Draw Nigh to God

VII.–18. For there is a disannulling of a foregoing commandment because of its weakness and unprofitableness
19. (For the law made nothing perfect), and a bringing in thereupon of a better hope, through which we draw nigh to God.

In verse 12 we read, **For the priesthood being changed, there
is made of necessity a change also of the law.** When the order of Aaron had to give way to that of Melchizedek, the law,
under which Aaron had ministered, had to give way to the new
order, to the law not of commandment, but to the law of the
power of the endless life. The reason of this is now given.
**There is a disannulling of the foregoing commandment, be-
cause of its weakness and unprofitableness, for the law
made nothing perfect.** Perfection was what God and man
sought as deliverance from sin and its effects; perfect restoration and perfect fellowship. The law could make nothing perfect, neither the conscience nor the worshipper. Jesus came to
work out, and reveal, and impart that perfection the law could
only foreshadow.

And what this perfection is, we are now told: "There is a disannulling of the commandment, **and a bringing in of a better
hope, through which we draw nigh to God.**" To bring man
nigh to God, into full favour and actual fellowship, is the object
of every priest. Aaron could not do it; Jesus has done it. This is
the glory of the New Testament; it brings in a better hope, a real

drawing nigh to the living God, a communion of the Holy Spirit with Him. This is the perfection which, not the law, but Jesus gives. In chapter vi. hope was already mentioned as that through which we enter within the veil, whither our Forerunner has gone for us. In the power of the endless life He has opened the veil and opened the way; He has brought in the better hope through which we draw nigh to God.

Draw nigh to God! This expression is one of the fingerposts on the way to the higher teaching that is to come. It gives us the main object of Christ's work: to enable us to live our life in the nearness of God. There are Christians who, in seeking salvation, only think of themselves and their own happiness: Christ is simply a means to an end. There are others who go farther: they feel a personal relation to Christ, and desire greatly to know and serve Him better. But even with these, there is something lacking which is indispensable to a whole and vigorous Christian character. They do not know that Christ is only the way, the door to the Father, and that His great desire is to lead us through and past Himself to the Father, really **to bring us to God!** He wants us to live the same life He lived upon earth—always looking up to, depending upon, and honouring a God in heaven above Him.

Draw nigh to God! Nothing but this can satisfy God and His love. He longs to have His children come to dwell in that love, and to delight in His presence. He sent His Son to bring us to Him. This is what constitutes full salvation. God as the author of our being longs to have us yield ourselves and wait upon Himself to work His work in us. As the righteous and holy One He seeks to have us wholly given up to His will and wisdom. As the unseen and hidden One, He asks that we should withdraw ourselves from the visible and hold fellowship with Him. Man was created for the presence of God. The nearness of God was to be his native atmosphere. It is this God is willing to vouchsafe to each of us; it is this the heavenly priesthood makes possible; it is this God would have us seek.

As God is no outward Being, so is nearness to Him nothing external, but an inner spiritual harmony of disposition, a fellowship and unity of will. As His spirit gives us more of the divine nature, and God works His will more freely and fully in us, we come nearer to Him, we become truly united to Him.

Draw nigh to God! Nothing less than this is what the redemption of Christ has won and set open for us. This was the weakness of the law, that it made no provision for God's people entering into His sanctuary, His immediate presence. The way into the Holiest has been opened by Jesus. We may boldly enter in and appear before God. Seated on the throne *our High Priest has the power by His Holy Spirit to make the drawing nigh to God our continual abiding experience.* He does this in the power of the endless life. Life never works from without, always from within. Our High Priest by His life-power enters our life, and renews it, and lifts it up; His heavenly life becomes our actual life, and the presence of God surrounds and shines on us as the sunlight shines on our bodies. He is able so to shed abroad the love of God in our hearts that His presence is our joy all the day.

Draw nigh to God! Nothing less than this must be what our faith claims. The redemption in Christ is so perfect and all-prevailing, His salvation so complete, the power of His life in us so heavenly and indissoluble, the action of His priesthood so unceasing and unbroken, and the working of His Spirit so sure and so divine, that it is indeed possible for us to dwell all the day in the enjoyment of God's love and fellowship. It is a life-state He has entered into, has opened to us, and lives to keep us in. Let us believe it. Yes, let faith be the one habit of our soul—a faith that honours our King-Priest on the throne in expecting from Him what is impossible to man, what is possible only to God, to keep our hearts all the day within the veil before the face of God.

Christ is the door. The door of what? the door of the heart of God. Through Him I can enter in and abide in God's love, can dwell in God and God in me. He is the living door, who takes me up, and brings me in to God. He does it most surely, because He is High Priest **in the power of the endless life.**

1. A life nigh to God: *This is the better hope, which enters into that which is within the veil. Hold fast* the glorying of this hope. *Give diligence unto* the fulness of the hope: *hope maketh not ashamed.*

2. God near, the world far; *the world near, God far. Jesus entered the presence of God in the path which He opened up for us. That path was humility and meekness, obedience and death. It cost Jesus entire and intense self-surrender to open the path and enter in. He has won for us the power to follow Him, and communicates it to all upright souls, in the power of an endless life.*

3. Nigh to God! *Is this thy life? Is this thy desire? Is this thy expectation? It is the salvation Christ has prepared for thee, and waits to give thee.*

LV.

Jesus, the Surety of a Better Covenant

VII.–20. And inasmuch as it is not without the taking of an oath
21. (For they indeed had become priests without an oath; but he
with an oath by him that saith of him,

> The Lord sware and will not repent himself,
> Thou art priest for ever);

22. By so much also has Jesus become the surety of a better
covenant.

In chapter vi. the deep meaning of God's oath was set before us.
On His side it is a proof of His unchangeable purpose concerning something which He binds Himself faithfully to perform.
On our side it points to something in which there is special need
of faith, and calls us to the exercise of full and unhesitating confidence as to the certainty of God's fulfilment of the promise. In
the words of the appointment of Christ as High Priest we have
already found three significant expressions—there is a fourth
one we are now to notice. **The Lord sware and will not repent
Himself:** this oath of God is a new proof of the glory of Christ's
priesthood and its superiority to the old. God confirmed His
blessing to Abraham with an oath; that blessing is eternal and
unchangeable. Aaron was made a priest without an oath: his
priesthood was only temporary, a shadow of what was to come.
At the first announcement of a priest after the new order, God
again interposed with an oath: **inasmuch as it was not without
the taking of an oath, by so much hath Jesus become the
surety of a better covenant.** The oath points us to the cove-

nant, to its being a better covenant, to Jesus being its surety, and to the priesthood as that in which the covenant and the suretyship have their power.

A better covenant. The object of a covenant is to define and settle the relation between the two parties who enter into it, and to give security for the faithful fulfilment of their engagements to each other. The old covenant which God made with Israel had proved a failure. At its establishment they were most ready to promise, *All that the Lord hath said will we do and be obedient.* But how soon was the covenant forgotten and the promise broken. They had undertaken what they could not perform; the vow and the purpose availed nothing without the strength. In course of time God promised to establish a new covenant, and in it to provide for what had been wanting, for the power to obey, and so to keep the covenant. It would be a covenant of life—giving that new life into the heart, out of which obedience would naturally spring. Of this better covenant, established on better promises, we shall hear in the next chapter.

The surety of a better covenant. It is this Jesus has come to do, to give the covenant its security, and to undertake that its engagements shall indeed be fulfilled. He is surety of the covenant on both sides. Surety to us that God will keep His promise, and give us His life and law and Spirit in our heart; surety to God for us, He will ensure our obedience and our keeping the covenant.

Become a Priest with an oath. It is in the priesthood of Jesus that the covenant and the suretyship have their power. It is the Priest for ever who deals with sin and takes it away in the power of an endless life. It is the Priest for ever, the Son of God, perfected for evermore, who has opened a new and living way, a new state of life, and works all in the power of an endless life, in whom we have a divine surety that every promise and every obligation of the better covenant will be fulfilled by God and by us.

It is to give us a living and most complete assurance that all this will be so, that the installation of Jesus in the Priest's office was announced by an oath from heaven. God does so long that we should in very deed become to the full partakers of the eternal redemption His Son has obtained for us, and because He sees it is impossible for Him to work out His will in us except as our hearts open to Him in faith and expectation, He is ready to do anything He can, to awake our confidence and compel us to trust Him perfectly. And so His Spirit reminds us that the priesthood of Jesus, and all the blessings which come from it in the power of our eternal life, are absolutely sure and certain. As if it is not enough that we know that as the Son of God He is the Almighty One, as Son of Man the merciful and faithful High Priest, as the Exalted One, a King upon God's throne, God calls us to consider the oath He took. **He swears by Himself.** He points to Himself and His honour as God, to Himself as the Eternal and Almighty God and charges us to believe that this **Priest for ever** He has given us does indeed save with an everlasting salvation, with a salvation in which the power of eternity works.

When God confirmed by oath to Abraham His promise of blessing, Abraham, though he knew but little of what that blessing would yet be, believed God: he was strong in faith, giving glory to God. And we, who know the Son in whom God has now revealed Himself, and in regard to the efficacy and eternal life-power of whose work for us God has now sworn His oath to us, shall we doubt or hesitate? God forbid! Oh that our hearts were opened to understand! *The one thing God asks of us, is the faith that sees what He has promised to do, and that sinks down before Him to let Him work what He has undertaken.* The one thing we have to strive after, as we move on in the path the Epistle opens up to the inner sanctuary, is that our faith stand not in the wisdom of men, in our own thoughts of the way or the measure in which God will fulfil His promise, but only and entirely in the power of God. What needed an oath of God to assure us of it, needs and has the power of God to work it.

1. Do hold fast these two things. Faith must see what God promises, and then allow God to fulfil the promise in us. Pray for the enlightening of the Holy Spirit, to get delivered from all partial and defective views of what our High Priest can work in us, and then regard as your highest work, to wait upon God and yield to His operation in adoring trust.

2. The content and substance of the oath of God is, the living personal Christ, as Son and Priest; that is, as Priest in the power of the divine and eternal life which He imparts. He that clings to Christ will be led on to know all that God has promised in Him.

LVI.

A Priest, Able to Save Completely

VII.–23. And they indeed have been made priests many in number, because that by death they are hindered from continuing:
24. But he, because he abideth for ever, hath his priesthood unchangeable.
25. Wherefore also he is able to save to the uttermost[1] them that draw near unto God through him, seeing he ever liveth to make intercession for them.

In the order of Aaron there was a continual succession of priests, one dying and another taking his place. That characterised the whole system; it bore the mark of change and weakness and death. It could not effect anything that was really abiding and permanent, much less anything that was eternal. The whole inner life of the worshipper was what the system was, subject to change and decay. **But He, because He abideth for ever, hath His priesthood unchangeable.** He Himself is the Eternal One, who abideth Priest for ever. His priesthood is unchangeable; the life, in the power of which He ministers, and the life which He ministers, is a life that abides unchangeable too. His priesthood is an everlasting one, ever living, ever active.

Wherefore also He is able to save completely them that draw near unto God through Him. Wherefore, that is **because He abideth for ever,** because there is never a single moment in which His priestly action, His watchful care of us, His loving sympathy and succour, His working in us in the power

1. Completely.

of our endless life, is not in full operation. Therefore **He can save completely,** that is, there need never be a moment in which the experience of His saving power is intermitted, in which the salvation He has wrought does not save. To confirm this, it is added, **seeing He ever liveth to make intercession for them.** Without ceasing there streams forth from Him to the Father the prayer of His love for every one and every need of those that belong to Him; His very person and presence is that prayer, so closely and so inseparably is He identified with those He calls His brethren. And without ceasing there streams forth to Him from the Father the answer of His good pleasure, and the power of the Holy Spirit, bearing that answer. And even so, without ceasing, there streams forth from Him to each member of His body the grace for the timely help. Because **He ever liveth to make intercession,** without one moment's intermission, therefore **He is able to save completely.**

He is able to save completely. The connection of the promise with the character and work of Christ shows us what it means. The great complaint of Christians is that their experience is so changeful—that the blessed sense of God's love and grace passes away, and that what they know of the keeping, cleansing, power of Christ does not last; the sense of nearness to God does not abide continually. It is somehow as if there is a necessity of its being lost. With change of circumstances, alas, comes too often change in the nearness of God and His saving power. Could what Christ does for them at times but be maintained continuously, could it but abide—their joy would be full, their salvation complete. We have here the very promise such Christians need. Because **He abideth for ever,** because **He ever liveth to make intercession,** because He is **a Priest for ever,** who exercises every function of His office in *an endless life-power,* that *never* for a moment intermits its action, **He is able to save completely.** In Himself He has been **perfected for evermore,** with Himself **He hath perfected for ever** them that are

272

sanctified. The salvation He has wrought out is a life in the opened sanctuary of God's presence in the power of God's Spirit; all that is needed is that the believer be kept abiding for ever, ever living in this salvation-life which Jesus has opened up. And this he can do, when once he learns to trust Jesus for it, because he understands that **He ever liveth to make intercession.** He prayed for Peter that his faith might not fail. Because His work of intercession never pauses or ceases, our faith and our experience of the power of that intercession need never fail. **He is able to save completely!**

Them that draw near unto God through Him. In verse 19 we saw that to enable us to **draw nigh to God** is the better hope the gospel brings—the one aim of Christ's priesthood. Here we have it again. One reason why so many have no conception of Christ as able to save completely is simply that they have never understood fully what salvation is. The following chapters will open it up to us—and may God's Spirit truly open it!—that **to come to God through Christ, to draw nigh to God** means nothing less than an entering into the Holiest of All, and dwelling there all the day, spending our life there, abiding there continually. It is only those who believe it possible, will give themselves up to it. It is only those who forsake all to give themselves up to it to whom it will be possible. But for all **who come to God** through Him the promise is sure: **He abideth for ever; He is able to save completely.**

Oh, let us fix our eyes and hearts on Jesus in heaven, our Melchizedek, our Priest-King on the throne of power, and on His unceasing intercession. And let our one desire be to believe that the God who hath sworn by Himself, by His own life as God, means to do for us something above all we can ask or think.

1. Able to save completely. *This is that solid food for the perfect which only the truly consecrated soul can apprehend. It is of the things "hard of interpretation, seeing ye are become dull of hearing."*

2. Like priest, like people. *The character of a priest determines the character of the people whose worship he leads.* The character of Christ's priesthood determines the character of those who belong to Him. *And our view of what that priesthood can effect will determine our religious character. Of what infinite importance to worship and to trust Him,* as able to save completely. *That will determine our Christian character and life.*

3. *What a view of the place and power of intercession! Christ's whole life is given up to it. His power as Priest-King on the throne has no other channel for its exercise. You long to save others. Give yourself to prayer and intercession. Present yourself before God as a sacrifice for your fellowmen, offering to be filled with His Spirit and consumed by His fire. Count intercession the secret of bringing down the blessing of heaven. Connect the two things inseparably together—unceasing intercession and power to save completely in Christ. Complete salvation and unceasing intercession in us.*

LVII.

Such a High Priest,
the Son Perfected for Evermore

VII.–26. For such a High Priest became us, holy, guileless, undefiled, separated from sinners, and made higher than the heavens;
27. Who needeth not daily, like those high priests, to offer up
sacrifices, first for his own sins, and then for the sins of the people: for this he did once, when he offered up himself.
28. For the law appointeth men high priests, having infirmity;
but the word of the oath, which was after the law, appointeth a
Son, perfected for evermore.

For such a High Priest became us—was suited to us, as being
what we needed. The words refer to the whole chapter, but specially to the verse that just precedes—**such a High Priest,** one
who **abideth for ever,** one who is **able to save completely.** It
also refers to what now follows, in which His personal characteristics are summed up. **Holy,** in fellowship and harmony with
God; **guileless,** in the purity of His disposition; **undefiled,** in
His having conquered all temptation from sin and the world;
separated from sinners, a true Man among men, and yet one
who had kept Himself free from their sin; **made higher than
the heavens,** now exalted in the glory of God, to communicate
to us the life and the blessings of the heavenly world.

**Who needeth not daily like those high priests, to offer up
sacrifices, first for His own sins, and then for the sins of the
people; for this He did once, when He offered up Himself.**
We saw that the glory of Christ's priesthood, in contrast with

that of the many who had, by reason of death, to succeed each other, was, that He alone is Priest, because He abideth ever. Here we have the same truth from another side: in contrast with the daily ever-repeated sacrifices, He accomplished all when **He offered Himself once.** That which has to be repeated is imperfect; that which need be done only once is perfect and lasts for ever. Farther on we shall find the word *once* again, as having the same meaning with regard to His sacrifice which *for ever* has with regard to His priesthood.

He offered up Himself. We have here the first mention of the sacrifice of Christ. In chapter ii. we had mention of His death, here we see that it was death upon the altar. He is both Priest and Victim. His divine priesthood, as it is exercised in heaven, is the application of the blood and the virtue of that sacrifice which He brought upon earth. The *once for all* of the sacrifice is the counterpart of the *henceforth for ever* of the throne of the heavens.

For the law, this is the conclusion of the whole, **appointeth men high priests, having infirmity; but the word of the oath, which was after the law, appointeth a Son, perfected for evermore.** The law was a preparation, to waken the need and the hope, of that true, supernatural, heavenly communion with God, which should be, not in words or wishes, but in the power of the eternal life. What the law could not do, God hath done, appointing as **High Priest, the Son, perfected for evermore.**

In these last words we have the summing up of the whole preceding teaching of the Epistle. In chapter i. it had spoken of the Son of God and His glory: He came from God, He is God, and has the life of God in Him; He is able to bring us near, into the true possession and enjoyment of the very life of God. In chapters ii.–v. we had His humanity, His being made perfect through suffering and obedience. He so perfected a new human nature, which from heaven He imparts to us in the power of the Holy Ghost. In chapter vii. we have now been taught what it

means that He is the **Priest for ever,** after the order of
Melchizedek, whose person and priesthood and work are all in
the power of the endless life, and who, because He ever abideth
and ever intercedeth, is **able to save completely,** and to make
our drawing nigh to God a life that abides continually. **Such a
High Priest became us, the Son, perfected for evermore.**

And if such a High Priest became us, what becomes us now
towards Him? Surely one thing, that we fully seek to know and
to trust and to experience His saving power. If your heart does
indeed long for deliverance from sin, for true near fellowship
with God, for complete salvation, for a life in the power and the
likeness of the Son of God, our Leader and Forerunner within
the veil—*you must learn to know Jesus both as Son of God and your
High Priest.* You must pray for the Spirit of wisdom and revelation, that you may know the exceeding greatness of God's power to us-ward who believe, according to the working of His
mighty power in Christ Jesus, when He raised Him from the
dead and set Him at His own right hand. You must believe that
the mighty power by which He was thus perfected for evermore,
and is seated at God's right hand, is working in you. Yield yourself up in faith to this mighty working of God in Christ, to the
power of the eternal life with which from heaven He will work
in you to draw you nigh to God, and keep you there. As you believe this, and trust Jesus for it, He Himself will make it your experience. Oh beware of thinking that these are beautiful words
and images that Scripture gives; they are meant by God as the
most downright actual realities for daily life and walk. God has
given you such a High Priest that you might live an impossible
life, a life above sense and reason, a supernatural life in the power of His Son. When Jesus ascended the throne His disciples
were to wait for a communication direct from Himself of the
spirit and power of the heavenly life into which He had entered
for them. It is the same Holy Spirit, dwelling in us in Pentecostal

power, who alone can make all the blessed objective truth of the Epistle a living reality within us.

1. *Ere we part from this chapter note well the three words in which its practical teaching gathers up what our Melchizedek, who abideth a priest continually, is to us.* The law of His working is: He does all after the power of an endless life. *The object of His work: the better hope, by which we draw nigh to God. The measure of His work:* able to save completely. *The power of eternal life, the nearness of God, and complete salvation are what He has to bestow.*

2. *The eternal priesthood of Christ: this is the first of the perfection truths that lead us to the perfection life. A Son,* perfected *for evermore, is our High Priest, who out of Himself and in Himself gives us the life we are to live.*

3. *The one thought of God in His word here is to make us feel what a complete salvation there is for us with such a Saviour. God speaks to us in His Son, giving us in Him His own life.*

LVIII.

The Priest-King on the Throne
in the Heavens

VIII.–1. Now in the things we are saying the chief point is this:
We have such a high priest, who sat down on the right hand of
the throne of the Majesty in the heavens.

In every pursuit it is always most important to keep the eye
fixed on that which is the main thing, and to make everything
else subservient to it. A Christian often feels perplexed by the
variety of truths and duties set before him in Scripture; to see
clearly what the central thought is, is like finding the key to
some building round which one had vainly wandered seeking
an entrance. Our author here is careful in summing up what we
have had thus far, to fix our view on what is **the chief point—**
We have such a High Priest, as has been set before us, the very
Son of God, a true Man in His obedience to God and sympathy
with us, become a Priest after the order of Melchizedek, in the
power of an endless life. And we have Him as one **who sat**
down on the right hand of the throne of the Majesty in the
heavens. It is as our faith apprehends and holds this truth that
we have the key which opens the door into the heavenly life
upon earth.

279

Jesus our Priest-King on the throne in the heavens. What does this mean, and teach, and give? It reminds of this, first of all, that Jesus is not only Priest but King. This was part of what was included in His appointment after the order of Melchizedek, whose name meant King of righteousness, and who was King of Salem, that is King of peace. The Psalm in which the word of the oath is spoken began thus: **The Lord said unto my Lord, Sit thou at my right hand.** In Israel the office of king and priest had ever been kept separate; it was only one of the latest prophets who foretold (Zech. vi. 13): *He shall be a priest upon the throne.* It was part of the defect in the character of the preparatory dispensation that the function of priest, the representative of the religious life, should be so distinct from that of the king, the guide of the civil life of the people. The priest represents purity, the king power; it is the glory of the new dispensation that the Priest is King—the cleansing from sin, and the access to God which that gives, is all in a power that goes through the whole life. Religion is no longer to be a thing of times and seasons, of special acts or emotions: in kingly power our High Priest rules over all. Blessed is the man to whom it is given to see that this is the chief point, that this is all.

And that, because He is a King **sat down on the right hand of the throne of the Majesty in the heavens.** The Son of God became Man that He might win for Himself and us, for humanity, His own and ours, the power He had with the Father before the world began, and so as our High Priest serve and rule us in the power of an endless life, in the power of the heavenly life. **He sat down on the right hand of the throne.** His position is now one of perfect fellowship with God, in a nearness in which nothing can intervene, in an equality which gives Him complete possession and disposal of all power in heaven and on earth. This is the chief point to know in faith, that **we have such a High Priest!**

On the throne of the Majesty in the heavens. We have said before that the great characteristic of our Priest-King, of His salvation and His life, is its heavenliness. It will reward the reader each time the thought occurs, to go over the passages we have marked, and seek to come fully under the power of the thought. Jesus is **passed through the heavens, made higher than the heavens, seated on the throne in the heavens,** in order that He might open the kingdom of heaven to us. Heaven, we have said before, is not only a place, but a state of life; the kingdom of heaven can come to us here on earth in power, and be set up within our hearts. The will of God can be done on earth as in heaven. All Jesus is, is heavenly; all the gifts He bestows, all the work He does, all the life He breathes, all the power He exercises is exclusively heavenly. This is the solid food for the perfect; as our faith receives and feeds upon this, it becomes partaker of the very spirit of heaven, in the power of an endless life. As the heavenliness of the redemption and the life in Jesus is revealed by the Holy Spirit in the heart, heavenliness, its purity, its power, its love, its worship, its blessedness, will be the characteristic of our religion.

He sat down on the throne of the Majesty in the heavens. We know how to the first disciples this blessed truth was revealed and sealed—it was by the Holy Spirit sent down from heaven. The Spirit of heaven is the Spirit in the power of which the angels do God's will there. The Spirit of heaven is the Spirit which came down from the opened heaven on the Son of Man. The Spirit of heaven was sent down to His disciples by the Son of Man, when He had sat down on the right hand of the throne in the heavens, as their share in His exaltation; not as the Spirit of conversion, but as the Spirit to seal their faith; as their experience of fellowship with Him in His glory; as their participation in the joy and holiness of the heavenly life; as their power to conquer sin and the world. To those who are willing to come and be separate and utterly forsake this world, this Spirit of heaven still comes as the gift of our heavenly Priest-King. Let us believe the Word, let us cling to Him and worship Him as seated on the throne in the heavens; it will become our blessed heart experience, not only that this is the chief point, **Such a High Priest became us,** but that *we have*—yes, not only in thought, in gift, but in living enjoyment—**we have such a High Priest, who sat down on the right hand of the throne of the Majesty in the heavens.**

1. *The spirit of a king imparts itself to his subjects. As he devotes himself to war or peace, to noble pursuits or to luxury and pleasure, his example leads his people. Perfect heavenliness, heavenly perfection, is the mark of our King; it is meant to be the mark of His people. The true knowledge of a heavenly Christ makes a heavenly Christian.*

2. *"Our Forerunner has carried away our hearts with Him. We have no heart left for any one but Him, or for anything without or within the veil that He is not, or is not in."*

3. *Ever connect Christ's entering the heavenly life and His ascending the throne with the descent of the Spirit to be the life of the disciples. And remember that all our knowledge and faith in the Priest-King is only preparatory to the true blessing—the Holy Spirit revealing Him and making Him present in the heart. Ascension and Pentecost are inseparable.*

LIX.

The Priest-King, the Minister of the True Sanctuary

VIII.–1. Now in the things which we are saying the chief point is this: We have such a high priest, who sat down on the right hand of the throne of the Majesty in the heavens.

2. A minister of the sanctuary, and of the true tabernacle, which the Lord pitched, not man.

3. For every high priest is appointed to offer both gifts and sacrifices: wherefore it is necessary that this High Priest also have somewhat to offer.

4. Now if he were on earth, he would not be a priest at all, seeing there are those who offer the gifts according to the law;

5. Who serve that which is a copy and shadow of the heavenly things, even as Moses is warned of God when he is about to make the tabernacle: for, See, saith he, that thou make all things according to the pattern which was shewed thee in the mount.

The chief point is this: We have such a High Priest, who sat down at the right hand of the throne of the Majesty in the heavens. Thus the writer had summed up his teaching. He has now one more thought to add, revealing still more distinctly and fully the work our Lord does for us in heaven. He is a **Minister of the sanctuary, and of the true tabernacle, which the Lord pitched, not man.** The heavens, with the heavenly life of Christ there, are here shown to be the true counterpart of the tabernacle Moses built, and He, the Priest-King on the throne, is seen to be the Minister of the sanctuary, of the true tabernacle which God pitched and not man.

He then proceeds to remind us, that as every high priest is appointed to offer gifts and sacrifices, so Christ must have something to offer too. **Now if He were on earth, He would not be a priest at all, seeing there are priests according to the law.** Christ belongs to an entirely different sphere. With the body which He offered on earth, and the blood He shed, He has passed away out of the visible into the invisible realm of spiritual worship and life. Heaven is the sphere of His ministry. When God said to Moses, to make all according to the pattern showed him in the mount, to serve as a shadow of **the heavenly things;** in the very appointment of the tabernacle, there was the indication that it was but a copy and promise of the true tabernacle, with its heavenly sanctuary. The heavens where Jesus sits on the throne, they are the **true tabernacle;** and the High Priest on the throne is at the same time the **Minster of the sanctuary.**

A Minister of the sanctuary. The King is still a servant. All the ministry or service of the priests in the tabernacle had its fulfilment in Him. The priests served in the tabernacle day by day, ordered everything for the service of God according to His will; as representatives of the people they received the assurance of God's favour, and brought them out God's blessing. Jesus is the Minister of the heavenly sanctuary. He represents us there. He has opened up the way, and brought us in, and sends down into our hearts the life and spirit of the true sanctuary; without ceasing He maintains the cleansing of His precious blood in our conscience, and, **in the power of an endless life,** enables us to worship in spirit and in truth, and to live our earthly life in the presence and the favour of God. As the exalted Priest-King He does it all in an infinite, a divine power. As the Minister of the sanctuary, He does it with all the sympathy and the gentle forbearance which we have seen to mark Him as made like to His brethren in all things.

A priest must have a sanctuary in which he dwells, to receive all who come to seek his God. Our great High Priest has His sanctuary in the heavens; there He dwells, there we find Him; there He receives us, there He introduces us to meet God; there He proves that He is a Priest who abides continually, and who gives those who come to God through Him the power to do it too—to abide continually in His presence. The nearness to God and fellowship with Him I cannot partake of except through my heart. My heart is my life, is myself; my only blessedness is in the state of the heart. And therefore Jesus as High Priest cannot do His priestly work of bringing me near to God except as He dwells in my heart by the power of the Holy Spirit. All our thought, and faith, and adoration of Him in heaven brings us back to the riches of the glory of the mystery—Christ in you. He is Priest after the power of *an endless life,* a Priest whose presence and power are known and enjoyed in the life of the heart.

These are indeed spiritual mysteries of which we speak—things hard to be understood of those who, through sloth or worldliness, are dull of hearing. Oh, let us not imagine that these are things which reason can grasp or hold; they are a supernatural wisdom, a divine revelation which none can receive but those who receive it from the Spirit of God. Let us remember that it is God, who has pitched this tabernacle; that it cost the Son of God a life of humility and suffering, cost Him His death and blood, to open it for us; that it needed the almighty power of God in the resurrection and ascension to bring Him there; that it needed ten days unceasing prayer, and the coming down of the blessed Spirit at Pentecost, before the High Priest could impart even to His elect circle the power of the life within the veil. And let us then pause to think that it is no wonder if most Christians rest content with the easier and more external worship as typified by Aaron, and never press on unto perfection, in the full knowledge of our Melchizedek and the mystery of the heavenly life into which He leads them. Let us, above all, remember that it was through death, through the offering up of Himself, that Jesus entered in, and opened a way for us to follow. To enter in demands a very entire renunciation of the world and of self, a very real and true participation in Christ's humbling of Himself and becoming obedient unto death, even the death of the cross—in His death to sin. And it demands no less a very real experience of the mighty operation of God, which raised Him from the dead, and set Him at His right hand. But let us praise God, too, that for every soul who truly wills it, our almighty King-Priest, able to save completely, will surely give it.

1. How many Christians think of heaven, as the place where Jesus is, as the place to which they have a title, and where they hope to go when they die. But they think not of heaven as a life, and of God's nearness as an experience for every hour of our daily walk. And how many who think of Jesus as the blessed One in whom they are there, by imputation, but know not of Him as lifting them and their whole life into heaven, and, by the Holy Spirit, bringing heaven into them.

2. Every priest has his temple, where he receives the worshippers, and leads them to find the God they seek. Jesus must have a temple too. The heavens are the true sanctuary. Do not attempt to separate between the priest and the place of his dwelling. As His life in heaven is the life of our heart, we know the power of His priesthood.

LX.

The Priest-King, the Mediator of the New Covenant

VIII.–6. But now hath he obtained a ministry the more excellent, by how much also he is the mediator of a better covenant, which hath been enacted upon better promises.

7. For if that first covenant had been faultless, then would no place have been sought for a second.

8. For finding fault with them, he saith,
Behold the days come, saith the Lord,
That I will make a new covenant with the house of Israel and with the house of Judah;

9. Not according to the covenant that I made with their fathers;
In the day I took them by the hand to lead them forth out of the land of Egypt;
For they continued not in my covenant,
And I regarded them not, saith the Lord.

In our chapter there are two titles given to our Priest-King, describing two functions which He discharges. The one is, **a Minister of the sanctuary,** the other, **the Mediator of the better covenant.** The Epistle, having mentioned the sanctuary in which Christ ministers, is about to proceed in the next chapter with the work that Christ did in opening and entering the sanctuary with His own blood. He does not, without good reason, first interpose here the member of the new covenant and Christ's work as its Mediator. The two designations, **Minister of the sanctuary, Mediator of the new covenant,** represent two aspects of Christ's work which are the complement of each other, and which are each necessary to the right understanding of the other. The sanctuary is God's dwelling; the **Minister of the sanctuary** has specially to do with bringing us nigh to God, and the blessedness we find there. The covenant deals with our relation and duty towards God; **the Mediator of the covenant** has specially to do with our preparation for entering the sanctuary, and being made fit to meet God.

In chapter vii. we heard that Jesus is **the surety of a better covenant.** We said there that a covenant is meant to define the mutual relation of the two contracting parties, and to secure the fulfilment of their engagements to each other. In the passage from Jeremiah quoted in our chapter we are told that the covenant God made with Israel, when He brought them up out of Egypt, was not faultless, and that therefore a second was needed. The fault or insufficiency of the first—its weakness and unprofitableness (vii. 18)—would be avoided in the new. A different provision would be made **The fault** of the old covenant is **stated to be** (ver. 9): **They continued not in My covenant, and I regarded them not.** Israel began well, and **accepted the covenant,** and promised obedience. **But they continued not.** There was no power to continue; no power to conquer temptation, or the evil heart; to remain faithful. Against this the new covenant would provide, because it was better, enacted in better promises. It would, by the blood of Christ, provide such an actual putting away and cleansing of sin that God would actually **remember them no more for ever.** With this He would, by His Holy Spirit, so **put His laws into their heart** that they should delight in doing them. God would Himself work both to will and to do. And then, in this power of Christ's blood and the renewal of the Holy Spirit, they would no longer be dependent on men for their knowledge of God, but have direct access and direct intercourse with Him. They would, in spiritual reality, draw nigh to God in the Holiest of All.

This is the new, the better covenant, of which Jesus was to be the Mediator. It is easy now to see of what importance it is that the Epistle should here introduce this name and function of our blessed Lord, the Mediator of the new covenant. When the message comes to us of drawing nigh to God, of entering into the Holiest and abiding there, the thought always comes that our sinful, faithless hearts render it impossible. It would be very easy, we say, and very blessed to dwell all the day consciously in God's presence, if we could all the day remain occupied with spiritual things. But we cannot—our earthly duties render unbroken communion an impossibility. And if it be said that, if we trust this to Jesus, He will care for us, even when we have to be occupied with earthly things, the answer comes again: But oh, the sinfulness of our heart! Ere we know, tempers and dispositions come which must bring a cloud; to abide always in the light of God, not only to enter God's presence, but to continue there—it is not possible!

Come and listen. **But they continued not in My covenant.** This is the experience of the old covenant, to which there now can be an end. The whole provision of the new covenant is to fit us for continuing in it, for abiding continually. It is indeed true that the sanctuary is the dwelling-place of the Holy One, the Holiest of All, and that sinning clouds God's presence. There must be correspondence, harmony, between the sanctuary, with the God that dwells there, and the worshipper. But it is for this very purpose that Jesus, **the Minister of the true sanctuary,** is also the **Mediator of the new covenant.** He engages so to reveal the power of His blood and the boldness of access it gives thee, so to put God's law into thy heart in that power of an endless life in which He does all His priestly work, so to fit thee to know the Lord, that thou shalt indeed know that as **Minister of the sanctuary** He does in very truth secure thy entrance and thy abiding there. The work done by Jesus in the heavenly sanctuary must have its counterpart in the heart that is to enter that sanctuary.

And because it is one Jesus who is both Minister of the new sanctuary and Mediator of the new covenant, we may be confident that He will do His work in our heart as effectually as He does it in heaven. And, therefore, the deeper our insight into the perfection of His work in heaven above, the more confident our expectation may be of the perfection in our life within.

1. *Let us pray God very earnestly that as we now proceed to study the* better *promises of the* better *covenant, our hearts may be opened to receive them in all their fulness.*

2. *"No omnipotence can make you partaker of the life of the outward world without having the life of this outward world born in your own creaturely being. And therefore no omnipotence can make you a partaker of the beatific life in presence of the Holy Trinity, unless that life stands in the same triune state* within you *that it does without you."*

3. *A heavenly sanctuary and a heavenly High Priest ask for a heavenly Christian and a heavenly heart. And this is what the new covenant promises, and the Mediator of the new covenant gives indeed.*

LXI.

The Central Blessing of the New Covenant—
the Law Written in the Heart

VIII.–10. For this is the covenant that I will make with the house
of Israel after these days, saith the Lord;
  I will put my laws into their mind,
  And on their hearts also will I write them.

We have seen what the fault was of the old covenant, **But they
continued not in My covenant.** We have seen that the one object of the new covenant is to repair the fault of the old. There is
henceforth no more need of the word, **But they continued not.**
The one distinguishing characteristic of the new covenant is to
be, There is grace for those who enter it to continue. The great
mark of the priest after the order of Melchizedek is—**He
abideth continually.** The great mark of each of His people is
meant to be too—**He abideth continually.**

But are we not, some one will say, all living under the new
covenant, and yet is not the ordinary experience of Christians
still the same as of old, **But they continued not?** Alas, it is so.
And how, then, with the provision of the covenant? Is it really
to be taken so literally? And if so, has not the new covenant
failed just as the old did, of securing the continual obedience
God desired? The answer will be found in what we have more
than once pointed out. The Hebrews were Christians under the
new covenant, but with their life in the old. The new covenant
does not do violence to man's will. It is only where the heart sees
and believes what God has promised, and is ready at any cost to

291

claim and possess it, that any blessing can be realised. With most Christians there is not even the intellectual belief that God means His promise literally. They are so sure that their views of man's sinfulness and the necessity of always sinning are correct, that the teaching of God's word in regard to His purpose to make an end of the **but they continued not** can never enter the mind. Others there are who accept the truth, but through unbelief enter not into the full possession. And the whole state of the Church of Christ is such that but few live in the full experience of what the covenant means.

Let us meditate on its promises, and specially on its chief promise, its central blessing, **I will put My laws in their mind, and write them in their hearts,** in the adoring faith of our great High Priest upon the throne, who as Mediator of the new covenant is its surety that every word will be made true. It is in Him, whom He hath by oath appointed Priest in the power of an endless life, that God says: **This is the covenant I will make after these days: I will put my laws into their mind and write them in their hearts.** In chapter 7 (ver. 16) we saw what the difference is between an external law and an inner life. The one is impotent, the other mighty. And we saw how even God's law failed of securing obedience, because the heart was not right. The promise of the new covenant is to convert the external law into an inner life, to put it so in the heart that it shall be its inmost life, so that, as naturally as the heart wills and lives and acts on earth, it shall will and live and do what God demands. Why does an acorn so spontaneously grow up into an oak? Because the law of the oak is written in the heart of the acorn. The life of every creature acts with delight in accordance with the law of its Creator, that is, its inner nature. God and His holiness, Christ and His Holy Spirit, if they belong to us, must be as near to us, as essentially within us, as truly inherent in our own life, as our own thinking, willing, and feeling. And so God promises that He will put His law in our minds and write it in our hearts, in such a way that it shall be our inner nature, our very life, and we shall act according to it as naturally as we think or live. Yes, He will do it. So that we can say, even as His Son did, *Thy law is within My heart; I delight to do thy will, O God.*

This is the covenant I will make, saith the Lord. And God hath given His own Son with an oath to be of that covenant the surety! And of that covenant He, the High Priest upon the throne, is the Mediator! Oh, what think you? Will God fail in the very thing the covenant was devised to provide? Will He disappoint us in the one thing in which, as it deals with our experience, the new covenant is to be better than the old? In the one thing His heart and our heart longs for, to serve Him in righteousness and holiness all the days of our life—is this one thing the very thing we are not to realise? God forbid. He hath said— **This is the covenant I will make;** and He will do it.

Let us look up to the Mediator of the Covenant, our High Priest upon the throne in the heavens. When He was with His disciples on earth, the law was not yet *put into* their hearts. How often they failed in humility and love and boldness. But when He sat down upon the throne, He sent down the Holy Spirit from heaven in their hearts, and all was new. They were full of humility and love and great boldness. The law of God was in their hearts as the power of a life that knew, and loved, and did His will. Christ dwelt in their hearts by faith. The power of the endless life from the throne of God had taken possession of them. Oh, let us not doubt. Let us plead God's promise, **I will make a new covenant.** Let us trust God's Son, the surety of the covenant, and receive God's Spirit—we shall be brought into the covenant, and into the sanctuary together, and have grace to *continue,* to *abide continually.*

1. Just as truly as there is a sanctuary above, there is a sanctuary within. In the old sanctuary the chief object in the Holiest of All was the law, in the ark covered by the mercy-seat sprinkled with blood. It is the law written in the heart sprinkled with the blood that makes it a sanctuary. It is the heart that is thus made a sanctuary that enters the true sanctuary.

2. Is not the reason that some who seek earnestly, fail of the blessing, that they seek to grasp it in their own power, and do not yield to the Holy Spirit to work it in them. It is God who says, I will make the covenant. He must by His mighty operation do it in each heart. Our place is deep dependence, patient waiting, and implicit reliance on His mighty power.

3. Remember that all He has to do as Mediator of the new covenant, He does because He is Minister of the true sanctuary. He sends out of the sanctuary the Spirit of heaven into our hearts—it is this that puts God's law within us.

4. The whole law is fulfilled in one word: Thou shalt love. Where the love of God is shed abroad in the heart by the Holy Ghost, the law of love is written in the heart.

5. The soul of man hath no other near or far from God, but as its will unites with God's will, and worketh with it.

LXII.

The Crowning Blessing of the New Covenant—Fellowship with God

VIII.–10. And I will be to them a God,
    And they shall be to me a people:
11. And they shall not teach every man his fellow-citizen,
    And every man his brother, saying, Know the Lord:
    For all shall know me,
    From the least to the greatest of them.

God created man to find his blessedness in Himself. This is the nobility and the greatness of man, that he has a heart capable of fellowship with God, a heart so great that nothing less than God can really satisfy it. This is held out to him as his highest blessedness through eternity.

There is but one thing can hinder the fellowship, and that is sin. Where there is no sin, the creature lives in the Creator as naturally as a bird in the air, or a fish in the water. For this reason the two promises of the new covenant go together as cause and effect: **I will write My law in their hearts,** and, **I will be to them a God, and they shall know Me.** The deliverance from the evil, wandering heart, will be followed by close personal access to God. **They shall not teach every man his brother, Know the Lord: for all shall know Me, from the least to the greatest of them.**

Personal, direct fellowship with God: this is the crowning blessing of the new covenant, to which the Epistle to the Hebrews very specially points the way. In Israel only the priests might enter the Holy Place: thence they went out again to teach the people. Into the Most Holy only the High Priest might come. In Christ every believer has access to the Holiest of All. Christ hath redeemed us, not to bring us to Himself, but to bring us to God. He is the door, in which we are not to remain standing, but through which we enter to God Himself, to His heart and His love. **God, having spoken in past times in the prophets, hath now spoken in His Son;** in Him there is an immediate living fellowship with the living God. All that the Epistle has to teach of the rending of the veil, and our boldness in the blood, and the entrance into the Holiest of All—it has all to do with this one thing, direct personal living fellowship with the living God. As the **Minister of the true sanctuary** Jesus sends the Spirit from thence to do the work He has in our heart as Mediator of the covenant, and prepare us to enter the sanctuary. As **Mediator of the covenant** He then reveals Himself more fully as the **Minister of the sanctuary,** who does indeed bring us nigh to God.

And how does He do this? In the way in which He Himself entered there, the way of obedience. **I will write My law in their hearts, and they shall know Me.** The law written on the heart is the condition of fellowship with God. "Without holiness no man shall see the Lord." "Blessed are the pure in heart for they shall see God." "Thy will be done on earth as it is in heaven." To be brought by the heavenly High Priest within the veil, and dwell before God's face, we must learn to do His will on earth as it is done in heaven. This is the true heavenly-mindedness that renders us capable of fellowship with the God of heaven. Union with God's will was the way by which Jesus entered. Union with God's will is the way by which Jesus brings us in to the love and the joy of the Father.

And how, again, do we obtain this double blessedness—of the law written in the heart, and the entrance into God's presence in Jesus? It is God must do it. It is He who sware to Abraham—**Blessing I will bless.** It is He who sware to our High

Priest—**Thou art a Priest for ever.** It is God Himself who will fulfil His oath. Jesus is not now on the throne to take the place of God, to be to us instead of God. Verily no; He brings us *to God.* Through Him we draw nigh to God, that God may perfect His work in us. Our first access to God in the pardon of sin, ere yet we know what the access of abiding fellowship is, has this one sole object that God may reveal His Son in us, so that we look up to and love and serve the Father, even as the Son did. And so the one thing required of us is, that we bow ourselves and abide and live in deep dependence and humility before God. However clearly we see the blessed truth of the promises of the new covenant, however earnestly we desire them, however firmly we think we grasp them as faith, all will not avail— God Himself must do it. God Himself must admit to His presence, and make His face to shine upon us. And as the path to this, God Himself must write His law in our hearts, give us the new nature in such power of the Holy Spirit, that He works both to will and to do. God Himself must by the Holy Ghost so shed abroad His love in our hearts, that to love becomes as natural to us as it is for the dove to be gentle. God has promised on His oath to do this for us, in Jesus the surety of the new covenant. It is God who strengthens us mightily by His Spirit, then gives Christ to dwell in our hearts by faith; it is in God that we are rooted in love; and then—this is the full entrance into His presence in the Holiest of All—then filled with all the fulness of God.

Once again, how do we obtain this double blessedness of the law of God written in the heart, and the presence of God filling our life? There is no way but utterly ceasing from ourselves, dying to self, and waiting in absolute dependence and deep humility upon God. Christ's priesthood is not of earth but of heaven. All means and ordinances, all thoughts and purposes in man are but the shadows of the heavenly things. It is from God in heaven that the heavenly life must come, through Christ who brings us nigh to Him. And Christ cannot bring us nigh to God, cannot make our drawing nigh acceptable in any other way than by working in our heart a faith, and love, and obedience which are pleasing to Him; that is, by His fulfilling, as Mediator of the new covenant, its promises within us. This brings us to the true knowledge of God.

1. *If you would realise the need of absolute dependence upon God, and His direct operation, I know not of anything that will be more helpful than to read what William Law says on humility, meekness, patience, and resignation to God's will, as the one only and infallible way to God. See "The Spirit of Love," Part II., Third Dialogue (WHOLLY FOR GOD, pars. 29–38).*

2. When He had effected the cleansing of sins, He sat down on the right hand of the Majesty on high. *The removal of sin is the path to God's presence with Christ and with us.*

LXIII.

The Initial Blessing of the New Covenant—the Pardon of Sin

VIII.–12. For I will be merciful to their iniquities,
   And their sins will I remember no more.
13. In that he saith, A new covenant, he hath made the first old.
But that which is becoming old and waxeth aged is nigh unto
vanishing away.

Of the blessings of the new covenant, the one which is here
mentioned last is in reality the first. **For I will be merciful—**
this is what precedes, and is the ground of the renewal of the
heart and the fellowship with God. *Pardon* is the door; *holiness
of heart and life* the pathway; the *presence of God* the blessedness
of the Christian life. The first leads to the second, the first and
second to the third. To live in God's presence and fellowship
two things must be clear: the thought of sin must be put away
out of God's heart, and the love of sin out of our heart. These
two blessings are together secured in the new covenant. First,
the forgiveness of sins so complete, that He remembers them no
more for ever; they never more enter into God's heart. And, second, the renewal of our heart and will so complete, that the law
of God is written there by the Holy Spirit, so that the will of God
is our will.

   The three blessings—the pardon of sin, purity of heart, and
the presence of God—are so joined, that as our views and our
acceptance of one is feeble, our hold on the others will suffer. In
Jesus the Mediator of the new covenant they are offered and se-

cured to us in their fulness, in the power of an endless life. But our experience of this depends upon our knowledge, our faith, our surrender. And it is because our understanding and acceptance and experience of the two first blessings is so defective that our fellowship with God, our entrance into the holy presence, and our abiding there, is still so much in Old Testament failure—**But they continued not.** Let us try and realise this.

Take the first of the three covenant blessings: **I will be merciful to their iniquities, and their sins will I remember no more.** In more than one respect the Christian's thought of what this pardon is may be defective. With some it is nothing more than the remission of punishment. They think only of acquittal; they know not that it implies acceptance, complete restoration to the favour, to the heart and the home of the Father. They are content with pardon, as the escape from a great danger; of the surrender to, and the life abiding in the love that pardoned, they know little. With others the thought of pardon is mostly connected with individual or with daily sin. They have no conception of the entire and eternal putting away of sin out of God's sight and thought, which is assured to us in the words: **Their sins will I remember no more.** And with still others, whose views may be more accurate, the pardon of God exercises so little power, because it has been accepted more with the mind than the heart. They consent to and claim what God's word says of it; but have never, mostly owing to the want of any deep sense of sin, or any powerful workings of the Holy Spirit, realised the overwhelming glory of God's mercy as they came to Himself to receive from His own mouth the pardon of their sins. In all these cases the farther blessings are scarce understood or sought, or if claimed, their full meaning and power are never known.

It is even so with the second covenant blessing. There are not a few who know indeed what the greatness of God's pardoning love is, who yet never reach out to claim, as equally sure, the greatness of His sanctifying grace. The necessity of daily sinning, the impossibility of living for one day without actual transgression is such a deeply-rooted conviction, and there is such confidence that God's word teaches it, that the mind cannot for a moment enter into what the word has said of the radical difference between the old covenant and the new in this respect. The confounding the freedom from any sinful tendency, and freedom in the power of Christ's indwelling from actual sinning, even with the sinful tendency still remaining, is so universal, that every attempt to press home the promise of the law written in the heart, in its contrast to the Old Testament life, is regarded as dangerous. The wonderful promise is levelled down to the ordinary experience of the ordinary Christian life. No wonder then that the crowning promise, **They shall not every man teach his brother, Know the Lord,** with its direct teaching of the Holy Spirit, and its direct fellowship with God through the Spirit, is neither valued nor claimed, and the entrance through the rent veil into the Holiest of All and the presence of God postponed to another world.

Let us pray the Father *to give us enlightened eyes of the heart, to know what is the hope of His calling,* to a life in His love and will, *and what the riches of the glory of His inheritance in* the saints—the direct and full access to His presence and fellowship, *and what the exceeding greatness of His power in us who believe, according to the working of His mighty power which He wrought in Christ, when He raised Him from the dead and set Him on His own right hand.* Let us believe that that exaltation of Christ out of the dead to His throne, and the assurance that that same mighty power works in us, means, even for this earth, a life of heavenly power and joy, of holiness and happiness which it hath not entered into the heart to conceive. Jesus, the Priest-King on the throne, is **the surety of the covenant.** Let us, like Him, yield ourselves to that death to sin and to self, out of which God raised Him. Let us sink into the death of emptiness and nothingness and helplessness; let us, as dead, wait for the mighty operation of God. He who gave Jesus as Mediator of the new covenant, and surety for its promises, will reveal Him, and fulfil them in us, will bring us in Him within the veil, and give us our life there in the secret of His blessed presence.

1. *Pardon of sin is the door, the entrance to the Father's home. The law in the heart is the life and walk there, the fitness to draw nigh to God. Direct fellowship with God; this is the blessedness to be found in God's presence.*

2. *All the three blessings in Him the surety of the covenant. In Him our justification and the assurance that our sins no more come up before Him. In Him our santification, with the Holy Spirit breathing His will into our very heart. In Him our complete redemption, the fitness to dwell in God's presence for evermore.*

The Power of Christ's Blood in the Opening of
the New Sanctuary and the New Covenant

LXIV.

The Holy Place and the Most Holy

IX.–1. Now even the first covenant had ordinances of divine service, and its sanctuary, a sanctuary of this world.

2. For there was a tabernacle prepared, the first, wherein were the candlestick, and the table, and the shewbread; which is called the Holy Place.

3. And after the second veil, the tabernacle which is called the Holy of Holies.

4. Having a golden censer, and the ark of the covenant overlaid round about with gold, wherein was a golden pot holding the manna, and Aaron's rod that budded, and the tables of the covenant;

5. And above it cherubim of glory overshadowing the mercy-seat; of which things we cannot now speak severally.

6. Now these things having been thus prepared, the priests go in continually into the first tabernacle, accomplishing the services;

7. But into the second, the high priest alone, once in the year, not without blood, which he offereth for himself, and for the errors of the people.

In chapter vii. the eternal priesthood of Jesus has been revealed to us. In chapter viii. we have seen Him, as Priest seated on the throne of heaven in His twofold work. He is the Minister of the sanctuary in the heavens. He is the Mediator of the covenant in the heart of man on earth. We thus know the Priest and the sanctuary in which He ministers; we are now invited in this chapter to look at the blood which He presents, and what it effects. The word Blood has not yet been used: in this chapter we have it twelve times. In the first half (1–14) we have its efficacy in opening the most holy place, and in sprinkling our conscience to enter there; then (15–22) in dedicating the covenant, and cleansing all connected with it; and after that again in opening heaven and putting away all sin (23–28).

The first portion begins with a description of the worldly sanctuary, the tabernacle and its furniture, *of which things,* the writer says, *we cannot now speak severally.* Just as he said, in chapter viii. 1, *This is the chief point: we have such an High Priest,* so here too, in speaking of the sanctuary, he has one great thought which he wishes to press home. The tabernacle was so constructed by Moses, after the heavenly pattern, as specially to shadow forth one great truth. In that truth lies the mystery and the glory of the New Testament, the power and joy of the Christian life. That truth is the opening of the way into the Holiest, the access into the presence of God.

We read: **There was a tabernacle prepared, the first, which is called the Holy Place. And after the second veil, the tabernacle which is called the Holy of Holies. The priests go in continually into the first tabernacle, accomplishing the service; but into the second, the high priest alone, once in the year, not without blood.** The one thing the writer wishes to direct our attention to is the difference and the relation between the two compartments into which the tabernacle was divided, and the meaning of the veil that separated them.

The inner sanctuary was called the Holiest of All, or, as it is in Hebrew, the Holiness of Holinesses. It was the highest embodiment there could be of holiness; it was the place where God Most Holy dwelt. His holy presence filled it. No man might enter there on pain of death but the high priest, and even he only once a year. In the Holy Place, separated from the Most Holy by a heavy veil, the priests entered and served. The truths embodied in the house thus made after a heavenly pattern were very simple. In the Most Holy God dwelt, but man might not enter. In the Holy Place man might enter to serve God, but God dwelt not there. The veil was the symbol of separation between a holy God and sinful man: they cannot dwell together. The tabernacle thus expressed the union of two apparently conflicting truths. God called man to come and worship and serve Him, and yet he might not come too near: the veil kept him at a distance. His worship in the tabernacle testified to his longing for the restoration to the fellowship with God he had lost in paradise, but also to his unfitness for it, and his inability to attain it. The two truths find their reason and their harmony in the holiness of God, that highest attribute of the divine Being. In it righteousness and love are combined. Love calls the sinner near; righteousness keeps him back. The Holy One bids Israel build Him a house in which He will dwell, but forbids them entering His presence there. The entrance of the high priest once a year for a few moments was a faint foreshadowing that the time would come when access to the Holiest would be given. In the fulness of time righteousness and love would be revealed in their perfect harmony in Him, in whom those types and shadows would find their fulfilment.

The first and second tabernacles are the symbols of two degrees of the divine nearness, two stages of access to God's presence, two modes of fellowship with God, two ways of serving Him. The one, to which the High Priest had access only once a year, is the promise of what would one day be in Christ: the nearer, the more direct and immediate approach into the presence and fellowship of God. The other is the symbol of the service of God as at a distance with a veil between, without the full light of His countenance. The one thing the writer wants us to learn is the difference between the two stages, and the way by which God leads us from the lower to the higher.

1. Of which things we cannot now speak severally, one by one. There is a time for doing this too. But when souls are to be led on into the perfection of Christ and His work, we must turn then from the multiplicity of truths to the simplicity and unity of one truth, that Christ has opened heaven. Let this be our one question, What has the heavenly High Priest effected for me?

2. I know what Christ has done. I need to know what He had to do. There was a Holy Place into which man might enter. There was a Most Holy into which he might not enter. The veil shut him out. And Christ's one work was to tear down that veil, and give us the right and the fitness to enter, yea to dwell always in that heretofore inaccessible place. The mystery of the rent veil, *of the opened entrance into the Holiest, is the one thing we need to learn.*

LXV.

The Holy Spirit and the Way into the Holiest

IX.–8. The Holy Ghost this signifying, that the way into the Holy Place hath not yet been made manifest, while as the first tabernacle is yet standing;

9. Which is a parable for the time now present; according to which are offered both gifts and sacrifices that cannot, as touching the conscience, make the worshipper perfect,

10. Being only (with meats and drinks and divers washings) carnal ordinances imposed until a time of reformation.

We said that *the Holiest of All,* or, as it is literally, the Holiness of Holinesses, was the very embodiment of the holiness of God, the place of His presence. *The Holy Spirit* specially bears the epithet Holy, because He is the bearer of the divine holiness to impart it to man—He is the Spirit of holiness. It will appear no more than natural that there should be a close connection between the sanctuary as the revelation of God's holiness, and the Holy Spirit as the revealer. This is what we are taught here: the whole construction of the tabernacle and the appointment of the high priest's entrance once a year was so ordered by the Holy Spirit as to be a great object-lesson in which the truth was taught that so long as the veil hung there, the way into the Holiest was not yet open. **The Holy Spirit signifying that the way into the Holiest was not yet opened.** The words teach us that the truth about the way into the Holiest was entirely in charge of the Holy Spirit. It was He who devised and revealed to Moses the heavenly pattern. It was He who ordered the veil as the to-ken that the way was not open. It was He who, by the yearly entrance of the high priest, gave the prophecy that it would one day be opened. It was He who prepared a body for Him, and later on filled Him who was to be the opener of the way. It was He, the Eternal Spirit, through whom Christ offered Himself as the sacrifice with whose blood He might enter in. It was He, the Spirit of holiness (Rom. i. 4), through whom Christ was raised from the dead and exalted to the throne of God. It was the Holy Spirit who, when the way had been opened, came out from the Holiest of All on the day of Pentecost, to impart to men the life and the power of the glorified Christ. It is He who today still presides over the way into the Holiest, leading in all who are willing to dwell there.

The lesson for our spiritual life is one of deep suggestiveness. The Holy Spirit has charge of the way into the Holiest; both while that way is not yet manifest and when it is opened up. He alone hath the knowledge and the power to reveal this mystery. For it is still a spiritual mystery. Though everything that Scripture reveals of it can be studied and understood by any man of intelligence, and a clear conception can be formed, or an exposition given of what it means, the living power of the truth, the actual experience of entering in through the opened veil into the presence of God, can only be communicated and wrought in the life within by the Holy Spirit. The Holy Spirit alone can reveal in the heart what the way means, both where it is not yet made manifest, and where it is. He can work in a man the deep conviction that he does, or does not know, the true nearness of God in his own experience.

We have seen that the two compartments of the tabernacle represent two degrees of nearness to God, two dispensations of God's grace, or two stages in the Christian life, a lower and a higher. Into the Holy Place every priest might come daily to do there the service God had appointed. Into the Most Holy he might not enter till Christ had opened it for all believers. Many believers never in experience enter into this life of the inner sanctuary, the more complete and abiding nearness to God. They have, in the outer court, seen the altar, and received the pardon of sin; they have entered upon the service of God, they seek to do His will, but the joy of His presence as their abiding portion they know not. And very often they do not know that there is a better life, that there is an entering within the veil, a real dwelling in the secret of God's presence; the need that the Holy Spirit signify to them, work in them the conviction that to them the way into the Holiest hath not yet been made manifest. They need—oh let us, if we have not yet entered in, let us give ourselves to pray for—the discovery that there is an inner chamber; that there is still the veil of the flesh, the life of the carnal Christian, that prevents the access; that only the possession of the Pentecostal blessing, the Spirit that came from the throne when Jesus had rent the veil, that reveals Him and links to Him, is what will bring us in.

When He has signified this to us, and we yield ourselves to the full conviction that we are still without the veil, and strong desire has been awakened at any cost to enter in, the same Spirit who at Pentecost, when our High Priest had just entered with His blood, came forth from the Holiest of All, will come to us in power and bring us in too. As He reveals Jesus Himself as having gone in for us; as He makes us willing for that perfect surrender, in which nothing less than the direct and continual fellowship with God can satisfy us; our hearts will open to the wondrous mystery, that what is impossible to men is possible with God, and that God of His free grace and in His mighty power does indeed grant it to His child, even now in Christ, to dwell with Him in unbroken communion.

O God! let the Holy Spirit witness to every reader who needs it, that to him the way into the Holiest hath not yet been made manifest; and to everyone who is ready for it, that in Christ the way into the Holiest is indeed open. With Pentecost, and the participation it brought of the Spirit of the glorified Jesus, began true Christianity, as a ministration of the Spirit. The enjoyment of the Pentecostal gift, as the communication of the heavenly life and the abiding presence of Jesus the glorified One, in all its Pentecostal freshness and fulness, is the only power that can enable us to live within the veil, in the living experience that the way into the Holiest has now been opened. It is the Spirit dwelling in us will fit us for dwelling in God's presence.

1. *Shall we any longer fear and doubt? The Father in heaven beckoning us into His presence; the Son, our Brother, Prophet, Priest, and King, pointing to the way He opened for us and the Holy Spirit within us to be our light and strength, to enable us to walk in that way—shall we fear? No, let us hear the voice that gives the power: Rise up and walk. Enter in.*

2. *Do get it very clear that the two compartments are two stages in religious life and worship and service. The one when the power of the rent veil is not yet understood; the other where the Holy Spirit has brought us in.*

LXVI.

The Opening Up of the Holiest

IX.–11. But Christ having come a High Priest of the good things to come, through the greater and more perfect tabernacle, that is to say, not of this creation,

12. Nor yet through the blood of goats and calves, but through his own blood, entered in once for all into the Holy Place, having obtained eternal redemption.

In studying the meaning of the Mosaic ritual, there are specially four things, through which the Holy Spirit shadows forth to us the mysteries of redemption, the good things to come of the new dispensation that Israel was to look for. These are the Priest, the Sanctuary, the Blood, and the Way into the Holiest. We have these four things here together. There is **Christ the High Priest of the good things to come,** there is **the greater and more perfect tabernacle,** there is **His own blood,** and there is His **entering in** into the Holiest. As we apprehend the power of these things, we shall know the meaning of **His having obtained eternal redemption.** Let us hear what the Holy Spirit speaks of the opening up the Holiest, and the wonderful path in which that was effected.

The writer uses a very remarkable expression, **Christ through the greater and more perfect tabernacle, entered into the Holiest.** The two compartments of the sanctuary are the symbols of two states of life, two degrees of fellowship with God. The Epistle teaches us that Christ knew this difference in His own life experience, and, in entering into and opening up the higher one for us, passed through the lower. He entered into the Holiest **through the greater and more perfect tabernacle,** through the experience of that spiritual reality of which the tabernacle was the shadow. The Holiest is God's immediate presence, the Holy Place a drawing nigh to God with a veil between. The flesh, man's fallen nature in its weakness and its exposure to all the consequences of sin, is the veil. Christ has dedicated for us a new and living way **through the veil, that is to say, His flesh.** When He came in the likeness of sinful flesh, that life in flesh, with its liability to temptation, and its weakness, with its possibility of suffering and death, with its life of faith and prayer and tears, with its need of learning obedience and being made perfect, with its subjection to the law and its curse, was the Holy Place, the first tabernacle, through which He had to pass to have the veil rent in His death, so to enter in and appear before God. Christ lived with His people in the Old Testament; He passed through the first tabernacle as a spiritual experience in perfect reality; it was only with His resurrection and ascension the New Testament began.

Yes, Christ passed from the Holy Place into the Holiest of All. When He died the veil was rent in twain; the two compartments were made one. The priest who was in the Holy Place could see, could enter into the Holiest. All that was in the Holiest, the light of God's presence between the cherubim, could shine unhindered into the Holy Place. In Christ the veil of the flesh was rent asunder and taken away. The free access to God was opened up, not only as a thing of right and title in virtue of our pardon, but as a thing of power and living reality. *Ye are not in the flesh, but in the Spirit, if so be the Spirit of Christ dwelleth in you.* When the veil was rent and Christ entered in, the two abodes, what had been the dwelling of God, and what had been the dwelling of the priests, were thrown into one. The eyes and the hearts of men might freely and boldly look up and rise up and greet their God and Father; in Christ they had their place before Him. All the light and love and holiness of the Most Holy shone into the Holy Place. The Spirit of God, as He was received by Christ from God the Father on His ascension, passed down into the worshippers. The Pentecostal gift brought down, from above, the higher life into which the blessed Son had entered; the Holy Spirit made the light and love and holiness of the inner sanctuary not only a vision, a revelation, but a possession and an experience.

The veil of the flesh has been rent; Christ has entered once for all, having obtained everlasting redemption; the dwelling of God and man has been thrown into one; the Spirit of heaven has been given to signify to us, and to give us the living experience, that **the way into the Holiest has been made manifest.** Our entering in, our dwelling in God's presence in the light and nearness and holiness of the Most Holy, is a spiritual, a heavenly reality. It can only be apprehended by the tender, by the perfect conscience, which the Holy Spirit gives to him who is willing to give up all to be saved completely, by the perfect whose senses are exercised to discern good and evil. But to all who are willing to pass through the rent veil of Christ's flesh, to die with Him as He died, and live with Him as He lived, the Holy Spirit will show it; the way into the Holiest is opened up.

Christ having come, entered in once for all. Four thousand years after man's loss of fellowship with God in paradise had to pass. Fifteen hundred years the veil had to hang with its solemn injunction not to draw near. Thirty-three years the Son of God Himself had to live on this side of the veil. But at length, once for all and for ever, the way was opened. Fear not, O Christian, to whom these things appear too high, fear not. Be thou faithful, through faith and longsuffering we inherit the promises. Persevere in the faith of what Christ has accomplished **once for all.** He entered in, the Second Adam, in whom our life is, whose members we are. Persevere in the faith of the infinite meaning of that great transaction. And to thee, too, will come a day when, in thy experience, thou shalt enter, and go out no more for ever.

1. This entering in and opening up of the Holiest was solely and entirely on our behalf, that we might live and serve there. *Therefore—the practical part of the Epistle commences at once—therefore,* having boldness to enter *into the Holiest,* let us draw nigh. *That is the summing up of the whole Epistle. God is not content that we should serve Him with a veil between. Let us know clearly which of the two positions we occupy as Christians—within or still without the veil.*

2. *"After I had lived for thirteen years in the Holy Place, seeking to serve God there, it pleased Him, who dwelleth between the cherubim, to call me to* pass through *the veil, and to enter the Holiest of All, through the blood of Jesus."*

LXVII.

The Power of Christ's Blood to Open the Holiest

IX.–12. But Christ, through his own blood, entered in once for all into the Holy Place, having obtained eternal redemption.

Through His own blood. We have seen our great High Priest on the throne of God, a Priest after the order of Melchizedek, in the power of an endless life. When He rose from the dead and ascended into heaven, it was according to that working of the strength of His might, whereby God had raised Him from the dead and set Him at His own right hand. He entered God's presence as the living One who was dead, and behold, He lives for evermore. And yet, strange to say, it was not enough that He should present Himself at the gate of heaven as the conqueror of death and hell, and ask admission. He had to take with Him **His own blood,** as it had been shed upon earth, as the power by which alone, as the surety of sinners, He could claim access to the presence of God. **Through His own blood Christ entered the Holiest of All.**

And what does this word, **His own blood,** mean? To Moses God had said that He gave *the blood upon the altar to be an atonement, because the blood is the life.* That is, the living blood in the body is the life. And the shed blood? That means death. More than that, it means an unnatural, a violent death. There are only two ways in which this unnatural blood-shedding comes: by malice or by justice. We have the two together in the words:

Whoso sheddeth man's blood, by man shall his blood be shed. In the death of Christ the malice of men and the righteousness of God met. He was slain, a sacrifice to the evil passions of men, because He resisted unto blood, striving against sin. He was slain, a sacrifice unto God, because He was the Lamb of God that taketh away the sin of the world. Death is inseparably connected with sin, and the curse which God pronounced upon it. When Jesus, as the Second Adam, tasted death for all; when, in Gethsemane, He with strong crying and tears besought His Father that the cup might pass from Him; when on the cross He cried, *My God! My God! why hast thou forsaken Me?* He tasted death in all its bitterness, both as the terrible fruit of sin, the revelation of what sin is in its very nature, and as the penalty God had attached to it. He died, as Scripture says, the just for the unjust; He bore our sins; His blood was shed for us; He gave His life a ransom for many. And the word "blood" in this Epistle includes all that is meant by the death of Christ; the blood is the expression and embodiment of His obedience unto death, of His death for our sins, of the atonement which He made for us as the victim on the altar, as our Substitute.

It is this blood now, of whose power our Epistle says such wondrous things. It was **in the blood of the eternal covenant that God brought again our Lord Jesus from the dead;** the blood was the power of the resurrection. It was through His blood He **cleansed the heavenly things themselves and entered the Holiest** on our behalf. In those heavenly places our sins were in God's book, our sins had as a thick cloud darkened God's presence; for the sake of the blood the sin was blotted out, and access given to Him, and in Him to us, to appear before the very face of God. And now, in the vision of the heavenly glory to which he has given us access, as we have it later in the Epistle, we find in heaven not only God the Judge of all, and Christ the Mediator of the new covenant, but also **the blood of sprinkling that speaketh better things than that of Abel.**

Everywhere we see, besides and along with Jesus Christ, the living One Himself, in His resurrection, in His entering heaven, in His sitting on the throne, as a separate existence and power, the blood, the symbol of the death in which we have our ransom and redemption.

Through His own blood. Let us specially note how the blood is connected with the heavenly priesthood of Christ. We are too apt to think only of the fulfilment of the type of Aaron, the blood-shedding on earth. The Epistle does not speak of it. Where it mentions the blood, it is in connection with the resurrection and the entrance into heaven, as it works in the power of an endless life. It is as the Holy Spirit reveals this to the soul, *the heavenly power of the blood,* as ministered by our Melchizedek, the minister of the heavenly sanctuary, that we see what a power that blood must have, as so sprinkled on us from heaven, in the power of the Holy Spirit, at once to give us a real, actual, living access into the presence of God.

His own blood. I know of no word in the Bible or in human speech that contains such mysteries! In it are concentrated the mysteries of the incarnation, in which our God took flesh and blood; of the obedience unto death, in which the blood was shed; of the love that passeth knowledge, that purchased us with His own blood; of the victory over every enemy, and the everlasting redemption; of the resurrection and the entrance into heaven; of the atonement and the reconciliation and the justification that came through it; of the cleansing and perfecting of the conscience, of the sprinkling of the heart and the sanctifying the people. Through that blood Christ entered once for all into heaven; through that blood we enter too, and have our home in the Holiest of All. As the Holy Spirit from heaven, dwelling in us, imparts to us the boldness the blood gives, and the love into which it opens the way, our whole inner being will be brought under its power, and the cleansing of the blood in its full extent be our experience.

317

1. *"As in heaven so in earth."* *Thou hast more interest than thou thinkest in knowing what the blood hath wrought in heaven. As thou enterest by the Spirit into its power there, will thy faith receive its power within thee.*

2. *The inner sanctuary—deeper, nearer to God. He that seeks after this will have the inner sanctuary opened within himself. The inner life, the law within the heart, in the inward parts, a deepening sense of the life of God in the soul will be give to such a one.*

3. *There are in Scripture two aspects of Christ's death—that of atonement and that of fellowship. He died for us, for our sin, that we might not die. What our Substitute did in bearing the curse of sin, we cannot do, we need not do. He died to sin, and we died with Him and in Him. The blood is the divine expression for the former aspect:* His own blood *is the power and the worth of His death taken up and presented and for ever preserved in its energy and action before God. The sprinkling with the blood includes the transition to the second aspect. As the blood, as a heavenly reality, through the Holy Spirit works in us, the very disposition that animated Jesus in the shedding of it will be imparted to us.*

4. *Christ can bring us into the Holiest in no other way than He went in Himself,* through His own blood. *Oh, seek to know the power of Christ's blood.*

LXVIII.

The Power of Christ's Blood to Cleanse the Conscience

IX.–13. For if the blood of goats and bulls, and the ashes of a heifer sprinkling them that have been defiled, sanctify unto the cleanness of the flesh:

14. How much more shall the blood of Christ, who through the eternal Spirit offered himself without blemish unto God, cleanse your conscience from dead works to serve the living God?

The High Priest went into the Holiest once a year, **not without blood.** Christ, the High Priest of good things to come, entered the greater and more perfect Holiest of All **through His own blood,** opening up to us in very deed the way into God's presence. The entrance of the high priest on earth effected a certain external and temporary cleansing and liberty of access. The blood of Christ which had power to open heaven, is able to effect, in its heavenly, eternal power, a heavenly, a divine cleansing in the heart.

To illustrate this, we are referred to Numbers xix. and the cleansing with the ashes of the heifer. Anyone who had touched a dead body was unclean, and had to be excluded from the camp. To meet the need, the ashes of a heifer that had been sacrificed, and of which the blood had been sprinkled towards the tabernacle, were mingled with water, and sprinkled on the one who had been defiled. The sprinkling restored him to his place and privileges; with a clear conscience he could now take part in the life and worship of God's people. And the question is asked—If the blood of a sacrifice had such power, **how much more shall the blood of Christ cleanse your conscience to serve the living God?** The infinite efficacy of Christ's blood, and the infinite blessedness of the cleansing it effects, can only be measured by what that blood really is.

The power of Christ's blood consists in two things. The one element that gives the blood its value is, the holy obedience of which its outpouring was the proof; the blood of Christ who **offered Himself without spot unto God.** He came to live the life of man, such as God had meant Him to be, in creating Him. He gave up His will to God, He pleased not Himself but sought only God's pleasure, He yielded His whole life that God might reveal Himself in it as He pleased: **He offered Himself unto God.** He took and filled the place the creature was meant to fill. And that **without spot.** His self-sacrifice was complete and perfect, and His blood, even as the blood of a man, was, in God's sight, inexpressibly precious. It was the embodiment of a perfect obedience. The other element is, that the Eternal Spirit was in the life of that blood. It was **through the Eternal Spirit He offered Himself.** It was the Word that became flesh, the Eternal Son of God who was made man. It was the life of God that dwelt in Him. That life gave His blood, each drop of it, an infinite value. The blood of a man is of more worth than that of a sheep. The blood of a king or a great general is counted of more value than hundreds of common soldiers. The blood of the Son of God!— it is in vain the mind seeks for some expression of its value; all we can say is, it is His own blood, the precious blood of the Son of God!

It was this twofold infinite worth of the blood that gave it such mighty power—first, in opening the grave, and then in opening heaven. It was this gave it the victory over all the powers of death and hell beneath, and gave Him the victor's place on high on the throne of God. And now, when that blood, from out of the heavenly sanctuary, is sprinkled on the conscience by the heavenly High Priest—how much more—with what an infinitely effectual cleansing, must not our conscience be cleansed.

We know what conscience is. It tells us what we are. Conscience deals not only with past merit or guilt but specially with present integrity or falsehood. A conscience fully cleansed with the blood of Christ, fully conscious of its cleansing power, has the sense of guilt and demerit removed to an infinite distance. And no less is it delivered from that haunting sense of insincerity and double-heartedness, which renders boldness of access to God an impossibility. It can look up to God without the shadow of a cloud. The light of God's face, to which the blood gave our Surety access, shines clear on the conscience, and through it on the heart. The conscience is not a separate part of our heart or inner nature, and which can be in a different state from what the whole is. By no means. Just as a sensibility to bodily evil pervades the whole body, so the conscience is the sense which pervades our whole spiritual nature, and at once notices and reports what is wrong or right in our state. Hence it is when the conscience is cleansed or perfected, the heart is cleansed and perfected too. And so it is in the heart that the power the blood had in heaven is communicated here on earth. The blood that brought Christ into God's presence, brings us, and our whole inner being, there too.

Oh, let us realise it. The power of the blood in which Christ entered heaven, is the power in which He enters our hearts. The infinite sufficiency it has with God, to meet His holy requirements, is its sufficiency to meet the requirements of our heart and life. It is the blood of the covenant. Its three great promises—pardon and peace in God's forgetting sin; purity and power in having the law of life in our heart; the presence of God set open to us, are not only secured to us by the blood, but the blood has its part too in communicating them. In the power of the Holy Spirit the blood effects a mighty, divine cleansing, full of heavenly life and energy. The Spirit that was in Christ, when

He shed the blood, makes us partakers of its power. His victory over sin, His perfect obedience, His access to the Father—the soul that fully knows the cleansing of the blood in its power will know these blessings too.

1. The blood that cleanses my conscience is the blood that gave Christ access into the Holiest. If I truly desire, if I know and honour and trust the blood, it will give me access too.

2. How completely every vestige of an evil conscience can be taken away and kept away by the redeeming power of this precious blood! Let us believe that our High Priest, whose entrance into the sanctuary and whose ministry there, is all in the power of the blood, will make it true to us.

3. This cleansing is what is elsewhere spoken of as Christ's washing us in His blood. A piece of linen that is to be washed is steeped and saturated until every stain be taken out. As we in faith and patience allow the blood to possess our whole inner being, we shall know what it means that it washes whiter than snow.

LXIX.

Through the Eternal Spirit

IX.–14. How much more shall the blood of Christ, who through the eternal Spirit offered himself without blemish unto God, cleanse your conscience from dead works to serve the living God?

One might well ask for the reason why the blood of Christ, which hath had such infinite power in conquering sin and death and in opening heaven to Christ and to us, does not exercise a mightier influence even in earnest Christians, in cleansing our heart and lifting us into a life in the joy of God's presence. The first answer must be, that we seek too little for a real insight into its divine and infinite worth. The blood of the heavenly Son, shed in the power of the Eternal Spirit, could not but again return heavenward: as God's Spirit leads us by faith to gaze on its power in heaven, and to see how through all heaven its power is manifest, we shall learn to expect and to receive its working to keep us in God's presence, in a power above all that thought can conceive. The same Eternal Spirit, through whom the blood-shedding took place, will effect in us the blood-sprinkling too, and make us indeed partakers of what it has accomplished in God's presence above.

This is a lesson of the utmost consequence. If the blood is His **who offered Himself to God through the Eternal Spirit,** if it is in the power and life of that Spirit that the blood was brought into heaven, and now has its place there, we may be sure that that Spirit will ever work with and in that blood. *There are three* that bear witness on earth: the Spirit and the water and the blood. The Spirit and the blood must and will ever go together. We must not limit our faith in the power of the blood in our heart to what we can understand. Our faith must ever be enlarging, to expect that the Holy Spirit, according to His hidden but almighty and uninterrupted working, can maintain the heavenly efficacy of the blood in a way to us inconceivable. Just as Christ is the visible revelation on earth and in heaven of the invisible God, so the Holy Spirit again is the communication of the life and redemption of the unseen Christ. The Holy Spirit is the power of the inner life. Within us, down in the inaccessible depths of our being, He is able, as the Eternal Spirit, to maintain, in them that yield to Him, the divine power of the blood to cleanse from sin and to give abiding access to the presence of God. Let him who would know to the full the mighty, the divine, the inexpressible power and blessing the blood each moment can bring in Him, remember, it was **through the Eternal Spirit** it was shed.

In connection with this there is still another lesson. The Spirit not only applies the power of the blood, but in doing so He reveals its spiritual meaning. The blood has its value, not from the mere act of physical suffering and death, but from the inner life and disposition that animated Christ in shedding it. It is the blood of the Lamb **who offered Himself without blemish unto God,** with which our heart is brought into a divine and living contact. *Self-offering, self-sacrifice,* was the disposition of which the blood was the expression, and from which alone it had its worth. Where the Eternal Spirit communicates the power of the blood, He communicates this disposition. Christ humbled Himself and became obedient to death. *Therefore,* as the Lamb of God, who gave His blood, He was the embodiment of meekness, and humility, and submissive surrender to God's will. It was our pride and self-will that was the very root and life of sin in us: as we are washed in the blood of the Lamb, His spirit of meekness and submissiveness and obedience will work in us, because the same Eternal Spirit, through which the blood was shed, applies it in our hearts. We know what it means to wash our clothes in water, how they are plunged into it and saturated with it, until the water carries off all defilement. The blood of Jesus Christ cleanses from all sin, because the Eternal Spirit imparts the very life and power of which that precious blood-shedding was the outcome and the fruit. This is the power that cleanses the conscience from dead works to serve the living God. Not the blood only, as shed upon earth, as the first object of our faith for pardon, but the blood as shed through the Eternal Spirit, and glorified in the spirit life of heaven, brings us truly into the inner sanctuary, and empowers us to serve Him as the living God. "As nothing but the Eternal Spirit could have overcome or redeemed fallen nature, as Christ took it upon Him, so nothing can possibly overcome or redeem the fallen soul or body of any child of Adam, but that same overcoming and redeeming Spirit, really living and acting in it, in the same manner as it did in the humanity of Christ."

We live in the dispensation of the Spirit—the Spirit of God's Son, who hath been sent for this *into our heart.* It is the dispensation of the inner life, in which we are brought into the inner sanctuary, the secret of His presence, and the inner sanctuary is found within us—in that secret inner place which none but God's Spirit can search out. In that hidden depth is the house God hath prepared for Himself; there, in the inner man, the Holy Spirit will reveal, in a way that sense and reason cannot apprehend, the power of Christ's blood to cleanse and bring God nigh. Oh let us believe the infinite mysteries with which we are surrounded. And above all, this mystery too, that within us, **the blood of Christ,** the Lamb of God—that mystery of mysteries—is being applied and kept in full action by the Eternal Spirit, cleansing us and revealing God's presence in us.

1. *What a mystery! what blessedness! a heart sprinkled with the blood of the Son of God! To walk before God day by day with the blood of His Son upon us! To know that the Lamb of God sees us washed in His own blood! Oh, we need, let us ask, the Eternal Spirit to make all this clear to us.*

2. *If our faith is only to believe what our reason can make clear to us—no wonder the power of the blood effects so little. Let us have faith, not in what we understand, but let us have faith in God, and the heavenly, the inexpressibly glorious realities, of the blood and Spirit of the Son.*

3. *What a tender, careful, holy fear comes upon a soul that lives in the full and living consciousness of the blessed reality—a heart sprinkled with the blood of the Lamb.*

4. *Beware of trying to comprehend all the blood means, or of being discouraged when you fail of doing so. The blood in heaven is a divine and inscrutable mystery: be content to believe in its efficacy. When the Holy Spirit comes into the heart in power, He applies the blood in a power far beyond what we can think or understand.*

LXX.

The Power of the Blood to Fit for the Service of the Living God

IX.–14. How much more shall the blood of Christ cleanse your conscience from dead works to serve the living God?

We must not regard the cleansing in the blood of Christ as the end, the final aim, of redemption. It is only the beginning, the means to a higher end—the fitness for the service of the living God. It is the restoration to the fellowship of Him who has life and gives life. The blood gives cleansing **from dead works**, the works of the law and of self, with its own efforts; it brings into a living relation to the living God. God and His fellowship, a life in His love and service, the living God and the enjoyment of His presence—this is the aim of redemption.

The living God! This name was used in the Old Testament as a contrast to the dead idols of the heathen. In the New Testament it points us to the danger of our forming an image of God, not in wood or stone, but in our mind and imagination—*a thought-image,* in which there is neither life nor truth. What we need first of all in religion is that **we believe that God is,** that our faith realise Him as the living One, who is all that He is, in the power of an infinite life and energy. He is **the living God!** He speaks and hears. He feels and acts. He has the power to make us know that He is near to us, and that He receives us when we come near to Him. The knowledge of the living God is the ground of a living faith, a living fellowship, a living service.

327

As the living God, He is all, and does all and fills all—the ever-present, ever-working God.

To serve the living God! The glory of the creature is to serve God, to be a vessel in which He can pour His fulness, a channel through which He can show forth His glory, an instrument for working out His purposes. This was what man was created for in the image of God. The whole object of redemption is to bring us back to a life in the living service of God. It is for this the Holiest of All was opened to us by the blood as the place of service. It is for this our conscience is cleansed in the blood, as the fitness for service. A life in the Holiest of All is a life in which everything is done under the sense of God's glory and presence, and to His glory; a life that has no object but the service of God.

It was thus with the priests in Israel. They were set apart by the sprinkling of blood (Ex. xxix. 19, 20). The object of this was (Deut. x. 8) to fit them *to stand before the Lord, to minister unto Him, to bless in His name.* One great reason why many Christians never enter into the full joy and power of redemption, into the life within the veil, is that they seek it for themselves. Let us beware lest we seek the access into the Holiest, the joy of unclouded fellowship with God, the power of the blood to cleanse, only for the sake of our advance in holiness or in happiness. The whole appointment of the sanctuary and the priests was that there might be men who could come before God to minister to Him, *and then go out and bless their fellowmen.* Christ entered through His blood within the veil, to go and serve; to be a minister of the sanctuary in the power of the blood, by which He could cleanse others and admit them too within the veil. To know the power of the blood to cleanse and admit within the veil, and give us part in the priests' ministry of blessing men: this will come as we seek it as fitness to serve the living God.

How much more shall the blood of Christ **cleanse your conscience from dead works to serve the living God?** The cleansing is for service. There was a great difference between the people in the outer court and the priests within the tabernacle. The former saw the blood sprinkled on the altar, and trusted for forgiveness; the blood was not applied to their persons. The priests were sprinkled with the blood; that gave them access to the sanctuary to serve God there. We still have outer-court Christians, who look at Calvary, and trust for forgiveness, but know nothing of the access to God which the more direct and powerful application of the blood from heaven by the Holy Spirit gives. Oh let us give ourselves to be priests, wholly separated to the service of God, wholly given up to God, for Him to work in us and through us what perishing men need—our consecration to this service will urge us mightily to claim an ever mightier experience of the blood, because we shall feel that nothing less than a full entrance into, and a true abiding in God's presence, can fit us for doing God's work. The more we see and approve that the object of the cleansing must only be for service, the more shall we see and experience that the power for service is only in the cleansing.[1]

How much more shall the blood cleanse from dead works to serve the living God! If we experience in ourselves, or in those around us, that there is little of the power and presence of the living God in our religious service, we have here the reason. If we find that in that service dead works still prevail, and that in prayer and preaching, in home life and work around us, the duties of the religious life are performed without the power of the life and Spirit of God, let us learn the lesson—it is only the effectual cleansing, through the Eternal Spirit, of the blood that

1. "The blood contains that which makes white (Rev. vii. 14). Not only the man, but his garments are made white. This is more than cleansing. It is the word used regarding Christ's transfiguration garments (Matt. xvii. 2); the angel robes (Matt. xxviii. 3); the heavenly clothing (Rev. iv. 4); the judgment throne (Rev. xx. 11), whiter than snow, white as the garments of Christ. What potency, what excellency, what virtue does this blood contain! How it beautifies! How it glorifies!"— H. Bonar

has taken into the Holiest, that can fit us to serve the living God. That blood, witnessed to by the Holy Spirit, brings us into the Holiest, and makes God to us **a living God!** That blood brings the life of the Holiest into our hearts, cleanses our conscience from every dead work, from every attempt and every hope to do anything in our own strength, gives the consciousness that we are now ransomed and set free and empowered from heaven to serve the God of heaven in the power of a life that comes from heaven. The blood of Christ doth indeed cleanse us to serve the living God!

1. How vain it would have been for anyone to seek the priestly consecration with blood, and the entrance into the sanctuary, if he were not to do the priest's service. Let us give up the vain attempt. Let us seek the power of the blood to serve the living God, as He ministers to our fellow-men. The whole inward life of our High Priest, which He imparts to us, consisted of these two things: it was a life in the will of God, and in self-sacrificing love to men.

2. The priests honoured the blood sprinkled on them by boldly entering the tabernacle. Oh let us honour the blood of the Lamb by believing that it gives the power for a life in the Holiest, in the service of the living God!

3. Conscience tells me what I must think of myself. The blood tells me what God thinks of me. A conscience cleansed with the blood is a conscience that glories in this, that in holiness and in sincerity of God we behave ourselves in the world.

4. Oh to realise it! Christ went into the Holiest, not for Himself, but for us. And we go in, too, by His blood and in His Spirit, not only for ourselves but for others.

LXXI.

The Power of Christ's Death Ratifying the Covenant

IX.–15. And for this cause he is the mediator of a new covenant, that a death having taken place for the redemption of the transgressions that were under the first covenant, they that have been called may receive the promise of the eternal inheritance.
16. For where a testament is, there must of necessity be the death of him that made it.
17. For a testament is of force where there hath been death: for doth it ever avail while he that made it liveth?

You remember how in chapter viii. we found two names given to our Lord Jesus, indicating the twofold work He does, with God in heaven and in our heart on earth. As a **Minister of the sanctuary,** He is in God's presence, ministering the grace of the sanctuary to us, and giving us the enjoyment of that presence. As **Mediator of the new covenant,** He works in our heart on earth, giving God's law within us, as the law of the Spirit of His own life, and fitting us for the worship and fellowship of the sanctuary. In the first half of this chapter we have had the exposition of how Christ, as **Minister of the sanctuary,** opened and entered into it through His own blood, and there ministers the everlasting redemption. He does it by cleansing our conscience, in the power of that blood that has prevailed to open heaven, to enter in boldly and freely to serve the living God. In the second half of the chapter He now proceeds to speak of Christ as the **Mediator of the new covenant.** With the same blood with which He dedicated the sanctuary He has dedicated the covenant too.

And for this cause He is the Mediator of a new covenant, that they that have been called may receive the promise of the eternal inheritance. The word *promise* reminds of what was said of the **better covenant, enacted upon better promises.** The word *inheritance* of the oath of God and the inheriting the promise through faith. The word *eternal* of all we have heard of our Melchizedek, as a Priest *for ever,* who does all His work in the power of an endless life. Christ has become a Mediator of this new covenant, that the promise of the eternal inheritance, that blessed heritage of eternal life even now made manifest in the promises of the law written in the heart and full personal fellowship with God, might be our portion; it is the work of the Mediator to ensure our inheriting the promises. But this could not be till **a death had taken place for the redemption of the transgressions that were under the first covenant.** The first covenant had its sanction in God's appointment; the new covenant could not take its place until the first had met with full satisfaction for its claims. There was no way for this, for the redemption of the transgressions it had seen and condemned, but by *a death.* All the writer had meant in speaking of *the blood,* he now includes in the expression, *a death.* The change of the expression reminds us how the two are one. The blood is through the death; the death is for the blood. The blood-shedding and the death are the redemption, the ransom, that by sin-bearing and atonement deliver from transgressions and their power. All the transgressions of the old covenant had been treasured up; the death of Christ gave satisfaction to all that that covenant could claim, and brought release. So the Mediator of the new covenant begins an entirely new economy, with sin put away by the sacrifice of Himself, and an open path to the beginning of a new life in the favour and power of God.

Now follow two verses which have caused no little difficulty. In English we have for one word in Greek two words of entirely different meaning. The word "covenant," a treaty between two parties, and "testament," the last will by which one party leaves his property to another, are the same in Greek. Through the whole of Scripture the word may always best be translated "covenant," with the exception of the two following verses. Here the argument renders the meaning "testament" or "will" necessary. **For where a testament is, there must of necessity be the death of him that made it. For a testament is of force where there hath been death: for doth it ever avail while he that made it liveth?** It is as if the author turns aside for a moment, led to it by what he had just said of them who receive the eternal inheritance, to use the other meaning of the Greek word in order to prove how, in every connection, a death is indispensable. He had spoken of Christ's death as the sacrifice by which the covenant was ratified. To confirm the thought he adds: "When one who has made a testament dies, he passes away, and the heir takes his place—even so Jesus, the Heir of all things, in His death gave up all, that we might stand in His place, and inherit all."

Would God that our hearts might take it in. *A death having taken place!* Now *the covenant is sure.* The redemption of past transgressions is sure; we may now claim and take the promise of the eternal inheritance. *A death having taken place!* Now *the testament avails.* The maker of the testament has died, to put us in complete possession of all He had and all He won for us. And, praise God! He lives again, as no other maker of a testament ever lives, to put us in full possession of the inheritance, and to be Himself its chiefest measure and joy; **as Minister of the true sanctuary** to keep us in God's presence; as **Mediator of the new covenant** to keep our heart in the full enjoyment of all its blessings.

1. *Everyone can understand how absolutely a last will or testament needs a death. This must help us to believe that a covenant needs it as much for the*

redemption of transgressions. As sure as the death of a maker of a testament puts the heir in complete possession of the promise, so surely has the death of the Mediator made a perfect redemption from all transgression.

2. Let us get firmly hold of this: in virtue of his death the first covenant could be set aside and the second dedicated with His blood. The second covenant has entirely to do with keeping our heart and life in a right state for entering the sanctuary and abiding there. Let me believe it can and shall be fulfilled.

LXXII.

Even the First Covenant—Not without Blood

IX.–18. Wherefore even the first covenant hath not been dedicated without blood.

19. For when every commandment had been spoken by Moses unto all the people according to the law, he took the blood of the calves and the goats, with water and scarlet wool and hyssop, and sprinkled both the book itself, and all the people, saying,

20. This is the blood of the covenant which God commanded to you-ward.

21. Moreover the tabernacle and all the vessels of the ministry he sprinkled in like manner with the blood.

22. And according to the law, I may almost say, all things are cleansed with blood, and apart from shedding of blood there is no remission.

The writer returns here to the idea of the covenant in verse 15. He had there said that a death was needed for the redemption of the transgressions under the first covenant, ere Christ, as Mediator of the new, could put the heirs in possession of the promise. In confirmation of this necessity, he reminds us how **even the first covenant was not dedicated without blood.**

God has made more than one covenant with man, but ever, **not without blood!** And why? We know the answer (Lev. xvii. 11): *The life* (soul) *of the flesh is in the blood; and I have given it to you upon the altar to make atonement for your souls: for it is the blood that maketh atonement by reason of the life.* The life is in the blood. The blood shed is the token of death, life taken away. Death is always and everywhere God's judg-

335

ment on sin: *The sting of death is sin.* The shed blood sprinkled upon the altar, or the person, is the proof that death has been endured, that the penalty of the transgressions, for which atonement is being made, has been borne. In some cases the hands were laid upon the head of the sacrifice, confessing over it, and laying upon it, the sin to be atoned for. The shed blood upon the altar was the pledge that God accepted the death of the substitute: the sins were covered by the blood, and the guilty one restored to God's favour. **Apart from blood-shedding there is no remission**; in the blood-shedding there is remission, full and everlasting.

Not without blood! This is the wondrous note that rings through all Scripture, from Abel's sacrifice at the gate of paradise to the song of the ransomed in Revelations. God is willing to receive fallen man back again to His fellowship, to admit him to His heart and His love, to make a covenant with him, to give full assurance of all this; but—**not without blood.** Even His own Son, the Almighty and All-perfect One, the gift of His eternal love, even He could only redeem us, and enter the Father's presence, in submission to the word, **not without blood.** But, blessed be God, the blood of the Son of God, in which there was the life of the Eternal Spirit, has been given, and has now wrought an eternal redemption! He did, indeed, **bear our sins**, and take them away. **He put away sin by the sacrifice of Himself.** The life He poured out in His blood-shedding was a life that had conquered sin, and rendered a perfect obedience. The blood-shedding as the completion of that life, in its surrender to God and man, has made a complete atonement, a covering up, a putting away of sin. And so the blood of the new covenant, in which God remembers our sins no more, cleanses our heart to receive His law so into it, that the spirit of His law is the spirit of our life, and takes us into full and direct fellowship with Himself. **It was in this blood of the eternal covenant** that God brought again from the dead our Lord Jesus: the blood had so atoned for sin and made an end of it that, in its power, Christ was raised again. It became the power of a new life to Him and to us. With it He opened the way into the Holiest for us; the way into our hearts for Himself.

Not without blood! In earth and heaven, in each moment of our life, in each thought and act of worship, this word reigns supreme. There can be no fellowship with God, but in the blood, in the death, of His blessed Son.

But, praised be His name, in that blood there is an access and a fellowship, a life and a blessedness, a nearness and a love, that passeth understanding! Let us seek to cultivate large thoughts of what the blood has effected and can effect. Men have sometimes rejected the word: its associations are so coarse and at variance with a finer culture. Others do not reject it, and yet have not been able to sympathise with or approve the large place it sometimes takes in theology and devotion. The strange fascination, the irresistible attraction the word has, is not without reason. There is not a word in Scripture in which all theology is so easily summed up. All that Scripture teaches of sin and death, of the incarnation and the love of Christ, of redemption and salvation, of sin and death conquered, of heaven opened and the Spirit poured out, of the new covenant blessings, of a perfect conscience and a clean heart, and access to God and power to serve Him, personal attachment to Jesus, and of the joy of eternity, has its root and its fruit in this alone: the precious blood of Christ; **the blood of the eternal covenant.**

1. *Hear what Steinhofer says: "One drop of that blood, sprinkled out of the sanctuary on the heart, changes the whole heart, perfects the conscience, sanctifies the soul, makes the garments clean and white, so that we are meet for fellowship with God, ready and able to live in His love. Such a heart, sprinkled and cleansed with the blood of Jesus, is now fitted for all the grace of the new covenant, all the heavenly gifts, all the holy operations of divine love, all the spiritual blessings of the heavenly places. The blood of the Lamb does indeed make the sinner pure and holy, worthy and fit to partake of all that the inner sanctuary contains, and to live in God. Therefore the apostle*

says: Let us, as those whose hearts are sprinkled from an evil conscience, boldly draw near before the face of God. *To be sprinkled with the blood, to have the living, cleansing, all-pervading power of the blood of Jesus in the heart—this fits us for serving God, not in the oldness of the letter but in the newness of the Spirit."*

LXXIII.

Heaven Itself Cleansed by the Blood

IX.–23. It was necessary therefore that the copies of the things in the heavens should be cleansed with these; but the heavenly things themselves with better sacrifices than these.
24. For Christ entered not into a holy place made with hands, like in pattern to the true; but into heaven itself, now to appear before the face of God for us.

In the previous verses we saw how, at the dedication of the first covenant with blood, both the book and the people and, later on, the tabernacle and all the vessels of the ministry, were sprinkled with blood. Even so, the writer tells us, the blood-shedding on earth was not enough, but there was a needs-be that **the heavenly things themselves be cleansed** with the blood of the better sacrifice, ere heaven could be opened to us, and we obtain access to a life in the presence of God. There must not a vestige or sign of sin be left there, to rise up against us. Such is the power of this better sacrifice and its blood, that **the heavenly things themselves were cleansed** by it, and that Christ our surety with His own blood, **entered into heaven itself,** now to appear before the face of God for us. **The heavenly things themselves cleansed,** and **Christ entered into heaven itself for us**—these are the two aspects of the eternal redemption here put before us.

The heavenly things themselves cleansed. What can this mean? We speak of the heavens being dark, black with clouds. The light of the sun is there, but clouded. When the clouds are gone the heavens are bright and clear. God's word speaks of our sins rising up as a cloud, as a smoke before Him. Our sins are come up before Him, are in His presence, written in His book of remembrance, calling for vengeance. God says to Israel: *I have blotted out as a thick cloud thy transgressions, and as a cloud thy sins.* Just as the tabernacle had to be sprinkled and *cleansed and hallowed from all the uncleanness of the children of Israel,* so the heavenly things themselves by the blood of Christ. As the blood was brought in, every vestige of a thought of sin was removed out of God's presence; the heavens were cleansed; the heavens are now clear and bright, and the love of God can shine out in noonday glory.

And this because Christ is not entered into the Holiest, made with hands, but **into heaven itself, now to appear before the face of God for us.** This is the great consummation to which all the teaching of the heavenly priesthood of Christ, and the true sanctuary, and the blood of the covenant leads up. **Heaven itself** is now opened up to us. Christ has entered, not simply on His own behalf, but entirely to **appear before the face of God for us.** Yes, **for us,** His entering in has obtained for us **boldness to enter in.** His entering in was through the rent veil; **there is no veil now between God and us.** We are called to draw nigh in the fulness of faith. We are taught, **Ye are come** to the heavenly Jerusalem, **and to God. Before the face of God,** in the presence of God, is now the home of the soul. Heaven is not only a locality, with its limitations, but a state of life, that condition of spiritual existence in the full enjoyment of God's love and fellowship, into which Christ entered. Christ **passed through the heavens, was made higher than the heavens.** *He ascended far above all the heavens, that He might fill all things.* **Heaven itself,** the Holiest of All, into which He entered, the presence of God, is now the sphere in which He exercises His heavenly ministry, into which He brings us in as an actual life and experience, in which we alone can truly serve the living God.

And what, we may well ask, what is the reason that so few of God's children can testify to the joy of entering in and having their abode here in the very presence of God? There can be but one answer. There is such a difference between being the heir of a promise and actually inheriting it. Each of the great words of our Epistle, as God's gift to each one of His children, has an infinitude of meaning and blessing and power in it. **Christ a Priest for ever; the power of an endless life;** He is **able to sympathise, able to succour, able to save completely;** the true sanctuary, the new covenant, the blood cleansing the heavens, cleansing the conscience—all these are divine realities, with a power and a glory that the heart of man cannot conceive. It is only by faith and longsuffering that we inherit the promises. It is as we give up our whole heart and life to be just one act of faith, looking up and longing, praising and expecting, believing and receiving what God gives and works in Christ, that this life in the Holiest will be ours. It is as our faith sees the divine unity of the **once for all** and the **for ever,** that we shall be bold to believe that the **for ever,** the abiding continually, has in Christ been made ours **once for all,** and can be made ours in an entering within the veil as clear as that of Christ's. This faith will prove itself in longsuffering. First, as we diligently, perseveringly hold fast, and gaze and draw nigh and wait on God to take us within the veil; and then, as within the veil, in deepest humility and meekness and patience and resignation to God, we wait upon Him in service, to perfect us in the work for which we were admitted into His very presence.

But remember where all this begins, and wherein it all consists. **Not without blood! With His own blood! How much more shall the blood of Christ!** These words are the key to this blessed chapter of the opening of the Holiest to us. As we yield to the Holy Spirit, the Eternal Spirit, to testify to us how the way into the Holiest has been made manifest, and what the blood is by which it was done, and what the cleansing of our conscience in that blood to enter in and serve the living God, we shall in fulness of faith be bold to draw nigh and enter in and abide.

1. *Think not that it will be too difficult for thee to dwell always with thy heart up yonder in heaven. When the sun shines on thee, thou dost not think of its distance; thou rejoicest in its warmth. It is so near to thee; thou enterest into it, and it enters into thee. Even so with Jesus and the heavenly life. Heaven comes down. The kingdom of heaven is come with power; the Holy Spirit gives and maintains it in thee. The veil is rent, and the light and life of heaven is come down here where we serve in the Holy Place.*

2. *To open the way to heaven and to God, Jesus died to sin. He that hates and loses his life will find the way to the life of God.*

3. *Just as the cleansing of the tabernacle was part of the dedicating of the first covenant, so the sprinkling the heavenly sanctuary, the cleansing of the heavens with the blood of the new covenant, is our assurance that the sanctuary is open to us, and that the covenant is sure and will be fulfilled to us.*

LXXIV.

Sin Put Away by the Sacrifice of Himself

IX.–25. Nor yet that he should offer himself often; as the high priest entereth into the Holy Place year by year with blood not his own;

26. Else must he often have suffered since the foundation of the world: but now once at the end of the ages hath he been manifested to put away sin by the sacrifice of himself.

27. And inasmuch as it is appointed unto men once to die, and after this cometh judgment;

28. So Christ also, having been once offered to bear the sins of many, shall appear a second time, apart from sin, to them that wait for him, unto salvation.

In the previous verses the spiritual and heavenly character of Christ's work was contrasted with the material and earthly figures of the old worship. Here the contrast will be between the unceasing repetition of the old and the **once** and **for ever** of the new. Repetition is the proof of imperfection: what needs doing only once is finished, is perfect, is for ever. **Now once at the end of the ages hath He been manifested to put away sin by the sacrifice of Himself. As it is appointed unto men once to die, and after this the judgment**—with death, life is finished and complete, and ripe for judgment; after that comes the full revelation of what that death was—**so Christ also, having been once offered to bear the sins of many, shall appear a second time**—in the full manifestation of what that death accomplished—**without sin, to them that wait for Him, unto salvation.** What is done once is done for ever: all it waits for is the everlasting manifestation of what is already perfect and complete.

Christ, now once manifested to put away sin by the sacrifice of Himself—this is the great lesson of our passage. What Christ effected by His dying once, is for ever. And what He did effect was this—**He put away sin by the sacrifice of Himself.** He was manifested to put it away out of God's presence, out of His book and His remembrance—to put it away from us, so that it has no more power over us, and we enter upon an entirely new state of life, with sin removed and God's law written in our heart.

The question comes up, Is not the expression too strong? Is not the experience of the Church a proof that it cannot be meant so literally? The solution of the difficulty will be found in a truth that leads us into one of the deepest mysteries of the spiritual life. As we saw in our last meditation, the words of God have a divine, an infinite fulness of meaning. They set before us what is an actual fact, a divine reality, a spiritual truth in the power of the endless life. But this truth is seldom fully understood or accepted by believers. And as their knowledge limits their faith, and their faith their experience, the human exposition and witness of what God means seldom if ever reaches to the fulness of what the word contains. We limit the Holy One of Israel perhaps most when we think we honour Him, by thinking that we know and hold in our formulas all His word means. With its divine contents the word infinitely exceeds our apprehension, and ever invites us to press on to perfection, and prove the deeper and higher truth there is still hidden in the old familiar words. It is as we yield ourselves to the Holy Spirit, whose it is to reveal the power of the blood and the opening of the way into the Holiest, that we shall be led to inherit this promise too, in all its divine significance—sin put away by the sacrifice of Himself.

By the sacrifice of Himself. The words reveal the inmost meaning of the death of Christ: it was self-sacrifice. Sin, in its deepest root, is a turning from God to self; rejecting God to please self. From the wilderness to the garden this was the one temptation with which Satan sought to lead Him astray. By doing not His own will but the will of His Father, by the sacrifice of Himself to God and His will, He conquered sin in His own person, and gained a victory over it whereby it was for ever vanquished and brought to nought. He gave Himself up to death, as His submittal to it to do its utmost, rather than yield to its temptation. He gave Himself up to death, as His submittal to God's righteous judgment upon sin. It was in this that His death *to sin,* as the obedient One, that His death *for sin,* as our Substitute, had its power, and His atonement its efficacy. To Him, our Head, death was a personal spiritual victory, and thereby a vicarious propitiation. In both aspects He made an end of sin, and of both we are made partakers.

And how? By the sacrifice of **Himself He put away sin.**[2] And now He offers us **Himself** to take the place of sin. He gives Himself, the sacrificed One, who has finished redemption, to us to put away sin within us, too. It is as the Son, the living One, that He is High Priest; it is in eternal life power, by a life working in us, that He brings us to God. And so, by His Spirit, He, in His self-sacrifice, lives in us, and makes it true in the experience of each true disciple—sin put away by the sacrifice of self. The law for the Head is the law for every member.

And now the alternative is put before us: Which shall it be? Sin and myself or Christ and His Self. Christ has opened for us a heavenly life-sphere, out of which sin has been put away—the sanctuary of God's presence. Which shall it be—self-pleasing or self-sacrifice—a life in self or a life in Christ. Though we may not always be able to see fully all that Christ's work means, or

---

2. *"The putting away of sin.* The thought goes beyond the redemption from transgressions (ver. 15). It is literally for the disannulling of sin (comp. vii. 18). Sin is vanquished, shown in its weakness, 'set at nought' (Mark vii. 9; Gal. iii. 15)"— Westcott

realise all the riches of blessing it brings, there is one word not difficult to carry in which all is centred. That word is *Himself*. He gave Himself a sacrifice for sin; He gives Himself the putter away, the conqueror of sin; He is Himself all we can desire or need. Blessed the soul that rests in nothing less than Himself.

1. *Sin is the refusal to sacrifice one's self to God. Self-sacrifice in the fellowship and Spirit of Jesus is the way out of sin to God.*

2. *Christ as our Head is our Substitute. The value of His work as Substitute rests in His personal character and obedience. The two aspects are inseparable both in Him and in us. We draw nigh to Him and accept Him, and are saved at once by Him as our Substitute. But then we are at once implanted into Him, and the spirit in which He worked our salvation is imparted to us. And so salvation by sacrifice, putting away sin by the sacrifice of self, rules our whole being.*

LXXV.

The Sacrifices of the Law Cannot Make Perfect

X.–1. For the law having a shadow of the good things to come, not the very image of the things, they can never with the same sacrifices year by year, which they offer continually, make perfect them that draw nigh.

2. Else would they not have ceased to be offered, because the worshippers, having been once cleansed, would have had no more conscience of sins?

3. But in those sacrifices there is a remembrance made of sins year by year.

4. For it is impossible that the blood of bulls and goats should take away sins.

We have now seen **the Priest for ever,** able to save completely (chap. vii.); **the true sanctuary** in which He ministers (chap. viii.); and **the blood** through which the sanctuary was opened, and we are cleansed to enter in (chap. ix.). There is still a fourth truth of which mention has been made in passing, but which has not yet been expounded, What is **the way into the Holiest,** by which Christ entered in? What is the path in which He walked when He went to shed His blood and pass through the veil to enter in and appear before God? In other words, what was it that gave His sacrifice its worth, and what the disposition, the inner essential nature of that mediation that secured His acceptance as our High Priest. The answer to be given in the first eighteen verses of this chapter will form the conclusion of the doctrinal half of the Epistle, and especially of the higher teaching it has for the perfect.

To prepare the way for the answer, the chapter begins with once again reminding us of the impotence of the law. **The law having a shadow of the good things to come, not the very image of the things.** The law had only the shadow, not the substance. The gospel gives us the **very image.** The image of God in which man was created was an actual spiritual reality. The Son Himself, as the image of the Father, was His true likeness— ever in possession of His Father's life and glory.

When man makes an image, it is but a dead thing. When God gives an image it is a living reality, sharing in the life and the attributes of the original. And so the gospel brings us not a shadow, a picture, a mental conception, but the **very image** of the heavenly things, so that we know and have them, really taste and possess them. A shadow is first of all a picture, an external figure, giving a dim apprehension of good things to come. Then, as the external passes away, and sight is changed into faith, there comes a clearer conception of divine and heavenly blessings. And then faith is changed into possession and experience, and the Holy Spirit makes the power of Christ's redemption and the heavenly life a reality within us. Some Christians never get beyond the figures and shadows; some advance to faith in the spiritual good set forth; blessed they who go on to full possession of what faith had embraced.

In expounding what the law is not able to do, the writer uses four remarkable expressions which, while they speak of the weakness of the law with its shadows, indicate at the same time what the good things to come are, of which Christ is to bring us the **very image,** the divine experience.

The priests **can never make perfect them that draw nigh.**
This is what Christ can do. He makes the conscience perfect. He
hath perfected us for ever. These words suggest the infinite difference between what the law could do, and Christ has truly
brought. What they mean in the mind of God, and what Christ
our High Priest in the power of an endless life can make them
to be to us, this the Holy Spirit will reveal. Let us be content with
no easy human exposition, by which we are content to count the
ordinary low experience of the slothful Christian—the hope of
being pardoned, as an adequate fulfilment of what God means
by the promises of **the perfect conscience.** Let us seek to know
the blessing in its heavenly power.

**The worshippers once cleansed would have had no more
conscience of sins.** This is the perfect conscience—when there
is **no more conscience of sins**—a conscience that, **once**
cleansed in the same power in which the blood was **once** shed,
knows how completely sin has been put away out of that sphere
of spiritual fellowship with God to which it has found access.

**In those sacrifices there is a remembrance made of sins
year by year.** The cleansing of the heavens and the putting away
of sin is so complete that with God our sins are no more remembered. And it is meant that the soul that enters fully into the Holiest of All, and is kept there by the power of the eternal High
Priest, should have such an experience of His eternal, always
lasting, always acting redemption, that there shall be no remembrance of aught but of what He is and does and will do. As we
live in the heavenly places, in the Holiest of All, we live where
there is **no more remembrance of sins.**

**It is impossible that the blood of bulls and goats should
take away sins.** What is impossible for the law is what Christ
has done. **He takes away** not only guilt but sins, and that in
such power of the endless life that those that draw nigh are
made perfect, that there is no more conscience of sins, that there
be no more remembrance of sins.

To how many Christians the cross and the death of Christ are nothing so much as a remembrance of sins. Let us believe that by God's power, through the Holy Spirit, revealing to us the way into the Holiest, it may become the power of a life, with no more conscience of sins, and a walk with a perfect conscience before God.

1. *Here we have again the contrast between the two systems. In the one God spake by the prophets, giving thoughts and conceptions—shadows of the good things to come. But now He speaks to us in His Son, the likeness of God, who gives us the very image, the actual likeness, in our experience of the heavenly things. It is the deep contrast between the outward and the inward—the created and the divine.*

2. A perfect conscience. No more conscience of sin. *Let me not fear and say, Yes, this is the conscience Christ gives, but it is impossible for me to keep it or enjoy its blessing permanently. Let me believe in Him who is my Priest, after the power of an endless life, who ever lives to pray, and is able to save completely, because every moment His blood and love and power are in full operation—the perfect conscience in me, because He is for me in heaven, a Priest perfected for evermore.*

LXXVI.

A Body Didst Thou Prepare for Me

X.–5. Wherefore when he cometh into the world, he saith,
Sacrifice and offering thou wouldest not,
But a body didst thou prepare for me;
6. In whole burnt offerings and sacrifices for sin thou hadst no
pleasure:
7. Then said I, Lo, I am come
(In the roll of the book it is written of me)
To do thy will, O God.

The writer has reminded us of the utter insufficiency of the sacrifices of the law to do what was needed to take sin away, or to perfect the worshipper. In contrast to these he will now unfold to us the inner meaning, the real nature and worth of the sacrifice of Christ. In speaking of the blood in chapter ix. he has taught us what its infinite power and efficacy is. But what we need still to know is this: what gave it that infinite efficacy; what is its spiritual character, and what its essential nature, that it has availed so mightily to open for us the way to God. Even when we believe in Christ's death, we are in danger of resting content with what is not much better than its shadow, the mere doctrinal conception of what it has effected, without entering so into its divine significance, that the **very image,** the real likeness of what it means, enters into us in power.

Our writer here again finds what he wants to expound, in the Old Testament. He quotes from Psalm xl., where the Psalmist uses words which, though true of himself, could only have their full meaning revealed when the Messiah came. Our author

351

makes special use of two significant expressions, **A body thou didst prepare for Me**, and, **Lo, I am come to do Thy will, O God.** Speaking of the sacrifices of the Old Testament, the Psalmist had shown that he understood that they never were what God really willed: they were but the shadows pointing to something better, to a spiritual reality, a life in the body given up to the will of God, as a divine prophecy of what has now been revealed in Christ.

A body didst thou prepare for Me. Instead of the sacrifices, **God prepared a body for Christ,** which He so offered up or sacrificed that we have now been sanctified **by the offering of the body of Jesus Christ** once for all. Christ's body was to Him just what any man's is to him—the dwelling and organ of the soul; the channel for intercourse with the outer world, susceptible of impressions of pleasure and of pain, and therefore one of the first occasions of temptation. His body was a part of His human personality and life. He was in danger, just as we are, of using the body for His own service or pleasure, a means of gratifying self. But He never did this. He was filled with one thought—God prepared Me this body; I have it for His disposal, for His service and glory; I hold it ready every moment to be a sacrifice to Him. The body comes from God; it belongs to Him; it has no object of existence but to please Him. The one value My body has is, that I can give it a sacrifice to God.

It was the purpose of the Old Testament sacrifices to waken this disposition in the worshipper. There was to be not only the thought—as specially in the sin offering—This sacrifice dies in my stead, so that I need not die. But the farther thought—this the burnt offering specially symbolised—The giving up of this lamb and its life in sacrifice to God, is the image and the pledge of my giving up my life to Him. I offer the sacrifice to God, in token of my offering myself to Him. Substitution and Consecration were equally symbolised in the altar.

This was the feeling of David in writing the Psalm. What he could only partly understand and fulfil has been realised in Christ. And what Christ accomplished for us, of that we become full partakers as it is wrought into us, in a life of fellowship with Him. The word comes to us, *Present your bodies a living sacrifice unto God.* The real essential nature of the sacrifice of Christ, what gives it worth and efficacy, is this: the body that God prepared for Him, He offered up to God. And just as David, before Christ, through the Spirit of Christ, said these words of himself, so every believer after Christ, in the Spirit and power of Christ, says them too: **A body hast thou prepared for me.** This is the new and living way that Christ has opened up. David walked in it by anticipation; Christ the Leader and Forerunner walked in it and fully opened it up; it is only as we, too, by participation with Him, walk in it, that we can find access into the Holiest.

Every believer who would be fully delivered from the Old Testament religion, the trust in something done outside of us, that leaves us unchanged, and would fully know what it means that we are **sanctified and perfected by the one offering of the body of Christ,** must study to appropriate fully this word as true of Christ and himself as a member of His body—**A body didst thou prepare for Me.** In paradise it was through the body sin entered; in the body it took up its abode and showed its power. In the lust for forbidden food, in the sense of nakedness and shame, in the turning to dust again, sin proved its triumph. In the body grace will reign and triumph. The body has been redeemed; it becomes a temple of the Spirit and a member of Christ's body; it will be made like His glorious body. **A body didst thou prepare for Me:** through the body lies, for Christ and all who are sanctified in Him, the path to perfection.

And yet how many believers there are to whom the body is the greatest hindrance in their Christian life. Simply because they have not learnt from Christ what the highest use of the body is—**to offer it up to God.** Instead of *presenting their mem-*

bers unto God, of *mortifying the deeds of the body through the Spirit,* of *keeping under the body,* they allow it to have its way, and are brought into bondage. Oh for an insight into the real nature of our actual redemption, through a body received from God, prepared by Him, and offered up to Him.

1. *The soul dwells in the body. The body has been well compared to the walls of a city. In time of war, not only the city and its indwellers must be under the rule of the king, but specially the walls. Jesus, for whom God prepared a body, who offered His body, knows to keep the body too.*

2. *The mystery of the incarnation is that Godhead dwelt in a body. The mystery of atonement, the one offering of the body of Christ. The mystery of full redemption, that the Holy Spirit dwells in and sanctifies wholly the body too.*

3. *"Know ye not that your body is a temple of the Holy Ghost, which is in you? Glorify God, therefore, in your body." Did you ever know that the Holy Spirit is specially given for the body, to regulate its functions and sanctify it wholly?*

LXXVII.

Lo, I Am Come to Do Thy Will

X.–8. Saying above, Sacrifices and offerings and whole burnt offerings and sacrifices for sin thou wouldest not, neither had pleasure therein (the which are offered according to the law),
9. Then hath he said, Lo, I am come to do thy will. He taketh away the first, that he may establish the second.
10. By which will we have been sanctified through the offering of the body of Jesus Christ once for all.

On the word, **A body didst thou prepare for Me,** as the expression of God's claim, there follows now in the Psalm that other on the surrender to that claim—**Lo, I am come to do Thy will.** In this, the doing of God's will, we have the destiny of the creature, the blessedness of heaven, the inmost secret of redemption. In this consists the worth of Christ's sacrifice, and this alone is the reason why His blood prevails. The path He opened up to God, the path He walked in and we walk in, to enter the Holiest, is—**I am come to do Thy will.** It is through God's will alone we enter in to God Himself. The central blessing, Jesus, the Mediator of the new covenant, gives us, when He gives us Himself, is a heart in which the will of God lives.

We have more than once spoken of the two aspects of Christ's death—substitution with the atonement it wrought, and fellowship with the conformity it brings. The two are inseparably connected. As long as we look to the substitution simply as an act accomplished outside of us, without seeking to know its inner nature and meaning, the fellowship and conformity of

355

Christ's death will be an impossibility. But as we enter into the real meaning of the death for us and in our stead, to that which constituted its divine life and power, we shall find that death and the life out of death becomes ours in truth, laying hold of us, and bringing us into the true life-fellowship with our blessed Leader and Forerunner; we shall see and experience that what was to Him the way into the Holiest will be to us the only but the certain, the living way thither.

Lo, I am come to do Thy will, O God. "He humbled Himself, and became obedient—*therefore* God hath highly exalted Him." Because God is the all-perfect fountain of life and goodness and blessing, there can be no life or goodness or blessing but in His will. The whole evil and ruin of sin is that man turned from God's will to do his own. The redemption of Christ had no reason, no object, and no possibility of success, except in restoring man *to do God's will*. It was for this Jesus died. He gave up His own will; He gave His life, rather than do His own will. It was this that gave value to His bearing our sins, with their curse and consequences, to His tasting death for every man. It was this that gave such infinite worth to His blood. It was this that made Him a real propitiation for the sins of the world. And it is this we are made partakers of—first, as an obedience for the sake of which we are made righteous; but, further also, in the fellowship of the very spirit of the death and the life in which He entered the presence of God. **I come to do Thy will**, is the way into the Holiest, for Him and for us.

By which will we have been sanctified. By which will, as willed by God, as done and fulfilled by Christ in His one offering, as accepted by us in faith. When we accept Christ, the will of God wrought out in Christ on our behalf, is accepted by us too; it becomes the power that rules in our life by the Holy Spirit. **In which will,** not as a dead past transaction, or as the mere performance of a certain work to be done, but as a living eternal reality restoring man into God's will in living power—this it is in which we have the new and living way to God.

In which will we have been sanctified. Sanctification in this Epistle is a word of larger meaning than what is meant by that title in ordinary Church doctrine. It includes all that is implied in bringing us into living fellowship with God. He is the Holy One. His life is His holiness. The inner sanctuary to which we enter in, is the Holiness of Holinesses. In chapter ii. we read: **Both He that sanctifieth, and they who are sanctified are all of one.** Our sanctification is rooted in our oneness with Jesus. **In the which will we are sanctified,** delivered from the power of sin and this evil world, brought into fellowship with the Holy One, and fitted for entering the Holiest of All.

In the which will we have been sanctified through the offering of the body of Jesus Christ. His offering has such power, because it was the doing of the will of God, the entering into the will of God, and through it into the holiness of God, into the very Holiest of All. And now, as no one but Christ had power of Himself to say, *Lo, I am come to do Thy will,* so no one can speak thus, or live thus, but because the divine nature of Christ is truly born and formed within him, and is become the life of his life and the spirit of his Spirit. It is thus that His priesthood manifests His power to bring us nigh to God.

Fellow-Christian! hast thou learnt to believe and to regard thyself as *sanctified in the will of God as done by Jesus,* admitted to the fellowship of the Holy One? Is not this possibly the reason that thou hast not yet entered the rest of God within the veil, because thou hast never, in accepting Christ, accepted that which really constitutes Him the Christ? He is the Christ who came *to do the will of God*—this constitutes Him a Saviour. Oh, come and believe that this is what He did for thee and on thy behalf, that thou mightest be able to do it too. The new and living way into the Holiest, which Jesus as Leader and Forerunner hath opened up, is the way of a body prepared for me by God, a body offered

357

to Him, and a life given to do His will. As I say with Jesus, I am come to do Thy will, I have no other object in life, for this alone I live, I shall with Him abide in God's presence.

1. The only way to God is through the will of God. *A truth so simple and self-evident! and yet so deep and spiritual that but few fully apprehend it. Yes, this is the way, the only way, the new and living way into the Holiest which Jesus opened up. Let us follow Him, our Leader and Forerunner, walking in His footsteps,* in the will of God.

2. *Be not afraid to say—Yes, O my God, here am I, absolutely given up in everything to do the will of God; by Thy grace and Holy Spirit, to make every part of my being a doing of the will of God! So help me, God!*

3. *For the penitent convert it is enough to know the beginning of the doctrine of Christ, His obedience has atoned and makes me righteous. The believer who seeks to grow and become conformed to the image of the Son, seeks and finds more. The obedience that gave the sacrifice its power in heaven, exercises that power in his heart. The adorable Substitute becomes the beloved Leader and Brother, the High Priest in the power of the heavenly life, bringing us near to God by leading us and keeping us in His will.*

LXXVIII.

Once and for Ever

X.–11. And every priest indeed standeth day by day ministering and offering oftentimes the same sacrifices, the which can never take away sins:

12. But he, when he had offered one sacrifice for sins for ever, sat down on the right hand of God;

13. From henceforth expecting till his enemies be made the footstool of his feet.

14. For by one offering he hath perfected for ever them that are sanctified.

In the last verses of chapter vii., where the eternal priesthood of Jesus had been set forth, He was spoken of as one who needeth **not daily** to offer, for this He did **once for all**, when He offered up Himself—a Son, perfected for **evermore.** And so in chapter ix., with its teaching of the efficacy of His blood, we had the thought repeated, Christ entered in **once for all.** Not that He should offer Himself **often,** else **must** He have **often** suffered; now **once** hath He been manifested; Christ **once** offered shall appear a second time. The contrast is put as strongly as possible between the sacrifices ever repeated, and the offering of Christ **once for all.** So, too, in the beginning of our chapter the impotence of the sacrifices **year by year continually** is proved from the fact, that the conscience **once** cleansed would need no new sacrifice; as a fact, they only renewed the remembrance of sins. And now, in the concluding verses of the argument, the thought is summed up and pressed home anew. The priest standeth **day**

by day offering **oftentimes;** Christ offered **one** sacrifice **for ever.** By one offering He hath perfected **for ever** them that are sanctified. The **once** of Christ's work is the secret of its being **for ever:** the more clear the acceptance of that divine **once for all,** the more sure the experience of that divine **for ever,** the continually abiding working of the power of the endless life.

Once and **for ever:** see how the two go together in the work of Christ in its two principal manifestations. In His death, His sacrifice, His blood-shedding, it is **once for all.** The propitiation for sin, the bearing and the putting away of it, was so complete that of His suffering again, or offering Himself again, there never can be any thought. God now remembers the sin no more for ever. He has offered one sacrifice **for ever;** He hath perfected us **for ever.** No less is it so in His resurrection and ascension into heaven. He entered **once for all** through His blood into the Holiest. When He had offered one sacrifice **for ever,** He sat down on the right hand of God. The **once for all** of His death is the secret of the **for ever** of the power of His sacrifice. The **once for all** of His entering through the blood, the power of the **for ever** of His sitting on the throne.

What is true of Christ is true of His people. The law of His life is the law of theirs. Of the **once for all** and the **for ever** of His work on earth and in heaven, their lives and spiritual experience will feel the power and bear the mark. See it in conversion. How many have struggled for years in doubt and fear, simply because they did not apprehend the **once for all** of Christ's atonement. They could not understand how it was possible for a sinner **once for all** to believe and be saved. No sooner was it made plain to them that the punishment was borne, that the debt was paid, **once for all,** all became clear and they counted it their duty and joy at once to accept what was so finished and so sure. And they could see, too, how the **once** was **for ever**—the power of the endless life bearing them on into the **for ever** of God's presence.

And no otherwise is it with the believers entering within the veil, into a life of unclouded and unbroken fellowship. We saw in Christ's work the two manifestations of the **once** and the **for ever**. It was not only in the death and blood-shedding, but in the entering into the Holiest and the blood-sprinkling in heaven. To many it appears at variance with all the laws of growth and development, that there should be a **once for all** of an entrance within the veil. And yet there are witnesses not a few who can testify that when the **once** of Christ's entering in was revealed in its infinite power as theirs, all doubt vanished, and not only boldness but power of access was given, which brought them into an experience of the eternal and unchanging power of the heavenly priesthood, and of the kingdom within as set up and kept by the Holy Spirit, which they never had thought of. And that **once** was followed by the **for ever** of the continually abiding, which the priesthood of Jesus was meant to secure.

But He, when He had offered one sacrifice for sins for ever, sat down on the right hand of God; from henceforth expecting till His enemies be made the footstool of His feet. We have said before, the Epistle would fill us with the thought of a heavenly Christ; nothing less than the knowledge of that can enable us to live as the partakers of a heavenly calling. Let us fix our eyes here again upon Christ as King. The **once** of sacrifice and death issues in the **for ever** of the nearness and the power of God. The **once** of our entrance into the death of Christ and His life, brings us back to the fellowship with Christ in the love and power of the Father in heaven. His **for ever** is one of victory, and of the blessed expectation of its full manifestation in the subjugation of every enemy. Our life within the veil may be one too of possession and expectation combined; the enjoyment of the overcoming life, with the going on from strength to strength in the victory over every foe. Between these two pillars—on the one hand, this once for all, on the other this for ever, the way into the Holiest passes and brings us to the throne of God and of the Lamb.

1. The time when the long and patient preparation was perfected in this once for all *was in God's hands. Christ waited on the Father. Even so, our full participation in it is not something we can count a thing to be grasped; in the faith of it we bide God's time, seeking each day to live in a redemption that is perfected and eternal. Through faith and longsuffering we inherit the promises.*

2. Once for all. *That covers my past completely—my past not only of guilt, but of sin with all its consequences.* For ever. *That covers my future, with all its possible needs. Between these two, in the present moment, the* Now *of daily life, I am saved with an everlasting salvation; the* Today *of the Eternal Spirit, even as the Holy Ghost saith,* Today—*makes the* Once *and the* for ever *a daily present reality.*

LXXIX.

The Sanctified Perfected for Ever

X.–14. For by one offering he hath perfected for ever them that are sanctified.

This verse is in reality the conclusion of the doctrinal part of the Epistle. The four following verses are simply the citation of the words of the new covenant to confirm its teaching with the witness of the Holy Spirit. The writer having, in the context, expounded the nature of Christ's sacrifice, as showing what the way into the Holiest is, sums up his proof of its worth and efficacy in the words: **By one offering He hath perfected for ever them that are sanctified.** We find here five of the most important words that occur in the Epistle.

Sanctified. That looks back to the great purpose of Christ's coming, as we had it in chapter ii. Sanctified is cleansed from sin, taken out of the sphere and power of the world and sin, and brought to live in the sphere and power of God's holiness in the Holiest of All. It looks back, too, to verse 10: **In which will we are sanctified by the offering of the body of Christ.**

He hath perfected them that are sanctified. It not only says that He has finished and completed for them all they need. The word points back to what was said of His own **being made perfect.** All He became was for us. In His one sacrifice He was not only perfected Himself, but He perfected us; He took us into the fellowship of His own perfectness, implanted His own perfect life in us, and gave His perfected human nature to us that we were to put on, and to live in.

For ever. He hath perfected us once for all and for ever. His perfection is ours; our whole life is prepared for us, to be received out of His hand.

By sacrifice. The death, the blood, the sacrifice of Christ, is the power by which we have been alike sanctified and perfected. It is the way which He opened up, in which He leads us with Himself into what He is and does as the One who is perfected for evermore, and the Holiest of All.

By **one** sacrifice. **One** because there is none other needed, either by others or Himself; **one** divine, and therefore sufficient and for ever.

The chief thought of the passage is: **He hath for ever perfected them that are being sanctified.** The words in verse 10, **In which will we have been sanctified,** speak of our sanctification as an accomplished fact: we are saints, holy in Christ, in virtue of our real union with Him, and His holy life planted in the centre of our being. Here we are spoken of as **being sanctified.** There is a process by which our new life in Christ has to master and to perfect holiness through our whole outer being. But the progressive sanctification has its rest and its assurance in the once and for ever of Christ's work. **He hath perfected for ever them that are being sanctified.**

In chapters ix. 9 and x. 1 we read that the sacrifices could **never, as touching the conscience, make the worshipper perfect, never make perfect them that draw nigh,** so that **they have no more conscience of sins.** Our conscience is that which defines what our consciousness of ourselves before God should be: Christ makes the worshipper perfect, as touching the conscience, so that there is no more conscience of sins. **He hath perfected for ever** them that are sanctified. At the close of the chapter in Christ's priesthood we read of Himself (vii. 28): **He is a High Priest, a Son, perfected for evermore.** Here at the close of the unfolding of His work, it is said of His saints: **He hath perfected them for ever.** The perfection in both cases is one and the same. As the Son of Man, as the Second Adam, who lives in all who are His, **He perfected Himself for them,** and them in Himself. His perfection and theirs are one.

And wherein His perfection consists we know too. (See in ii. 10 and v. 9.) A Leader in the way of glory, **God made Him perfect through suffering;** perfected in Him that humility and meekness and patience which mark Him as the Lamb, which are what God asks of man, and are man's only fitness for dwelling with God. **Having offered up prayer, and having been heard for His godly fear, though He was a Son, yet He learned obedience by what He suffered, and was made perfect.** His godly fear, His waiting on God in the absolute surrender of His will, His submitting to learn obedience, His spirit of self-sacrifice, even unto death—it was by this that as man He was perfected, it was in this He perfected human nature, and perfected His people too. In His death He accomplished a threefold work. He perfected Himself, His own human nature and character. He perfected our redemption, perfectly putting away sin from the place it had in heaven (ix. 23), and in our hearts. He perfected us, taking us up into His own perfection, and making us partakers of that perfect human nature, which in suffering and obedience, in the body prepared for Him, and the will of God done in it, He had wrought out for us. Christ Himself is our perfection; in Him it is complete; abiding in Him continually is perfection.

Let us press on to perfection, was the call with which we were led into the higher-life teaching of the Epistle. Here is our goal. **Christ, by one offering, hath perfected us for ever.** We know Him as the Priest for ever, the Minister of the new sanctuary, and the Mediator of the new covenant, who by His blood entered into the Holiest; there He lives for ever, in the power of an endless life, to impart to us and maintain within us His perfect life. It is the walk in this path of perfection, which as our Leader He opened up in doing the will of God, which is the new and living way into the Holiest.

1. *The work of Christ is a perfect and perfected work. Everything is finished and complete for ever. And we have just by faith to behold and enter in, and seek and rejoice, and receive out of His fulness grace for grace. Let every difficulty you feel in understanding or claiming the different blessings set before you, or in connecting them, find its solution in the one thought— Christ has perfected us for ever; trust Him, cling to Him, He will do all.*

2. *One sacrifice for ever. We perfected for ever. And He who did it all, He for ever seated on the throne. Our blessed Priest-King, He lives to make it all ours. In the power of an endless life, in which He offered Himself unto God, in which He entered the Holiest, He now lives to give and be in our hearts all He hath accomplished. What more can we need?* Wherefore, holy brethren! partakers of a heavenly calling, consider Jesus.

LXXX.

The Witness of the Holy Spirit

X.–15. And the Holy Ghost also beareth witness to us: for after he hath said,

16. This is the covenant that I will make with them
> After those days, saith the Lord;
> I will put my laws on their heart,
> And upon their mind also will I write them; then saith he,

17. And their sins and their iniquities will I remember no more.

18. Now where remission of these is, there is no more offering for sin.

The writer has concluded his argument. He has made clear that the sacrifice of Christ, as the offering up of His body to the will of God, had opened for us a new way into the Holiest. **Through the offering of the body of Jesus Christ we have been sanctified. When He had offered one sacrifice for ever, He sat down on the right hand of God. By one offering He hath perfected for ever them that are sanctified.** His sacrifice is over, and has everlasting power; in virtue of it He sits on the throne, expecting His final triumph; those He has sanctified are perfected for ever. The sacrifice is of infinite worth; it has opened the entrance to a state of perfect and everlasting holiness and glory; nothing is now needed but to rejoice and wait and see the King on the throne applying and revealing the power of His finished work.

The writer appeals to the words of the institution of the new covenant (viii. 6–13), in support of what he has said. He does so with the words, **And the Holy Ghost also beareth witness**

to us. The words of Jeremiah are to him the words of the Holy Spirit. He believes in a direct inspiration. It was the God who knows the end from the beginning, who had planned all from the least to the greatest in the preparation of redemption, who had revealed to Jeremiah the new covenant that would be made centuries later. It was the same Holy Spirit who had inspired the first record of Melchizedek, and the Psalm with the oath of God, who had ordered the tabernacle and the veil to signify that the way into the Holiest was not yet open, and had watched over the first covenant, and its dedication not without blood, through whom the promise of the new covenant was spoken and recorded. Our writer appeals to Him and His witness.

He does so as one who himself has the teaching of that Spirit. Anyone might read the words of the covenant, and of the death of Jesus; no one could connect and expound them in their divine harmony and their everlasting significance but one taught by the same Spirit. These men *preached the gospel with the Holy Ghost sent down from heaven;* the Spirit, from the King sat down upon the throne, revealed in and to them the will of God, and the eternal power of the one sacrifice, to open the way into the Holiest.

And what is now the witness of the Holy Ghost in the new covenant? The witness to the two blessings of the covenant in their divine inseparable unity. **I will put My laws in their heart, and their sins will I remember no more.** The complete remission of sins, the removal of sin out of God's sight and remembrance for ever, was promised. **Now,** our writer argues, **where remission of these is, there is no more offering for sin.** The one offering hath perfected for ever them that are sanctified. The death of Christ has opened up and introduced us into a relationship to God, a state of life before Him, in which sin has been finally put away, and God receives us into His fellowship as those who have been sanctified in Christ. He receives us into the Holiest of All through the blood. The blood that sprinkles the mercy-seat also sprinkles and cleanses our conscience, bringing the full remission, the full deliverance from sin and its power, into our inmost being; and, fitting our heart to receive that Spirit of heaven which witnesses with the blood, as a Spirit of life, puts the law within us, as the law of our life.

And so we enter into the finished work of Christ, and the rest of God in it; enter the perfection with which He Himself was perfected for evermore, and hath perfected us for ever; into that Holiest of All, into which God fulfils the promise, **I will be to them a God, and they shall be to Me a people.** And the offering of the body of Christ once for all, the one sacrifice for ever, becomes, in ever-growing blessedness, the one thought, the one trust, the one joy, the one life of the believer. His salvation and redemption are finished and eternal realities, His perfection and sanctification too. Our one need is to believe and abide in and receive what our Priest-King on the throne imparts through His Spirit: a full entrance into the **no more offering for sin**, with all that flows from it, in the person and throne and work of our Priest for ever: this is the entrance into the Holiest.

And the Holy Ghost also beareth witness to us. It is easy to understand the truth of the forgiveness of sin as one of the elementary foundation truths, of which we read in chapter vi. (ver. 1). But if we seek to press on to perfection, and to know what the fulness of salvation is into which it leads, we may count upon the Holy Spirit to reveal it, to witness to it, in our inner life. He reveals it not to the mind, or as the reward of earthly study, but to the poor in spirit and them that are of a lowly heart. It is in the heart God sends forth the Spirit of His Son; the heart that longs for and chooses and loves and waits for this life of perfect fellowship with God more than its chief joy, shall have it witnessed by God's Spirit that the **no more offering for sin** is indeed the opening up of the Holiest of All. The Holy Ghost who comes from heaven, bears witness of what is in heaven. We can know nothing really of what takes place in heaven but by the Holy Ghost in our heart. Dwelling in us He gives in our inmost life the full witness to all the efficacy of Christ's atonement and His enthronement in the presence of God.

1. *The one central truth to which the Holy Spirit testifies is this: that the old way of living and serving God is now completely and for ever come to an end. Death and the devil are brought to nought; the veil is rent; sin is put away; the old covenant is disannulled, vanished away, taken away. A new system, a new way, a new and eternal life has been opened up on the power of Christ Jesus. Oh to have our eyes and hearts opened to see that is not merely a thought, a truth for the mind, but a spiritual state of existence which the Holy Ghost can bring us into.*

2. The Holy Ghost beareth witness. *For this He came down on the day of Pentecost out of the heavenly sanctuary and from our exalted Priest-King, to bring down the heavenly life, the kingdom of heaven to the disciples, and make it real to them, as a thing found and felt in their hearts. Each one of us needs and may claim the Holy Spirit in the same Pentecostal power, and the new, the eternal, the heavenly life will fill us too.*

Second Half—Practical—Chap. x. 19—xiii. 25

The Call to a Life in Harmony with the Glory of God's Revelation of Himself in the Son

Ninth Section—x. 19-25
Of Life in the Holiest of All

It may help us the better to master the rich contents of this central passage, containing a summary of the whole Epistle, if we here give the chief thoughts it contains.

    I. The four great Blessings of the new worship:
        1. The Holiest opened up.
        2. Boldness in the Blood.
        3. A New and Living Way.
        4. The Great High Priest.
    II. The four chief Marks of the true worshipper:
        1. A True Heart.
        2. Fulness of Faith.
        3. A Heart sprinkled from an Evil Conscience.
        4. The Body washed with Clean Water.
    III. The four great Duties to which the opened Sanctuary calls:
        1. Let us draw nigh (in the fulness of *faith*).
        2. Let us hold fast the profession of our *hope*.
        3. Let us consider one another to provoke unto *love*.
        4. Let us not forsake the assembling of ourselves together.

LXXXI.

The Entrance into the Holiest

X.–19. Having therefore, brethren, boldness to enter into the Holy Place;[1]

22. Let us draw near.

Enter into the Holiest. With these words the second half of the Epistle begins. Hitherto the teaching has been mainly doctrinal. The glory of Christ's person and priesthood, of the heavenly sanctuary which He, through His own blood, has opened and cleansed and taken possession of for us, of the way of obedience and self-sacrifice which led Him even to the throne, has been unfolded. Now comes the practical part, and our duty to appropriate the great salvation that has been provided is summed up in the one thought: **Having boldness to enter into the Holiest; let us draw nigh.** Access to God's presence and fellowship, the right and the power to make that our abiding dwelling-place, to live our life there, has been provided in Christ: let us draw nigh, here let us abide.

Enter into the Holiest. It is a call to the Hebrews to come out of that life of unbelief and sloth, that leads to a departing from the living God, and to enter into the promised land, the rest of God, a life in His fellowship and favour. It is a call to all lukewarm, half-hearted Christians, no longer to remain in the outer court of the tabernacle, content with the hope that their sins are pardoned. Nor even to be satisfied with having entered

1. Holiest.

373

the Holy Place, and there doing the service of the tabernacle, while the veil still hinders the full fellowship with the living God and His love. It calls to enter in through the rent veil, into the place into which the blood has been brought, and where the High Priest lives, there to live and walk and work always in the presence of the Father. It is a call to all doubting, thirsting believers, who long for a better life than they have yet known, to cast aside their doubts, and to believe that this is what Christ has indeed done and brought within the reach of each one of us: **He has opened the way into the Holiest!** This is the salvation which He has accomplished, and which He lives to apply in each of us, so that we shall indeed dwell in the full light of God's countenance.

Enter into the Holiest. This is, in one short word, the fruit of Christ's work, the chief lesson of the Epistle, the one great need of our Christian life, the complete and perfect salvation God in Christ gives us to enjoy.

Enter into the Holiest. What Holiest? To the reader who has gone with us through the Epistle thus far, it is hardly needful to say, No other than that very same into which Christ, when He had rent the veil in His death, entered through His own blood, to appear before the face of God for us. That Holiest of All is the heavenly place. But not heaven, as it is ordinarily understood, as a locality, distinct and separate from this earth. The heaven of God is not limited in space in the same way as a place on earth. There is a heaven above us, the place of God's special manifestation. But there is also a spiritual heaven, as omnipresent as God Himself. Where God is, is heaven; the heaven of His presence includes this earth too. The Holiest into which Christ entered, and into which He opened the way for us, is the, to nature, inaccessible light of God's holy presence and love, full union and communion with Him. Into that Holiest the soul can enter by the faith that makes us one with Christ. The Holy Spirit, who first signified that the way of the Holiest was not yet open; through whom Jesus shed the blood that opened the way; who, on the day of Pentecost, witnessed in the heart of the disciples, that it was now indeed open; waits to testify to us what it means to enter in and to bring us in. He lifts the soul up into the Holiest; He brings the Holiest down into the soul.

Enter into the Holiest. Oh, the glory of the message. For fifteen centuries Israel had a sanctuary with a Holiest of All into which, under pain of death, *no one might enter.* Its one witness was: man cannot dwell in God's presence, cannot abide in His fellowship. And now, how changed is all! As then the warning sounded: *Enter not!* so now the call goes forth: *Enter in!* the veil is rent; the Holiest is open; God waits to welcome you to His bosom. Henceforth you are to live with Him. This is the message of the Epistle: Child! thy Father longs for thee to enter, to dwell, and to go out no more for ever.

Oh the blessedness of a life in the Holiest! Here the Father's face is seen and His love tasted. Here His holiness is revealed and the soul made partaker of it. Here the sacrifice of love and worship and adoration, the incense of prayer and supplication, is offered in power. Here the outpouring of the Spirit is known as an ever-streaming, overflowing river, from under the throne of God and the Lamb. Here the soul, in God's presence, grows into more complete oneness with Christ, and more entire conformity to His likeness. Here, in union with Christ, in His unceasing intercession, we are emboldened to take our place as intercessors, who can have power with God and prevail. Here the soul mounts up as on eagle's wings, the strength is renewed, and the blessing and the power and the love are imparted with which God's priests can go out to bless a dying world. Here each day we may experience the fresh anointing, in virtue of which we can go out to be the bearers, and witnesses, and channels of God's salvation to men, the living instruments through whom our blessed King works out His full and final triumph.

O Jesus! our great High Priest, let this be our life!

1. *"One thing have I desired of the Lord, that will I seek after; that I may dwell in the house of the Lord* all the days of my life, *to behold the beauty of the Lord, and to enquire in His temple."* Here the prayer is fulfilled.

2. *"Did not Jesus say, 'I am the door of the sheepfold'? What to us is the sheepfold, dear children? It is the heart of the Father, whereunto Christ is the gate that is called Beautiful. O children, how sweetly and how gladly has He opened that door into the Father's heart, into the treasure-chamber of God! And there within He unfolds to us the hidden riches, the nearness and the sweetness of companionship with Himself."—TAULER*

3. We have read of a man's father or friends purchasing and furnishing a house for a birthday or a wedding gift. They bring him there, and, handing the keys, say to him: "This is now your house." Child of God! the Father opens unto thee the Holiest of All, and says: "Let this now be thy home." What shall our answer be?

LXXXII.

Boldness in the Blood of Jesus

X.–19. Having therefore, brethren, boldness to enter into the
Holy Place,[1] by the blood of Jesus;
22. Let us draw near.

Enter into the Holiest. This word brought us the message of
the Epistle. Christ has in very deed opened the Holiest of All for
us to enter in and to dwell there. The Father would have His
children with Him in His holy home of love and fellowship,
abiding continually all the time. The Epistle seeks to gather all
in. Having boldness to enter, **let us draw near!**

It may be that some, as in the study of the Epistle the wondrous mystery of the way into the Holiest now opened was revealed to them, have entered in; they have said, in faith: Lord,
my God; I come. Henceforth I would live in Thy secret place, in
the Holiest of All. And yet they fear. They are not sure whether
the great High Priest has indeed taken them in. They know not
for certain whether they will be faithful, always abiding within
the veil. They have not yet grasped what it means—**having
boldness** to enter in.

And there may be others, who have with longing, wistful
hearts, heard the call to enter in, and yet have not the courage
to do so. The thought that a sinful worm can every day and all
the day dwell in the Holiest of All is altogether too high. The
consciousness of feebleness and failure is so strong, the sense of

1. Holiest

377

personal unfaithfulness so keen, the experience of the power of the world and circumstances, of the weakness of the flesh and its efforts, so fresh, that for them there is no hope of such a life. Others may rejoice in it, they must even be content without it. And yet the heart is not content.

To both such, those who have entered but still are full of fears, and those who in fear do not enter, the Holy Spirit speaks—**Today, if you shall hear His voice, harden not your hearts; Having boldness in the blood of Jesus** to enter into the Holiest, let us draw nigh. The boldness with which we are to enter is not, first of all, a conscious feeling of confidence; it is the objective God-given right and liberty of entrance of which the blood assures us. The measure of our boldness is the worth God attaches to the blood of Jesus. As our heart reposes its confidence on that in simple faith, the feeling of confidence and joy on our part will come too, and our entrance will be amid songs of praise and gladness.

Boldness in the blood of Jesus. Everything depends upon our apprehension of what that means. If the blood be to us what it is to God, the boldness which God means it to give, will fill our hearts. As we saw in chapter ix., what the blood has effected in rending the veil and cleansing the heavens, and giving Jesus, the Son of Man, access to God, will be the measure of what it will effect within us, making our heart God's sanctuary, and fitting us for perfect fellowship with the Holy One. The more we honour the blood in its infinite worth, the more will it prove its mighty energy and efficacy, opening heaven to us and in us, giving us, in divine power, the real living experience of what the entrance into the Holiest is.

The blood of Jesus. *The life is the blood.* As the value of this life, so the value of the blood. In Christ there was the life of God; infinite as God is the worth and the power of that blood. In Christ there was the life of man in its perfection; in His humility, and obedience to the Father, and self-sacrifice, that which made

Him unspeakably well-pleasing to the Father. That blood of Jesus, God and man, poured out in a death, that was a perfect fulfilment of God's will, and a perfect victory over all the temptations of sin and self, effected an everlasting atonement for sin, and put it for ever out of the way, destroying death and him that had the power of it. Therefore it was, that in the blood of the everlasting covenant Jesus was raised from the dead; that in His own blood, as our Head and Surety, He entered heaven; and that that blood is now for ever in heaven, in the same place of honour as **God the Judge of all, and Jesus the Mediator** (xii. 24). It is this blood, now in heaven before God for us, that is our boldness to enter in, even into the very Holiest of All.

Beloved Christian! The blood of Jesus! The blood of the Lamb! Oh think what it means. God gave it for your redemption. God accepted it when His Son entered heaven and presented it on your behalf. God has it for ever in His sight as the fruit, the infinitely well-pleasing proof, of His Son's obedience unto death. God points you to it and asks you to believe in the divine satisfaction it gives to Him, in its omnipotent energy, in its everlasting sufficiency. Oh, will you not this day believe that that blood gives you, sinful and feeble as you are, liberty, confidence, boldness to draw nigh, to enter the very Holiest? Yes, believe it, that the blood and the blood alone, brings you into the very presence, into the living and abiding fellowship of the everlasting God. And let your response to God's message concerning the blood, and the boldness it gives you be nothing less than this, that this very moment you go with the utmost confidence, and take your place in the most intimate fellowship with God. And if your heart condemn you, if coldness or unbelief appear to make a real entrance impossible, rest not till you believe and prove to the full the power of the blood indeed to bring you nigh. **Having boldness by the blood of Jesus**—what then—**let us draw nigh!**

1. Which is now greater in your sight: your sin or the blood of Jesus? There can be but one answer. Then draw nigh, and enter in, into the Holiest of All. As your sin has hitherto kept you back, let the blood now bring you nigh. And the blood will give you the boldness and the power to abide.

2. "One drop of that blood, coming out of the Holiest on the soul, perfects the conscience, makes that there is no more conscience of sin, and enables us to live in the fellowship of God and His Son. Such a soul, sprinkled with the blood, is able to enjoy the heavenly treasures, and to accomplish the heavenly service of the living God."

3. And that blood, such is its heavenly cleansing power, can keep the soul clean. "If we walk in the light, as He is in the light," if we live in the Holiest, in the light of His countenance, "we have fellowship one with another, and the blood of Jesus Christ, His Son, cleanseth us from all sin," so that no sin touch us, whereby we lose the fellowship with the Father.

4. Understand how the Father's heart longs that His children draw near to Him boldly. He gave the blood of His Son to secure it. Let us honour God, and honour the blood, by entering the Holiest with great boldness.

LXXXIII.

The New and Living Way

X.–19. Having therefore, brethren, boldness to enter into the Holy Place by the blood of Jesus,

20. by the way which he dedicated for us, a new and living way, through the veil, that is to say, his flesh;

22. Let us draw near.

The Holiest of All is opened for us to enter in and appear before God, to dwell and to serve in His very presence. The blood of the one sacrifice for ever, taken into heaven to cleanse away all sin for ever, is our title and our boldness to enter in. Now comes the question, What is the way that leads up and through the opened gate, and in which we have to walk if we are to enter in. This way, the only way, the one infallible way is, **a new and living way, which Jesus dedicated for us, through the veil, that is to say, His flesh.** *The boldness* we have *through the blood* is the right or liberty of access Jesus won for us, when we regard His death as that of our Substitute, who did what we can never do— made redemption of transgressions, and put away sin for ever. **The new and living way, through the rent veil, that is, His flesh,** has reference to His death, regarded as that of our Leader and Forerunner, who opened up a path to God, in which He first walked Himself, and then draws us to follow Him. The death of Jesus was not only the dedication or inauguration of the new sanctuary and of the new covenant, but also of the new way into the holy presence and fellowship of God. Whoever in faith accepts of the blood He shed as His boldness of entrance, must accept, too, of the way He opened up as that in which he walks.

And what was that way? **The way through the veil, that is, His flesh.** The veil is the flesh. The veil that separated man from God was the flesh, human nature under the power of sin. Christ came in the likeness of sinful flesh, and dwelt with us here outside the veil. *The Word was made flesh. He also Himself in like manner partook of flesh and blood.* **In the days of His flesh,** He was tempted like as we are; He offered prayer and supplication with strong crying and tears. He learned obedience even to the death. Through the rent veil of His flesh, His will, His life, as yielded up to God in death, He entered into the Holiest. *Being made in likeness of men, He humbled Himself, becoming obedient even unto death. Wherefore also God highly exalted Him.* Through the rent veil He rose to the throne of God. And this is the way He dedicated for us. The very path in which, as our Substitute, He accomplished redemption, is the path which He opened for us to walk in, the path of obedience unto death. "Christ suffered for you, leaving you an example that ye should follow His steps." Christ our High Priest is as literally and fully Leader and Forerunner as He is Substitute and Redeemer.

His way is our way. As little as He could open and enter the Holiest for us, except in His path of suffering and obedience and self-sacrifice, as little can we enter in unless we walk in the same path. Jesus said as much of His disciples as of Himself: *Except a corn of wheat fall into the ground, and die, it abideth alone. He that hateth his life in this world shall keep it unto life eternal.* Paul's law of life is the law of life for every believer: *Bearing about in the body the dying of Jesus, that the life also of Jesus may be manifested in our body.* The way into the Holiest is the way of the rent veil, the way of sacrifice and of death. There is no way for our putting away sin from us but the way of Jesus; whoever accepts His finished work accepts what constitutes its Spirit and its power; it is for every man as for the Master—to put away sin by the sacrifice of self. Christ's death was something entirely and essentially new, and so also His resurrection life; a life out of death, such as never had been known before. This new death and new life constitute the new and living way, the new way of living in which we draw nigh to God.

Even as when Christ spoke of taking *His flesh* as daily food, so here where the Holy Spirit speaks of taking the rent veil of His flesh as our daily life, many say: *This is a hard saying; who can bear it? Who then can be saved?* To those who are willing and obedient and believe, all things are possible, because it is **a new and living way. A new way.** The word means ever fresh, a way that never decays or waxes old (viii. 13) but always retains its first perfection and freshness. **A living way.** A way always needs a living man to move upon it; it does not impart either life or strength. This way, the way of obedience and suffering and self-sacrifice and death, however hard it appears, and to nature utterly impossible, is *a living way.* It not only opens a track, but supplies the strength to carry the traveller along. It acts in the power of the endless life, in which Christ was made a High Priest. We saw how the Holy Spirit watches over the way into the Holiest, and how He, as the Eternal Spirit, enabled Christ, in opening the way, to offer Himself without spot unto God; it is He whose mighty energy pervades this way, and inspires it with life divine. As we are made partakers of Christ, as we come to God through Him, His life, the law of the Spirit of life in Christ Jesus, takes possession of us, and in His strength we follow in the footsteps of Christ Jesus. The way into the Holiest is the living way of perfect conformity to Jesus, wrought in us by His Spirit.

The new and living way through the rent veil into the Holiest. We now know what it is: it is the way of death. Yes, the way of death is the way of life. The only way to be set free from our fallen nature, with the curse and power of sin resting on it, is to die to it. Jesus denied Himself, would do nothing to please that nature He had taken, sinless though it was in Him. He denied it; He died to it. This was to Him the path of life. And this is to us the living way. As we know Him in the power of His resurrection, He leads us into the conformity to His death. He does it in the power of the Holy Spirit. So His death and His life, the new death and the new life of deliverance from sin, and fellowship with God, which He inaugurated, work in us, and we are borne along as He was to where He is. **Having therefore boldness, to enter in by the new and living way, let us draw nigh.**

1. When first a believer avails himself of the boldness he has in the blood, and enters into the Holiest, he does not understand all that is meant by the new and living way. It is enough if his heart is right, and he is ready to deny himself and take up his cross. In due time it will be revealed what the full fellowship is with His Lord in the way He opened up, of obedience unto death.

2. The new and living way is not only the way for once entering in, but the way for a daily walk, entering ever deeper into God's love and will.

3. The way of life is the way of death. This fallen life, this self, is so sinful and so strong, there is no way of deliverance but by death. But, praise God! the way of death is the way of life; in the power of Christ's resurrection and indwelling we dare to walk in it.

LXXXIV.

A Great Priest over the House of God

X.–21. And having a great Priest over the house of God; let us draw near.

We said before that in the symbols of the Mosaic worship there were specially four things that, as types of the mystery of the coming redemption, demand attention. These are—*the Sanctuary, the Blood, the Way into the Holiest, the Priest.* The first three, all heavenly things, we have had; we now come to the fourth, the chief and the best of all—a *living Person, Jesus, a great High Priest over the house of God.* The knowledge of what He has won for me, the entrance into the Holiest; of the work He did to win it, the shedding of His blood; of the way in which I am to enter into the enjoyment of it all—all this is very precious. But there is something better still: it is this, that the living, loving, Son of God is there, personally to receive me and make me partaker of all the blessedness that God has for me. **This is the chief point: we have such a High Priest, who sat down on the right hand of the Majesty in the heavens. Wherefore, brethren, having a great Priest over the house of God, let us draw near.**

And what is now the work we need Jesus to do for us? Has it not all been done? The Holiest is opened. Boldness through the blood has been secured. The living way has been dedicated to carry us in. What more is there that Jesus has to do for us? Nothing more; it has all been finished, once and for ever. And why is it then we are pointed to Him as the great Priest over the house of God? And what is it we may expect of Him? What we need, and what we must look to Him for is this, so to work in us that the work He has done for us may be made real *within us,* as a personal experience of the power of an endless life in which He was constituted priest. **Because He liveth ever,** we read, **He is able to save completely.** Salvation is a subjective, experimental thing—manifest in the peace and holiness of heart He gives. We, our life, our inner man, our heart, our will and affections, are to be delivered from the power of sin, and to taste and enjoy the putting away of sin as a blessed experience. In our very heart we are to find and feel the power of His redemption. As deep and strong as sin proved itself in its actual power and its mastery within us, is Jesus to prove the triumph of redeeming grace.

His one work as Priest over the house of God is to bring us into it, and enable us to live there. He does this by bringing God and the soul into actual harmony, sympathy, and fellowship with each other. As Minister of the sanctuary He does all that is to be done in heaven with God; as Mediator of the new covenant He does all that is to be done here on earth, in our heart—the one as effectually as the other. The two offices are united in the one great Priest; in each act of His He unites both functions, to the soul that knows what to expect, and trusts Him. Every movement in the presence of God can have its corresponding movement in the heart of man.

And how is this effected?—In virtue of His union with us, and our union with Him. Jesus is the Second Adam; the new Head of the race. He is it in virtue of His real humanity, having in it the power of true divinity that filleth all. Just as Adam was our forerunner into death, and we have all the power of his sin and death working in us and drawing us on, so we have Jesus as our Forerunner into God's presence, with all the power of His death and His resurrection-life working in us, and drawing and lifting us in with divine energy into the Father's presence. Yes, Jesus with His divine, His heavenly life, in the power of the throne on which he is seated, has entered into the deepest ground of our being, where Adam, where sin, do their work, and is there unceasingly carrying out His work of lifting us heavenward into God's presence, and of making God's heavenly presence here on earth our portion.

And why is it we enjoy this so little? And what is needed that we come to its full enjoyment? And how can Jesus truly be to us a great High Priest, giving us our actual life in the Holiest of All? One great reason of failure is what the Epistle so insists on: our ignorance of the spiritual perfection-truth it seeks to teach, and specially of what the Holy Spirit witnesseth of the way into the Holiest. And what we need is just this, that the Holy Spirit Himself, that Jesus in the Holy Spirit, be waited on, and accepted, and trusted to do the work in power. Do keep a firm hold of this truth, that when our great High Priest once for all entered the Holiest, and sat down on the throne, it was *the Holy Ghost sent down in power into the hearts of His disciples, through whom the heavenly High Priest became a present and an indwelling Saviour,* bringing down with Him into their hearts the presence and the love of God. That Pentecostal gift, in the power of the glorified Christ, is the one indispensable channel of the power of Jesus' priesthood. Nothing but the fulness of the Spirit in daily life, making Jesus present within us, abiding continually, can keep us in the presence of God as full experience. Jesus is no outward High Priest, who can save us as from a distance. No, as the Second Adam, He is nowhere if He is not in us. The one reason why the truth of His heavenly priesthood is so often powerless, is because we look upon it as an external distant thing, a work going on in heaven above us. The one cure for this evil is to know that our great Priest over the house of God is *the glorified Jesus, who in the Holy Spirit is present in us,* and makes all that is done in heaven above for us to be done within us too by the Holy Spirit.

He is Priest over the house of God, the place where God dwells; we are His house too. And as surely as Jesus ministers in the sanctuary above, He moment by moment ministers in the sanctuary within. **Wherefore, brethren, having**—not only in gift, not only in the possession of right and thought, but in our hearts—**having a great Priest over the house of God, let us draw near.**

1. Having a great Priest! *You know a great deal of Jesus, but do you know this—that His chief, His all-comprehensive work, is to bring you near, oh so near, to God? Has He done this for you? If not, ask Him, trust Him for it.*

2. *It is Jesus Himself I want. Himself alone can satisfy me. It is in the holy faith of Jesus, the compassionate sympathiser, in the holy love of Jesus who calls us brethren, that we can draw near to God. It is in a heart given up, with its trust and love and devotion to Jesus, that the presence of God will be felt.*

3. We have such a High Priest! *Yes, say, I have Him; in all His power and love He is mine; and yield to Him to do His work.*

LXXXV.

With a True Heart

X.–22. Let us draw near with a true heart.

We have been looking at the four great blessings of the new worship by which God encourages us to draw near to Him. We shall now see what the four chief things are that God seeks for in us as we come to Him. Of these the first is, **a true heart.**

In man's nature the heart is the central power. As the heart is so is the man. The desire and the choice, the love and the hatred of the heart prove what a man is already, and decide what he is to become. Just as we judge of a man's physical character, his size and strength and age and habits, by his outward appearance, so the heart gives the real inward man his character; and "the hidden man of the heart" is what God looks to. God has in Christ given us access to the secret place of His dwelling, to the inner sanctuary of His presence and His heart; no wonder that the first thing He asks, as He calls us unto Him, is the heart—a true heart; our inmost being must in truth be yielded to Him, true to Him.

True religion is a thing of the heart, an inward life. It is only as the desire of the heart is fixed upon God, the whole heart seeking for God, giving its love and finding its joy in God, that a man can draw near to God. The heart of man was expressly planned and created and endowed with all its powers, that it might be capable of receiving and enjoying God and His love. God's great quarrel with His people is that their heart is turned from Him. In chapter iii. we heard Him complain of the hardening of the heart, the wandering heart, the unbelieving heart. No wonder that the first requisite for entering the Holiest of All should be a true heart. It is only with the heart that religion, that holiness, that the love and the will of God can be known. God can ask for nothing else and nothing less than the heart—than **a true heart.**

What the word *true* means we see from the use of it made previously (viii. 2 and ix. 24), **the true tabernacle,** and, **the Holy Place,** which are figures of **the true.** The first tabernacle was only a figure and a shadow of the true. There was, indeed, a religious service and worship, but it had no real abiding power; it could not make the worshipper perfect. **The very image,** the substance and reality, of the heavenly things themselves, were only brought by Christ. And God now asks that, to correspond with the true sanctuary, there shall be a true heart. The old covenant, with its tabernacle and its worship, which was but a shadow, could not put the heart of Israel right. In the new covenant God's first promise is, *I will write My law in the heart: a new heart will I give thee.* As He has given His Son, full of grace and truth, in the power of an endless life, to work all in us as the Mediator of a new covenant, to write His law in our hearts, He calls us to draw nigh with **a true heart.**

God asks for the heart. Alas, how many Christians serve Him still with the service of the old covenant. Religion is a thing of times and duties. There are seasons for Bible-reading and praying and church-going. But when one notices how speedily and naturally and happily, as soon as it is freed from restraint, the heart turns to worldly things, one feels how little there is of the heart in it: it is not the worship of a true heart, of the whole heart. The heart, with its life and love and joy, has not yet found in God its highest good. Religion is much more a thing of the head and its activities, than of the heart and its life, of the human will and its power, than of that Spirit which God gives within us.

The invitation comes: **Let us draw near with a true heart.** Let no one hold back for fear, my heart is not true. There is no way for obtaining the true heart, but by acting it. God has given you, as His child, a new heart—a wonderful gift, if you but knew it. Through ignorance or unbelief or disobedience it has grown feeble and withered; its beating can, nevertheless, still be felt. The Epistle, with its solemn warnings and its blessed teaching, has come to bring arousing and healing. Even as Christ said to the man with the withered hand, Stand forth, He calls to you from His throne in heaven, Rise, and come and enter in with a true heart. As you hesitate, and look within to feel and to find out if the heart is true, and in vain to do what is needed to make it true, He calls again, **Stretch forth thy hand.** When He spake that to him of the withered arm, whom He had called to rise up and stand before Him, the man felt the power of Jesus' eye and voice, and he stretched it forth. Do thou, likewise. Stretch forth, lift up, reach out that withered heart of thine, that has so been cherishing its own impotence—stretch forth, and it will be made whole. Yes, in the very act of obeying the call to enter in, it will prove itself a true heart—a heart ready to obey and to trust its blessed Lord, a heart ready to give up all and find its life in the secret of His presence. Yes, Jesus, the great Priest over the house of God, the Mediator of the new covenant, with the new heart secured thee, calls, **Draw nigh with a true heart.**

During these last years God has been rousing His people to the pursuit of holiness—that is, to seek the entrance into the Holiest, a life in full fellowship with Himself, the Holy One. In the teaching which He has been using to this end, two words have been very much in the foreground—Consecration and Faith. These are just what are here put first—a true heart and the fulness of faith. The true heart is nothing but true consecration, the spirit that longs to live wholly for God, that gladly gives up everything that it may live wholly for Him, and that above all yields up the heart, as the key of the life, into His keeping and rule. True religion is an inward life, in the power of the Holy Spirit. Let us enter in into the inner sanctuary of God's love, and the Spirit will enter into the inner sanctuary of our love, into our heart. Let us draw nigh with a true heart—longing, ready, utterly given up to desire and receive the blessing.

1. *If you look at your own constitution, you see how the head and the heart are the two great centres of life and action. Much thought and study make the head weary. Strong emotion or excitement affects the heart. It is the heart God asks—the power of desire and affection and will. The head and the heart are in partnership. God tells us that the heart must rule and lead, that it is the heart He wants. Our religion has been too much that of the head—hearing and reading and thinking. Let us beware of allowing these to lead us astray. Let them stand aside at times. Let us give the heart time to assert its supremacy. Let us draw nigh with a true heart.*

2. *A true heart—true in what it says that it thinks of itself; true in what it says that it believes of God; true in what it professes to take from God and to give to Him.*

3. *It is the heart God wants to dwell in. It is in the state of the heart God wants to prove His power to bless. It is in the heart the love and the joy of God are to be known. Let us draw near with a true heart.*

LXXXVI.

The Fulness of Faith

X.–22. Let us draw near, in fulness of faith.

This translation, **the fulness of faith,** is not only more correct than that of, full assurance of faith, but much more significant. Full assurance of faith refers only to the strength and confidence with which we believe. The truth we accept may be very limited and defective, and our assurance of it may be more an undoubting conviction of the mind than the living apprehension of the heart. In both respects the **fulness of faith** expresses what we need—a faith that takes in objectively all that God offers it in its fulness, and subjectively all the powers of our heart and life in their fulness. **Let us draw near, in fulness of faith.**

Here, if anywhere, there is indeed need of fulness of faith, that we may take in all the fulness of the provision God has made, and of the promises that are waiting for us to inherit. The message comes to a sinful man that he may have his continual abode in the **Most Holy;** that, more real and near than with his nearest earthly friend, he may live in unbroken fellowship with the Most High God. He is assured that **the blood of Christ** can cleanse his conscience in such power that he can draw nigh to God with a perfect conscience and with undoubting confidence, and can ask and expect to live always in the unclouded light of God's face. He receives the assurance that the power of the Holy Ghost, coming from out of the Holiest, can enable him to walk exactly in the same path in which Christ walked on His way to God, and make that way to him **a new and living way,** with

393

nothing of decay or weariness in his progress. This is the **fulness of faith** we are called to. But, above all, to look to Jesus in all the glory in which He has been revealed in the Epistle, as God and Man, as Leader and Forerunner, as Melchizedek, as the Minister of the sanctuary and Mediator of the new covenant—in one word, as **our great Priest over the house of God.** And, looking to Him, to claim that He shall do for us this one thing, to bring us nigh, and even on earth give us to dwell for ever in the presence of God.

Faith ever deals with impossibilities. Its only rule or measure is what God has said to be possible to Him. When we look at our lives and their failures, at our sinfulness and weakness, at those around us, the thought will come up—Is it for me? Dare I expect it? Is it not wearying myself in vain to think of it or to seek for it? Soul! the God who redeemed thee, when an enemy, with the blood of His Son—what thinkest thou? would He not be willing thus to take thee to His heart? He who raised Jesus, when He had died under the curse of thy sins, from the death of the grave to the throne of His glory, would He not be able to take thee, too, and give thee a place within the veil? Do believe it. He longs to do it; He is able to do it. His home and His heart have room for thee even now. **Let us draw near in fulness of faith.**

In fulness of faith. The word has also reference to that full measure of faith which is found when the whole heart is filled and possessed by it. We have very little idea of how the weakness of our faith is owing to its being more a confident persuasion of the mind with regard to the truth of what God says, than the living apprehension and possession of the eternal spiritual realities of the truth with the heart. The Holy Spirit asks us first for a true heart, and then at once, as its first exercise, for **fulness of faith.** There is a faith of insight, a faith of desire, a faith of trust in the truth of the word, and a faith of personal acceptance. There is a faith of love that embraces, a faith of will that holds

fast, and a faith of sacrifice that gives up everything, and a faith
of despair that abandons all hope in self, and a faith of rest that
waits on God alone. This is all included in the faith of the true
heart, the fulness of faith, in which the whole being surrenders
and lets go all, and yields itself to God to do His work. **In fulness of faith let us draw nigh.**

In fulness of faith, not of thought. What God is about to do
to you is supernatural, *above what you can think.* It is a love *that
passes knowledge* is going to take possession. God is the incomprehensible, the hidden One. The Holy Spirit is the secret, incomprehensible working and presence of God. Do not seek to
understand everything. Draw nigh—it never says with a clear
head, but with a true heart. Rest upon God to do for you far
more than you understand.

In fulness of faith, and not in fulness of feeling. When you
come, and, gazing into the opened Holiest of All, hear the voice
of Him that dwells between the cherubim call you to come in;
and, as you gaze, long indeed to enter and to dwell there, the
word comes again, **Draw nigh with a true heart!** Your answer
is, Yes, Lord; with my whole heart—with that *new heart* thou
thyself hast given me. You make the surrender of yourself, to
live only and always in His presence and for His service. The
voice speaks again: Let it be Today—Now, **in fulness of faith.**
You have accepted what He offers. You have given what he asks.
You believe that He accepts the surrender. You believe that the
great Priest over the house takes possession of your inner life,
and brings you before God. And yet you wonder you feel so little changed. You feel just like the old self you were. Now is the
time to listen to the voice—**In fulness of faith,** not of feeling!
Look to God, who is able to do above what we ask or think.
Trust His power. Look to Jesus on the throne, living there to
bring you in. Claim the Spirit of the exalted One as His Pentecostal gift. Remember these are all divine, spiritual mysteries of
grace, to be revealed in you. Apart from feeling, without feeling,

in fulness of faith, in bare, naked faith that honours God, enter in. Reckon yourself to be indeed alive to God in Christ Jesus, taken in into His presence, His love, His very heart.

1. Be followers of those who, through faith and longsuffering, inherited the promises. Faith accepts and rejoices in the gift; longsuffering waits for the full enjoyment; and so faith in due time inherits, and the promise becomes an experience. By faith at once take your place in the Holiest; wait on the Holy Spirit in your inner life to reveal it in the power of God; your High Priest will see to your inheriting the blessing.

2. In the fulness of the whole heart to accept the whole fulness of God's salvation—this is what God asks.

3. As in heaven so on earth. The more I look at the fulness of grace in Christ, the more the fulness of faith will grow in me. Of His fulness have we received, and grace for grace.

4. A whole chapter is to be devoted to the exhibiting of what this fulness of faith implies. Let us go on to study it with the one object for which it is given—our entering into that life in the will and love of God which Jesus has secured for us.

LXXXVII.

Our Hearts Sprinkled

X.–22. Let us draw near . . . our hearts sprinkled from an evil conscience.

In verse 19 we had **boldness through the blood of Jesus,** as one of the four precious things prepared for us by God. It is that actual liberty or right which the blood of Jesus gives, apart from any use we make of it. Along with the opened sanctuary, and the living way, and the great Priest, the blood and our boldness in it is a heavenly reality waiting our faith and acceptance. Here the blood is mentioned a second time, and our being sprinkled with it as one of the things God asks of us. It is in the personal application and experience of the power of the blood we are to draw nigh. This second mention of the blood is in accord with what we had in chapter ix. of its twofold sprinkling. First, Christ entered with it into heaven, to cleanse the heavenly things, and fulfil the type of the sprinkling on the mercy-seat. It proved its power with God in putting away sins. And then we read of its cleansing our conscience. The blood which has had its mighty operation in heaven itself has as mighty power in our hearts. It makes us partakers of a divine and eternal cleansing. In heaven the power of the blood is proved to be infinite and immeasurable, never-ceasing and eternal, giving boldness to enter even as Christ did. As the soul learns to believe and rejoice in this heavenly power of the blood, it will claim and receive the very same power in the heart; as Jesus washes us in His blood, we know by faith what it is to have, in a heavenly reality, **a heart sprinkled from an evil conscience.**

There will ever be harmony between a home and those who dwell in it, between an environment and the life that is sustained by it. There must be harmony between the Holiest of All and the soul that is to enter in. That harmony begins with, and has its everlasting security in, the blood of sprinkling. The ever-living and never-ceasing energy of the blood, ever speaking better things than the blood of Abel and keeping heaven open for me, has a like effect on my heart. The blood has put away the thought of sin from God; He remembers it no more for ever. The blood puts away the thought of sin in me too, taking away the evil conscience that condemns me. The better things which the blood speaks in heaven, it speaks in my heart too; it lifts me into that heavenly sphere, that new state of life and intercourse with God, in which an end has been made of sin, and the soul is taken in to the full and perfect enjoyment of the love of God.

The action of the blood in heaven is unceasing—never a moment but the blood is the delight of the Father and the song of the ransomed. Draw nigh when thou wilt, the blood is there, abiding continually; not a moment's interval. And even so will it be in the soul that enters in. The difficulty that staggers the faith of many lies just here: they cannot understand how one who has to live amid the cares and engagements and companionships of this daily life can every moment maintain a heart sprinkled from an evil conscience. They do not know that, if once, with a heart sprinkled they enter in, they are in an inner sanctuary, where everything acts in the power of the upper world, in the power of an endless life. They breathe the inspiring, invigorating air of the Holiest of All; they breathe the Holy Spirit, and enjoy the power of the resurrection life. The Minister of the heavenly sanctuary is also the Mediator of the new covenant in our hearts. All He does in heaven He does each moment on earth in our hearts, if faith will trust Him; for the blood of sprinkling is the blood of the covenant.

And what may be the reason that so few Christians can testify of the joy and the power of a heart at all times sprinkled from an evil conscience? The answer is, That in the apprehension of this, as of every other truth, there are stages according to the measure of faith and faithfulness. See it in Israel. There you have three stages. The Israelite who entered the outer court saw the altar and the blood sprinkled there, and received such assurance of pardon as that could give him. The priest who was admitted to the Holy Place not only saw the blood sprinkled on the brazen altar, he had it sprinkled upon himself, and might see it sprinkled on the golden altar in the Holy Place. His contact with the blood was closer, and he was admitted to a nearer access. And the access of the high priest was still more complete; he might, with the blood for the mercy-seat, once a year enter within the veil. Even so there are outer-court Christians, who trust in Christ who died on Calvary, but know very little of His heavenly life, or near access to God, or service for others. Beyond these there are Christians who know that they are called to be priests and to live in the service of God and their fellow-men. They know more of the power of the blood as setting apart for service; but yet their life is still without the veil. But then come those who know what Christ's entering with His blood implies and procures, and who experience that the Holy Spirit applies the blood in such power, that it indeed brings to the life in the inner sanctuary, in the full and abiding joy of God's presence.[1]

Let us draw near, with a true heart, in fulness of faith, having our hearts sprinkled from an evil conscience. Oh, let

---

1. *"The blood contains life* (John vi. 53). The blood not only removes death (judicial and spiritual), but it gives and preserves life (judicial and spiritual). It quickens. We are not only to be sprinkled with it outwardly, but we are to receive it inwardly, to drink it. As with the water, so with the blood, they are for inward as well as outward application."—H. Bonar

us not bring a reproach upon the blood of the Lamb by not be-lieving in its power to give us perfect access to God. Let us listen and hear them sing without ceasing the praise of the blood of the Lamb in heaven; as we trust and honour and rejoice in it we shall enter the heaven of God's presence.

1. *"Wherein is the blood of Jesus better than the blood of goats and bulls, if it cannot free us from the spirit of bondage and the evil conscience, if it cannot give us a full glad confidence before God? What Jesus hath perfected we can experience and enjoy as perfect in our heart and conscience. You dishonour your Saviour when you do not seek to experience that He has perfected you as touching the conscience, and when you do not live with a heart entirely cleansed from the evil conscience."—STEINHOFER*

2. *A true heart—a heart sprinkled: you see everything depends upon the heart. God can do nothing for us from without, only by what He can put into the heart. Of all that Jesus is and does as High Priest in heaven I cannot have the least experience, but as it is revealed in the heart. The whole work of the Holy Spirit is in the heart. Let us draw nigh with a true heart, a sprinkled heart, our inmost being entirely and unceasingly under the heavenly power of the blood.*

LXXXVIII.

Our Body Washed

X.–22. Let us draw near . . . our body washed with pure water.

Man belongs to two worlds, the visible and the invisible. In his constitution, the material and the spiritual, body and soul, are wonderfully united. In the fall both came under the power of sin and death; in redemption deliverance has been provided for both. It is not only in the interior life of the soul, but in that of the body too, that the power of redemption can be manifested.

In the Old Testament worship the external was the more prominent. It consisted mostly in carnal ordinances, imposed until a time of reformation. They taught a measure of truth, they exercised a certain influence on the heart, but they could not make the worshipper perfect. It was only with the New Testament that the religion of the inner life, the worship of God in spirit and truth, was revealed. And yet we need to be on the watch lest the pursuit of the inner life lead us to neglect the external. It is in the body, as much as in the spirit, that the saving power of Christ Jesus must be felt. It was with this view that our Lord adopted one of the Jewish washings, and instituted the baptism with water. He that believed with the heart, came with the body to be baptized. It was a token that the whole exterior physical life, with all its functions and powers, was to be His too. It was in this connection John wrote: *There are three who bear witness, the Spirit and the water and the blood.* The same Spirit who applies the blood in power to the heart, takes possession and mastery of the body washed with water. And where in Scripture the word and water are joined together (Eph. v. 26; John xiii. 10; xv. 3), it is because the word is the external manifestation of what must rule our whole outer life too.

It is in this connection the two expressions are used here: **Our hearts sprinkled** from an evil conscience, **our bodies washed with pure water.** The thought was suggested to our author by the service of the tabernacle. In the court there were only two things to be seen—the brazen altar and the laver. At the one, the priest received and sprinkled the blood; at the other, he found the water in which he washed, ere he entered the Holy Place. At the installation of the priests in their office they were first washed and then sprinkled with blood (Ex. xxix. 4, 20). On the great day of atonement the high priest, too, had first to wash ere he entered into the Holiest with the blood (Lev. xvi. 4). And so the lesson comes to us that if we draw near with **hearts sprinkled from an evil conscience,** we must also have **the body washed with pure water.** The liberty of access, the cleansing the blood gives, can only be enjoyed in a life of which every action is cleansed by the word. Not only in the heart and the disposition, but in the body and the outer visible life, everything must be clean. *Who shall ascend into the hill of the Lord? or who shall stand in His Holy Place? He that hath clean hands,* and a *pure heart.* A heart sprinkled with the blood, a body washed with pure water from every stain—these God hath joined together; let no man separate them. There have been some who have sought very earnestly to enter into the Holiest of All and have failed. The reason was that they had not clean hands, they were not ready to have everything that is not perfectly holy discovered and put away. *Cleanse your hands, ye sinners, and purify your hearts, ye double-minded*—is a word that always holds. The blood of Christ has unspeakable and everlasting power for the soul that, with a true heart, is ready to put away every sin. Where this is not the case, and the body is not washed with pure water, the perfect conscience which the blood gives cannot be enjoyed.

Our body washed with pure water. It is not only in spirit, *but with the body too,* we enter into the Holiest of All. It is on us here, where we are *in the body,* that the presence of God descends. Our whole life in the flesh is to be in that presence; the body is very specially the temple, and in charge of the Holy Spirit; in the body the Father is to be glorified. Our whole being, body, soul, and spirit, is in the power of the Holy Spirit, a holy sacrifice upon the altar, a living sacrifice for service before God. With the body, too, we live and walk in the Holiest. Our eating and drinking, our sleeping, our clothing, our labour and relaxation—all these things have more influence on our spiritual life than we know. They often interrupt and break the fellowship we seek to maintain. The heart and the body are inseparably joined—a heart sprinkled from an evil conscience needs a body washed with pure water.

When He cometh into the world He saith, A body didst thou prepare for Me. This word of Christ must be adopted by each of His followers. Nothing will help us to live in this world, and keep ourselves unspotted, but the Spirit that was in Christ, that looked upon His body as prepared by God for His service; that looks upon our body as prepared by Him too, that we might offer it to Him. Like Christ we too have a body, in which the Holy Spirit dwells. Like Christ we too must yield our body, with every member, every power, every action, to fulfil His will, to be offered up to Him, to glorify Him. Like Christ we must prove in our body that we are holy to the Lord.

The blood that is sprinkled on thy heart came from the body of Jesus, prepared by God, and, in His whole life, even to His one offering, given up to God. The object of that blood sprinkling is that thy body, of which the heart sprinkled with the blood is the life, should, like His, be wholly given up to God. Oh, seek to take in this blessed truth, and to accept it fully. The heart sprinkled from the evil conscience will then become an unbroken experience, and the blood of the Lamb the ever-living motive and power for a life in the body, like Christ's, a sacrifice holy and acceptable to God.

1. *I am deeply persuaded that in the self-pleasing which we allow in gratifying the claims of the body, we shall find one of the most frequent causes of the gradual decline of our fellowship with God. Do remember, it was through the body that Satan conquered in Paradise; it was in the body he tempted Christ and had to be resisted. It was in suffering of the body, as when He hungered, that Christ was perfected. It is only when the law of self-denial is strictly applied to the body, that we can dwell in the Holiest.*

2. *He was tempted in all points, like as we are—in His body very specially, and is able to succour us. Let the committal of our body into the keeping and the rule of Jesus be very definite and entire.*

3. *"If Miranda was to run a race for her life, she would submit to a diet that was proper for it. As the race which is set before her is a race for holiness and heavenly affection, so her everyday diet has only this one end—to make her body fitter for this spiritual life."*

LXXXIX.

Let Us Draw Near

X.–22. Wherefore, brethren, let us draw near.

We have studied the four great blessings of the new worship, as the motives and encouragements for us to draw nigh. They are—the *Holiest opened up, Boldness through the blood,* the *New and living way,* and the *Great Priest over the house of God.* And we have considered the four great marks of the true worshipper— *A true heart, Fulness of faith, The heart sprinkled,* and *The body cleansed.* We now come to the four injunctions which come to us out of the opened sanctuary—and specially to the first—**Let us draw near.** Both in speaking of the entering in of Christ, and the power of His blood in chapter ix., and in the exposition of our context, we have had abundant occasion to point out what is meant by this entering in, and what is needed for it. And yet it may be well to gather up all we have said, and in the very simplest way possible, once again, by the grace of God, to throw open the door, and to help each honest-hearted child of God to enter in, and take his place for life in the home the Father has prepared for him.

And first of all I would say: *Believe that a life in the Holiest of All, a life of continual abiding in God's presence, is most certainly your duty and within your power.* As long as this appears a vague uncertainty, the study of our Epistle must be in vain. Its whole teaching has been to prove that the wonderful priesthood of Christ, in which He does everything **in the power of an endless life, and is therefore able to save completely;** that His having

405

opened a way through the rent veil into the Holiest, and entered in with His blood; that His sitting on the throne in heavenly power, as Minister of the sanctuary and Mediator of the covenant; that all this means nothing if it does not mean—*the Holiest is open for us.* We may, we must, and we can live there. What is the meaning of this summing up of all, **Wherefore brethren, having boldness to enter—let us draw nigh**, if a real entrance into and abode in the Holiest is not for us? No, beloved Christian, do believe, it can be. Let no thought of thy weakness and unfaithfulness hold thee back. Begin to look at God, who has set the door open and calls thee in; at the blood that has prevailed over sin and death, and given thee a boldness that nothing can hinder; at Christ the almighty and most loving High Priest, who is to bring thee in and keep thee in; and believe: yes, such a life is meant for me; it is possible; it is my duty; God calls me to it; and say, then, whether thy heart would not desire and long to enter into this blessed rest, the home of God's love.

The second step is, *the surrender to Christ,* by Him to be brought into the life of abiding fellowship with God. This surrender implies an entire giving up of the life of nature and of self; and entire separation from the world and its spirit; an entire acceptance of God's will to command my life, in all things, down to the very least. To some this surrender comes as the being convicted of a number of things which they thought harmless, and which they now see to have been in the will of the flesh and of man. To others it comes as a call to part with some single doubtful thing, or some sin against which they have hopelessly struggled. The surrender of all becomes only possible when the soul sees how truly and entirely Jesus, the Mediator of the new covenant, has undertaken for all, and engages to put His own delight in God's law into the heart, to give the will and the strength to live in all God's will. That faith gives the courage to place oneself before Christ and to say—Lord, here am I, ready to be led by Thee in the new and living way of death to my will, and a life in God's will alone: I give up all to Thee.

Then comes, accompanying this surrender, *the faith that Jesus does now accept and undertake for all.* The more general faith in His power, which led to the surrender, becomes a personal appropriation. I know that I cannot lift or force myself into the Holiest. I trust Jesus, as my almighty and ever-living Priest on the throne, even now, at this moment, to take me in within the veil, to take charge of me there, and enable me to walk up and down before the face of the living God, and serve Him. However high and impossible such a life appears, I cannot doubt but that He who with His blood opened the Holiest for me will take me in; and that He who sits on the throne as my great High Priest is able and faithful to keep me in God's presence. Apart from any feeling or experience of a change I believe He takes me in, and I say: Thank God, I am in the Holiest. **Let us draw nigh in fulness of faith.**

And then follows, *the life of faith in the Holiest,* holding fast my confidence and the glorying of hope firm to the end. I believe Jesus takes me in to the fulfilment and the experience of all the new covenant blessings, and makes me inherit all the promises. I look to Him day by day to seal my faith with the Holy Ghost sent down from heaven in my heart. The disciples, when their Lord ascended the throne, kept waiting, praising, praying, till the Spirit came as the witness and the revealer within their hearts of the glory of Jesus at the right hand of God. It was on the day of Pentecost that they truly entered within the veil, to which the Forerunner had drawn their longing hearts. The soul that gives itself over to a life within the veil, in full surrender and in simple faith, can count upon this most surely, that, in the power of the eternal, the Pentecostal Spirit in the heart, faith will become experience, and the joy unspeakable be its abiding portion—**Wherefore, brethren, let us draw near.**

1. Having boldness to enter in *is the summary of the doctrinal teaching of the first half of the Epistle;* let us draw nigh, *the summary of the life and practice which the second half expounds.*

2. *The faith that appropriates the blessing—Jesus now takes me in and gives me my place and my life in the Father's presence, is but a beginning. Faith must now count upon the Holy Spirit, in His Pentecostal power, bringing down the kingdom of heaven to us, to make it a personal experience. Until this comes, faith must in patience wait till it obtains the promise, in accordance with the teaching we had: "Cast not away therefore your boldness. For ye have need of patience, that, having done the will of God, ye may receive the promise."*

XC.

The Confession of Our Hope

X.–23. Let us hold fast the confession of our hope that it waver not; for he is faithful that promised.

The three chief words of this injunction we have had before— *Hold fast, Confession, Hope.* If we **hold fast** the glorying of our **hope** firm to the end. Give diligence to **the fulness of hope.** Christ the **High Priest of our profession.** Let us **hold fast** our **confession.** A **better hope,** by which we draw nigh to God. We have now been brought to see what Christian perfection is, in that perfect life in God's presence to which Jesus brings us in: here, more than ever, we shall need to hold fast our hope.

Faith and hope ever go together. *"Faith* is the substance of things *hoped* for." Faith accepts the promise in its divine reality, hope goes forward to examine and picture and rejoice in the treasures which faith has accepted. And so here, on the words **Let us draw near in fulness of faith,** there follows immediately, **Let us hold fast the confession of our hope.** Life in the Holiest, in the nearness of God, must be characterised by an infinite hopefulness.

It is not difficult to see the reason of this. Entering into the Holiest is only the beginning of the true Christian life. As we tarry there God can begin to do His work of grace in power. There the holiness of God can overshadow us, and can be assimilated into our life and character. There we can learn to worship in that true humility and meekness and resignation to God's will, which does not come at once, but in which we may grow up even as Jesus did. There we have to learn the holy art of intercession, so as to pray the prayer that prevails. There we wait to receive in larger measure, in ever-fresh communication, that fulness of the Spirit which comes and is maintained only by close and living contact with Jesus on the throne. The entrance into the Holiest is only a beginning. It is to be a life in which we every hour receive everything from God, in which God's working is to be all in all. Here, if anywhere, we have need of an infinite hopefulness. After we have entered in, we shall very probably not find what we expected. The light and the joy and the power may not come at once. Within the veil it is still, nay rather it is eminently, a life of faith, not looking to ourselves, but to God, and hoping in Him. Faith will still be tried, will perhaps most be tried when God wants most to bless. Hope is the daughter of faith, the messenger it sends out to see what is to come: it is hope that becomes the strength and support of faith.

Let us hold fast the confession of our hope. Men always speak out of the abundance of the heart of that which they hope for. We, too, must confess and give expression to our hope. The confession strengthens the hope; what we utter becomes clearer and more real to us. It glorifies God. It helps and encourages those around us. It makes God, and men, and ourselves, see that we are committed to it. Let us hold fast the confession of our hope, that it waver not. Let the better hope by which we draw nigh to God, by which we enter within the veil, be the one thing we hold fast and confess with a confidence that never wavers.

For He is faithful that promised. Study the references on the word "promise" in this Epistle, and see what a large place they take in God's dealings with His people, and learn how much your life depends on your relation to the promises. Connect the promises, as is here done, with the promiser; connect the promiser with His unchanging faithfulness as God, and your hope will become a glorying in God, through Jesus Christ our Lord. **Faithful is He that promised:** that word lies at the root of the life within the veil. Just as it is God who speaks in Christ, who sent Him, who appointed Him Priest, who perfected Him, so it is God to whom Christ brings us into the Holiest, for Him now to work directly and continually in us that life in which, as His redeemed creatures, we are to live. This is the blessedness of being brought into the Holiest: Christ has brought us *to God.* And we are now in the right place and spirit for honouring Him as God—that is, for allowing Him to work freely, immediately, unceasingly in us such a life as He wrought in Christ. He is faithful that promised. God is going to fulfil His promises of life and love, of blessing and fruitfulness, in a way we have no conception of. **Let us hold fast the confession of our hope, for He is faithful that promised.**

My reader, thou hast heard the call, **Let us draw near in fulness of faith.** And hast obeyed? And hast believed that Jesus takes thee into a life of abiding in God's presence? And art, even amid the absence of feeling or experience, even amid the doubts and fears that threaten to press in, holding fast the confession of thy hope?—Listen, look up—**He is faithful that promised!** Let this be thy rock. Say continually—*O my soul, hope thou in God, for I shall yet praise Him. Thou art my hope, O God! I will hope continually, and praise Thee yet more and more.* This is the blessing of the inner sanctuary, that thou hast found thy true place at God's feet, there to wait in absolute dependence and helplessness on His working. Look up in the boldness the blood gives thee. Look up with a true heart, in which the Holy Spirit dwells and works. Look up with a heart sprinkled by thy blessed High Priest with the blood—and hope, yes hope, in God to do His divine work in thy soul. Let Him be to thee more than ever the God of hope. Claim the fulfilment of the promise of His word: *The God of hope fill you with all joy and peace in believing, that ye may abound in hope, in the power of the Holy Ghost.* The infinite faithful God, as the God of our hope, filling us with joy and peace in believing, and we learning to abound in hope through the power of the Holy Ghost: Be this our life in the secret of God's presence!

1. *Fulness of faith and fulness of hope are two dispositions that mark the true heart. It is because we are to have nothing in ourselves, and God is to be all and to do all, that our whole attitude is to be looking up to Him, expecting and receiving what He is to do.*

2. That ye may abound in hope, through the power of the Holy Ghost. *See how the life of hope in the Holiest depends entirely upon the Holy Spirit dwelling within us. To live this life, we need to be filled with the Spirit. Not a moment can we dwell in the Holiest, but by the Holy Spirit. Not a moment but we can dwell in the Holiest, by the Holy Spirit. Let us abound in hope, through the power of the Holy Spirit.*

XCI.

Love and Good Works

X.–24. And let us consider one another, to provoke unto love and good works.

We have had the *fulness of faith* in which we are to draw nigh, and the *confession of hope* we are to hold fast, now follows the third of the sister graces: **Let us consider one another**—let us prove our love and care for each other in the effort—**to provoke unto love and good works.** These three thoughts form the subdivision of the practical part of the Epistle. Chapter xi. may well be headed, *The fulness of faith;* chapter xii. 1–14, *The patience of hope;* and chapter xiii., *Love and good works.*

And let us consider one another. He that enters into the Holiest enters into the home of eternal love; the air he breathes there is love; the highest blessing he can receive there is a heart in which the love of God is shed abroad in power by the Holy Ghost, and which is on the path to be made perfect in love. *That thou mayest know how thou oughtest to behave thyself in the house of God*—remember this, *Faith and hope shall pass away, but love abideth ever. The chief of these is love.*

Let us consider one another. When first we seek the entrance into the Holiest, the thought is mostly of ourselves. And when we have entered in in faith, it is as if it is all we can do to stand before God, and wait on Him for what He has promised to do for us. But it is not long before we perceive that the Holiest and the Lamb are not for us alone; that there are others within with whom it is blessed to have fellowship in praising God; that

413

there are some without who need our help to be brought in. It is into the love of God that we have had access given us; that love enters our hearts; and we see ourselves called to live like Christ in entire devotion to those around us.

Let us consider one another. All the redeemed form one body. Each one is dependent on the other, each one is for the welfare of the other. Let us beware of the self-deception that thinks it possible to enter the Holiest, into the nearest intercourse with God, in the spirit of selfishness. It cannot be. The new and living way Jesus opened up is the way of self-sacrificing love. The entrance into the Holiest is given to us as priests, there to be filled with the Spirit and the love of Christ, and to go out and bring God's blessing to others.

Let us consider one another. The same Spirit that said, **Consider Christ Jesus**—take time, and give attention to know Him well—says to us, **Consider one another**—take time, and give attention to know the needs of your brethren around you. How many are there whose circumstances are so unfavourable, whose knowledge is so limited, whose whole life is so hopeless, that there is but little prospect of their ever attaining the better life. For them there is but one thing to be done: *We that are strong ought to bear the infirmities of the weak, and not to please ourselves.* Each one who begins to see what the blessedness is of a life in the full surrender to Christ should offer himself to Christ, to be made His messenger to the feeble and the weary.

Consider one another, to provoke unto love and good works. Love and good works: These are to be the aim of the Church in the exercise of its fellowship. Everything that can hinder love is to be sacrificed and set aside. Everything that can promote, and prove, and provoke others to, love is to be studied and performed.

And with love good works too. The Church has been redeemed by Christ, to prove to the world what power He has to cleanse from sin, to conquer evil, to restore to holiness and to goodness. Let us consider one another, in every possible way, to provoke, to stir up, to help to love and good works.

The chief thought is this: Life in the Holiest must be a life of love. As earnest as the injunction, *Let us draw nigh* in fulness of faith, *Let us hold fast* the confession of our hope, is this, *Let us consider one another* to provoke unto love and good works. God is love. And all He has done for us in His Son, as revealed in this Epistle, is love. And Christ is love. And there can be no real access to God as a union with Him in His holy will, no real communion with Him, but in the Spirit of love. Our entering into the Holiest is mere imagination, if we do not yield ourselves to the love of God in Christ, to be filled and used for the welfare and joy of our fellow-men.

O Christian! study what love is. Study it in the word, in Christ, in God. As thou seest Him to be an ever-flowing fountain of all goodness, who has His very being and glory in this, that He lives in all that exists, and communicates to all His own blessedness and perfection as far as they are capable of it, thou wilt learn to acknowledge that he that loveth not hath not known God. And thou wilt learn, too, to admit more deeply and truly than ever before, that no effort of thy will can bring forth love; it must be given thee from above. This will become to thee one of the chief joys and beauties of the Holiest of All, that there thou canst wait on the God of love to fill thee with His love. God hath the power to shed abroad His love in our hearts, by the Holy Spirit given unto us. He has promised to give Christ, so dwelling in our heart by faith, that we shall be rooted and grounded in love, and know and have in us something of a love that passeth knowledge. The very atmosphere of the Holiest is love. Just as I breathe in the air in which I live, so the soul that abides in the presence of God breathes the air of the upper world. The promise held out to us, and the hour of its fulfilment, will come, when the love of God will be perfected in us, and we are made perfect in love. Nowhere can this be but in the

Holiest; but there most surely. Let us draw nigh in the fulness of faith, and consider one another. While we are only thinking of others to bring God's love to them, we shall find God thinking of us, and filling us with it.

1. *It is the very essence, the beauty, and the glory of the salvation of Christ, that it is for all. He that truly receives it, as the Holy Spirit gives it, receives it as a salvation for all, and feels himself impelled to communicate it to others. The baptism of fire is a baptism of redeeming love, but that not as a mere emotion, but a power at once to consider and to care for others.*

2. *How impossible to love others and give all for them in our strength! This is one of the real gifts to be waited for in the Holiest of all, to be received in the power of the pentecostal Spirit—the love of God so shed abroad in the heart, that we spontaneously, unceasingly, joyfully love, because it is our very nature.*

XCII.

The Assembling Together

X.–25. Not forsaking the assembling of ourselves together, as the custom of some is, but exhorting one another; and so much the more, as ye see the day drawing nigh.

The inward and the outward must ever go together. As there is in every man a hidden inner life of the soul, along with the outer life of the body, so too in the Church of Christ. All its members are one body; the inward unity must be proved in active exercise, it must be seen in the assembling together. The assembling of His saints has its ground in a divine appointment as well as in the very nature of things; all who have entered into the Holiest to meet their God must turn to the meeting of His people. The tabernacle of old was the tent of meeting; to meet God and to meet our fellow-men are equally needful. Among the Hebrews it was already the custom with some to forsake the assembling together; it was one of the dangerous symptoms of backsliding. They are reminded, not only of the personal duty of each to be faithful, but also to care for others, and to exhort one another. For exercise and strengthening of the faith and hope and love, to which we have just been urged; for the full development of the life in the Holiest of All; for the helping and comforting of all who are feeble; for the cultivation of the fellowship of the Spirit and the Word—the assembling of ourselves together has unspeakable value. Let us listen to the exhortation, in connection with our entrance into the Holiest. **Not forsaking the assembling of ourselves together, as the custom of some is.**

If we would rightly apprehend the import of this word let us not forget the link to its context. Our section has been teaching us what life in the Holiest is to be. As those who have drawn near to God we are to draw near to our fellow-men. Meeting God is a thing of infinite blessedness and peace and power. Meeting our fellow-men is often accompanied with so much of weakness, distraction, and failure that some have thought it indeed better to forsake the assembling together. Let us see how life in the Holiest of All points to both the duty and the power of our assemblies.

It suggests the duty. The Holiest of All is the home of eternal love. It is love dwells there. It is love that came forth from there to seek me and bring me in. It is into the everlasting love I have been welcomed and taken in. It is love that has been shed abroad in my heart. My entrance in was only in the path of self-sacrifice; my abiding there can only be as one dead to self and filled with love. And love seeketh not its own; it gives itself away, and only lives to make others partakers of its happiness. And it loves the assembly of God's people, not only for what it needs and hopes to receive, but for the communion of saints, and the help it can give in helping and encouraging others.

It not only does this, but obeys the added injunction—**Exhorting one another**. It seeks to watch over those who are in danger of becoming unfaithful. It cares for those who have grown careless in their neglect. True love is quick of invention; it devises means for making smaller or nearer or more attractive assemblies for those who have become estranged. It counts nothing too humble or too difficult if it may but win back to the gathering of God's children those who may there be blessed and saved. It lives in the Holiest of God's love; it gives itself up to the one work of winning others to know that love.

The life in the Holiest is thus not only the motive but the power for doing the work aright. Yes, it is as those who profess to have entered the Holiest of All truly draw near to God, and prove the power of fellowship with Him, that they will have power in prayer and speech and service among their fellow-Christians. The Holiest of All is the place for daily worship and consecration and intercession; even a little band in the assembly will have power to make the divine presence felt. The worship in the place of prayer may become so linked to the secret worship of the Holiest of All that its blessing may come to those who have never known of it. God is willing so to bless the fellowship of His redeemed that the assembly shall be crowned with a fuller sense of His love and presence than ever can be found in the solitary approach to Him. **Wherefore, brethren, having boldness to enter into the Holiest, let us draw near; not forsaking the assembly of ourselves together, but exhorting one another.**

And so much the more as ye see the day approaching. The writer has doubtless in view the then approaching day of judgment on Jerusalem. We know not in how far the perspective of prophecy was clearly revealed, and that day was connected with the coming of the Lord Himself. It is enough for us to know that the fear of an approaching day of judgment was the motive to which appeal is made; and that, not only to move the indifferent, but specially to urge the earnest to exhort others. Christians need to be reminded of the terrible doom hanging over the world, and of all the solemn eternal realities connected with our Lord's coming in their bearing upon our daily life. So will our efforts for helping and saving others all be under the power of the thought of how short the time is, how terrible the fate of those who perish, and how urgent the call for everyone who knows redeeming love to do its work with all his might. In the Holiest of All we hear the voice of warning, and come out to save ere it be too late.

1. Note the intensely practical character of the gospel. Our section (19–25) is only one sentence. It begins with spiritual, heavenly mysteries; it ends in the plainest rules for our conduct to our fellow-men. Let us be sure that the deeper we enter into the perfection-teaching of chapters vii.–x. the fitter we shall be to be a blessing in the world.

2. When Christ spoke His farewell discourse to His disciples one of the things He pressed most urgently was that they should love one another. He loves all His redeemed ones, however feeble or perverse they be, so intently, that He tells us that we cannot prove our real love to Him in any other way than by loving them; the proof of a real entrance into the Holiest of All, the humility and gentleness and self-sacrifice with which we speak and think and prove our care of one another.

3. Study carefully the connection between these last twelve meditations, and see to get a clear hold of the unity of thought in this portion, the living centre of the Epistle.

The Fourth Warning

Chap. x. 26-39

Of Them That Sin Wilfully and Draw Back

XCIII.

Of Wilful Sin

X.–26. For if we sin wilfully after that we have received the knowledge of the truth, there remaineth no more a sacrifice for sins,

27. But a certain fearful expectation of judgment, and a fierceness of fire which shall devour the adversaries.

In mentioning those who forsake the assembling together of God's people, the writer has touched one of those sore places which, to him, are the symptom of imminent danger. This neglect of Christian fellowship is at once the indication of that indifference which is so dangerous, and the cause of further backsliding. All this leads him once again to sound the alarm, and to point out how neglect of outward, apparently secondary duties, opens the way to positive sin and eternal loss. He has scarcely finished his wondrous exposition of the glory of the heavenly Priest and the heavenly sanctuary and the way into it, he has only just begun to speak of the life and walk to which that opened sanctuary calls us, when, thinking of the state of the Hebrews, he sounds a trumpet-blast of warning more terrible than any we have heard yet. In the three previous warnings he had spoken first of neglect (ii. 1–4), then of unbelief and disobedience (iii. 1; iv. 13), then of sloth, leading to hopeless falling away (v. 13; vi. 19): here he now speaks of wilful sinning, with the awful rejection of God's mercy it implies, and the sore and certain punishment it will inevitably bring. John Bunyan, in his dream, saw a way leading from the very gate of heaven down to the pit. It is not only the Holiest of All that is set wide open for us; the gate of hell is opened wide, too, to receive all who neglect or refuse to enter the gate of mercy and of heaven. Let all who believe that it is indeed God who, by His Spirit speaks in this word, listen with holy fear.

For if we sin wilfully after that we have received the knowledge of the truth, there remaineth no more a sacrifice for sins. As we had in chapter vi. mention of **those who were once enlightened, and tasted the heavenly gift and the good word of God,** and who yet fell away, so here he speaks of those **who, after having received the knowledge of the truth,** yet sin wilfully. The expressions used show us that in the case of these the enlightening and the acceptance of the truth had been more with the mind than with the heart. Their judgment had been convinced, through the mind their desire and will had been affected and wrought upon; and yet, the heart, the whole inner life, had never been truly regenerate, had never received that eternal life, which cannot be taken away. And so there was a possibility of their still sinning wilfully and being shut out for ever from the one sacrifice for sin. As we saw before, the true assurance of salvation, the assuring of our hearts before God, can only be enjoyed in a life under the teaching of the Spirit, and a walk in obedience to God's will (1 John iii. 19–24.) True assurance of faith is the witness of the Holy Spirit that is given in living fellowship with and obedience to Christ as Leader.

If we sin wilfully. The question will be asked, But what is wilful sin? How are we to know when we are guilty of it? No answer can be given; no one on earth can draw the line between what is and what is not wilful sin. Only He who sits on the throne, and who knows the heart, can judge. But how will this warning profit, if we cannot see what wilful sin is? The warning will just thus profit us most—it will make us fearful of committing any sin, lest it might be, or lead us into wilful sin. He that would know what wilful sin is, with the thought that he is safe, as long as he keeps from that extreme, deceives himself. *The only sure way of being kept from wilful sin is to keep far from all sin.*

A captain of a ship, sailing between two harbours on a rocky coast, was once asked by an anxious passenger if the coast was not very dangerous. The answer was, Very. And was he not afraid?—No; our way is perfectly safe; you can be at ease. But how, if the rocks are so dangerous? Oh, very simply!—I put out to sea, and *keep far from the rocks.* O Christian! here is thy only safety: launch out into the deep of full obedience to all the will of God; keep far from all sin, and thou shalt be kept from wilful sinning.

For if we sin wilfully, there remaineth no more a sacrifice for sins. What a terrible contrast to the same expression as we had it before (x. 18): **No more offering for sin.** There it was the blessed secret of the glory of the gospel and redemption, the joy of Christian faith and life—**no more offering for sin:** salvation finished and perfected for ever. Here it is the awful revelation of the highest sin and its terrible doom: the one sacrifice rejected, and now **no more a sacrifice for sins** ever to be found. How awful to sin wilfully.

There remaineth no more a sacrifice for sins, but a certain fearful expectation of judgment, and a fierceness of fire, which shall devour the adversaries. Fearful judgment, fierceness of fire, devouring the adversaries—these words are in God's gospel; they follow close on its highest teaching; they are words He speaks to us in His Son. In the religion of the world—alas, in a great deal of the Christian teaching and the religious literature of our day, professing to honour the God of love whom the Bible reveals—these words are set aside and rejected. And yet there they stand, and behind them stand the divine realities they express. God help us to believe them with our whole heart, and to exhort one another, if so be we may save some, snatching them out of the fire!

1. *Let all who have entered the Holiest of All turn round and look to the hole of the pit—the horrible pit—whence they have been drawn up. And as they see the multitudes going down to the pit, oh let them remember that the highest glory of life in the Holiest is, even as it is of Him who opened it with His blood and sits on the throne, to go out and bring others in.*

2. *Even though thou knewest, through grace, that thou hadst escaped the judgment and the fire, take time to gaze upon them. Take upon thee the burden of those who are asleep, and plead with Christ to use thee to warn and to save them.*

XCIV.

The Sin Against the Triune God

X.–28. A man that hath set at nought Moses' law dieth without compassion on the word of two or three witnesses:
29. Of how much sorer punishment, think ye, shall he be judged worthy, who hath trodden under foot the Son of God, and hath counted the blood of the covenant, wherewith he was sanctified, an unholy thing, and hath done despite unto the Spirit of grace?
30. For we know him that said, Vengeance belongeth unto me, I will recompense. And again, The Lord shall judge his people.
31. It is a fearful thing to fall into the hands of the living God.

The Epistle has set before us the more excellent glory of the New Testament. We can draw near to God as Israel never could; God hath indeed made His grace to abound more exceedingly. But let no one think that greater grace means less stringency with sin, or less fierceness of the fire of judgment. Nay, the very opposite. Greater privilege brings greater responsibility, and, in case of failure, greater judgment. As elsewhere (ii. 2; xii. 25) we are reminded that the New Testament exceeds the Old not only in its blessing but also in its curse. As he had asked **"How much more** will the blood of Christ cleanse?" so here he asks, **"How much more** sore will the punishment be?" Oh that men would believe it; the New Testament, with its revelation of God as love, brings on its rejectors a far more fearful judgment than the Old. May God in mercy show us what it means, for our own sakes and that of others.

A man that hath set at nought Moses' law dieth without compassion—note this terrible word, **without compassion: of how much sorer punishment, think ye, shall he be judged worthy, who sins against New Testament grace?** The measure of the superior greatness of the New Testament will be the only measure of the greater fearfulness of the punishment sent; as in the first warning the greatness of salvation was connected with the part each person in the Holy Trinity had taken in it, so here too. The Father gave His Son: **of how much sorer punishment shall he be counted worthy, who hath trodden under foot the Son of God.** The Son gave His blood: here is one **who hath counted the blood of the covenant, wherewith he was sanctified, an unholy thing.** The Father and the Son gave the Spirit: he **hath done despite to the Spirit of grace.** Under Moses' law a man died **without compassion:** how much sorer punishment, without compassion, shall be the fate of them that reject Christ. Hear what all this means.

Who hath trodden under foot the Son of God! There was once an aged father, who had often pleaded in vain with a dissipated son to forsake his evil ways. One night, as the son was preparing again to go out, the father, after renewing his entreaties, went and stood in the door, saying, "My son, I cannot let you go—if you do, it will be over my body." The son tried to push the father aside. The old man fell, and in rushing out he trod on the father! Jesus Christ, God's Son, comes and stands in the sinner's way, pleading with him to turn from his evil way. He casts Himself in the way, with His wounded, bleeding body. And the sinner, not heeding what he does, passes over it: **he hath trodden under foot the Son of God!** What a sin against the Father and the love that gave the Son!

And hath counted the blood of the covenant, wherewith he was sanctified, an unholy thing. The Father gave the Son. And the Son gave His blood—the blood of the covenant, securing and conveying to us all its wondrous privileges—**the blood**

with which he was sanctified, admitted to the Holiest of All and the Holy One, he **hath counted an unholy thing.** When I come to water in which I wish to wash, and find it impure, I reject it; I throw it out. Christ calls the sinner to wash in His blood and be clean. He rejects it as an unclean thing. Yes, the blood that speaks of the love of Jesus, and remission of sins, and the opened heaven, is rejected and cast aside! Oh, what sin! If the rejectors of the blood of bulls and goats died without compassion, **how much more**—the despisers of the blood of the Son of God!

And hath done despite unto the Spirit of grace! I can put no greater affront on my king, or my father, than by shutting my door in his face. If they come to me with a message or a gift of love in my wretchedness, to turn them away is to do them despite. The Spirit comes as the Spirit of grace, to convince of sin and stir to prayer and lead to Jesus. To close the door, to refuse surrender, to open the heart to the spirit of the world instead of Him, is to do despite to the Spirit of grace! The Son trodden under foot, the blood counted unclean, the Spirit of grace despised and rejected—alas, what terrible sin!

For such **there remaineth no more a sacrifice for sins!** And such are they among us and around us who reject the Christ of God! And such their fate! **For we know Him that said, Vengeance belongeth unto Me, I will recompense. And again, the Lord shall judge His people.—For we know Him!** How many there are who profess to believe in Scripture, and to worship God, but who do not know this God. They have framed to themselves a God, after their own instincts and imagination; they believe not in the Holy One in whom righteousness and love meet in perfect harmony. They refuse to say, **We know Him that said, Vengeance belongeth unto Me, I will recompense.** Oh, let us seek so to know Him, that our hearts may be filled with compassion for all who are still exposed to this fearful vengeance. **For it is a fearful thing to fall into the hands of the living God.** Let us think in love on all who are still exposed to this judgment, until it stir us to thanksgiving for our own redemption, to an infinite compassion for all who are in danger, to new fervency of prayer for their salvation, and to a consecration of ourselves to the one work of warning them of their danger and leading them to Christ.

1. *In accepting God's word let us remember that as little as we could have devised or understood the glorious redemption in Christ, such as God's love has provided, without a divine revelation, can we arrange for or understand a judgment day such as God's righteousness requires. The one is a mystery of love and the other a mystery of wrath, beyond all we can think or know.*

2. *It was to meet the judgment and the wrath of God Christ's blood was needed. The blood stands midway between the judgment threatened and the judgment yet to be poured out. As we believe in the judgment we shall honour the blood; as we believe in the blood we shall fear the judgment.*

XCV.

The Former Days

X.–32. But call to remembrance the former days, in which, after ye were enlightened, ye endured a great conflict of sufferings;
33. Partly, being made a gazing-stock both by reproaches and afflictions; and partly, becoming partakers with them that were so used.
34. For ye both had compassion on them that were in bonds, and took joyfully the spoiling of your possessions, knowing that ye yourselves have a better possession and an abiding one.

The solemn warning now, just as was the case in chapter vi. (ver. 9), turns to encouragement and exhortation. As there, the Hebrews are reminded of the former days, when they were first enlightened—the time of their first love. But, in the previous instance, they were told that **God was not unrighteous to forget their work and love;** here they are urged themselves not to forget what had taken place. **Call to remembrance the former days.** The retrospect would call up the joy with which they once had sacrificed all for the name of Jesus, would humble them in view of past backsliding and present coldness, would stir within the desire and the hope of regaining the place they once had occupied. **Call to remembrance,** he says, **the former days, in which ye endured a great conflict of sufferings,** in not only **bearing reproaches** and **taking joyfully the spoiling of your possessions,** but also in **compassion towards and being partakers with others who were in bonds.**

It is a sad thought that a community that had so remarkably proved its faithfulness to the Lord, in the midst of persecution and suffering, should in a few years have gone so far back as to need the warnings that have just been given. And yet it has often been so. In some cases it happened that the persecution ceased, and the spirit of ease and of sloth, or of worldly prosperity, obtained the mastery. In others, the persecution lasted too long, and those who had appeared to forsake all, succumbed to the severity and length of the trial. The Hebrews were not only an instance of such defection, but of so many other cases, in which Christians, after having begun well, **wax weary, fainting in their souls.** They stand out as beacons to warn us of the danger the Epistle so strongly urges—that the best beginning will not avail unless we endure to the end (iii. 14; vi. 11; xii. 3). They call us to remember that we need a faith and a religion that stands fast and lasts; because it has its steadfastness, as the Epistle teaches, in the promise and the oath of God; in the hope within the veil; in Him the surety of the covenant, who is seated on the right hand of God, the Priest after the power of an endless life, the surety of an everlasting covenant.

In reminding them of the past a very remarkable expression is used to indicate what the power was that enabled them at first to endure so bravely. **Ye took joyfully the spoiling of your possessions, knowing that ye yourselves have a better and abiding possession.** The Christian stands between two worlds; each offers him its goods as possessions. In unceasing conflict the two compete for mastery. The one has the advantage of being infinitely more worthy than the other—giving infinite satisfaction, and lasting for ever. The other is in no wise to be compared with it—it cannot satisfy, and it does not last. But, in the conflict, it has two immense, two terrible advantages. The one is, it is nearer; it is visible; it has access to us by every sense; its influence on us is natural and easy and unceasing. The other, that our heart is prepossessed; the spirit of the world is in it. And so it comes that the possessions of this world with the most actually win the day, even against the better and abiding possession.

Ye took joyfully the spoiling of your possessions, knowing that ye have a better and abiding possession. What is this better and abiding possession? It is the love and grace of God. It is the eternal life within. It is Christ as our heart's treasure. It is a life and a character in the likeness of Christ. The old heathen moralists teach us most striking lessons as to the nobility of a man who knows that all earthly possessions are as nothing compared with the being master of himself. How much more reason the Christian has to rejoice in the good things, in the eternal realities which Christ bestows, both in the heaven above and the heart within. The world may rob you of personal liberty or earthly goods; it cannot compel you to commit sin or separate you from the living God in Christ Jesus. Heaven and its blessing in your heart can fill you with a joy that counts every sacrifice a privilege, that makes every loss a gain, and that turns all suffering into an exceeding weight of glory.

Alas that the Hebrews, after knowing this better and abiding possession, and having, for its sake, joyfully taken the spoiling of their possessions, should yet, many of them, have waxed weary, and fainted and turned back! Alas for the terrible possibility of making sacrifices, and enduring reproach for Christ, and then falling away! No wonder that our author at once follows up his appeal to the former days with the exhortation: **Cast not away your boldness—ye have need of patience.**

Let us learn the solemn lesson: the lawful possessions and pleasures and occupations of this world, its literature and its culture, are unceasingly and most insidiously seeking to undermine the influence of the better and abiding possession. This influence is greater than we know, because they are seen and near and ever active. Nothing can secure us against their power but a life of faith, a life in the Holiest, a life in the power of Christ, the Priest for ever, who works all in the power of the endless life.

Alone through Him who abideth continually can we abide continually too, can we endure unto the end.

1. *If there be any reader who has to look back with shame and regret on his first love, and his leaving it, let him listen to the call:* Remember the former days. *Think of them. Face the fact of your having gone back. Confess it to God. And take courage in the assurance, there is restoration and deliverance. Trust Jesus.*

2. A better and abiding possession. *A rich man counts his money. He spends time and thought on preserving it safe, and making it more. Our power to resist the world, so that its possessions shall not tempt us, nor its threats terrify us, lies in the full consciousness and enjoyment of our heavenly treasures. Take time to know your possessions, draw out an inventory of what you have and what you expect, and all the world offers will have no power.*

XCVI.

Boldness and Patience

X.–35. Cast not away therefore your boldness, which hath great recompense of reward.

36. For ye have need of patience, that, having done the will of God, ye may receive the promise.

We know how often we have had the word **boldness** in our Epistle. **If we hold fast our boldness** (iii. 6); **Let us draw near with boldness to the throne of grace** (iv. 16); **Having boldness to enter into the Holiest through the blood of Jesus** (x. 19). The boldness and confidence toward God is one of the strongest roots of the Christian life. Without it there is no strength to persevere, no power to draw nigh to the throne of grace in prayer, no liberty to enter into the full fellowship of God in the Holiest. And so the Hebrews are urged not to cast away their boldness, because it has great recompense of reward. In the vigour and joy of the Christian life, in the bright and joyous fellowship with God, in the courage for meeting the battle with the world and sin, the reward of boldness is great.

Cast not away your boldness. When I have my hands filled, and something more tempting is offered, I may either directly cast away what I have, or, by trying to take the new object into hands already full, may gradually lose hold of what I first held fast. Casting away our boldness always has its cause in something else that we allow to take its place in the heart. It may be sin, whether only rising in the heart or breaking out into act, if it be not immediately confessed and cleansed away. It may be

433

something in itself lawful, but which is allowed too large a share in our interest or affections. It may be something doubtful, so insignificant that it hardly appears worth considering, and yet which somehow robs us of perfect liberty in looking up into God's face. It may be care or fear, it may be self-effort, or self-seeking, self-trust; anything that is not in the perfect will of God loosens our hold on the boldness before God, and, ere we know, we have cast it away: it is lost.

But we must not only know how we lose it; we want as much to know how to keep and increase it. The texts we quoted tell us. Among the foundation truths we had it: **We have a High Priest able to sympathise, let us come with boldness.** And in the fuller teaching it came again: **Having boldness to enter through the blood, let us draw nigh.** The High Priest and the blood—these are the everlasting and unchanging ground of our confidence. It is as we consider Christ Jesus, and follow Him; as we grow in the knowledge and the faith of His blood, and enter through it into God's presence, that we shall hold fast our boldness with an ever firmer grasp. As with a true heart we draw nigh, and in the consciousness of our integrity, that in holiness and sincerity of God we are walking in the world, place ourselves in the light of God, we shall receive even in this life something of the great recompense of reward the boldness of faith ever brings.

Cast not away your boldness, for ye have need of patience. Your boldness you cannot dispense with for a single moment; to the end of life it is your only strength. Cast it not away; remember that without patience, in the persevering exercise and daily renewal of faith, you cannot inherit the promise. Between the faith that accepts a promise, and the experience that fully inherits or receives it, there often lie years of discipline and training needed to fit and perfect you for the inward possession of what God has to give. Whether it be a promise to be realised in this world or the coming, you have need of patience.

Therefore cast not away, never for a moment lose hold of, hold fast firm to the end, your boldness—**ye have need of patience.** In chapter vi. it was said: **Be imitators of them who through faith and longsuffering inherited the promise.** This is one of the great practical lessons of the Epistle. Without perseverance, endurance, steadfastness, faith is vain; the only proof that it is a living, saving faith, is that it holds fast its boldness firm unto the end.

Ye have need of patience, **that, having done the will of God,** ye may receive the promise. *Doing the will* is the way to receive the promise. *Doing the will* is to be the one thing that is to occupy us while we patiently wait. Between God's giving the promise to Abraham and his receiving its fulfilment there lay years of the obedience of faith. And each new act of obedience was crowned with new and larger blessing. Doing the will was the proof of his faith, the occupation of his patience, the way to his blessing. It was even so with our blessed Lord. Between the promise given Him of the Father and His inheriting it in the resurrection and ascension there lay—what? His life of obedience: *Lo, I am come to do Thy will, O God.* With every Christian who puts his trust in the living Christ, and enters the Holiest of All to live there, *doing the will of God* must be the link that unites the end to the beginning. Between the faith that accepts the promise and the experience that fully inherits it, there may to us, too, be years of waiting and trial. These must be marked by the obedience of faith, by "patient continuance in well-doing," or we never can reach the promised end. If we see to the doing of God's will, He will see to our inheriting the promise. The sure mark of true faith, the blessed exercise of life within the veil, the proof of the power of Christ, the obedient One within us, the blessedness of fellowship with God will all come with this—doing His will. To do the will of God is the only way to God and His presence. Therefore, day by day, hour by hour, let this be our motto: *Patience, that having done the will, ye may inherit the promise.*

435

1. *We have been so little accustomed in our Christian life to give the doing of God's will its right place, and there is so much misconception about it, as if it is not actually expected of us, that it will take time and trouble to get the heart under the complete mastery of the thought—I am every moment to be doing nothing but the will of God. Jesus Christ lived so. He, our Leader, will teach it us. He, our life, will live it in us. He, our High Priest, will by His Spirit, in this new and living way, bring us in very deed nigh to God.*

2. *Boldness, courage, bravery, the chief of the manly virtues. Patience, one of the loveliest of the gentler sisterhood of passive graces. In each full Christian character the two must be combined. Cast not away your boldness, for—Ye have need of patience. Boldness to undertake, patience to carry out the doing of God's will.*

3. *O believer, let the truth enter deep into thee—boldly, patiently doing the will is the way to inherit the promise.*

XCVII.

Believing or Drawing Back

X.–36. For ye have need of patience, that, having done the will
of God, ye may receive the promise.

37. For yet a very little while,
   He that cometh shall come, and shall not tarry.

38. But my righteous one shall live by faith:
   And if he shrink back,[1] my soul hath no pleasure in him.

39. But we are not of them that shrink back unto perdition; but
of them that have faith unto the saving of the soul.

In the summary we had (19–25) of what life in the Holiest
means, the last word, after we had been urged to exhort one another, was: **And so much the more as ye see the day drawing
nigh.** And then came the warning of the fearful expectation of
judgment, and the terror of falling into the hands of the living
God. Here the warning closes with once again pointing to the
Lord's coming as not far off. Christian faith lives not only in the
unseen present but also in the future; more especially in the future of the coming of Him who shall appear a second time to
them that wait for Him, Him who is now seated on the throne,
expecting till all His enemies be made His footstool. Let our faith
so live in the future, that all our life may be in the power of eternity, and of Him in whom eternity has its glory.

The passage quoted is from Habakkuk, the same that forms
the text of the Epistles to the Galatians and Romans. The
prophet is told by God, in the midst of the oppression of Israel

1. Draw back.

by the Chaldæans, that the vision will surely come. Two classes among the people are spoken of. Of one it is said: *His soul is puffed up, it is not upright in him.* Of the other: *But the righteous shall live by his faith.* Our writer uses the words to contrast the two classes among the Hebrews. On the one side, those who are not upright; on the other, the righteous who live by faith. The righteous man will in the midst of trouble, and while the vision is delayed, put his trust in God, and live in that trust. He shall live by it too, the God whom He trusts will not fail him but send deliverance.

Our writer introduces the passage of set purpose, to serve as the text of the following chapter. He had in chapters iii. and iv. spoken of unbelief as the great sin through which Israel had perished in the wilderness, of faith as the one thing needful if we are to enter into the rest of God. In chapter vi. of the faith by which the fathers inherited the promises. He had in our chapter, in his summing up of the Epistle, said: **Let us draw nigh in the fulness of faith.** He wishes, after his exposition of what the purpose and the work of Jesus can be to us, to show us the way to a full personal experience and enjoyment of it all, through faith alone. He proposes to do so by proving how all the Old Testament saints had lived and conquered through faith, and how it is the one only thing God asks if we are to experience His mighty saving power and the blessedness of His good pleasure. He is going to point out all the variety of circumstances and difficulties in which faith will give us God's help and sure deliverance, as well as all the various tempers and dispositions with which it will be accompanied. For all this he finds a most suggestive text in the words: **My righteous one shall live by faith.**

That means a great deal more than what many think—the sinner shall be counted righteous by faith; more, too, than the righteous shall have eternal life by faith. It means, the righteous shall live, his whole life shall be, by faith. This is just the lesson we need. The righteous who lives by faith is contrasted with him who draws back, of whom God says: *My soul shall have no pleasure in Him*. The one cause of backsliding is the want of faith in the unseen, a yielding of the heart to the visible, and, in the battle against it, a trusting in our own strength and not in Christ. We see here again that there is no other alternative—either believing or drawing back. In the Christian life nothing will avail to keep us from backsliding but the fulness of faith—always and in everything to live the life of faith. It is only when faith gives itself up entirely to Christ for Him to do all in us, to keep us standing too, and when faith so dominates our life that every moment and every engagement shall all be under its influence, that we can hope to be safe from drawing back. If I am to be sure of salvation, if I am to be strong against every temptation, if I am to live daily as one in whom God's soul has pleasure, I must see to one thing—to be a man of faith.

Let us prepare ourselves for the wonderful chapter that is coming, and all its blessed teaching, by looking back on what has been set before us of Christ and His redemption as the object of our faith. He is the Priest for ever, the Priest of God's oath, able to save completely—shall we not throw our whole being wide open to Him in trust? *We have* Him, a Priest-King upon the throne, the Minister of the sanctuary He has opened for us, and where He presides, to bring us in—oh, shall we not be strong in faith, giving glory to God? We have Him, the Mediator of the new covenant, who with one sacrifice hath perfected Himself and us for evermore, and whose work it is to write and put God's law within us as the power of a living obedience—again, I say, shall we not believe, and allow this mighty Saviour to do His perfect work in us? We have entered the Holiest of All, we have in faith claimed God's presence, and the life of abiding continually in it as our portion, and we have the great Priest over the house of God to make it all true and sure to us; surely it needs no words to urge us to make faith, faith alone, the faith of the heart, the unceasing sacrifice we bring our God. So may we too say, We are not of them that draw back, but of them that believe to the saving of the soul.

1. The only cure for all the coldness and backsliding in the Church is "the preaching of faith." Holiness by faith, standing by faith, being kept by the power of God through faith, having Christ dwell in our heart by faith—this must be the daily food of the Christian. A preaching that insists upon salvation by faith chiefly as pardon and acceptance must produce feeble Christians. The fulness of faith is indispensable to the full Christian life.

2. Believing or drawing back—there is no other alternative. Look back over the warning of which these words form the conclusion, and let us fear at the terrible possibility for ourselves and others. And look forward to the coming chapter, with the one prayer that our whole life may be in the fulness of faith, in the very presence and power of God.

XCVIII.

Faith—the Sense for the Unseen

XI.–1. Now faith is the assurance of things hoped for, the proving of things not seen.

2. For therein the elders had witness borne to them.

3. By faith we understand that the worlds have been framed by the word of God, so that what is seen hath not been made out of things which do appear.

The previous chapter closed with the solemn lesson: There is no alternative, believing or drawing back; there is no safety or strength for the Christian, but to be strong in faith; there is no way of pleasing God, of abiding in His presence and favour, but by faith. **If any man draw back, My soul hath no pleasure in him.** And so, after the teaching of the Epistle as to what God hath done, we are now to see that for our enjoyment of its power and blessing but one thing is needed—the fulness of faith. It will be shown us how this is the key to the life of all God's saints, and to all that God did for them.

The writer begins by a general statement of what faith really is in its nature and action. **Now faith is the assurance of things hoped for, the proving of things not seen.** Faith is the spiritual faculty of the soul which deals with the spiritual realities of the future and the unseen. Just as we have our senses, through which we hold communication with the physical universe, so faith is the spiritual sense or organ through which the soul comes into contact with and is affected by the spiritual world. Just as the sense of seeing or hearing is a dormant power till the objective reality, the light or the sound, strikes it, so faith in itself is a sense with no power beyond the possibility or capacity of receiving the impressions of the eternal. It is as an empty vessel which wants to be filled with its unseen contents. It is only when the eternal realities draw near and exercise their power that faith becomes and is the substance of things hoped for, the foundation which they lay in the soul, the proof or conviction of things unseen, the convincing power with which they give evidence and proof of their own supernatural existence.[1] Faith as a dormant faculty is the capacity for receiving this communication; faith as an active power is what it is in virtue of the overshadowing of the Invisible. The Invisible takes the initiative and wakens faith; faith receives the impression and seeks for ever fuller union with it.

Faith is thus much more than trust in the word of another. That trust is of extreme importance as its initial exercise, but the word must only be the servant leading in to the divine truth it contains, the living person from whom it comes. To deal too exclusively with the word as the ground of faith will lead to a faith

---

1. The two words *substance* and *proof* are used both in the objective and subjective sense. The word for substance properly means the foundation, and is used of the real nature of a thing as opposed to appearance. So, in chapter i. 3, of the *substance* of God, the divine essence. Or it is used of the confidence which knows that it rests on a sure foundation. So, in chapter iii. 14, *the beginning of our confidence.* It is of importance to hold fast the connection between the two meanings. So the word *proof,* or conviction, from the verb used in passages, as, *The Spirit shall convince of sin,* and often elsewhere of reproof, chiding, means both the conviction of guilt, or the conviction of a truth which is brought from without, and the subjective conviction which comes when one submits and allows himself to be convicted. It thus means both the means of proof and the proof itself. See 2 Tim. iii. 16—*Scripture profitable for reproof.*

that is more intellectual than spiritual, a faith that, as the Church so universally shows, rests more in the wisdom of men, in the power of reason, than in the power of God. We need to be persuaded very deeply that faith is not only a dealing with certain promises, but an unceasing spiritual intercourse with the unseen world around us. Just as in breathing, our lungs, or in seeing, our eyes, hold themselves open to receive unceasingly, from the air or the light, what they without ceasing in the literal sense press upon us, so faith is the unceasing reaching out heavenward of that spiritual sense to which things future and unseen reveal themselves as near and present, as living and powerful. Faith must in the spiritual life be as natural, as unceasing, as our breathing and seeing when we are doing our ordinary work.

For therein the elders had witness borne to them. Of Abel we read: **He had witness borne to him that he was righteous, God bearing witness in respect of his gifts.** And Enoch: **He had witness borne to him that he had been well pleasing to God.** And so it is said of all, verse 39: **These all had witness borne to them through their faith.** Faith does not depend for its blessing on the intensity of its effort; the unseen world, the eternity that surrounds us, is all filled by the living God; and to the faith that opens itself heavenward He bears witness. Let us be sure of this: faith can grow into firm and full assurance, it finds in confidence not in itself but in God. Let us count upon it, the faith that seeks for the eternal will be met by God and have the witness borne by Himself that God counts us righteous, that we are well-pleasing in His sight.

By faith we understand that the worlds have been framed by the word of God, so that what is seen hath not been made out of things which do appear. This visible world is to man his great temptation to forget God. Faith is the eye with which he can see God in all, which makes every part of it the transparent revelation of the nearness and goodness of God. By faith we understand that all was framed by God; by faith we see divinity and omnipotence in all, so that what is seen is known as made out of things that do not appear. *The invisible things of Him from the creation of the world are clearly seen, even His eternal power and Godhead.* Faith sees His superscription on every part of His handiwork, sees it all pervaded by the living God; surrounded by the things that perish and pass away, it yet stands in the midst of eternity, it knows itself allied to the unchangeable One. The world, instead of being a hindrance, becomes a help in revealing the everlasting God. And faith finds its life and its delight and its ever-increasing strength in meeting everywhere the God who delights to bear witness of Himself to them that seek after Him.

1. *Faith is mostly thought of as a power by which we grasp the heavenly things, and we weary ourselves in vain attempts to do so. No, faith is the substance, the substructure, that the divine things lay in me, the proof they give in me of their actual reality. Just as the light of the sun is its own evidence and proof, so with the light of God. The more we see this, the more confident will our hope be that they will prove themselves to us, and the more meek and patient and humble will be the spirit in which we wait for their self-revelation.*

2. *The rules for the strengthening of faith are thus very simple. Regard the unseen world as an actually existing kingdom of divine truth and power, which seeks to conquer and get possession of and bless you. Accept the measure of faith there is within you as the proof of its existence and operation, the pledge of a fuller revelation. Accept all that is revealed of it in the word as a finger-post to wake the longing and to show the way to the full possession. Set the heart open, in holy separation, from the world; in meditation and adoration and expectation the unseen world can become more real and more near than the seen.*

3. *Nothing can be a proof of anything but that which partakes of the nature of the thing proved. Thus it is with faith and the spiritual world.*

XCIX.

Abel–the Sacrifice of Faith

XI.–4. By faith Abel offered unto God a more excellent sacrifice than Cain, through which he had witness borne to him that he was righteous, God bearing witness in respect of his gifts: and through it he being dead yet speaketh.

One of the chief words of the Epistle is **offering, sacrifice.** Christ *"offered* Himself unto God." "He put away sin by the *sacrifice* of Himself." "By one *offering* He hath perfected for ever them that are sanctified." The inner spirit and power of that life by which Christ pleased His Father, and put away sin, and gained His seat on the throne of the Majesty on high, was—the offering of His body. As the Leader of our salvation He guides His people in the same, the new and living way, that of self-sacrifice.

It is a most remarkable and deeply suggestive fact that among those who have preceded us in the way of faith, we should find that with the very first one, Abel, the first fruit of faith was to sacrifice. The disposition, of which sacrifice is the expression, lies at the very root of the life of faith. If I would in this chapter learn what faith is, and how I can grow strong in faith, I must mark well what the very first step is: **By faith Abel offered a more excellent sacrifice.**

We know what the double meaning was of Abel's sacrifice. It was, on the one hand, his offering to God of a life to be given up to death, and so in his stead to bear the death which is in its very nature the punishment of sin. It was an acknowledgment of the righteous judgment of God against sin; the confession that without blood-shedding there could be no remission of sins. It was an act of faith; he counted that the sacrifice would be acceptable, and that with it he would be accepted too. On the other hand, the sacrifice was the offering and yielding up himself to God and His service. He knew it was something that lay in the very nature and spirit of a true sacrifice, that it could not be pleasing to God if he offered the lamb, and kept back himself. No, the sacrifice was the double confession—that he was unworthy to offer himself to God without atonement, but that, believing that in the sacrifice he was accepted, he gave himself to God's worship and service, he gave himself to the very death, to die to self and live to God. And it was as if his own death had to confirm and seal the truth; the man who had offered the sacrifice of faith, had founded his worship in the death of a lamb, had to die himself to find the way to God. The atoning sacrifice has ever two sides; the lamb was at once a substitute and a symbol, its death an atonement and a consecration.

Faith draws nigh to God through sacrifice; in Christ this truth finds its full realisation. **By one offering He hath perfected for ever them that are sanctified.** Our access to God and our fellowship with Him can only be in Christ's finished work. We have boldness through His blood. His blood cleanses and perfects the conscience. The first great work of faith is to appropriate the sacrifice and obedience and righteousness of Christ as accepted for us, to hold it up before God, and by the Holy Spirit to have the witness given, and to experience how acceptable we are. But faith cannot fully do this without at the same time entering into the inner spiritual significance of the sacrifice, and becoming partaker of the spirit and disposition it breathes, and in which alone it has its value. Faith sees that the law of self-sacrifice, under which the Head went in to God, is the law for each of the members. There is no way out of sin and sinful flesh, but through death to life. And as faith sees the beauty and the power of the truth in Christ, it hungers for conformity to Him in this His highest moral glory, and becomes itself the root of an inward self-sacrifice, a continual offering of itself to God and His holiness; because it is nothing less than a real, living union with Christ the High Priest Himself. Christ became our Substitute because He was Our Head; faith begins with the knowledge of him as Substitute, but grows up into Him, the Head of all things, and specially in the fellowship of His death. We find this truth throughout Scripture. All that is said in Romans vi. and Colossians iii. of our being dead to sin in Christ, and alive to God, in 2 Corinthians iv. of bearing about in the body the dying of Jesus that His life may be manifested in us, in Galatians ii. and vi. of our being crucified with Christ, being crucified to the world, in Philippians iii. of our being made conformable to His death, points to this—the inward spirit and disposition of self-sacrifice is born within us by His Spirit, is breathed in us every day where there is true communion with Him. The blessing of Christ's death as atonement is only surpassed because it is only fulfilled in that of His death as fellowship.

Beloved Christian, we know what the great lesson of the Epistle is: the way into the Holiest is opened up, we can live and abide continually in the presence of God. And now the chapter is to teach us how the power to come thus near and abide near to God, to enjoy the full salvation provided for us, is given to faith alone. And Abel, the first of the men of faith, teaches us just what the Epistle, what Christ our High Priest has taught— that the way to God, that the way of faith, is the way of sacrifice, of death. Christ entered in to God in the way of self-sacrifice; in faith I accept of Him, and His entrance into God's presence is mine; in union with Him, once and for ever mine. His self-sacrifice becomes the spirit and the power of my life, and the life of faith in me becomes the union of the two—His and my self-sacrifice.

God said: *No man shall see Me and live.* Through death, the death of Christ, our death in and with Him, is the way to God.

This is the new and living way, the way into the Holiest. Let us walk in it, in the power of the Holy Ghost. Let us yield ourselves in great simplicity and humility to die to self, as we confess our helplessness, and look to God to quicken us in Christ. Let us tarry in childlike dependence and patience, with the one desire, to please the Father as Jesus pleased Him. And as we wait, and patiently do the will of God, He may show us how, in the *once* and *for ever* of His death and resurrection, there is for us a perfect entrance into the perfect life that has been offered to our faith.

1. *Abel had witness borne him that he was righteous. As he bowed to God's righteous judgment on sin, and trusted in God's righteous deliverance from it through sacrifice, he was righteous in God's sight. As he worshipped with his eye on the dying lamb, he had witness borne to him. How I know not. As with my eye on the dying Lamb I worship, the witness comes to me by the Holy Ghost that I am righteous.*

2. *Let me believe in the immeasurable power of the blood of the Lamb, until my whole being is filled with the witness of the Holy Ghost.*

3. *The more I gaze, in confession and trust, on the dying Lamb, the more may I claim the spirit of His sacrifice to enter into me, and make me conformed to His likeness.*

4. A more excellent sacrifice. *Cain brings his offering without death, without blood—the spirit and religion of the world. With Abel and the hosts of heaven it is all—the blood of the Lamb.*

C.

Enoch—the Walk of Faith

XI.–5. By faith Enoch was translated that he should not see death; and he was not found, because God translated him: for before his translation he hath had witness borne to him that he had been well-pleasing unto God.
6. And without faith it is impossible to be well-pleasing unto him: for he that cometh to God must believe that he is, and that he is a rewarder of them that seek after him.

The sacrifice of faith is the entrance to the life of faith, and ever remains its chief characteristic. On the sacrifice of faith there follows the walk of faith—abiding, continuous fellowship is the fruit of Christ's self-sacrifice and ours. On Abel follows Enoch. Abel shows how death is the entrance to life: he triumphs over death by submitting to it. In Enoch, we see how life triumphs over death: he does not see death. Through faith Abel being dead yet speaketh; Enoch speaks as one who ever liveth. In Abel we see how death leads to life. In Enoch we see the life that never dies. In Abel we see Christ the crucified, and the boldness we have through the blood to enter in in the new and living way that goes through the rent veil. In Enoch we see Christ glorified and have life in the Holiest—the walk with God, the living One.

In connection with Enoch there are three things taught us in regard to faith. The first is, as to its nature. **He that cometh to God must believe that He is, and that He is a rewarder of them that seek after Him.** Faith is the spiritual sense by which we recognise the presence and character of the unseen God;

both that He is, and that He rewards the seeker. Desire is the root of faith; without a hunger for God His existence is a matter of indifference; the knowledge of His being does not affect the soul. Faith seeks for God; it believes that He is; it keeps the heart open towards Him; it bows in humility and hope for Him to make Himself known. To know God, to see God in everything and everywhere, in our daily life to be conscious of His presence so that we always walk with Him—this is the true nobility of man; this is the life that faith lives; this is the blessedness Jesus has now fully revealed in the rending of the veil. Faith can walk with God. He that cometh to God must believe that **He is.** And also **a rewarder of them that seek after Him.** Faith believes that God can be found; that He can and will make Himself known; that He cares for everyone who truly longs for Him; that He has a divine reward for the seeker after Him. In seeking Him the way may at times be dark and long, and the progress slow; faith honours God with its confidence as the God of love and truth; He will reward and bless. Let the deep restfulness of this assured conviction be the root of all your seeking after God.

The second lesson we have is as to what the reward of faith will be. **Before his translation he had been well-pleasing to God. Without faith it is impossible to be well-pleasing.** God created us for Himself: it is our destiny, we were made with the one object of pleasing Him, and being His delight. God is perfect goodness: a state of life in which we please God must be one of goodness and perfect blessedness. In our fallen state we are well-pleasing by faith. Faith is the surrender to God. Faith honours God by acknowledging and seeking His presence, by expecting everything from Him alone, by resting on Him. Faith gives God His place and His glory; faith wills what God wills; faith lets God have His own way, and makes Him all in all. No wonder that faith is infinitely well-pleasing to Him. If Christians only believed this, and only made it their one study to draw nigh and enter in, and walk before Him in the fulness of faith.

Then comes the third lesson—faith knows that it pleases God. Enoch **had witness borne to him that he had been well pleasing to God.** It was by faith that this witness came (see vers. 2, 4, 39). It is of the very essence of a healthy faith: God does not leave Himself without a witness to the soul that trusts in Him, least of all in the New Testament. The Lord Jesus promised to send from the Father in heaven the Holy Spirit, as a witness of all that took place in heaven on His ascension. All that the Epistle has taught us of the rent veil and the opened sanctuary and the entrance into God's presence, of Christ's perfect work and complete salvation as the Priest in the power of an endless life, has its seal and its worth and its power and its reality in our heart, from the Pentecostal gift. The Holy Spirit brought down, **out of that Holiest of All within the veil,** as an actual reality, the kingdom of heaven into men's hearts, so that the presence of God, and the Father's delight in His Son, and the Father's love now shed abroad in their hearts become their everyday experience and consciousness. And even so now still, to them who seek and receive and yield to the Holy Ghost, in His full indwelling and witness, faith receives and gives the witness that we are well-pleasing.

By faith Enoch walked with God. My brother, who with Abel hast drawn nigh to God in the infinite self-sacrifice of Jesus, learn with Enoch to walk with God the walk of faith. Let the presence of God by thy one desire; the will of God thy one choice; the help of God thy one trust; the likeness to God thy one hope. Let every day, the most ordinary one, the most difficult one, be a day with God, as one of the days of heaven upon earth, a day of which faith is the beginning and the end. Let all the teaching of the Epistle, as to the wonderful, the perfect, the everlasting redemption in the Son of God, have this one result—that it make thee full of faith in God, and guide thee to draw nigh to God, to walk with God; and thou, too, shalt know what it is not to see death; by faith to be translated, and have it written—He was not, for God took him.

1. Jesus said that John the Baptist was the greatest of all the prophets, greater than Enoch too. And yet, the least in the kingdom was greater than John. And must it then be counted impossible for men even now to walk with God, and to have the witness that they are well-pleasing to Him? Alas for the Church that scarce believes it.

2. The one great work of Jesus is to bring us near to God, in the nearness of unity of will and heart. And what He does is in the power of an endless life; He abides continually, and what He gives abides continually too. We can ever abide in God's presence and walk with Him.

3. By faith, that lives in the unseen; that allows Christ to do His mighty work; that believes that the presence of God is now its home; and so enters into its rest.

Cl.

Noah—the Work of Faith

XI.–7. By faith Noah, being warned of God concerning things not seen as yet, moved with godly fear, prepared an ark to the saving of his house; through which he condemned the world, and became heir of the righteousness which is according to faith.

In Abel we see how faith makes death the path to life. In Enoch, how faith conquers death. In Noah, how faith saves others from death by the work it does for them. The moment the entrance into the Holiest through the blood had been set open to us, we were called to the work of love (x. 19, 24, 25). If with Abel we have drawn nigh to God, in the death of Christ and the death to self—this is the root of the tree; if with Enoch we have given ourselves to a walk with God, in His presence and good pleasure—this is the tree growing from the root; let us, with Noah, do the work of faith, that can bless and save those around us—this is the fruit of the tree. In his story we find all the essential elements of faith combined.

By faith Noah, being warned of God concerning things not seen as yet. Faith has ever to do with the future and the unseen. It lives in God's word and thoughts; it sees what the world cannot see: it sees all, the future too, in the light of God. When God reveals His terrible, almost incredible judgment, it simply believes. It trusts not to its own experience or instinct, its thoughts or wishes. It believes in the inconceivable fearfulness of a judgment to come. O believer! if thou wouldst live and save

453

men, believe what God has said of the impending doom that is coming on the world.

Moved with godly fear. When Jesus prayed in Gethsemane (v. 9), under the sense of what sin and death are, it was with *godly fear.* We are exhorted (xii. 28) to **offer service well-pleasing to God with godly fear, because our God is a consuming fire.** It is a fearful thing to fall into the hands of the living God. How awfully and repeatedly our Epistle speaks of the fate of the disobedient. Surely it becomes us, whose eyes have been opened, with godly fear to listen to God's warnings, and then, under the mighty impulse of that motive, **moved with godly fear,** on some to have mercy with fear, snatching them out of the fire.

By faith Noah prepared an ark. Faith wrought fear, and fear wrought diligence, and faith guided heart and hand for the work of deliverance. No one had ever heard of a coming flood, and the destruction of a world by water. No one could ever have thought, if the world were drowned, of an ark escaping alone. But faith lives in fellowship with God; it knows His secrets of judgment and of salvation; it so possesses a man that he gives up his life to act it out. In the face of the mockery of men, and the long delay of the day, and all the difficulties of the work, Noah held fast to God's word. Simply to listen to what God says, and in the obedience of faith to give up our whole heart and life to carry it out: this is faith.

To the saving of his house. The believer is blessed by God, to be made a blessing. The faith of Noah, made perfect by works, saved his family; and with the family he saved the race, and became the father of us all. His preaching appeared to have little fruit, and yet the whole Church of God, since his day, owes its life to his faith too. Man was created in God's likeness in this too, that he has power over other lives. The power begins with the family, but reaches farther. The man of faith who with Abel, in the one sacrifice, has passed through death to life, and with

Enoch walks with God, has power with God, the power of life and of blessing.

Through which faith he condemned the world. The difference between the unbeliever and the believer is this: the one is a man of the world, and lives here; the other is a man of God, and lives in heaven. His whole life is a protest and a condemnation of the world. Abel, Enoch, Noah—all three were equally rejected and despised by the world, because they condemned its works. God grant that the life of his believing children may be so clear and bright, that the world may feel itself condemned by them!

And became heir of the righteousness which is according to faith—the righteousness of standing in the right relation to God, of a life of which faith is the root and power. Righteousness has been defined the giving each his due. This is the worth of faith in the sight of God: it gives Him His place as God, in it the soul confesses that it is nothing, and that God is all. This faith God counts for righteousness.

The faith that Noah manifested with regard to the ark, and the salvation it was to bring, we must show in relation to Christ and His salvation. The opened sanctuary is an ark of refuge: Christ has completed and perfected all. But what work there is for us to do, in gathering into it all that can be saved! Let us, like Noah, give our lives to this. Let us listen to God's awful threatenings on a sinful world, and be moved with fear. Let us believe in the infinite power of the great salvation provided, with the love that waits to dispense and apply it. Let us believe in the call of God, that invites and enjoins each one of His redeemed children to be a messenger of mercy to the perishing, and that assures us that He will abundantly use everyone that trusts Him.

By faith Noah prepared an ark to the saving of his house: does not this give faith a new attractiveness and value. By the prayer of faith and the labour of faith, by the death to self in Christ, and by the walk in the presence of God, our hearts can

455

be filled with a love and a power that cannot be fruitless. The Holy Spirit that came from our beloved Priest-King on the throne in the Holiest, as a witness to God's pleasure in us, and to the indwelling of our Lord, came specially as an enduement of power, to make us in our turn witnesses for Him. Oh all ye who, by faith, have entered into the Holiest and its blessings, go forth and work the work of faith; by faith bring in those who are still without. This is the faith that makes you an heir of the righteousness which is according to faith.

1. *Abel, Enoch, Noah: all types of Jesus. Abel: the righteous one, hated and slain by his brethren, coming to God with sacrifice. Enoch: the beloved son, in whom God is well pleased, walking with Him on earth, and taken up into heaven. Noah: preparing salvation, saving His people, condemning the world.*

2. *The one thing God gives me is, Jesus the dying One, the living One, the redeeming One. The one thing He asks of me is faith. Faith will make me like Him. Beginning with the Abel-blessing drawing nigh to God through death, I come to the Enoch-blessing, the life of unbroken fellowship. And so I learn the secret of the Noah-blessing, and become a saviour of others. And all, By faith.*

CII.

Abraham—the Obedience of Faith

XI.–8. By faith Abraham, when he was called, obeyed to go out
unto a place which he was to receive for an inheritance; and he
went out, not knowing whither he went.

9. By faith he became a sojourner in the land of promise, as in a
land not his own, dwelling in tents with Isaac and Jacob, the
heirs with him of the same promise:

10. For he looked for the city which hath the foundations,
whose builder and maker is God.

There is no child of Adam who is held in honour by such a large
portion of the human race as Abraham. Jews, Christians, Mo-
hammedans, look up to him as the father of the faithful. And
God honours him as His friend! If anyone, this hero of the obedience of faith can tell us what the secret is of a life of faith. Our
Epistle has called us to be **imitators of them who through faith
and longsuffering inherit the promises,** with special mention
of Abraham as one, who, **having suffered long, obtained the
promise** (vi. 12–15). As Paul, too (Rom. iv. 12), speaks of those
*who walk in the steps of that faith of our father Abraham which he
had.* Let all who have with purpose of heart determined, like
Abraham, to be strong in faith, giving glory to God, listen to the
lesson of his life. God expects from us, we do indeed need, and
there is within our reach, the very same faith which he had.

**By faith, Abraham, when he was called, obeyed to go out
to a place which he was to receive for an inheritance, and he
went out not knowing whither he went.** What was the object

of God's thus dealing with Abraham? And what, in real truth, the worth and the blessing of his obedience? The call of God was no arbitrary one; as we see into its divine meaning we shall understand what God asks of us and what our faith must lay hold of. Man stands between the visible and the invisible. His sin and fall consisted in his having turned from God to the world. His redemption from the power of sin could only be found in his giving up the world and setting his whole heart upon God. It was to train him to this, to teach him to find his life and his happiness in God Himself, that the call came: *Get thee out from thy country, and from thy kindred, unto the land that I will show thee.* God wanted to have him alone with Himself, separated from all he could cling to or trust in, that He might teach him to find his all in Himself. And it was *by faith,* faith that not only saw the land, and the promise connected with it, afar off, but saw the living God near to fulfil the promise, that Abraham obeyed. The call of God is ever accompanied by the promise; true faith in the promise is ever joined to obedience to the call. Obedience is of the very essence of faith. Faith is always the power by which a man gives himself up to an unseen object, and receives it into his heart and being. It is in the very nature of things impossible, to receive God without receiving His will.

By faith Abraham obeyed. We have seen how it was by obedience, by the doing of God's will, the Son Himself was perfected, and perfected us: becoming the author of salvation to them that obey Him. Let us learn that obedience is the very life of faith, and the only way into the Holiest. Let immediate, unreserved, joyful obedience be the one thing our heart is set upon. And let it specially manifest itself in this, one of the root principles of God's will, His call to come out and be separate, and give ourselves to walk with Him whithersoever He leads.

He went out not knowing whither he went. Say not that you cannot understand what it is to come out and forsake all. You do not need to know. You need to know something else—

that you have a God, who is watching and guiding you, and working out in you a character fit for heaven and eternity. The one great mark of that character, of likeness to the Son and fitness for heaven, is very absolute surrender to God, to let Him be all. Of that surrender deep humility, that only wants to obey and to trust, is the first essential. Therefore say to God, that at every cost, and in any way—you are ready to obey. He will never disappoint the trust of a soul fully committed to Him and His will.

By faith he became a sojourner in the land of promise. He not only went out from Haran, but into Canaan. And not even this alone, but **he sojourned,** he abode, he lived there. He not only began well, but in faith and longsuffering he inherited the promise. It is the great lesson of perseverance again. Every day, over again, it must just be obedience and faith, until God has brought us into closer communion with Himself, and can speak to men of us or through us as those who are His tested and trusted friends—men who live only to honour Him.

For he looked for the city, whose builder is God. By faith He saw the unseen; in hope he lived in the future. He had his heart as little in Canaan as in Haran; it was in heaven; it was with God. And we, who have been called to enter into the true tabernacle which God hath pitched—oh, shall we not obey, and go out, even though it be not knowing whither we go. Let us separate ourselves entirely from the world and its spirit; let us, like the Son, die to the creature, that we may live to God. A worldly spirit in the Church or the Christian is a deadly disease: it makes the life of faith impossible. Let us count it our worst enemy, and live as foreigners, who seek the city which is to come. Let us hear the voice calling us out to Himself, to close fellowship, to obedience as of the angels in heaven, to be a testimony and a blessing for the world. And let it be said of us too: **By faith he obeyed, and he went out, and he sojourned in the land of promise, for he looked for a city.**

1. See in Abraham how the whole life of faith is supernatural. His call, the promise of a country, of a son, of a seed—all is distinctly divine, above all sense and reason. It is only when the soul looks steadily at the really supernatural things God is to do for us and in us and through us, that its faith will rest entirely on the power of God, and obey at any cost.

2. God will hold as personal intercourse with thee as with Abraham. God will be all to thee as to him. Let thy life be supernatural; perfect impotence under the operating of divine omnipotence—God by His Spirit working out in thee His own life.

3. Be a sojourner in the land of promise—in the life opened up to us by the promises of God—the life in the Holiest of All, through the Holy Spirit. Live in the promises.

4. He went out, not knowing whither he went. *Christ is not only Priest but Prophet, Teacher, and Leader. Trust Him to bring thee within the veil, and to guide thee all through life in the new and living way. It is a peace that* passeth all understanding, *a love that* passeth knowledge, *a power that is able to do exceeding abundantly* above all we can think, *that marks the life of faith in the land of promise. Let us go out,* not knowing whither we go.

CIII.

Sarah—Faith in the Faithfulness of God

XI.–11. By faith even Sarah herself received power to conceive seed when she was past age, since she counted him faithful who had promised:

12. Wherefore also there sprang of one, and him as good as dead, so many, as the stars of heaven in multitude, and as the sand, which is by the sea shore, innumerable.

By faith Sarah received power to give birth to Isaac. To judge by nature and its possibilities, there was no hope of a son. But the birth of Isaac was to be a work of God's power: He had promised and He would perform. Sarah believed the promise, because she believed God the promiser; by faith she received power to become Isaac's mother; and **of one who was as good as dead, there sprang up as many as the stars of heaven in multitude.**

We are told wherein it was that, in sight of what was impossible with man, her faith found its strength: **she counted Him faithful who had promised.** She looked to the promise; she considered Him who had given it; she rested on His faithfulness. The faithfulness of God was the rest of her heart and her faith.

What is the lesson Sarah teaches us in regard to the life of faith, and the work that God would work in us through faith? From one who was as good as dead there sprang as the stars in multitude. God is the living God, who delights to give life in death. When Adam sinned, he and the whole race died; they lost the life of paradise and of God. God's great work is to restore that life. In the Old Testament He showed this in a case like that of Isaac, by proving that the new race He was going to prepare must have a life from Himself, a life born of one as good as dead. Isaac's life was to be in a special sense a God-given life. In the New Testament He showed it by the miraculous birth of Jesus Christ: God's mighty power revealing the divine life in the babe of Bethlehem. What God would teach us is: the new life must come from God; His mighty power must alone and directly work it, or all is vain. It is for this our faith must trust Him.

Just as really as the life of Adam, the life of Isaac, the life of Christ, was the immediate work of God's almighty power, is the divine life in our souls His work. And it is not only His work in its beginning, as if He bestowed upon us a life that we had to keep in safety, and to nourish and bring to perfection. No, as the tree grows every day on that root from which it sprang, so our spiritual life must every day stand and grow in God and Christ. One great cause of the weakness of the spiritual life of earnest Christians, notwithstanding their prayers and efforts, is that they seek to do the work that God alone can do. They know not that God, whose Spirit dwells in us, will maintain our life in a divine power, working in us that which is pleasing in His sight. If they knew this aright, they would see that their one duty was in utter helplessness, in deep humility and dependence, to wait upon God and to trust and count upon Him to do His blessed work.

It is this Sarah teaches us. She knew what God had promised. For twenty-five long years her heart yearned for the son of whom God had spoken. At times her faith was sorely tried, but she ever came back to this one thing: **He is faithful that promised!** And in due time God did His omnipotent quickening work, and Sarah received power to become the mother of Isaac and of Jesus. And down the ages her voice of witness is heard: Trust God; He is faithful; He is the living God; He gives life from the dead.

The teaching of the Epistle speaks to us of **the living God** and **the city of the living God to which we are come; of a**

High Priest who liveth, and **liveth for ever,** and of a work that He does within us, **the power of an endless life;** of a **new and living way,** in which we are borne into God's presence; of the law of life **written in the heart,** and of a life **within the veil, in the Holiest of All.** This new and wondrous life it has revealed is nothing less than the life and work of God in the soul. To the question which is so often asked, Why we do not experience that life more mightily, there can be but one answer: We do not allow God in Christ to work it in us; we do not believe in the continual indwelling and working of the Holy Spirit. Even as Sarah failed when she sought for the promised son by giving Hagar to Abraham, we fail because we seek by our effort to do what God will not allow any but Himself to do. Let us, like Sarah, come back from our self-devised ways, and enter by the new and living way; the way of death to nature and to self; the way of life through the Holy Spirit, into the life which God alone can maintain.

Faith is the power by which we take up into our being, and yield ourselves up to and become one with the object our heart clings to and reposes on. God hath spoken to us in His Son. His Son is the great promise to us, the token and the pledge of what God will make us. Let us look to the promise, let us look to the Son, let us look to the faithful One who has promised, and with whom *it is impossible to lie,* and we shall receive power to receive and bring forth the new life that is of God. Let us, above all, take the place before God that Sarah did as of one dead, hopelessly, helplessly dead, as far as the prospect of bringing forth a new life was concerned, and we may count upon it, God will do His work. Impotence is ever one of the conditions of true faith. Sink down before God in utter emptiness; bow before Him and wait upon Him, and walk with Him, in deep humility and meekness of soul, as having nothing and being nothing; fall down as dead at His feet, and He will say: Fear not, I am He that liveth, and maketh alive.

1. Now, bow down, say to God that you trust Him for the wonderful new life the Epistle has revealed in Christ. Trust Him to reveal Christ, in the power of an endless life, within you.

2. Let every doubt and fear be met by looking afresh to the promise, to God the promiser, and to the faithfulness of Him who by an oath has confirmed His promise of blessing and of the power of the eternal priesthood of Christ to thee.

3. In this trust take thy place of deep helplessness and dependence and humility. Be nothing that God may be all. Just yield thyself for the living God through His Son and Spirit to do His mighty work in thee.

4. The full blessing of Sarah's faith was not only Isaac, but as many as the stars in multitude. So with thee. As thou givest thyself wholly to be filled directly from God Himself with the divine life, it will break forth in blessing around. Blessing I will bless, and multiplying I will multiply.

CIV.

Faith—and Its Pilgrim Spirit

XI.–13. These all died in faith, not having received the promises, but having seen them and greeted[1] them from afar, and having confessed that they were strangers and pilgrims on the earth.
14. For they that say such things make it manifest that they are seeking after a country of their own.
15. And if indeed they had been mindful of that country from which they went out, they would have had opportunity to return.
16. But now they desire a better country, that is a heavenly: wherefore God is not ashamed of them, to be called their God: for He hath prepared for them a city.

Most instructive is the description given us here of the way in which faith prepared the saints of old for the fulfilment of God's promises. First comes—**Having seen them afar off:** faith was to them the revelation of unseen things. Then follows—**And having embraced them,** they gladly greeted, welcomed, accepted, and appropriated them, and lived as those to whom they belonged. Then follows the receiving. Of the Old Testament saints it is here said, **not having received the promises.** Some of the promises they did indeed receive, as we have seen in the birth of Isaac. But the promises, in their full meaning, they did not receive; this is our privilege. Seeing, embracing, receiving are the three great steps in the life of faith.

On this follows a description of the life in which their faith was made manifest, **Having confessed that they were strang-**

1. Embraced.

ers and pilgrims on the earth. Faith is such a power that it rules the whole life. It is the faith of a man that makes him forsake his home for our goldfields. If he sees his way to make a fortune, and return to some great centre of attraction, it is this faith maintains in him the spirit of a stranger and a pilgrim, whose heart is in the home land. So these saints proved that they were **seeking after a country of their own,** that they had no mind **to return to that from which they went out, they desire a better country, that is, a heavenly.** Faith made them pilgrims and strangers, and secured them the divine blessing. **Wherefore God is not ashamed to be called their God, for He hath prepared for them a city.**

Our great lesson is: Faith makes us pilgrims and strangers here on earth. Such was Christ; such are we to be. The moment we begin to press home the message to our own heart, many questions arise. Will it not unfit us for daily life? What if all men were to live in this pilgrim spirit, as strangers and sojourners? What would become of the development of the world? Do we not see that in science and politics and literature the men who give themselves wholly to these things, accomplish most? Those who come to a colony, and return home to spend their money there, never take the interest those do who give themselves to settle here. Is the true, intense, pilgrim spirit, really a duty for all? There is no more subtle temptation than to wait with what God calls us to do till we are first informed what others are to do, or what God is to do with the rest of the world. We may safely leave to Him who is ruler of all, the All-wise, what will come of obedience to His commands. To every question, *And what shall this man do?* Christ's answer is, *What is that to thee! Follow thou Me.* If we are disciples of Christ, each one of us must seek to have as much of His Spirit as can be. If we are to be led by Him in the new and living way, to live with Him in the Holiest of All, we must, like Him, live here as pilgrims and strangers.

Faith makes heavenly-minded. As partakers of a heavenly calling we look to Jesus, who endured the cross and despised the shame. Separation from the world is essential to a life of faith. Adam's fall was a fall under the power and spirit of this visible world. Christ gave Himself that He might deliver us from this present evil world. The world we live in, the so-called Christian world, is still the same that rejected Christ. While professing His name, its spirit of devotion to the things that are seen, its pursuit of pleasure and riches and honour, its delight and its boasting of culture and prosperity, is a spirit utterly at variance with the Christlike, with the heavenly-minded spirit. This is the reason why so many seek to grow in faith, and fail. They would fain live in the Holiest, but they would do so without forsaking the world. Abraham and his seed lived as men **seeking after a country of their own,** as those who **desire a better country, that is, a heavenly.** Until the kingdom of heaven in its power, as it came down from the throne of God in heaven, becomes our one desire, and until we leave all and sell all for this pearl of great price, our faith cannot stand in the power of God, or overcome the world. If it be not our one desire to live as those who are **partakers of a heavenly calling,** yea, **partakers of Christ,** as those who are pilgrims and strangers, and make it manifest that they are seeking after a country of their own, as those who desire a heavenly country, no wonder if God is ashamed to be called our God, and our souls cannot taste the joy of a walk in His presence.

There is nothing so heart-searching as faith. If we profess to believe all that this Epistle has revealed, let us prove it by following our Leader in the new and living way, and by living with Him in the Holiest of All. As we give ourselves wholly to this our faith will grow; we shall become men of faith, marked by this one thing—a faith that lifts us into the heavenly world, and makes us pilgrims and strangers here.

The eye of faith will become ever clearer, seeing perhaps at first, afar off, what so many cannot see—the promise and the reality and the possibility of abiding continually in the Holiest of All in the power of an endless life, separated and made free from the world and its spirit. The boldness of faith will become ever stronger—we shall greet and embrace, we shall claim and hold fast, all that God hath spoken in Christ of a life in the city of the living God here below as our very own. And we shall in patience persevere in doing the will of God, knowing that the power of God Himself and the Son of God is surety that we shall receive the promise. True faith begins with counting upon what God has promised, but it does not end there—it leads into the actual possession and enjoyment, in the power of God, of all it had embraced in His word. What God hath spoken to faith, His hand will perform.

1. Note well the three steps of faith. I must first see what God has promised. I must believe in the blessed life Christ can give and maintain within me. Let us pray for the Spirit's enlightening (Eph. i. 14–20). Then I embrace, greet, welcome, claim as my own the promise, and expect its fulfilment. This in due time I receive, in heart and experience. Whatever God has promised me I must expect to experience.

2. The promise is ever the expression of what God's omnipotence is going to work; our faith must ever be the expression of what we expect that omnipotence to work.

CV.

Faith Counting on the Power of God

XI.–17. By faith Abraham, being tried, offered up Isaac: yea, he that had gladly received the promises was offering up his only begotten son;

18. Even he to whom it was said, In Isaac shall thy seed by called:

19. Accounting that God is able to raise up, even from the dead; from whence he did also in a parable receive him back.

As the characteristic of Abraham's faith we have here again the great word—**offering**. Abel offered; Christ offered Himself; Abraham offered his only begotten, and, in doing so, himself too. In some shape or other intercourse with God, the life of faith, always means sacrifice. In a sinful world there is no way of drawing nigh to God, of coming out of the sinful nature, but by dying to it, and receiving a new life from God Himself, or rather by God giving His own life into the dead one to raise it again. There is no way to God but by giving up our own life, and what is as dear as life, unto death.

This sacrifice is only possible to faith. The faith that has seen and embraced the promise, that knows God as the living and life-giving God, and that dares claim and count upon His power to do to me what He has spoken, is the faith that has the courage for the altar and the knife and the fire. God's great object in leading His people in the path of faith is to train them for ever larger sacrifice. It was a sacrifice of all he held dear when Abraham left his kindred and his father's home. It was a sacrifice of all his own thoughts and wishes, when he was kept waiting for Isaac twenty-five years. But all this was only to prepare him for the crowning sacrifice—the giving up of his only son, the son of the promise, to the death.

And what was it that gave faith its strength and its victory here in this his severest trial? It was faith in God as the almighty One, **able to raise up even from the dead.** In the birth of Isaac he had learnt to know God as the giver of life, even where he was as good as dead. He knew and trusted his God, as *God who quickeneth the dead and calleth the things that are not as though they were.* And what is it that will give our faith the same all-victorious strength, and prepare us for the same mighty exhibition of God's quickening power on our behalf? If we are to have the same faith, and the same experience of God, we must be prepared to make the same sacrifice. Our lesson of today leads us to the very deepest roots of the life of faith. The deeper we are willing to enter into the death to self, the more shall we know of the mighty power of God, and the perfect blessedness of a perfect trust.

In the faith of Sarah we saw what the meaning and the power was of faith in the living and life-giving God. But Abraham on Moriah carries us much further. Sarah trusted God to supply a power that was wanting in nature; Abraham to restore a life that had been taken away. Sarah is the type of a soul that waits on God for His quickening power, as an act of grace and faithfulness, ere it thinks much of the death of self. With her the quickening came to meet a deadness that appears simply the result of the weakness of nature. With Abraham all is different. Isaac, the God-given life, must be sacrificed, ere this new display of power can be expected. That sacrifice was to teach that even the God-given life is still subject to the power of fallen nature; that only through death can it be delivered from the power of sin and death; that only so can it become a life wholly possessed of God. The first time quickened by Him, and yet under the power of sin; the second time, dead to sin, and alive to God in the perfect life of eternity. It was the symbol of what was to take place in Christ Jesus and everyone who is made like Him in the fellowship of His death.

We see where this leads us in the Christian life. Even as Christ in His birth received His life from the Father, so we, too, in our new birth. But that life had to be sacrificed, ere He could enter the full life in the glory of the Father. Even so with us. The life God gives us in the new birth is only to prepare us for understanding and deserving and accepting and entering into a perfect voluntary conformity to Christ's death. As we see how much there still is of self, we begin to learn and long for what is implied in the death to self. It means a deeper insight into our own entire and complete inability to do any good. It means a willing and a hearty consent to be and to do nothing, and to let God be and do all. It means a real ceasing from our own works, and an entire surrender to the immediate and unceasing operations of God by His Holy Spirit, for Him to work both to will and to do that which is pleasing in His sight. It means such a hating of one's own life, such a denial of one's self, that one is content with nothing less than death to it.

It is the soul that seeks to follow its Lord in this new and living way, that feels the need of the faith in the living God who raises the dead, that will be fitted to exercise it. It is the trial of faith calls out its power; it is the need of faith calls down the power of God. Oh, if we did but hear the call of God to bring the life He has Himself given us, with all its blessed experience, and yield it up to the death, how we should learn to know Him in His mighty quickening power. Instead of the life with something of God, but far more of man, He who led Abraham would bring us to the place of death, where He would give us the assurance that henceforth His almighty power would do all, and we should find our blessedness in being nothing and allowing God to be our life.

Christian! **Abraham offered up Isaac, accounting that God is able to raise him up, even from the dead.** Take the place of death; trust God who raises the dead, and gives life in death; believe and thou shalt see the glory of God.

1. *The highest manifestation of God's power is the raising of Christ from the dead. The highest exercise of faith by Christ was in death—He committed His Spirit into the Father's hands. The highest exercise of faith in a believer—the daily surrender of the life God has given us to death, in the faith that He will quicken it each moment by His indwelling Spirit.*

2. *Before Isaac's birth Abraham had nothing to lean upon but the promise. After it he was in danger of leaning on Isaac: therefore, Isaac had to be given up. All gifts of God received in faith may become our trust, and must be given up to Him in a higher faith.*

3. *Our whole life every day, every moment, is to be the work of Almighty God within us by His Holy Spirit.*

CVI.

Faith Blessing the Children

XI.–20. By faith Isaac blessed Jacob and Esau, even concerning things to come.

21. By faith Jacob, when he was a-dying, blessed each of the sons of Joseph; and worshipped, leaning upon the top of his staff.

22. By faith Joseph, when his end was nigh, made mention of the departure of the children of Israel; and gave commandment concerning his bones.

23. By faith Moses, when he was born, was hid three months by his parents, because they saw he was a goodly child; and they were not afraid of the king's commandment.

It is remarkable how much, both in this chapter and through all Scripture, faith has to do with the relationship of parents and children. In nature the life of the parents is imparted to the children. In the spiritual world it may be so too; the intercourse of faith with God reaches the children too; the man of strong faith is a blessing to his children. We have seen in Noah and Abraham and Sarah how largely their faith in God had to do with their children. And here we find four more examples.

By faith Isaac blessed Jacob and Esau. His blessing on his children was the manifestation of his faith in the promise of God to his father and himself, and the transmission of the blessing to them. **By faith Jacob blessed each of the sons of Joseph,** giving each of them their place in the future that was coming. **By faith Joseph made mention of the departure of the children of Israel** saying, "I die, but God will surely visit you, and bring you up out of this land." **By faith Moses was hid three months**

by his parents, because they saw he was a goodly child.
Their faith in the destiny they knew was waiting for the children
of Israel, and in the mercy of God watching over his people,
gave them the courage not to fear the king's commandment. In
all these cases faith was the secret inspiration of their treatment
of their children, and the source of blessing. Faith never con-
fines itself to the person of the believer himself, but takes in his
home and children.

And how is it that the Christian parent can secure this
longed-for blessing for his children? There is but one answer: *By
faith.* Our life must be all faith—that is, the unseen things must
be our life, yea, rather, the unseen God must be our life. The
blessing and the power are His; and it is as we have more of God
in our life and in our home, there will be the hidden power resting on our children. Faith does not only mean a knowing that
there is a covenant promise for our children, and a pleading of
it in prayer. This is an exercise of faith, and has its great value.
But the chief thing is the life; faith is the making way for God
and giving Him place in our life. And when at times the vision
tarries, and the promise appears to fail, faith understands this as
only a call to trust God more completely and more confidently.
As we hold fast our confidence firm to the end, as in patience
and longsuffering we are strong in faith, giving glory to God, we
shall know for certain that we shall inherit this promise too. I
will be thy God and the God of thy seed.

From the patriarchs we learn what the atmosphere and what
the soil is in which there grows such a faith that blesses the children. They were living in the land of promise as strangers and
pilgrims, or in Egypt as strangers and pilgrims too, longing for
the return to the land. Their whole life was hope in God and
what He would do. They were men whom God had taken hold
of, to prove in their history how gloriously he would fulfil His
promise. And they had nothing to live on but God. It is a law of
nature that no body can be in two places at the same time. This

is just as true of the heart. When God took Abraham and his seed out of their country, it was that the land of promise, the land of separation from men, of separation unto God, might be to them the training-school of faith. They went out from the fellowship of home and family, to live in the fellowship of God. It was there they learned by faith to bless the children.

Separation from the world, a being set apart unto God, the denial of self and its life, the imitation of Abraham in his going out, of Christ in His self-sacrifice—this is the only way to the land of promise where the faith-life flourishes. To live wholly for God, to hope alone in God, always to walk with God, in all things to hearken to God—this is the new and living way into the inner sanctuary, in which Jesus our High Priest leads us. What the land of promise was to the patriarchs, as the place for the life of separation and obedience and faith, that the Holiest of All is to us. That is the place of which God has said to us: *Get thee out of thy land, to a place that I will show thee, and I will bless thee*—that is the only place where our faith can grow freely, and God can prove all His power in us, so that we, like they, can be a display of what God can do. And that is the place where our faith will in full measure be a blessing to our children.

It is only by faith we can bless. God is willing to bless us to larger circles than our own house. He is calling for vessels, empty vessels not a few, in which He can multiply his blessing. He is the only fountain of blessing; as our faith yields to God, and allows Him to be all, His blessing will flow. Let the Christian who would be a blessing be a man of faith—that is, a man who has nothing and is nothing in himself, and in whom God has free scope to work, and the blessing will not be wanting. Oh that God might have the place that belongs to Him in this His own world. And if that may not yet be—oh that He might have that place in the hearts of His people. And if it is as if even that will not yet be—oh let Him have that place, my reader, in your heart and in mine. Let faith see and consent and prove that God is all, and He will prove that He is a God of blessing for thee and all around thee.

1. Parent, teacher, worker, the secret of blessing in the work, the power to influence, is—faith. Not simply the faith in some promise at times, but the habit of a holy faith that makes God the All of our life. Have faith in God as the God of thy life, the God who maintains His life and presence within thee. He will work through thee.

2. How blessed to be an instrument in the hands of God, with which He works out His purpose; to be a vessel He fills with His love.

3. Learn to regard thyself as set to be a blessing, and let faith and love mark thy whole life.

CVII.

Moses, and the Decision of Faith

XI.–24. By faith Moses, when he was grown up, refused to be called the son of Pharoah's daughter;

25. Choosing rather to be evil entreated with the people of God, than to enjoy the pleasures of sin for a season;

26. Accounting the reproach of Christ greater riches than the treasures of Egypt; for he looked unto the recompense of reward.

We all live by faith. What we love and live in we believe in. He that trusts and yields himself to the visible and the temporal lives an earthly, fleshly life. He that looks to the unseen and the eternal, and joins himself to it, lives a divine, a heavenly life. Between these two faith has ever to make its choice. The clearer and more deliberate, the more conscious the decision is for the unseen, the more will the faith in God be strengthened and rewarded. The great difficulty in making the right choice lies in the fact that, by the victory which things seen and sensible gained in paradise, our eyes have been blinded, and the things of time, even where we acknowledge them to be of less value, have acquired, in virtue of their continual presence and their pressing claims, superior power. The great work faith has to do, and the best school for its growth and strength, is the choice of the unseen.

Of this choice Moses is a striking illustration. Just see what there was on the one side. The lust of the flesh: **the pleasures of sin for a season.** The lust of the eye: **the riches of Egypt.** The pride of life: **to be called the son of Pharaoh's daughter.**

And, on the other side, **to be evil entreated,** to **bear reproach.** And what was it that enabled him to make a wise choice? He saw that **to be evil entreated with the people of God** is to have God as his portion and defence. He bore the reproach of Christ, in the power of the Spirit of Christ from heaven, lifting his heart above earth. Even as Christ, for the joy set before Him, endured the cross, so he **looked to the recompense of the reward.** Faith in the blessing of God on the people of God; union in spirit with the Christ of God; the assurance of a coming world, with its reversal of the judgments of earth;—no wonder that all this guided and strengthened him to the choice he made—the good part never to be taken away.

We are studying this chapter in its connection with the Epistle, and its teaching as to a life under the leadership of Christ—a life in the new and living way of conformity to Him, leading into the Holiest of God's presence. We long to know how we can grow strong, and live in the full exercise of a faith that inherits the promise and enters into the rest of God. Moses' witness is clear: Let faith prove itself in choosing, once for all and for always, at any cost, the unseen—the reward will be sure and large. In Abraham we saw this choice when there was no special opposition or persecution. This is the feature in Moses' choice we must notice: with the danger threatening us of being evil entreated, and bearing reproach, and having to face the loss of all, faith must not hesitate or halt. To be evil entreated with God's people, to bear Christ's reproach, and count these greater riches than all the treasures of Egypt—this is what faith enables a man to do, this is the spiritual discipline which makes faith strong. Faith looks at everything in the light of eternity, judging of it as one will do when the judgment day is past, and the glory begun; everything is seen in its true value, and sacrifice and suffering and loss and trial are welcomed as the training in which the glad decision, and the firm will, and the strong character, and the victory of faith are attained.

We have here the great cause of the weakness of faith in our days. *There is no separation from the world.* So many Christians seek to have as much of its pleasure and honour and riches as they possibly can, consistently with their profession of religion. In such an atmosphere faith is stifled. Many hardly believe, or never remember, that the world, with its arts and culture and prosperity, amid all its religious professions, is still the same world *that rejected Christ.* The disciple who would be as his Lord, "not of the world, *even as He* was not of the world," seeks to say with Paul, "Far be it from me to glory, save in the cross of our Lord Jesus Christ, *through which the world hath been crucified unto me, and I unto the world.*"

How wonderful is the place Moses occupies in the kingdom of God. A pattern of Jesus as a prophet, as a mediator, as an intercessor, in his meekness and his faithfulness, there are few of God's servants that stand higher. And what fitted him to take this place? Just this—the choice to give up everything for the reproach of Christ. Christian, wouldst thou live in the favour of God, and enter into His tent to meet Him as Moses did? wouldst thou be an instrument and a power of blessing, a man strong in faith?—seek to be perfectly separate from the spirit of the world, refuse its pleasure and honour and riches; count the contempt of God's people and the reproach of Christ thy treasures. Ask for the enlightening of the Holy Spirit to teach thee what true conformity to Christ is, in thy relation to the world, its culture, its possessions, its friendship. Beware of judging of what is lawful by any human standard: Christ alone can teach thee what it means to forsake all, to sell all, to deny thyself, and take up the cross, and follow Him. Count all things loss to be conformed to Him. It was in bearing the reproach of Christ a character like that of Moses was formed. This is the sure path of faith to power and to blessing.

Follow thou Moses, accounting the reproach of Christ thy riches, and thou shalt share with him the recompense of the reward. **Let us therefore go forth unto Him, bearing His reproach.**

1. *Examine very carefully where thy danger lies. Is it the friendship and honour of men? Is it pleasure? Is it the cares of the world? Whatever it be, give it up. It is only an unworldly spirit that can be strong in faith.*

2. *What is the faith that enables a man to bear all and to sacrifice all? Nothing but an eye that sees into the true nature and value of things, that judges of them as God does. Yea, rather that we see God to be all, and the creature nothing except as it leads to Him.*

3. *Exercise thyself in this faith by retirement into solitude and fellowship with the invisible. Beware of too free intercourse with the literature of this world: its spirit enters into thee. The world knows not God: make thy choice and maintain it.*

CVIII.

Israel, and Redemption by Faith

XI.–27. By faith he forsook Egypt, not fearing the wrath of the king: for he endured, as seeing him who is invisible.
28. By faith he kept the passover, and the sprinkling of the blood, that the destroyer of the firstborn should not touch them.
29. By faith they passed through the Red Sea as by dry land: which the Egyptians assaying to do were swallowed up.
30. By faith the walls of Jericho fell down, after they had been compassed about for seven days.
31. By faith Rahab the harlot perished not with them that were disobedient, having received the spies with peace.

In these verses we have, in five examples, from the history of Israel on its way from Egypt to Canaan, the truth confirmed anew that in all that God does in redemption, on man's part faith is the beginning and the ending. Whether we look at His revelation as a whole, or at its individual parts, everywhere the one thing He asks, the one thing that pleases Him, the one thing that secures His blessing is—faith. In the five times repeated *by faith* we see that in the greatest variety of circumstances and duties the first of all duties always is—faith in the invisible One. Oh that we might at length learn the lesson: as there is one God, and one redemption, so there is but one way to Him and to it—faith in Him. As absolute and universal and undisputed as is the sole supremacy of God, is to be the supremacy of faith in our heart. Because, when faith reigns supreme, it makes way for God, and God can become within us what He is in the universe, what He is in His very nature—the all in all.

The history of Israel, under the guidance of the Holy Spirit of God, is a real type and figure of the life of Christ in the soul. In the illustrations taken from the beginning of that history, we have some of the chief steps of the Christian life strikingly illustrated. **By faith Moses, with Israel, left Egypt, not fearing the wrath of the king** who would pursue them. That is ever the first step—coming out, being separate, parting with sin, bidding farewell to Egypt, the land of our birth, and not fearing the wrath of Satan or the world. It is by nothing but faith that this can be done, definitely and perseveringly. But faith can enable us to do it, as it did Moses. **For he endured, as seeing Him who is invisible.** Here is the mighty power of faith; it sees what others cannot see. It sees, amid the thousand things others see and are guided by, something infinitely greater—**it sees God.** No wonder it leads a man to act differently from other men. On everything it looks at, the bright light of eternity, of God, is shining. No wonder that under the inspiration of that Vision it can do mighty deeds, for it sees God its helper and strength.

Let me here say to every believer that just as, in any pursuit, the eye by practice can be trained to see what others cannot see, so the eye of faith can be trained to see God everywhere. Abide in His presence till the heart is filled with it. Recognise Him in every thing that happens. Seek to walk in the light of His countenance. Seeing the Invisible will make it easy to forsake the world and do the will of God.

By faith he kept, with Israel, the passover and the sprinkling of blood, that the destroyer should not touch them. When faith is ready for the first step, the forsaking of Egypt, God meets it with His divine provision, and faith finds perfect safety and rest under the shelter of the blood. And if Israel thus honoured God's word and trusted in the blood of a lamb—oh, shall we not ten thousand times more honour the blood of the Lamb, and believe and claim that eternal salvation it brings us. We have been taught its wonderful power in conquering sin and death, in opening heaven, in cleansing and perfecting our conscience and heart, and bringing us nigh to God; let us open our whole being to the power of the blood that cleanses from all sin. Let our faith rejoice in the invisible God and the precious blood of the Lamb of God.

By faith they passed through the Red Sea as by dry land. On the sprinkling of the blood there follows the entrance on a new life, the surrender to be led by God in a way that we know not, through difficulties to us insurmountable. **By faith they passed through** between the waters in a way man had never trod, in a way that their pursuers in vain sought to follow. Where nature fails faith triumphs, for it follows in a way where God leads.

By faith the walls of Jericho fell down. The strength of the enemy, in which he trusted, in view of the impotence of God's people, availed nothing before the power of faith. When shall we learn, in quiet patience and perseverance, to wait upon God our seven days too, the circle of a completed time, until He gives the possession of the promised rest. Let our faith claim it; we are the children of God who does impossibilities; we are called to a life of faith that expects and receives them. Let our life be—faith in God.

By faith Rahab perished not. Salvation by faith was not for Israel only but for the heathen too. By faith Rahab was not only saved, but became one of the ancestors of Jesus, and one of the cloud of witnesses that tell of the blessedness of faith. With one accord they call to us: Have faith in God, all things are possible to him that believeth. Let faith be all with us, and God will be all. Let God be all and He will do all.

By faith. Let this be the motto of our life. In every need and perplexity, with every desire and prayer, with every work and trial, with every thought of ourselves and of God, let this be the one thing we seek—ever to breathe a living faith in a living God. Once again I say: As absolute and universal and undisputed as is the supremacy of God, is to be the supremacy of faith in our heart and life. We can only have as much of God in our heart as we have of faith. And because God is All, and must be All to us, faith in us must be all too.

1. *The old saints had less light than we—how is it they had more faith than so many? It is because we trust in the light we have, as we hold it in our mind and reason. They were thrown upon God and trusted Him. Let us but give ourselves over to the perfect life Jesus has revealed—what power faith would give us.*

2. *But notice everywhere how it was only in obedience faith could act. In leaving Egypt, and sprinkling the blood, and passing through the Red Sea, and going round Jericho, and Rahab's deliverance—it was all, wholly and entirely, in obedience that faith acted and triumphed.*

3. *Faith is the power of the will choosing God's will, entering into it and yielding to it. Wouldst thou be strong in faith, stand perfect in all the will of God.*

CIX.

Faith, and Its Power of Achievement

XI.–32. And what shall I more say? for the time will fail me if I tell of Gideon, Barak, Samson, Jephthah; of David and Samuel and the prophets:

33. Who through faith subdued kingdoms, wrought righteousness, obtained promises, stopped the mouths of lions,

34. Quenched the power of fire, escaped the edge of the sword, from weakness were made strong, waxed mighty in war, turned to flight armies of aliens:

35. Women received their dead by a resurrection.

With the entrance into Canaan and the fall of Jericho the first period of Israel's history closes. It would take too much time for the writer to proceed as he had done; he now mentions a few of the most prominent names from among the Judges, the Kings, and the Prophets, and then passes on to a general view of the very wonderful proofs that faith had given of what it could do or suffer. His desire is to take the veil from the heart of the Hebrews, and show them, what so many who know Scripture history will never see, that under and behind and within all the outward events recorded, there lives, as the vital principle, faith in God. The history is, on the one hand, the record of what God has done through and for those who have trusted Him; on the other, the proof that in God's leading of His people, the one token of His presence and working was always the spirit of faith which He gave. Faith in exercise is the breaking out of the divine life within, the very substance of things hoped for, the proof of the presence of things not seen.

In mentioning the great achievements of faith, our writer gives three separate trios. In the first we find mentioned what the heroes of faith had accomplished. In combat with their enemies, they **subdued kingdoms**; in ruling the people and opposing evil, they **wrought righteousness**; in dealing with God, **they obtained promises.** In the second, personal deliverance from wild beasts, from the powers of nature, from the violence of men, is in the foreground. They **stopped the mouths of lions, quenched the power of fire, escaped the edge of the sword.** In the third, we have the experience of the power of faith for personal strengthening: **From weakness were made strong, waxed mighty in war, turned to flight armies of aliens.** And then there is added one thing more: **Women received their dead by a resurrection.** By faith women conquered the power of death. There is no power on earth that can stand before the power of faith, because the power of faith is the power of God working in us.

The memory of the heroes and heroisms of the olden time may be most instructive, if we regard them in their true light. One thing that impresses us is, how little God has promised to faith that it will be freed from difficulty and danger. It would be as easy to God to prevent the enemy coming as to give the victory over him. To do this would be infinite loss; faith would never be called into exercise; man would never learn to know either his God or himself as His child. Every trial accomplishes a double purpose. It gives us the opportunity of honouring God by the trust with which we wait on Him. And it gives God the opportunity of showing how faithful He is in watching over His child, and how truly He is working for him and in him. It is in trial that all the heart of the child is drawn out towards the father, in dependence and humility and trust. It is in trial that God can reveal in the opened heart of His child all the tenderness and all the saving power of His love. Without trial there could be no school of faith, no growth of spiritual character, no strength of will given up to God and clinging to Him. Let us bless God for every trial, small or great: it gives us a grand opportunity for putting the crown upon the head of God, and of being made fit that He crown us too.

Another thought of no less importance, that comes as we think of the achievements of faith in the history of Israel, is how closely they were all identified with the public welfare, with lives devoted to the cause of God and the people. Selfishness is the death of faith. *How can ye believe who take honour one of another?* As long as we seek to be strong in faith, for the sake of our own comfort and goodness, and the possession of power, even if we dream of using it all for others, when once we obtain it, we shall fail. It is the soul that at once, in its weakness, gives itself up for the sake of God and others, that will find in that self-sacrifice the need and the right to claim God's mighty help. Gideon and Barak, David and Samuel, they were all men whose names and whose faith would never have been known, but that they lived for their nation and God's cause in it, that they were God's chosen instruments for doing His redeeming work in His people.

The sphere of God's special revelation is now no longer Israel, but the world. What a work there is to be done in it! Among Christians and heathen, in church and mission and school, in temperance and purity work, in the great fight against iniquity and worldliness in every shape, in larger and smaller circles— what room, what need for the heroes of faith to subdue kingdoms, to work righteousness, to obtain promises! Let each of us offer himself to God for the struggle. And as we do so, let us remember well the double lesson: No faith without difficulties for it to conquer. No difficulty but faith can surely conquer. In this connection let us cease seeking faith in our own interest: let us lose ourselves in the work for God and souls. We shall lose ourselves to find ourselves back in God and His love.

1. Wherefore, brethren, having boldness to enter into the Holiest, let us draw near in fulness of faith. *Live the life of faith in the Holiest with God: then thy whole life on earth will be one of faith.*

2. *Give thyself wholly to God—thy faith will have the confidence to ask that God give Himself wholly to thee.*

3. *In the little things of daily life we need faith as much as in larger interests. Faith counts nothing insignificant, because nothing is good in which God is not. Faith yields itself to God for Him most literally and completely to be All.*

4. *Remember the real value of strong faith is—to gain victories for God, to live for the salvation of souls and the extension of His kingdom.*

CX.

Faith, and Its Power of Endurance

XI.–35. And others were tortured, not accepting their deliverance; that they might obtain a better resurrection:

36. And others had trial of mockings and scourgings, yea, moreover of bonds and imprisonment:

37. They were stoned, they were sawn asunder, they were tempted, they were slain with the sword: they went about in sheepskins, in goatskins: being destitute, afflicted, evil entreated

38. (Of whom the world was not worthy), wandering in deserts and mountains and caves, and the holes of the earth.

Faith has a twofold victory. In one case, it conquers the enemy or the difficulty by securing its removal or destruction. In the other, there is no deliverance from the trouble, and yet faith conquers in the power it receives to endure, and to prove that its spirit is superior to all that men and devils can do. The triumphs of faith are often seen as remarkably in those who obtain no deliverance from the threatened evil, as in those who do. After the mention of the heroes whose faith was rewarded with success, we have here the mention of those who, in the midst of suffering that was not removed, proved that their faith lifted them up above all the pains with which earth could threaten them. **They were tortured, not accepting their deliverance** when offered them at the price of their faithfulness, **that they might obtain a better resurrection.** Spiritual and eternal realities were by faith so clear and near that they reckoned not the sufferings of this present time worthy to be compared with the glory which shall be revealed. The triumph of faith is seen as much in bearing a temporary defeat as securing a victory. The victory of the vanquished is often the highest achievement.

In these men and women, leaders in the noble army of the martyrs, rejected and despised by the world, God sees the heavenly beauty of a faith that honours Him, and that counts His will, His favour, His righteousness, as more than all earthly happiness. By faith they had such a sight of God and His good pleasure, that they could with joy sacrifice everything to secure it. By faith they could, for the joy set before them, in the assurance of a heavenly recompense, count all the pleasures of earth as less than nothing. It is one of the highest and noblest exercises of faith to suffer aright. And the blessing that comes through suffering is one of the richest rewards that faith can win.

God has given us these examples of those who by faith triumphed over the extremities of suffering, that we might from them learn how to bear our lesser trials. Their faith in extraordinary suffering must strengthen ours in ordinary. It is in the little common trials of daily life that every believer can follow in the footsteps of these saints, in the footsteps of the great Leader of our salvation. By faith alone are we able to bear suffering, great or small, aright, to God's glory or our own welfare.

Yes, by faith alone, Faith sees it in the light of God and eternity; its short pain, its everlasting gain; its impotence to hurt the soul, its power to purify and to bless it. It sees Him who allows it, with us in the fire, as a refiner watching our purging and perfecting, as a helper of our strength and comfort. It sees that the forming of a character like that of the Son of God, maintaining at every cost the Father's will and honour, is more than all the world can give. It sees that to be made partaker of His holiness, to have the humility and weakness and gentleness of the Lamb of God inwrought into us, and like Him to be made perfect in suffering, is the spirit of heaven, and it counts nothing too great to gain this treasure. By faith alone, but by faith most surely, we can, in the midst of the deepest suffering, be more than conquerors.

We live in a world of suffering. What a privilege that suffering, instead of unfitting or excluding us, is God's special invitation, to trust and glorify Him. As we read of all that the men of faith had done, more than one has thought of his own unfavourable circumstances and his feeble strength; never could his faith reach to the achievements of the men who are set before him as an example. What a privilege that there is no suffering so great and depressing, so little and harassing, but can be a school of faith, a heavenly instruction in the blessed art of making God all; of proving that, for God's will and submission to it, we are willing to bear all. Faith transfigures suffering, makes it transparent with the love of God, the presence of Jesus, the beauty of holiness, the blessing of heaven.

As long as we live under the influence of the world and the flesh, all this appears but as a beautiful thought, without reality or possibility. Our Epistle is speaking to those whom it has led into the Holiest of All, who are walking in the new and living way of the will of God, of the obedience and the self-sacrifice and the death of Jesus. It is as we tarry in God's presence, and seek, above everything, His holiness and His will, that we shall look at things as God does, and regard suffering in His light. Let this be our aim. Our passage gives new confirmation to the one lesson: By faith alone! Would you please God, would you conquer sin and the world, would you be holy and perfect, would you live as the heir of heaven and eternity—live as a man of faith, meet every trial in the spirit of a joyful faith in God; every trial will make thee more meet for, and bring thee nearer to, God's blessed presence.

1. In the Old Testament prosperity was promised. And yet faith could endure adversity. In the New, we are taught to expect adversity: the cross is the symbol of our faith; the Man of Sorrows is our Leader; how much more ought we to be able to endure.

2. Let every suffering one, everyone who is bound to a sick-bed or bowed down under some cross, learn to believe that in the affliction we can greatly glorify God by faith, and that by faith we can become teachers and helpers of others, fulfilling, by example and intercession, in our measure, a very blessed part of the work of the body of Christ.

CXI.

Some Better Thing for Us

XI.–39. And these all, having had witness borne to them through their faith, received not the promise,

40. God having provided some better thing concerning us, that apart from us, they should not be made perfect.

In these closing verses we have the summing up of the chapter. The superior excellence of the New Testament is stated to be this, that we have *some better thing,* something *perfect,* which the saints had waited for but had never seen. We are told of them what it was that they had, and what they had not. **These all, having had witness borne them through their faith, received not the promise.** They received not the promise. There were indeed certain promises of which they received the fulfilment (see vi. 15; xi. 33). But the great promise of Jesus Christ and His redemption and the outpouring of the Holy Spirit, *the better promises of the better covenant,* these they received not. **They died in faith, not having received the promises, but having seen them from afar and embraced them.** They saw, and rejoiced in the promises, into the full possession of which it is our privilege to enter.

They received them not, but **they had witness borne to them through their faith** (see xi. 2, 4, 6). The living God, who had given them the promise, and was waiting His own time for the fulfilment, gave them witness through faith that they were pleasing to Him. The witness borne to Abel that he was righteous, and to Enoch that he pleased God, was given to them all.

God was not ashamed to be called their God, and to let them know it. With all the difference between their faith and ours, in regard to the clearness of the revelation and the actual possession of the promise, in this their faith was one with ours—the unseen God revealed Himself to them and was their God.

They received not the promise, God having provided some better thing concerning us, that they apart from us should not be made perfect. The two words here, *better* and *perfect,* are the words which characterise the new dispensation, the time of the fulfilment of the promise. We said before, the word "better" occurs thirteen times. Christ has inherited a better name; He has brought us a better hope; He is the surety of a better covenant enacted in better promises; in Him we have the better country and the better substance. To them God spake in the prophets; to us in the Son. To them was offered the rest of Canaan; to us the rest of God. Their high priest was a man who died; ours is a Priest for ever, in the power of an endless life. Their sanctuary was on earth, and even that had its veil; ours is the true sanctuary, with the veil taken away. Theirs was the old covenant, in which there was no power to continue; ours is the new, with the heart made new by the Spirit. Theirs was the blood of bulls and of goats, ours is the blood of Jesus. Theirs was a sanctifying cleanness of the flesh; ours is the cleansing of the heart from the evil conscience. Theirs a worship which made nothing perfect; in ours we are perfected for evermore. Their worship was a witness that the way into the Holiest was not yet open; ours is the blessed experience that in the new and living way we have living access into the very presence and love of the Father. God hath indeed provided *some better thing* for us.

That apart from us they should not be made perfect. The better thing God has provided is *perfection.* The word *perfect* is used fourteen times in the Epistle (see v. 14). The law made nothing *perfect.* Jesus was Himself, in His obedience and suffering, *made perfect* in His human nature, in His will and life and character, that He might have a true, new, *perfect* human life to communicate to us. As the Son *perfected* for evermore He is our High Priest, who having *perfected* us for ever in His sacrifice, now brings us, in the communication of that *perfection,* into real, inner, living contact with God. And so He is the *Perfecter* of our faith; makes us His *perfect* ones, who press on unto *perfection.* And our life on earth is meant to be the blessed experience that God *perfects* us in every good thing to do His will, working in us that which is pleasing in His sight. Apart from us they might not be made *perfect;* to us the blessing of some better thing, of being made *perfect,* has come.

My fellow-Christians, the old saints had only the promise; we have the thing promised, the divine reality, the full inheritance of what were to them only the good things to come. The promise was sufficient to make them live a wonderful life of faith. What ought not the effect to be in our lives of having obtained the promises, having entered on the possession of that of which the mere promise stirred them so? As much greater as deliverance is than the hope of it, as a divine possession is than the promise of it, so much greater is the better, the perfect thing God has provided for us, so much greater ought to be the joy and the holiness and the nearness to God, and the power of our lives. Is it so?

If not, the reason must be plain. We do not accept the possession with the intensity with which they accepted the promise. Our whole Epistle was written to expose this evil, and to set before us the glory of the better, the perfect thing God has provided for us in Christ. Shall we not listen to the witness of the heroes of our faith in the days when the sun had not yet risen, and let ourselves be ashamed out of our worldliness and sloth? If we will but yield ourselves to the glorious perfection-truths of our Epistle, the perfection of our High Priest and His work, and press on unto it, He to whom it has been given to work His work in us in the power of an endless life, and so to save completely,

495

will reveal in us that better and perfect thing as we have never yet known it. **By faith they obtained the promises.** By faith the fulfilment of every promise will be made true to us in the power of the Pentecostal Spirit, who comes from the throne of our great High Priest.

1. *Wherefore holy brethren, partakers of a heavenly calling, consider Jesus. It is He has done all:* it is He who, as much, must do all now. *It is He makes the Holiest of All, and the entrance into it, and the life there to serve the living God, a living continual reality. If hitherto thou hast been living without the veil, do believe God has provided some better thing for thee too.*

2. *He does this in the power of the Holy Spirit dwelling within us.* Christ redeemed us, that we might receive the promise of the Spirit through faith. *The Holy Spirit is the all-inclusive blessing of the better covenant. It is His to bring Jesus and heaven and the power of an endless life into us, and keep us in it.*

3. *May God reveal to us what Abraham's going out from his country, what Moses' choice of suffering and reproach, what Israel's leaving Egypt means. If we are ready to forsake all, we shall inherit all.*

The Patience of Hope

CXII.

Let Us Run with Patience the Race

XII.—1. Therefore let us also, seeing we are compassed about with so great a cloud of witnesses, lay aside every weight, and the sin which doth so easily beset us, and let us run with patience the race that is set before us.

The Epistle has taught us that one of the greatest dangers in the Christian life is the remaining stationary, and not advancing beyond the beginnings of Christ. It leads almost inevitably to backsliding and sin. The great virtue the Epistle has sought to inculcate, next to faith, is patience, the perseverance and long-suffering that holds fast the beginning firm unto the end, and diligently presses on to perfection. After having shown us, in his wonderful picture gallery, what the fulness of faith is, he now calls us, in view of all the trials life may bring, and with them the temptation to grow disheartened and faint, to patience as the virtue by which faith is to prove its persistence and secure its reward. True religion is not only drawing nigh to God once in the Holiest, but a life to be renewed there every day; it is not only the entrance upon the new and living way, but a continually abiding life and walk in it. It is running a race with patience. We have seen what life in the Holiest is, in the place where the power of the eternal life enters and possesses us. Let us now look at

497

that life in its visible manifestation as a race we run, and learn what is needed to run well and win the crown.

Therefore, let us, **Seeing we are compassed about with so great a cloud of witnesses, run the race.** The first encouragement to run the race with patience is to yield ourselves to the influence of the cloud of witnesses that encompass us, and to follow their example of faith and patience. We had the word "witness" five times in the previous chapter: *through faith they received witness.* And so they become witnesses to its power and the good pleasure of God it brings to the soul. They all with one accord, Abel and Enoch and Noah, Abraham and Sarah, Moses and the prophets, as with one heart and mouth witness to us: *Be of good courage, fear not; be strong in faith, and persevere.* The victory and the reward are sure and glorious. We are one with them and they with us. They could not be perfected without us; in us is to be perfected what they began. They held fast the promise when all was dark: they plead with us, now the full light has come, to hold fast the faith firm unto the end.

Therefore let us also, even as they, **lay aside every weight, and the sin which doth so easily beset us.** Here is our second lesson. One of the first thoughts connected with a race is the laying aside of everything that can hinder. In the food he eats and the clothing he wears how resolutely the runner puts aside everything, the most lawful and pleasant, that is not absolutely necessary to his success. Sacrifice, self-denial, giving up, laying aside, is the very first requisite on the course. Alas, it is this that has made the Christian life of our days the very opposite of running a race. The great study is, both in our religious teaching and practical life, to find out how to make the best of both worlds, how to enjoy as much as possible of the wealth and the pleasure and the honour which the world offers. With many Christians, if their conversion ever was an entering through a strait gate, their life since never was, in any sense, a laying aside of everything that might hinder their spiritual growth. They never heeded the word: *He that forsaketh not all that he hath cannot be My disciple.* But this is what we are called to as indispensable: **Laying aside every weight, and the sin which doth so easily beset us.** Yes, laying aside every sin—however little it seems, however much it be our special weakness—it may not be spared. Sin must be laid aside, if we are to run the race. It is a race for holiness and perfection, for the will of God and His favour; how could we dream of running the race without laying aside the sin which doth so easily beset us.

Therefore, let us run the race set before us. A race means, this is our third lesson, concentration of purpose and will, strenuous and determined effort. It means that a man while he is on the course gives himself wholly to one thing—running with all his might. It means that for the time being he forgets everything for the all-absorbing desire—to gain the prize. The Christian course means this *all through life:* a whole-hearted surrender of oneself, to put aside everything for the sake of God and His favour. The men who enter the course are separated from the crowd of idle spectators: they each of them can say, *One thing I do*—they run.

Let us run with patience the race. *Ye were running well, who did hinder you?* This was as true of the Hebrews as of the Galatians: many, many had gone back. Alas, alas, is it not true of multitudes of Christians in our days? They began well, everything was so hopeful; but it would be utterly untrue to say of them today that they are running a race for eternal life. And there is no way for us, and those for whom we labour, to be saved this terrible fate but for us to learn the lesson which this word *Patience* (endurance,[1] perseverance), is meant to teach us. Under the inspiring influence of the cloud of witnesses, to lay aside every weight and sin, to enter and begin the race is not enough—we must run *with patience.* Day by day, our separation

---

1. The word is the same as *endured,* in vers. 2, 3, 7.

from the world and sin, our giving up of every weight and every sin, must be renewed. Day by day our desire and our will to live wholly for God must be reaffirmed. Day by day we must wait on God afresh, to receive grace with all our heart and all our strength; with undivided purpose and in the boldness of faith, still to run in the race for God. Therefore let us also run the race with *patience.*

1. *Get clear hold of the three elements of success in a race: self-denial, that gives up everything that hinders; decision, that puts the whole heart into the work, and runs; patience, that day by day afresh enters the course.*

2. *It is the heart of him that runs that is the power that urges him on. Whether it be for a prize or a pleasure—his heart is the driving power. The Holy Spirit is the only power that can keep our heart daily fresh and bright in the race.*

3. The new and living way. *The race is but another aspect of it, to bring out the thought of devotion and earnestness and energy.*

CXIII.

Looking unto Jesus

XII.–2. Let us run with patience the race that is set before us, looking unto Jesus the author[1] and perfecter of our faith, who for the joy that was set before Him endured the cross, despising shame, and hath sat down at the right hand of the throne of God.

The practical and the contemplative Christian life are often spoken of as if they were at variance. Here we see them in their perfect harmony. **Let us run**—there we have intense exertion, claiming body and soul; **looking to Jesus**—there we have the inner life of the spirit, a heart always fixed on Jesus in faith and worship, drawing inspiration and strength from His example and His love. **Let us run, looking to Jesus.** Let all that we have learnt of Him in the Epistle, all the faith and joy with which we have seen and considered Him, bear this fruit: let us with patience, perseverance, run the race.

Looking unto Jesus, the Leader and Perfecter of our faith. Jesus is **the Leader of our salvation** (ii. 10), **the Forerunner, who hath entered within the veil for us,** leaving behind His track and footsteps for us to walk in. This is the new and living way which, through obedience and death, leads to life and to God. And so He is **the Leader of our faith,** too. He leads in the way of faith, He walked in it Himself, He opened it for us, He draws and helps us in it. The old saints had given us examples of faith; Jesus is the Leader of *our faith,* the faith that through

1. Leader.

death enters into resurrection life and the Holiest of All, that better and perfect thing which God hath provided for us.

The Leader and Perfecter of our faith. Jesus is the Perfecter of our faith. He perfected it in His own person, by acting it out to its fullest possibility, when in the darkness of death He entrusted His Spirit into His Father's hands. He perfected it when He was Himself perfected by it, and proved that faith is the highest perfection, because it gives God room to be all. He perfected it when, having perfected us in Himself, He became the perfect object for our faith. He perfects it in us, because He who is the perfect object of our faith is the living One, who lives and works in us in the power of our endless life. He is *the Perfecter of faith*—the faith that looks away to Him the perfect One and the Perfecter, is the secret of Christian perfection. He has not only perfected Himself and us, He perfects our faith too. Let us entrust our faith to Him above everything; He will make it His care, the chief and most blessed work of His Spirit. **Let us run, looking to Jesus;** in His life on earth the Leader, in His glory on the throne the Perfecter, of our faith. Let us look to Jesus. There is life in a look, and power too; the life and the power of a divine transformation, in which, as we behold, we are changed into the same image from glory to glory.

Let us run, looking to Jesus, who for the joy that was set before Him. Like Moses, He had respect unto the recompense of the reward. He triumphed over suffering and death by the faith that lived in the future and the unseen. It was in faith He lived and endured and conquered. **Who for the joy that was set before Him endured the cross, despising shame, and hath sat down on the right hand of the throne of God.** Let us look to Jesus in His path on earth, and on His throne in glory. In His path on earth, as He endured the cross, He is **the Leader of our faith,** only in the path in which he walked Himself. In His life of self-denial and humility, of obedience and death, He showed us that there is no way to God but that of sacrifice, resisting the world and self unto death; no way of deliverance from fallen nature but by dying to it. He is **the Perfecter of our faith,** as He sits on the throne. Looking to Him we see what the sure reward is of dying with Him, what the divine power and glory are to which He invites our trust and the committal of our souls, what the heavenly life is that His Spirit will bring down into our hearts. Let every thought of Him on the throne remind us of the path that brought Him there and brings us too; and every thought again of Him in that path of trial lift our hearts in loving, steady gaze to the throne, where He reigns, to communicate to us, in unbroken continuity, the power of His glorified life, His complete and eternal salvation.

Yes, **let us run, looking to Jesus.** Looking, not to ourselves or our sins, but to Him who hath put away sin for ever. Not to ourselves or our faith, whether in its weakness or its strength, but to Him whose presence is the life of our faith. Not to the world or its temptations, but to Him who hath said: *Be of good cheer, I have overcome the world.* Not to Satan or his threats, but to Him who hath brought him to naught. Not to men, their fear or their favour, but to Jesus, the God-Man, Immanuel, God with us, our Brother and our King. Looking to Jesus and Jesus alone.

Looking to Him always and in all. In trial and trouble, as in joy and prosperity; in solitude and repose, as in company and business; in religious worship, as in daily life;—always, only, looking to Jesus. Looking to Him, to see what He is, to hear what He speaks, to do what He says, to follow where He leads, to trust for all He waits to give. Looking to Him and His love, till my heart burns with that love. Looking to Him, till His eye meets mine, and I know that He watches over me. Looking to Him in the power of His love and Spirit, knowing that He Himself is drawing me to Himself, leading and perfecting my faith. Looking to Him, to be changed into His likeness from glory to glory. **Let us run the race with patience, looking to Jesus.**

1. "Looking to Jesus, *with the look of faith, because our salvation is in Him alone; with the look of love, because He alone can satisfy our heart; with the look of strong desire, longing to know Him better; with the look of soul devotion, waiting only to know His will; with the look of gladness, because we know He loves us; with the look of wonder and admiration, because He is the brightness of the Father's glory, our Lord and our God."*

2. *Let us say it once again: the whole secret of the Christian life consists in the personal relationship to Jesus. Not what Jesus has done or does for me can be my salvation, except as He Himself has my heart, and binds me to Himself in dependence and attachment, and trust and love.*

3. Let us run. *The gospel is intensely practical. It means for every day, let us live like men who are running a race for life, and laying aside everything that can in the least hinder them. We judge everything by this one standard: can it help me in the race.*

The Fifth Warning

Chap. xii. 14-29

Against the Rejection of God's Son

CXIV.

Follow after Sanctification

XII.–14. Follow after peace with all men, and the sanctification without which no man shall see the Lord.

The Section on Patience in Tribulation (the Patience of Hope), is concluded, and there now remains the subject of Love and Good Works. It is as if the writer began here what he gives in chapter xiii., but was led into his last warning by the thought of so many who fail in the pursuit of holiness and fall back. When the warning is concluded he returns to his subject in chapter xiii.

Follow after peace with all men, and sanctification. My relation to my fellow-men is most intimately one with my relation to God. In the Beatitudes we have mercy and purity following each other: *Blessed are the merciful—Blessed are the pure in heart. The wisdom that is from above is first pure, then peaceable.* Where there is no peace with men, peace with God cannot be enjoyed. Paul writes: *If it be possible, as much as lieth in you, be at peace with all men.* In our summons to dwell in the Holiest, we remember how the call to faith, **Let us draw nigh,** was at once followed by that to love, **Let us consider one another, to provoke to love and good works.**

Follow after sanctification, *lit.* "holy-making." We know this word. Holiness is the highest glory of God, and so holy-making is the being taken up into His fellowship, and being made partakers of His holiness. It is receiving into our nature and character the spirit of that heavenliness and holiness in which He dwells. **Follow holy-making, without which no man shall see the Lord.** Holy-making is the spiritual preparation, the inner capacity for meeting the Lord, and being at home with Him. The passages in the Epistle, in which we have already had the word, will be our best instruction as to the way in which we are to follow after holiness.

He that sanctifieth, and they who are sanctified, are all of one. It is Jesus who makes holy. *Of God are ye in Him, who is made of God unto us sanctification.* It is the living Christ who is our sanctification; the more deeply we enter into His life on earth, His obedience, His doing God's will, His giving Himself up to God alone, the more we have this His life abiding in us, the holier shall we be. Holiness is the losing of self and being clothed upon with the spirit and likeness of Jesus.

Jesus spake: **I come to do Thy will, O God. In which will we have been sanctified. By one offering He hath perfected for ever them that are sanctified.** The more deeply I enter into the truth, or rather the truth enters into my life, that the sacrifice of Jesus is the crowning act of His perfect surrender to God's will and giving up everything to be one with it, and that it is in His doing of that will, that *I have been sanctified*—the clearer will my insight grow that holiness is the actual living in the will of God with my will, having the will of God the moving power of my life. Jesus doing the will of God, and sanctifying me in it, has taken me up into it, and planted me for ever in it. As I live in living union with it, doing it and rejoicing in it, that holy will becomes my holiness. It was in the doing of God's will, and glorifying God thereby, that He was prepared for the glory; the heavenly life, which He sends down by His Spirit into my heart, is a life in which God's will is always and perfectly done; to live in God's will is the true following after sanctification.

Having boldness to enter into the Holiest—the Holiness of Holinesses—**let us draw nigh.** The Holiest into which we have been taken in to dwell, and the holiness which is to be our characteristic, are closely linked. There, where God dwells in His holiness—even there, is the dwelling of the sanctified one, who enter in by faith. There is the place where we are made holy, where the Son who sanctifies, and the will in which we are sanctified, and the presence of the Holy One, all are met and known in power. He who does not know what it is to enter in, and tarry and worship in the Holiest, to separate himself from the world and its fellowship, to hold communion with the Holy One, will seek in vain by his prayers or efforts to become holy. Holiness is found nowhere but *with God in the Holiest of All.* Union with Jesus the Son who sanctifies us, union with the will in which we have been sanctified by loving and doing it, union with God Himself in the Holies—in these is the power of sanctification.

Follow after peace with all men, and sanctification, without which no man shall see the Lord. Seeing the Lord! What blessedness and what glory to the soul that has once learnt to love Him! As the bride puts on her beautiful garments, to meet him she loves and to whom she is to be united, the call comes to us to put on our holy garments, to array ourselves in the beauty of holiness to meet our Lord. Let our whole heart respond in the prayer: Lord! make me holy, that I may be found ready to meet thee when thou comest.

1. This sanctification is as much by faith as justification. Both are received in union with Christ: the peace of the one and the power of the other are found in the abiding union through an abiding habit of faith.

2. Follow after—the same words as in Phil. iii. 12, 14: I press on, if that I may apprehend; I press on toward the goal. It is the thought of the race—pressing on after holiness, fellowship with God, with Jesus, with God's will.

CXV.

Of Falling Short of the Grace of God

XII.–15. Looking carefully lest there be any man that falleth short of the grace of God; lest any root of bitterness springing up trouble you, and thereby the many be defiled.

16. Lest there be any fornicator, or profane person, as Esau, who for one morsel of meat sold his own birthright.

17. For ye know that even when he afterward desired to inherit the blessing, he was rejected (for he found no place for repentance), though he sought it diligently with tears.

Take heed, brethren, lest there be in any one of you an evil heart of unbelief, was the warning in chapter iii. And in chapter iv., **Let us fear lest any one come short of the rest.** And in chapter x., **Let us consider one another, exhorting one another.** Here it is the same thought—**Looking carefully**—the word really means taking oversight—**lest there be any man:** each is not only to care for himself, but for his brother too; **lest there be any man**—there must not, through our lack of faithfulness, be one—**that falls short of the grace of God.** Here we have again the great danger against which the Epistle warns us earnestly. It is the terrible complaint from which every congregation suffers. There are so many who, just as Israel left Egypt, but came short of the promised rest, for a time make an earnest Christian profession, and yet come short of the grace of God—receive the grace of God in its beginnings in vain: never truly become possessed of it and by it. As it was true of the Galatians, with all their zeal for religion and its forms, so of these too: *Ye are fallen away* *from grace* (Gal. v. 4). The running of the race with patience; holiness, or even the earnest pursuit of it; the joy and the power and the fruit of the Christian life—all are wanting. Let us look carefully lest anyone fall short of the grace of God.

Three things are mentioned as causes and marks of this falling short of grace. **Lest any root of bitterness springing up trouble you, and thereby the many be defiled.** The root of bitterness may refer to a person, who by wrong conduct or doctrine causes trouble, and leads others astray. Or it may refer to the error itself, some mode of thought or behaviour by which the many are defiled. The spirit of the world; too great interest in temporal things; bitterness in religious differences; being led by the carnal reason more than by God's word or Spirit; giving way to sin; any of these things may be the root of bitterness, in regard to which the call sounds: Be careful, look round, and watch.

Lest there be any fornicator. Here is a special sin is mentioned. Each church as a whole must watch against this sin, not waiting till it is found, but looking carefully, and doing everything to prevent, *lest there be any.* Christians must maintain in society the high moral tone which refuses to condone sin in either high or low. In all its members, and among its young people, it must be a witness for purity of life and lips and heart. And to all who are fallen it must seek, in the power of the gospel, to offer the helping hand of love. **Lest there be any fornicator.**

Or profane person, as Esau, who for one mess of meat, sold his own birthright. We have seen that faith is ever the separation from the visible. Abraham and Isaac and Jacob sacrificed all to become heirs of the heavenly city of the future, and the heavenly blessing. Esau lived in the present: for a momentary satisfaction he parted with his blessing, the promise of God, and his inheritance in the future. And even so there are numbers who are called Christians, and yet are profane. There is nothing sacred or holy in their spirit or life. They are absorbed in the present of the possessions and pleasures of the world. To speak of their pursuit of holiness would be a mockery. Let us think of such, and mourn and pray and labour for them. Looking carefully lest there be any one of you a profane person, like Esau.

For ye know when he afterward desired to inherit the blessing, he was rejected (for he found no place for repentance), though he sought it diligently with tears. We remember the *yet afterward* of faith. What a contrast here, the *afterward* of the worldling. For the present with its pleasures, the divine birthright, the promise of God, and the future inheritance is neglected. And when it is too late, when the heart is shrivelled up, and the power of the will and the power of faith is lost, the thought of something better is awakened—but, alas, it is found to be too late! Many shall seek to enter in, and shall not be able, when once the Master of the house is risen up, and hath shut the door! He *afterward* desired to inherit, but was rejected!

Looking carefully, lest any man fall short of the grace of God. What a solemn thing the Christian life is, the race for life we have to run! With what dangers we are surrounded! Our daily needs and our daily food may be our destruction. It was eating that lost Esau his birthright. It was eating that lost Adam and his seed the kingdom of God. It was in refusing to eat, when Satan tempted Him in the wilderness, that Jesus won back heaven for us. In our home, in our body, in our daily need, the temptations to ease and enjoyment, to sloth and standing still are ever around us and in us; let us take heed lest we fall short. Let us look carefully, and see if there are not others around us who are fainting and turning back, and let us count it our duty and privilege to care for them. Let us beseech grace of God to give us power in faith and love to be the deliverer of our people and our brethren. If we feel powerless to speak to others or to influence them, let us lay ourselves before God with the cry that He would use us to save some: He can fill us with His Spirit and His love.

1. Looking carefully—*the word is the same as bishop, overseer.* Lest any man. *We are all to watch over each other. Do we really take the state*

of Christians to heart? Do we indeed look round carefully and lovingly, to consider what can be done? Consider Jesus! consider one another!—*the two commands are inseparable.*

2. Afterward, he was rejected! O my brother, if you have escaped this danger, I beseech you, by the mercy of God, think of those who are in it, and say to God that you will do anything He wishes you to save them from that terrible fate.

CXVI.

Not Sinai, but Sion

XII.–18. For ye are not come unto a mount that might be touched, and that burned with fire, and unto blackness, and darkness, and tempest,

19. And the sound of a trumpet, and the voice of words; which voice they that heard intreated that no word more should be spoken unto them:

20. For they could not endure that which was enjoined, If even a beast touch the mountain, it shall be stoned;

21. And so fearful was the appearance, that Moses said, I exceedingly fear and quake.

In confirmation of the call to follow after sanctification, and the warning against falling short of the grace of God, or despising the birthright blessing, we are now reminded of what our true position is as believers, and what the fulness of blessing of which we have been made partakers. This is set before us first by way of contrast: We **are not come** to Mount Sinai (18–21) the place and state of Israel at the giving of the law. Then we are told (22–24) what the wonderful life is to which we now have access: We **are come to Mount Sion.** It is only the living faith that realises our true position and privileges, that will nerve us in the pursuit of holiness, and keep us from falling short.

Our whole Epistle has taught us that all God's dealing with man is founded on the principle of two dispensations—the one of preparation and promise, of weakness and failure; the other of fulfilment and perfection, of life and power, the power of the endless life. The Epistle has taught us, too, that though we now have our place in the new dispensation, we, just as the Hebrews, may be living in the old, through ignorance and unbelief, experiencing nothing of the power and the life of the better covenant. As a consequence, all the weakness and sin of Israel of old still continues in the Christian; he knows not what the eternal redemption is, and cannot live in it. We have the difference between these two dispensations in the suggestive words: **Ye are not come** unto a mount that might be touched: **Ye are come** unto Mount Sion. *Which things contain an allegory: for these are two covenants; one from Mount Sinai, bearing children unto bondage, and answereth to the Jerusalem that now is. But the Jerusalem that is above is free, which is our mother* (Gal. iv. 22–26). The whole secret of the Christian life lies in the right apprehension of the difference between the two systems, the one with the spirit of bondage and fear, the other with its boldness and liberty.

Ye are not come to the mount that might be touched,[1] with its fear and terror, with its command not to draw nigh under pain of death, and its words which only made them that heard entreat that no word more should be spoken to them, with the mediator of the covenant himself saying, **I exceedingly fear and quake.** All this is a symbol of what the law does; it works wrath and fear and death. It comes with demands we cannot fulfil; with its threats it rouses to effort and performance, but gives neither the love of God's will nor the power to do it. It only discovers and condemns sin; the sense of self-reproach and self-condemnation is all it can bring. Read Romans vii. and see there, where the law alone, and not the Spirit, is mentioned, the impotence and the wretchedness which it reveals. Read Romans viii. and see there what the liberty and the peace, the life and the

---

1. "The apostle reminds us of seven things in connection with the giving of the law—(1) The mount touched by God; (2) Fire; (3) Blackness of cloud; (4) Darkness; (5) Thunder; (6) The sound of a trumpet; (7) The voice of God."—Saphir. Notice in the next passage the sevenfold glory of Mount Sion.

love, the joy and the strength is which comes with the Spirit of life in Christ Jesus.

Ye are not come to the mount that might be touched. Why should it be necessary to tell the Christian this? If Sinai is so terrible, who could wish to live there? who would not gladly accept the first message that God calls him away from there? Strange to say, the awakened soul is ever in danger of thinking that there is no way to pacify Sinai but by fulfilling its demands. God's grace is so wonderful, the way in which He has met the claims of Sinai is so divine and beyond man's comprehension, that the human heart, when it begins to seek salvation, ever does so in the way of effort. And even after we have believed in Jesus, we are always inclined to look to what we can do to satisfy the demands of God. We know not that in calling us away from Sinai to Mount Sion, God not only gives us a free and full pardon for sin, but the law written in the heart, the power for a new obedience by the Holy Spirit, and the fitness for entering into His presence, and dwelling in unbroken fellowship with Him.

Ye are not come to Mount Sinai. This is just the word every Christian needs who is in danger of being discouraged and fainting in the race. You are not under the law. Your complaints that when you would do good, evil is present with you, prove that you are still under the law, trying to fulfil it. It is all in vain. You must ask for the Holy Spirit's teaching, to show you how entirely you are taken from under the shadow of Sinai, and placed on Mount Sion. Oh, try to understand what God is speaking to you in His Son. Christ is to be your life. In the power of an endless life He is your High Priest, bringing you near to God; He is your covenant Mediator, putting in divine reality the law into your inmost parts; your Priest-King, sending from His throne the Holy Spirit to reveal Himself as the law of your life.

Ye are not come to Mount Sinai; its fear and terror are exchanged for faith and trust. Come and live by faith, and Christ will be your life.

1. *In studying the meaning of a word or truth, it is often most helpful in cases where we are in danger of confounding, owing to apparent resemblances, things that differ, to find out what it is not.* There is so much in salvation by the law that looks like true salvation, that many are all their life led astray. It is, therefore, of infinite consequence to know well what this means: Ye are not come to. The place to which Christ brings you to, not in the least Mount Sinai. *Say now, I have nothing to do with Mount Sinai.*

2. *Mount Sinai means, as man takes it, life by self-effort, by our own goodness, God helping us; by a religion of self, with God's grace to fill out what self cannot do. Mount Sinai, as God means it, is sin and wrath and condemnation: the death and the end of self, to prepare the way for Christ. Mount Sinai points away to Mount Sion and to Christ.* There He does all.

CXVII.

Ye Are Come unto Mount Sion

XII.–22. But ye are come unto Mount Sion, and unto the city of the living God, the heavenly Jerusalem, and to innumerable hosts of angels,

23. To the general assembly and church of the firstborn who are enrolled in heaven, and to God the Judge of all, and to the spirits of just men made perfect,

24. And to Jesus the Mediator of a new covenant, and to the blood of sprinkling that speaketh better than that of Abel.

Ye are come unto Mount Sion. A traveller by train has often reached a place without his knowing that he is there. The guard or a friend has to tell him. Often it is because that he had expected the journey to last longer. So deep is there in us the spirit of salvation by effort and attainment, by what we are and feel, that the rousing call is needed continually. Here you are, sooner than you thought, in very deed, come to Mount Sion! Come, let us walk about Sion, and go round about her. Beautiful in elevation, the joy of the whole earth, is Mount Sion. God has made Himself known in her palaces for a refuge! Let us consider its sevenfold glory as here set before us. And may God, in the power of His Holy Spirit within us, reveal to us what it means, that we **are come unto Mount Sion,** that we have been made meet for dwelling there, that Mount Sion is an actual spiritual reality our dwelling-place, where the powers of the heavenly world rest upon us and work in us.

1. **Ye are come unto Mount Sion, and unto the city of the living God, the heavenly Jerusalem.** Read the description of the heavenly Jerusalem in Revelations (xxi. 1–3, 10, 11; xxii. 27, xxii. 1–5), and listen to the voice: *Behold! the tabernacle of God is with men, and He shall dwell with them, and they shall be His people, and God Himself shall be with them, and be their God. The Lord God Almighty, and the Lamb are the temple thereof. The glory of God did lighten it, and the light thereof is the Lamb. The throne of God and of the Lamb shall be therein; and His servants shall do Him service; and they shall see His face.* This is the glory to which Jesus has brought thee in, when He took away the veil. In the power and experience of that opened way the Holy Spirit enables thee to live. This is the city which Abraham looked for, which hath the foundations. Thou art come to it. Of this city thou art now a citizen. In it thou canst live, for thou hast been brought into the Holiest, the very centre of the city, the very presence of God. **Ye are come unto Mount Sion.**

2. **And to innumerable hosts of angels.** These are they who stand around the throne of God, and who fulfil His will. These are they through whom the power of God works in all nature. These are they who are sent out to minister to the heirs of salvation. With these, their worship and obedience, we are now in fellowship, doing the will of our Father as it is done in heaven.

3. **To the general assembly and Church of the first-born who are enrolled in heaven.** That is, the Church on earth, enrolled in heaven, but not yet gathered in. They are the firstborn—destined, as having the image of the firstborn One, to take the first place in creation among all the creatures of God (Col. i. 15; Jas. i. 18). God keep us from despising this our birthright—let us

live as God's firstborn, in living union with all His saints on earth.

4. **And to God the Judge of all.** It is not only to the living God, dwelling in the city of God, that we are come, but to Him who is Judge of all. Our redemption gives us such deliverance from sin, that we have already been admitted to the home of our Judge.

5. **And to the spirits of just men made perfect.** These are the saints in heaven. There are those on earth who are called perfect (v. 14), but these are they who, like Christ, have been wholly *perfected*. These spirits, too, waiting for the redemption of the body, belong to the blessed fellowship to which we have been admitted.

6. **And to Jesus, the Mediator of a new covenant.** Moses was the mediator of the covenant on Sinai; Jesus, of the better covenant, enacted upon better promises. The covenant, we saw (viii. 6–13), has specially to do with our heart, with our fitness for holding fellowship with God, with a will and a life in perfect unison with God's will. In Mount Sion we are come to Jesus, who, in the power of the Holy Spirit, lives and does all His saving work within us.

7. **And the blood of sprinkling, which speaketh better than that of Abel.** What a heavenly mystery! It is not enough that for our life in the city of God we have Jesus, the living One, as our life; we find there too the token of His death—the blood of sprinkling, speaking, pleading for us each moment. Speaking, not as Abel's, of wrath, but of atonement and eternal redemption. We are come to the blood, not only as shed on earth, but as sprinkled in heaven—our boldness, our cleansing, our sanctification; speaking to God for us, speaking for God to us, of peace and love; speaking in divine, in heavenly power within us.

Christian, to all this **you are come.** Just as sure as you are come to God in the Holiest, to dwell with Him, **you are come**[1] to all this, and dwell in the midst of it. God hath brought you to it by the Holy Spirit, and will, by the Holy Spirit, reveal it in your heart, so that you know the things which are freely given you of God. Can it be, that any are content to sleep on, while the call is heard: **You are come** to the heavenly Jerusalem—enter in and dwell here. There is no other choice—can it be that any will prefer to live under Sinai and its bondage? Can it be that any will count the price too great, and, because they love the world, refuse, with Abraham and Moses, to go out and live by faith, in this city of God. God forbid that it should be so with us. Let Sion, the city of God, with its heavenly joy, and its beauty of holiness, and its eternal life power, be the place of our abode. The Holy Spirit, sent down when Jesus had entered and opened the gates for us, brings down into our hearts the very life and light of heaven, brings us into the experience of it all.

1. *Salvation brings to the city of God, to a fellowship of the saints, to a social life of mutual intercourse and help. To find our happiness in the welfare of others, for the sake of Jesus Christ, is of the essence of religion, is a condition of the dwelling in Mount Sion.*

2. *I saw the New Jerusalem come down from heaven: that took place in part on the day of Pentecost. The kingdom of heaven descended upon earth, in the power of the Holy Spirit, into the hearts of those praying disciples. It is only in the power of the Holy Spirit that this* Ye are come unto Mount Zion *can be more than a beautiful imagination.*

3. *The Holy Spirit makes all the work and glory of Jesus an inward life in our heart. Let every word like this,* Ye are come, *that is too high for us, make us believe more firmly in His hidden inward teaching. He will work in our heart more than our mind can understand.*

---

1. The word *come* is the same as in iv. 16; vii. 25; x. 1, 22, *draw nigh.*

CXVIII.

Our God Is a Consuming Fire

XII.–25. See that ye refuse not him that speaketh. For if they escaped not, when they refused him that warned them on earth, much more shall not we escape, who turn away from him that warneth from heaven:

26. Whose voice then shook the earth: but now he hath promised, saying, Yet once more will I make to tremble not the earth only, but also the heaven.

27. And this word, Yet once more, signifieth the removing of those things that are shaken, as of things that have been made, that those things which are not shaken may remain.

28. Wherefore, receiving a kingdom that cannot be shaken, let us have grace, whereby we may offer service well-pleasing to God with reverence and awe:

29. For our God is a consuming fire.

See that ye refuse not Him that speaketh. The writer is full of the danger of their falling short, tarrying under Sinai, and perishing there. For the third time (see ii. 2; x. 26) he urges the Hebrews to remember how much more terrible the punishment of sin will be under the New than under the Old. The certainty and the sureness of the punishment under the law give us terrible warning of the danger we incur. Greater privileges bring greater responsibility; the neglect of these, greater punishment. *If they escaped not,* when they refused Him that warned them on earth, *much more shall not we escape,* who turn away from Him that warneth from heaven. The terrors of Sinai will be far surpassed by the awful judgment on those who refuse Him that speaks from Mount Sion. Mount Sion has its terrors too; let these, far more terrible than Mount Sinai, rouse us to accept its wonderful blessing. **He whose voice then shook the earth, hath spoken, Yet once more, I will make to tremble not the earth only, but the heaven also. And this word, Yet once more, signifieth the removing of those things that are shaken, as of things that have been made, that these things which are not shaken may remain.** In that final shaking all created things will be removed, that only the things which cannot be shaken, the city that hath foundations, may remain. In that day nothing will stand but that Mount Sion, which shall never be moved, and they that dwell there.

Wherefore, receiving a kingdom that cannot be shaken. There is only one thing that cannot be shaken: the kingdom of God—that spiritual world in which His will is done and His love revealed. That kingdom we receive by faith into our hearts. *The kingdom of God is within you.* And the more our faith knows and owns, amid the things that are shaken and shall not remain, the unmovable kingdom, the more will itself become firm and steadfast, and enable us to stand unshaken and immovable too.

Wherefore, receiving a kingdom that cannot be shaken, let us have grace, whereby we may offer service well-pleasing to God, with godly fear and awe. Let us have grace—let us accept, and realise, and always hold fast the grace promised at the throne of grace (iv. 16) for every time of need. **Whereby we may offer service well-pleasing to God.** We have been cleansed by the blood from dead works to serve the living God. Our entrance into the Holiest and our drawing nigh was that we might serve Him day and night in His temple—serve Him so that we obtain the witness that our service is well-pleasing. Nothing less can satisfy either our heart or His heart. But this is what grace will indeed effect. It will not only pardon, and not only accept and cover what is defective; it will enable us to offer service well-pleasing to God. Let us have grace and faith for this; without faith it is impossible to please God.

That we may offer service well-pleasing to God with godly fear and awe: for our God is a consuming fire. Jesus was heard *for His godly fear.* Noah was *moved with godly fear.* The Father of Jesus, the God of Noah, is our God; surely it becomes us to serve Him with godly fear. It will be one of the sure fruits of grace in us. The awful realities of sin and judgment that Noah and Christ had to deal with still exist and surround us. The holiness and the glory of God, the power and the curse of sin, our own utter weakness and the terrible danger of the multitudes around us, call every Christian to offer his service to God with godly fear and awe.

For our God is a consuming fire. The fire and blackness and darkness of Sinai were but shadows—the reality will be seen when God breaks forth in His judgment on those who reject His Son. His holiness is a fire, which, by the eternal law of His nature, must consume all that is evil. His love is a fire, which must burn up and destroy all that hinders or refuses the triumph of love.

Fire may be either a blessing or a curse. All depends upon my relation to it whether it meets me as a friend or an enemy. The fire of God, as it comes to purify, to consume the sacrifice and convert it into its own heavenly light-nature, to baptize with the Holy Ghost and with fire, to transform our being into flames of love—blessed the man who knows His God as a consuming fire. But woe to him on whom the fire of God descends, as on Sodom and Gomorrah, in wrath and judgment. Oh that in the fulness of faith all believers might see and fear this impending judgment, and, moved with the compassion of Christ, give themselves to warn men and snatch them from the fire. **For our God is a consuming fire.**

1. I know almost nothing that makes one feel his own impotence more than when a sight is given of the approaching fate of so many around us, and it is as if nothing avails to arouse or save them. *Our only hope is to place ourselves persistently at His feet who is mighty to save, and wait on Him for the fire of His zeal and love to burn within us.*

2. Godly fear and awe. *"For as good as God is, so great is He; and as much as it belongeth to His Godhead to be loved, so much it belongeth to His greatness to be dreaded. And this reverent dread is the fairest worship that is in heaven before God's face. And as much as He shall be loved, overpassing that He is now, insomuch shall He be dreaded overpassing that He is now. And well I wot that the Lord has shown me no souls that love Him but those that dread Him."* (TREES PLANTED BY THE RIVER.)

CXIX.

Of Love

XIII.–1. Let love of the brethren continue.

2. Forget not to shew love unto strangers: for thereby some have entertained angels unawares.

3. Remember them that are in bonds, as bound with them; them that are evil entreated, as being ourselves also in the body.

4. Let marriage be had in honour among all, and let the bed be undefiled: for fornicators and adulterers God will judge.

At the door of the Holiest, coupled with the invitation to enter in (x. 19–25), we heard the name of the three sisters—Faith, Hope, and Love. The life into which faith leads us has been set before us in chapter xi.; that of hope and its patience in chapter xii. 1–13. We now have the life of love and good works. Our author begins with pointing out four of the chief characteristics of the life of love. These are, the love of the brethren, hospitality, sympathy with those who are in bonds or persecuted, and the love of the married state.

Let love of the brethren continue. The word love, used of God or Christ, is not found in the Epistle. It was not needed: its whole teaching is the revelation of that love. Of the love and loving care of the saints for each other mention has more than once been made. He that enters the Holiest finds there the God of love. The life and the blessing he receives is nothing but the nature of God, the love of God shed abroad in his heart. He cannot truly enter the presence of God or enter His love without finding his brethren there: he cannot but prove his love to God and his joy in God in love to his brethren. On Mount Sion is the city of God, where God makes the solitary to dwell in families: we cannot share its blessings in any way but as we share them with our fellow-citizens.

The command of our text reminds us of how love may wax cold, and how it may be sadly wanting in the Church. In divisions and separations, in indifference and neglect, in harsh judgments and unloving thoughts—alas, how little has Christ's Church proved that it has its birth from the God of love, that it owes its all to Him who loved us, gave us the new commandment of love, and asked us to prove our love to Him by bestowing it on our brethren. If our study of the Epistle has not been in vain, if we have seen or tasted aught of the power of the eternal redemption it reveals, let us yield ourselves to live lives of love. Let every child of God, be he ever so feeble or erring or unlovable, be to us the object of a deep, Christlike love. Let us show it in the humility and gentleness, the kindliness and helpfulness, with which we give ourselves to care for them and to comfort them. The life in the city of the living God is a life of love: the more we love, the more the mists will roll away and our souls see it in sunshine and beauty. The greatest of all is love: he that dwelleth in love dwelleth in God, and God in him.

Forget not to shew love unto strangers: for thereby some have entertained angels unawares. Love must prove itself in deeds. Our Lord's words: *I was a stranger, and ye took Me in,* teach us the sacredness and the blessedness of hospitality, shown not only to friends, but to those whose only claim is that they are Christ's. It is too sadly true that, with the increase of riches and luxury, the simplicity that loves to entertain strangers is often lost. Scripture lays down no rules, it only points us to the law of love. It addresses us as those who have entered the Holiest, who are come to Mount Sion, and asks us, who, apart from all worthiness or merit, have been so freely and wonderfully loved and received into the home of God, that we in turn should open our home to the stranger and the needy. The Holiest is the abode of perfect love: let him who enters live in love. Let us remember the deep spiritual mystery, that our actions often mean more than we know; we may be entertaining angels, or even their Lord: *He that receiveth you, receiveth Me.*

Remember them that are in bonds, as bound with them; them that are evil entreated, as being yourselves also in the body. We know so well in our own body that when one member suffers all the members suffer with it. The word points to loving union with Jesus and His body on earth as close and real. This feeling of sympathy may and must be as quick and real in the spiritual as in the natural body. We are to feel towards the prisoners and the persecuted as if we ourselves were suffering. We have been admitted to a life in the home and the love of God; they who abide there will learn thus to love.

Let marriage be had in honour among all, and let the bed be undefiled: for fornicators and adulterers God will judge. From the wider we are now led to the inner circle. Marriage is the God-ordained type of the love of Christ to His Church. Alas, how its holy union has been abused and defiled! Christianity raised marriage out of the deepest degradation, and made it, with the home that gathers round it, what it has been in the Christian Church. Love, the love of God in Christ alone, can keep it pure and holy.

Ye are come to the city of the living God. Let your life be one of love. Its claims appear too high and exacting, they appear impossible to one who stands outside the gate. They become the joy of him who knows what it is to have entered the rest of God, where He works all. They become the very nature of Him who has, *in fulness of faith,* accepted Jesus as His High Priest, in the power of the endless life, bringing him nigh, giving him entrance into the life of God. The covenant, of which He is the Mediator, has written on the new heart the one law of love, has given us the spirit of love.

1. *The first half of the Epistle opened our eyes to the heavenly glory of Jesus, and of that heavenly sanctuary into which He lifts us. The second shows us how we are to live that heavenly life on earth. The more a man lives in heaven, the better fitted he is to live on earth.*

2. *Love is the new nature we receive from heaven, and is renewed from heaven day by day. The fruit of the Spirit is love. When the Spirit was poured out from heaven, love filled the hearts. Let us beware of attempting to fulfil these commands of love by our own will: it is only a love given from God that can love all, at all times and in all circumstances.*

3. *Ye are not come to Mount Sinai, the life of law and effort, of strain and failure. But ye are come to Mount Sion, a life in the Holy Spirit, in the power of Jesus, in joy and strength and perfect love.*

CXX.

Of False and True Riches

XIII.–5. Be ye free from the love of money; content with such things as ye have: for himself hath said, I will in no wise fail thee, neither will I in any wise forsake thee.
6. So that with good courage we say,
   The Lord is my helper; I will not fear:
   What shall man do unto me?

The first duty the Christian who has drawn near to God in Christ has to learn is, what his relation is to his fellow-men, how his life is to be one of love. The second concerns his relation to the world and its goods. The outer world surrounds him on every side, he is in contact with it every moment. With a never-ceasing solicitation it asks his care, his interest, his affections. It tempts him with its offer of pleasure and its threat of pain; it comes to him holding life and death in its hand. The world, which was meant to be transparent with the light of God's presence and goodness, has, since sin blinded man's eyes, become the veil that hides God from him. One of the first things the Christian, who is running the race, must watch most carefully, is the power that the world has, with its lawful needs and interests and pleasures, to become the weight that keeps him back, and too often cause the loss of the prize.

In money we have the concrete embodiment of all that the possessions of the world can offer. And so in the love of money we have the very spirit of the world. Our text says: **Be ye free from the love of money.** The temptation comes so unobservedly, both to the rich man who has money, and to him who is still seeking for it. The tempter comes like a very angel of light. In money itself there is no sin. Is it not one of God's good gifts? May not the possession of it be the proof of honest labour and diligence and forethought, of self-denial and wise economy; a token of God's blessing on our work; a power to help others and benefit society. Is not poverty frequently a sign of sloth and sin? Is not money one great means for attaining God's purpose, that man should bring the whole world into subjection to himself?

Scripture knows and teaches all this. And yet it raises its voice aloud and cries: *Beware of covetousness. The love of money is a root of all kinds of evil* (1 Tim. vi. 9, 10, 16, 17, 18). So insidious is the approach and entrance of this sin, so many and specious are the arguments by which it can be cloaked and made to wear the garments of the truest virtue, that the Christian, to whom prosperity comes, needs ever to be on his guard. It is only the man who truly seeks first the kingdom of God, who longs after the utmost conformity to the Master, and seeks to be taught by Himself what and how to own, who holds all He has, not in name but in actual practice, at the disposal of Jesus, who will escape the snare. **Be content with such things as ye have.** Here is the safety of the Christian. Study well the Master's teaching in the Sermon on the Mount; learn from His Spirit in thee to breathe its spirit. Let the treasure in heaven, the being rich in God and in good works, let the blessedness of living in the love and the will of God, in the heavenly riches of a holy character, and a life of Christlike beneficence, fill the heart, and we shall be content in any lot, and shall in contentment find our safeguard against anxious care or love of money.

For Himself hath said, I will in no wise fail thee, nor in any wise forsake thee. Yes, when God is the portion of the soul, it may well be content with what it has of earth. It is the consciousness of the favour and nearness of God that makes the soul rise above all that the world can offer. To lead the truly

Christian life, the life of faith amid daily duties and daily care, we need the presence of God as our better and abiding possession. Our earthly and our heavenly life are more closely linked than we know. Too much of interest in or attachment to earthly things inevitably weakens our hold on God. True fellowship with God at once brings us into the right relation to earthly things. Let our faith study and feed on the promise: **Himself hath said, I will in no wise leave thee, nor in any wise forsake thee.** The faith that clings to its fulfilment will overcome the world.

So that with good courage we say, The Lord is my helper; I shall not fear: what shall man do unto me? God's promise ever claims an answer. Here the answer is given us with which our hearts ought to respond to His **I will in no wise leave thee;** with good courage we say, **the Lord is my helper, I shall not fear.** Let us speak the words out loud, and repeat them until we feel that they are ours. Whether it be in temporal need, or in our many spiritual requirements, we are often tempted to faint and fear. A promise of God, such as we have here, is meant for the hour of trial. Everything may at times appear very dark; we cry and no answer comes; it almost looks as if God had forgotten us. Let, in the fulness of faith, the voice of the cloud of witnesses, all bidding us be of good courage and to wait patiently, enter our hearts, and let us say: **Himself hath said, I will in no wise leave thee. Let us hold fast the confession of our hope that it waver not, for He is faithful that promised,** and boldly say, **The Lord is my helper, I will not fear.**

Free from the love of money, content with what he has, holding fast what Himself has said, and with good courage answering, **The Lord is my helper,** such is the life which the man who has entered the Holiest is able to live amid the cares and needs of daily life.

1. *The promise*—I will in no wise leave thee *was first given to Jacob, then to Joshua, and again to Solomon, and afterwards to Israel. It teaches us*

how every promise of the Old Testament may be appropriated by us. We in our daily life are to God of as deep interest as those on whom of old the working out of His purpose depended. The abiding, uninterrupted presence of God is our one great need in daily life. It is the one great blessing which in Christ is made doubly clear and sure.

2. Himself hath said: So that we say. *As we listen to and repeat what God the Everlasting has said, we shall know what to say in response, and say it with good courage.*

3. Be content: *the power that conquers the love of money, and opens the heart for the faith in God's promise and abiding presence.*

CXXI.

Jesus Christ, the Same for Ever

XIII.–7. Remember them that had the rule over you, which spake unto you the word of God; and considering the issue of their life, imitate their faith.

8. Jesus Christ is the same yesterday and today, yea and for ever.

Remember them that had the rule over you, and imitate their faith. The reference may be to teachers who had been with them for a time, and then had gone elsewhere, or to those who had been called away by death. The Hebrews are called to consider what the issue, the result, of their life had been, the impression they had left, and to imitate their faith, as the power that brought forth their life. Happy the church where the holy life and manifest faith of the leaders can be pointed to, even more than their teaching. Happy the church that imitates and emulates the faith of its leaders.

We remember the contrast we had in chapter vii. between the priests who die and are succeeded by others, and the unchanging priesthood of Jesus. The thought here of the loss of those who had taught them, but had now left them, appears to suggest the words that follow: **Jesus Christ is the same yesterday and today, yea and for ever.** There may be loss and change of men who are beloved and of great worth as teachers. Jesus we can never lose—in Him there is no change. **Jesus Christ is the same yesterday and today, yea and for ever.** Through all the changes in the Church around us, through all the changes in the spiritual life within us, He changeth not—He is ever the same.

As our faith sees and seizes hold upon this, and rests upon Him as the same for ever, it will participate in His unchangeableness; like Him it will know no change, but always be the same.

Throughout the Epistle we have now so often seen that the great defect in Christians is that there is no steadfast, certain progress, no holding fast firm to the end—they abide not continually. As with Israel in the old covenant—**they continued not in it.** And the great difference of the new covenant, the wonderful perfection of Christ's redemption and eternal priesthood is to be, that now there is to be an end to backsliding. The new life is no longer to be fitful and changing and intermittent; its measure and its power, its anchor within the veil is to be—the unceasing action of Jesus the High Priest after the power of an endless life, maintaining for us in heaven, and within us in the heart, the free, undisturbed, abiding fellowship with God. And, as we have more than once said, the only reason why so many young or earnest Christians never attain to this unchanging life is—*They do not know Jesus.* They do not know him by faith, as the Epistle has set Him before those who are pressing on to perfection—as a Priest for ever, who ever liveth to pray, and therefore every moment will watch over and keep the soul that trusts Him for it. They do not know that what He has done for one day, or one hour, He will do every day and every hour, because *yesterday and today, yea and for ever, He always is the same.*

All that He was yesterday, he is today. All that He was yesterday, in the past of the great eternity, as the object of the Father's delight, and the bearer and dispenser of the Father's life and love, He is today. All that He was yesterday, in His life upon earth, with His meek and gentle and sympathising heart, He is today. All that He has been on His throne, in sending down His Spirit, in working mighty things in and on behalf of His Church, in revealing Himself in joy unspeakable to trusting souls, in meeting and blessing you who read this—He is today. All that He is, He can be to you today. And the only reason that you ever had to look back to a yesterday that was better than today, was that you did not know, or that you failed to trust, this Jesus, who was waiting to make each today a new revelation and a larger experience of the grace of yesterday.

The same yesterday and today, **and for ever.** Yea, all that He has been He will be for ever, even from henceforth, from the present moment, and for evermore. And all that He will be for ever He is at this moment for you. Think of Him in the fullest revelation of His glory, in the inconceivable closeness of the union with Him and His love which shall be yours hereafter, and let faith say, All that he ever will be, He is today. In the external revelation there may be change and advance, in Jesus Christ Himself—none. All that He can in eternity be He is to you today—the same today and for ever. Amid all the changes in the Church and the circumstances around us, or in our heart within us, in this one word is a strength and a joy nothing can take away: **Jesus Christ, the same yesterday and today, yea and for ever.**

Today!—Even as the Holy Ghost saith, Today! Yes, *Today,* claim and trust this unchanging Jesus as your life. His unchangeableness enters into the faith that feeds upon it, and communicates itself to it; yea, imparts itself to the soul that clings to Him as such. Look not at yourself, your feelings or attainments, but at Him who changeth not. In the power of the Holy Ghost, strengthening us with might in the inner man, He, this unchanging Christ, dwells in the heart *by faith.* Let the faith that worships Him on the throne, the same for ever, rejoice in Him as the indwelling Saviour, who abideth continually, who changeth not. According to your faith be it unto you. **Even as the Holy Ghost saith, Today!**

1. Jesus Christ, for ever the same. *The power in which He gave His blood, and rose again and entered heaven, is the power in which He is working each moment in us. The reason we do not experience it is simply, because of our unbelief. Let us open our heart, the hidden depth of our inner life, to worship and receive and experience.*

2. Jesus Christ ever the Same: then my life, too, ever the Same; for Christ is my life.

3. Let us pray for the Holy Spirit's teaching, let us turn inward in stillness of soul, that He may reveal in us this unchanging Saviour as our life. There is no true knowledge of Christ but through the life of Christ in us.

4. As the Holy Jesus is but one—the same yesterday, today, and for ever—so His quickening, sanctifying Spirit in fallen man is but one, always working in one and the same power.

CXXII.

Let Us Go Forth, without the Camp

XIII.–9. Be not carried away by divers and strange teachings: for it is good that the heart be stablished by grace; not by meats, wherein they that occupied themselves were not profited.

10. We have an altar, whereof they have no right to eat, which serve the tabernacle.

11. For the bodies of those beasts, whose body is brought into the holy place by the high priest as an offering for sin, are burned without the camp.

12. Wherefore Jesus also, that He might sanctify the people through his own blood, suffered without the gate.

13. Let us therefore go forth unto him without the camp, bearing his reproach.

14. For we have not here an abiding city, but we seek after the city which is to come.

Among the Hebrew Christians many still clung to the temple and its ritual. And there were among them teachers who inculcated obedience to the laws in regard to food and to eating of the sacrifices as necessary. The writer warns against these strange teachings. **For it is good that the heart be stablished by grace, not by meats.** No outward observances can sustain the inner life: it is by grace alone, grace that comes from the throne of grace, that the heart must be established. **Let us have grace,** we read, **whereby we may offer service well-pleasing to God.** All that Christ has and gives and works in us by the Holy Spirit—this is the grace by which the heart can be confirmed, and kept from falling.

The Hebrew Christian might not think of returning to fellowship with the old sacrifices. **We have an altar, whereof they have no right to eat, which serve the tabernacle.** Our altar is the cross: the Levitical priesthood does not share in what it gives; the old and the new worship are utterly different. The old priesthood has no part in the sacrifice of the cross: the new worship no part in the old sacrifices. What is more, even **the sin-offering, of which the blood was brought into the Holy Place by the High Priest, was**—not eaten, but—**burnt without the camp.** It is not a question of eating, but of understanding what it means, the burning of the body without the camp. This we shall see in Jesus. The sin-offering, if you understand it aright, leads you to separation and rejection. **Wherefore Jesus, that He might sanctify the people through His own blood, suffered without the gate.** He was cast out of the city, as one who was indeed made sin for us. **Let us therefore go forth unto Him without the camp, bearing His reproach.** We now belong to Jesus, and fear not the rejection of those who rejected Him. **For we have not here an abiding city, but we seek after the city which is to come.**

Without the camp. This expression, which occurs three times, gives us the chief thought. We are ever inclined to seek our religion and its enjoyment in something external. And it is only to be found in *fellowship with Jesus.* His death is not only an atonement for our sins—it is that, praise God!—but only as an entrance into what is a great deal more and better. It is the way and the power, a living way of fellowship with Him, so that like Him we come to God in the path of self-sacrifice and separation from the world and death to sin. His death and life work in us as the power that makes us ready and able, even like Him, to go without the gate, to be crucified to the world, bearing his reproach.

To understand this aright, let us look at the two distinguishing features of the sin-offering on the day of atonement. The blood was brought *into the Holy Place;* the body was burnt *outside the camp.* Even so Christ's blood was brought into heaven, and is the power of our entrance and our abode there: the sign that that is our place. And the call comes: *Let us draw nigh, let us enter.* But Christ's body was brought without the camp: the sign that that is our place too. Heaven has received Him and us in Him: we belong there. The world has cast Him without the camp, and us with Him: we belong there. In heaven we share His honour; on earth His reproach. **Let us therefore go forth unto Him, without the camp, bearing His reproach.**

The camp was not Rome with its heathenism, but Jerusalem with its religion and its revelation from God. There Jesus was rejected of the Jews, because He condemned their self-righteousness and formality. It is not the irreligious but the religious world from which we must go out—that is, from everything that is not in harmony with His cross and its spirit of self-sacrifice. **Let us go forth:** not from one religious connection to another, which in time proves to have as much of the spirit of the camp. No, let us go forth **unto Him!** to closer fellowship, to more entire conformity to Him the Cross-bearer, to His meek and patient and loving spirit. Let us not cast our reproach on those we leave behind, but let us **bear**—His reproach.

Let us go forth. In the summing up of the Epistle (chap. x.) it was, **Let us draw nigh, let us enter in;** here it is, **Let us go forth.** The two words gather up all the teaching of the Epistle, all the need of the Christian life. There are two places appointed for the believer in the power of Christ's redemption—**within the veil,** to worship; **without the gate,** to witness. In both places he can count upon Christ to keep him. The deeper he enters into the spirit of the one, the more will he realise of the other. The deeper he enters within the veil, the more will he feel withdrawn from the spirit of the camp and the party. And the more he goes forth unto Him, bearing His reproach, the more will he find access through Him to enter in into His glory. In both places the boldness of which the Epistle has spoken so much will be found: the boldness in God's presence to claim Christ and be one with Him; the boldness in presence of the world to witness for Christ as one with Him. **Let us therefore go forth unto Him.**

1. *Separated from the world, separated unto God—the negative and the positive side of the Christian life; inseparably and most blessedly joined to each other. If we die with Him we shall also live with Him.*

2. *There is perhaps no greater need in our day than that God should open the eyes of His people to the solemn truth that the so-called Christian world is the very same world that rejected Christ. We are to bear to it the same relation He did.*

3. *Christ the rejected One, Christ the glorified One: the disciples were not fit to testify of Him till the Holy Spirit from heaven had revealed Him in their hearts. Much less can we, who have never seen Him, know Him in truth and power without the Holy Spirit, in the same Pentecostal fulness of life, revealing Him within us.*

CXXIII.

Well-Pleasing Sacrifices

XIII.–15. Through him then let us offer a sacrifice of praise to God continually, that is, the fruit of lips which make confession to his name.

16. But to do good and to communicate forget not: for with such sacrifices God is well pleased.

17. Obey them that have the rule over you, and submit to them: for they watch in behalf of your souls, as they that shall give account; that they may do this with joy, and not with grief: for this were unprofitable for you.

18. Pray for us: for we are persuaded that we have a good conscience, desiring to live honestly in all things.

19. And I exhort you the more abundantly to do this, that I may be restored to you the sooner.

The Hebrews were in danger, we saw this in the previous verses, of being led to seek the strengthening of their religious life in returning to the old sacrifices. They have been reminded that of the sin-offering of old, the type of Christ, nothing was eaten; it was burnt without the camp. The fellowship of Christ must be sought in another way. By His blood He sanctifies us and leads us into the Holiest; by His example and His life He leads us without the camp. This is the true fellowship of the offering of Christ. The writer will now tell us what the sacrifices are in which we may still take part. In the fellowship of Jesus and His one sacrifice, we may bring the sacrifices of praise, of deeds of love and kindness, of humility and of prayer.

Through Him then let us offer up a sacrifice of praise to God continually, that is, the fruit of lips which make confession of His name. In Hosea we find Israel saying that when God puts away their iniquities, they will render Him the offering of the fruit of their lips. These are the sacrifices God asks and is well pleased with. These we may bring continually—the fruit of lips which make confession of His name. Speech is one of man's most wonderful endowments; the power of revealing and committing himself. Christ has redeemed us wholly for Himself; our lips belong to Him, and He claims that we shall speak of Him and praise him continually. For our own sake, for His sake, for the sake of those who hear us, it is an indispensable element of a vigorous Christian life. There can be no continuous joyful life within the veil, if we do not as priests continually bring these sacrifices.

But to do good and to communicate forget not. In our Christian fellowship, and in the world around us, Christ has given us the poor and needy that we may show in them what we would like to do to Him, if He were on earth. Let the Christian study to combine a life with God in the Holiest with lips that praise and confess Him. And this, again, with deeds of love and kindness and Christian help that prove that the Spirit of Jesus is in us, that we are walking in practical fellowship with His self-sacrifice. And let every act of love and kindness be laid at God's feet as a sacrifice to Him. **For with such sacrifices God is well pleased.** They are to Him a sweeter savour than the sweetest incense. And as we offer them indeed to Him in faith, they will bring our hearts the assurance that we are well-pleasing.

Obey them that have the rule over you, and submit to them. Obedience and submission, even to men, for the Lord's sake; these, too, are elements of the self-sacrifice, which is well-pleasing to God. In the New Testament we have no longer a priestly caste, to intervene between God and men; all God's saints are priests. But we have a God-ordained ministry with the gifts and the setting apart, and the duties and the authority, of which the Acts and the Epistles teach us so fully. This is no mere human arrangement, but an appointment of Christ by the Holy Ghost, through which he carries out His work as the great Priest over the house of God. Such rulers are no lords over God's heritage, and yet have a claim to the honour due to them. The relation between the teacher and the taught is of such importance in the Church, the power of the teaching and the watching depends so much on the spirit of harmony and love, that this element of the Christian life must be carefully cultivated if we are to suffer no harm. **Obey and submit:** these are words that may not be forgotten, **for they watch in behalf of your souls, as they that shall give account.**

Pray for us: And I exhort you the more abundantly to do this, that I may be restored to you the sooner. Prayer, too, is one of the sacrifices we may offer; Jesus Himself in the garden **offered prayers and supplications.** The writer, in the very spirit in which Paul writes, not only asks for prayer, but believes that the intercession of the Church will hasten his restoration to them. Our life in the Holiest is indeed to be no selfish luxury; there is work there for us—work that calls for self-denial and self-sacrifice. Let us pray much for God's servants and all His saints; and let us be sure that nowhere may greater wonders be wrought by faith, than as it deals with God in prayer.

Christian, you are a priest! You have access into the Holiest! Christ went in with the blood of His sacrifice. Enter you continually with your sacrifice—the praise of God and the confession of His name; deeds of charity and beneficence; obedience and submission to those over you in the Lord; prayer and intercession—**through Him let us continually offer.**

1. Through Him! *God can have no communication with the creature but through Him, that is, as He is in His Son. And we can have no access to God with our service but* through Him, *that is, as we are in the Son, and He is in us. God can delight in nothing but the perfect image of His Son. Let us, by*

faith, abide in Him, and so through Him *offer continually sacrifices that are well-pleasing.* As the great High Priest, He works it in us through His Spirit.

2. Through Him *a sacrifice of praise: that is, in the joy which He gives we praise God continually.*

3. *Self-sacrifice—the power and the glory of Christ's life upon earth.* What a privilege that our whole life, like His, may be one of sacrifice too: the sacrifice of praise and confession, of love and beneficence, of humility and submission, of prayer and intercession.

CXXIV.

The God of Peace—
and What He Has Done for Us

XIII.–20. Now the God of peace, who brought again from the dead the great shepherd of the sheep in the blood of the eternal covenant, even our Lord Jesus,
21. Make you perfect.

The Epistle began by telling us that in all that Christ is and does it is God speaking in us. The great work of Christ is to bring us to God; His death and His blood, His ascension and sitting on the throne, all mean one thing—our being brought nigh to dwell in God's presence. And with what object? That God may have us, to perfect us, and work in us that which is well-pleasing in His sight. Let no one think that the entrance into the Holiest is the end, it is only the beginning of the true Christian life. It brings us into the right place and the right position, in which God now, in His divine power, can work out His own power in us, can make us in full truth one with Christ, can work the likeness of Christ into us.

We have reached the close of the Epistle. The writer gathers up all his teaching in the two verses of this beautiful closing prayer. As in it he commits his readers to God, the mention of God's name calls up all that he has said of God's work, and the first of the two verses is a summing up of all that God *has done for us* to bring us to Himself. Then follows, in the second the prayer, with its promise of all that we can count upon this God *to do in us,* that we may live worthy of Him. He points to the work God has *done for us,* as the ground and pledge of what He *will do in us.* The Epistle has revealed to us God in Christ; it seeks to send us out into life with the assurance that as wonderful and mighty and perfect as was the work of God in Christ for us, will be His work through Christ, by the Spirit, in us. Let each one who has listened to the call, **Let us draw nigh,** remember that he has been brought to God, that God may now reveal Christ in Him, and, as completely as He perfected Christ, perfect each one of us to do His will. The more we look to what God has done in Christ, as the pledge of what He will do in us, with the more confidence will our faith accept and expect it. And the more our desire is set upon the wonderful work God is yet to do in us, the more will our heart be fixed in adoration on God Himself as our hope and our joy.

The God of peace. This is the name by which we are invited to call upon and trust our God. Peace is the opposite of enmity, of war, of care, of unrest. Where everything is finished and perfect, there is peace and rest. God hath set the Holiest open for us, in token that we may enter into His rest, and trust Him to perfect His work in us. The peace of God, which passeth all understanding, can now keep our hearts and minds by Christ Jesus. Peace, an end of all care and fear and separation, has been proclaimed; the God of peace is now waiting to do His work in us.

Who brought again from the dead the great Shepherd of the sheep, in the blood of the everlasting covenant. The Epistle has nowhere directly made mention of the resurrection of Christ. But this was not needful: all its teaching was based upon the fact that He who died and shed His blood is now living in heaven. We have studied the Epistle in vain, and we shall in vain attempt to live the true Christian life, if we have not learnt that our salvation is not in the death of Jesus but in His life—in His death only as the gate to the risen life. And so the God of peace, whom we are now invited to trust in, is spoken of as He who raised Jesus, the Shepherd of the sheep, who gave His life for them, from the dead. Scripture ever points to the resurrection as the mightiest part of God's mighty power; the God of the resurrection is to be the God in whom we trust for the work to be done in us. He has raised Christ, as the Shepherd, who watches and tends His sheep, through whom He will do His work.

In the blood of the everlasting covenant. We know how the blood has been coupled in the Epistle with the redemption of transgressions, the opening of the entrance into heaven, and the cleansing of the heart from all conscience of sin. Were it not for that blood-shedding Christ had never risen from the dead. In that blood, even the blood of the everlasting covenant, which could only be made after there had been a redemption for transgressions, God raised Jesus from the dead. It was the blood that sealed the covenant, by which the covenant blessings of perfect pardon, of the law written in the heart, and direct fellowship with God were secured to us. It was the blood that had conquered sin and death and hell, that could give the entrance into heaven, and cleanse the sinner's heart for the reception and experience of the heavenly life. And as those who are sprinkled with this blood, the secret of resurrection power, we are invited to trust the God of the resurrection to work in us.

The God of peace, who hath raised Jesus from the dead in the blood of the covenant, **make you perfect in every good work to do His will.** The God who perfected His Son through suffering to do His will, until He raised Him in triumph over death to His own right hand—O soul! this same God is waiting to do this same work in thee in the same power. What He did in Christ for thee is *all for the sake of what He is now day by day to do in thee.* All that thou hast learnt of the wonders of His redeeming work, and His receiving thee into the Holiest, is that thou mightest now confidently trust and expect Him to take possession of thee and perfect His work within thee. Oh, let us draw nigh and enter in, in the restful, adoring assurance that God will perfect us in every good thing.

1. Peace is rest. To know the God of peace is to enter the rest of God. And until the soul rests in Him in Sabbath peace, God cannot do His higher, His perfect work.

2. The work of the Father and the Son for us find their completion in the work of the Holy Spirit within us. All the objective revelation is for the sake of the subjective experience, the mighty power of God working in the heart of His child what He longs to see. It is in what God makes us, that the power of the redemption in Christ is proved.

3. By faith. Here more than ever this must be our watchword. Faith that sees and accepts and dwells in all God has done for us in Christ, and then counts upon His faithfulness and power to make it all real within us in Christ through the Spirit.

4. As it was through the Spirit that God wrought that perfect work in Christ by which fallen human nature, as He had taken it upon Himself, was redeemed and raised up and glorified, so nothing can make us partakers of that redeeming and quickening power but that same Spirit, truly living and working in our soul and body, in the same manner as it did in the humanity of Christ.

CXXV.

The God of Peace—What He Will Do in Us

XIII.–20. The God of peace. . . .

21. Make you perfect in every good thing to do his will, working in us that which is well-pleasing in his sight, through Jesus Christ; to whom be the glory for ever and ever. Amen.

In our last meditation we saw what the link is between the two verses of this wonderful benediction. All that God has done in the redemption in Christ is for the sake of what He wishes to effect in our heart. All that He makes known to us of that redemption is to bring us to trust and yield ourselves to Him—to work out the inner, the subjective redemption in the same power in which the objective, the heavenly redemption, has been effected. The Father longs to have back again the man He lost in paradise, His image and likeness restored within us. All that Christ hath done on earth and in heaven, even to His sitting at His right hand, cannot satisfy the heart of God until He sees the kingdom set up within our heart. There the true power and glory of the Son are manifested.

The God of peace make you perfect in every good thing to do His will. To do His will. This, then, is the object of all that God has done. That the Son, who is God, should be our Redeemer; that the stupendous miracles of the incarnation and the atonement, the resurrection and the seating of a man on the throne of God, should be wrought, that the Holy Spirit of God should be poured out from heaven—all was with one view, that we should *be brought to do the will of God.* The whole relation between God and the creature depends on this one thing: without it there can be no true fellowship with God. It was for this Jesus became man: *Lo, I come to do thy will, O God.* It was through this He redeemed us. It is to make us partakers of the power to do this, that, as Mediator of the covenant, He puts the law in our heart, that we may do the will of God on earth as in heaven. *It is for this alone He lives in heaven:* the only proof and measure of the success of His work is *that we do the will of God.* Without this, all His work and ours is in vain.

Now the God of peace make you perfect in every good work to do His will. The doing of God's will depends entirely upon God's fitting us for it. As truly as God Himself perfected Christ and wrought out the redemption in Him, must God perfect us to do His will. As surely as He did the first, He will do the second. The word "perfect" used here means, to put into the right position or condition, to readjust, to equip, to fit a thing perfectly for its purpose. The prayer, **God make you perfect in every good thing,** teaches that the work of God is not only a general enabling or endowing with power, leaving to us its use and application, but that He must perfect us in each one of the good things we have to do; so alone can we do His will. It calls us to an absolute dependence upon the Father, as Jesus meant, when He said, *The Son can do nothing of Himself.* It seeks to bring us to a helplessness and a humility that just yields itself to God for every moment, and counts upon Him, even as He wrought out the great salvation in Christ as a whole, to work it in us in each minutest particular. With God nothing is small or insignificant. He must be in things, little as great, All in All.

Working in you that which is pleasing in His sight, through Jesus Christ. Here we have the explanation of how He perfects in us every good thing: *He works in us through Jesus Christ.* The three persons of the Godhead are indivisibly and inseparably one. The Father works through the Son and the Holy Spirit. When Jesus, our Priest-King, ascended the throne, He sent from the Father the Holy Spirit to be within us, the power and life of His redemption in heaven. Then the ministration of the Spirit, of the inner life, began upon earth—God working in men what is pleasing in His sight, through Jesus Christ dwelling in the heart. Then the fruit of Christ's work was made manifest; men on earth in very deed doing the will of God, and working what was pleasing in His sight, because He Himself worked it in them, through Jesus Christ.

Let this parting prayer teach us a double lesson, It is a promise of what God will do. *He will perfect us*—put us in the right position, and give us the right condition of heart—**in every good thing, to do His will**—Himself **working in us that which is well-pleasing in His sight, through Jesus Christ.** Let us read the words until we know in truth what God is waiting to do. The prayer becomes then a call to us to prayer and faith. Let us fix our hearts in faith on God and what He has wrought through Christ for us. Let us fix them in faith on what He will do in us through Christ, as surely and as mightily. *All that God has done in Christ is only a beginning, a promise, a pledge of what He will do in us.* Let that faith stir our desire to rest content with nothing less than the actual experience of the truth of this prayer-promise. Let that faith begin in prayer to claim and embrace and own it as our very own, waiting in deep dependence and humility on God to do it. And let every thought of the teaching of the Hebrews just culminate in a blessed act of adoring surrender. O Thou, God of Peace! here I am, thou wilt do it.

1. God working in us. *Look upward in wonder and worship. Turn inward in stillness and meekness of heart, taking time to yield to the Spirit's working. And regard thy heart as indeed the sphere of the working of the living God.*

2. Pray, pray, pray! *The blessing of the Epistle, the power of redemption, must come from above. It comes certainly to the heart open towards God and thirsting for Him.*

3. Make you perfect: *fit you perfectly to be subject to Him, and in dependence and humility and faith to work what He works in you. It is often a*

misapprehension or a difficulty that hinders. God can restore you in one moment to the right relation or position.

4. A road is only good for that to which it brings as its end. The whole gospel is nothing but a way to this end; God finding His place in our heart to dwell and work there that which is pleasing in His sight, so that we do His will.

CXXVI.

To Whom Be Glory for Ever

XIII.–21. Working in you that which is pleasing in His sight, through Jesus Christ; to whom be the glory for ever and ever. Amen.

To whom be the glory for ever and ever. No wonder that the heart of the author bursts out in adoration. In the closing prayer he had summed up all the glory of what God had done in Christ, and was now waiting to work in us. He has pronounced over his readers the blessing of the God who hath revealed Himself in His Son, and longs to reveal Himself in us for our complete deliverance, and his whole soul blows in wonder, joy, and worship. The sight of the God who has raised Jesus from the dead, drawing nigh to do His mighty work in us too, brings the song to His lips: **To Him be glory for ever and ever!** Oh that we may ever learn so to study and admire and appropriate the mysteries of redeeming grace that every mention of it leads to the spontaneous outburst: *Glory be to God!*

It is doubtful whether the **whom** refers to God or to Christ. It appears more probable that the writer meant God, to whom and whose glorious work the whole prayer refers. But the question will cause us no difficulty. In Scripture the same adoration is given to the Son as to the Father (see 2 Tim. iv. 13; 2 Pet. iii. 18; Rev. i. 6). The throne is that of God and the Lamb. All the honour that goes up to the Father goes through the Son; He shares in it. And all the honour given to the Son, goes through

Him to the Father. It is ever of God in Christ we say, **To whom be glory**.

Without this note of praise it is as if there would have been something wanting in the Epistle. In God's temple the chief thing is the praise and honour of Him who dwells there. The Epistle has opened up to us the way into the Holiest. It has spoken to us of the glory of the Priest-King whom God has set at His own right hand, for our sakes, and of His all-prevailing blood, and of the entrance we have into God's presence for Him to reign and work in us, and fit us to enjoy and to serve Him. It has spoken of the continual sacrifice of praise we ought to render. And yet the writer has never sounded a note of praise. But here, at last, when he calls us to look back to all that God has done for us, and forward to all that He will do in us, the voice of adoration sounds forth: **To Him be glory for ever and ever.** The joy of heaven consists in this that they rest not day nor night in the worship and praise of God and the Lamb; if we are indeed come to Mount Sion, and into the very presence of God Himself, let our life and walk ever be in the spirit of adoration: **To Him be glory for ever!** The man who has not learned to praise, with whom it never breaks out spontaneously, has not learned to know his God aright, has not yet tasted the joy of a full salvation.

If we would learn the secret of a life giving glory to God, on earth as in heaven, it must be found in the faith and the experience spoken of in the prayer to which this doxology belongs. The praise was born out of it, in the heart of the writer; it must be so with our hearts too. The more we gaze upon Christ our Priest-King, and upon His precious, cleansing, saving blood, and upon the new covenant, sealed in that blood, and the new heart with God's Spirit in it as our law, and upon God Himself who hath done it all, the more we shall feel urged to fall down and worship, **To Him be glory for ever and ever.** But especially as we claim and realise and yield ourselves to the promise which is the outcome of this great redemption, **God perfect you in ev-**

ery good thing to do His will, working in you that which is pleasing in His sight, our hearts will swell with joy unspeakable and praise unutterable, that can only find relief in the cry, To Him be glory, to Him be glory!

I know that it is just here a difficulty will come to many. The promise appears so high, and its fulfilment in their experience, God perfecting them in every good thing, so impossible, that even the praise which came, when they thought upon what God had done, passes away. Let me speak one word to such. Just look at this great universe. The God who made it all, the sun and moon and stars, the mighty mountains and the great ocean; this God cares for every blade of grass and gives it its life and beauty. The greatest and the least are alike to Him; He cares for the whole and for each minute detail. And, even so, He who wrought out the mighty redemption in Christ is now still working out, in the same power and love, its application in every soul, in every moment and in every circumstance. God has not done part, and left part dependent on us. God is all, and must in very deed do all. As the God of peace, who raised Christ from the dead, He must work in you every good thing that can be pleasing in His sight. And He will do it. What He began in Christ, He will finish in you. A great artist attends to the minutest details. God is engaged, as He perfected Christ the Head, in perfecting every member of His body. He does this by Himself working in us. The Spirit of God's Son sent into our heart as an inward life, Christ dwelling in our heart, God working in us— oh, it is when this is believed, and waited for, and in some measure experienced, that the whole life becomes a song of praise: To Him be glory for ever and ever!

Brother! Having boldness through the blood, let us draw nigh, and dwell in God's presence. Let us worship Him for what He hath done. Let us in tenderness of spirit adore Him as the God who is working in us through Christ Jesus. Let us in deep humility yield ourselves to Him, to be made so fully one with

Christ that Christ may be seen to dwell in us. And the flame of God's love will break out and burn and rise heavenward without ceasing: **To Him be glory! to Him be glory for ever and ever!**

1. As in heaven so on earth. *What God hath wrought in heaven, through Christ, is the pledge of what He will work in my heart. As I receive this into my heart, His will will be done in me, on earth as in heaven, because He does it Himself. And as in heaven, so in my heart, the praise will never end.*

2. My heart, *the temple where God dwells and reveals His work and His glory; all in the hidden power of the Holy Spirit.*

3. To Him be glory for ever and ever! *Lord Jesus! the great High Priest beside the altar, the minister of the sanctuary, it is Thy care that the fire ever burns, and the song never ends, to the glory of the Father.*

CXXVII.

Parting Words

XIII.–22. But I exhort you, brethren, bear with the word of exhortation: for I have written unto you in a few words.

23. Know ye that our brother Timothy hath been set at liberty; with whom, if he come shortly, I will see you.

24. Salute all them that have the rule over you, and all the saints. They of Italy salute you.

25. Grace be with you all. Amen.

These closing verses are so entirely in the spirit of Paul, that involuntarily we feel as if we were listening to him. The mention of a Timothy, of his deliverance and of the hope of accompanying him, the greeting to the rulers in the Church and to all the saints, the greetings from the saints of Italy, and the final benediction, all remind us of what we find in his Epistles.

I exhort you, brethren, bear with the word of exhortation. Ere the writer closes, one more word of exhortation, and that is, to bear, to submit to and accept the exhortation he has sent them. The word he uses means both admonition or reproof (so xii. 5), and encouragement (so vi. 18). The Epistle has combined both elements most remarkably. In the five warnings, and in its hortatory parts, its tone has been one of faithful reproof, with a view to convict of sin, to awaken to a sense of danger, and to urge to repentance. At the same time, everything has been done to quicken faith and hope, and to urge to steadfastness by pointing to the strong encouragement to be found in the word of God and the power of Christ.

557

To us the closing message comes too: **Bear,** yield yourselves to, **the word of exhortation.** Exhortation is indeed the main characteristic of the Epistle. It comes to us as an intensely practical, personal appeal, to give ourselves wholly to the Son of God from heaven, and to live the heavenly life He offers to work within us. We may gather up its chief thoughts in four of the words it has used more than once.

Take heed! Its tone is one of solemn warning against the danger of negligence and sloth, disobedience and double-mindedness, unbelief and falling away. Let us yield to its discovery of sin and danger. Let us beware lest the contentment with beginnings, a resting short of an entire devotion to God and perfect conformity to Jesus, a selfish desire to have salvation and heaven without the very Spirit of Christ and of heaven, deceive us, so that, like Israel, we perish half-way between Egypt and Canaan.

Press on! Let us accept its teaching of what the true aim of the Christian life is. We are to give due diligence to enter and dwell in the rest of God. We are to press on to perfection; to be like men running a race for life. We are to take Jesus as our Leader and Forerunner, to follow Him in the path of perfect obedience to God's will, and entire self-sacrifice. We are to enter with Him into the Holiest, to make God's presence our home, and His fellowship our daily portion and our chief joy. We are to be like the old saints, to go out from our home, to live in the pilgrim spirit, seeking a heavenly country. Yea, we are to live as those who are come to the heavenly Jerusalem. We are to go forth to Him without the camp bearing His reproach, wholly identified with Him. Let us press on. Let us run. Let us enter in. Let us go forth. This is what the exhortation means.

Consider Jesus. The one sure and effectual remedy the Epistle offers for all the prevailing feebleness and danger of the Christian life, we know. It has been said to us, You do not know Jesus aright. The knowledge that sufficed for conversion, does

not avail for sanctification and perfection. You must know Jesus
better. **Consider Jesus!** As God! As Man! In His sympathy! In
His obedience! In His suffering! In His blood! In His glory on
the throne; opening heaven; bringing you in to God; breathing
the law of God and the Spirit of heaven into your heart, as your
very life! As little as you can reach heaven with your hand, can
you of yourself live such a heavenly life. And yet it is possible,
because God has borne witness to the Gospel of His Son with
the gift of the Holy Ghost. The Priest-King, on His ascension to
the throne, sent down the Holy Spirit into the hearts of His disciples, and with Him returned Himself to dwell in them, that in
the power of His heavenly life they might live with Him. **Consider Jesus!** and you will see that you can live in the heavenlies
with Him, because He lives in you.

By faith! This word is the key to all. **By faith! in fulness of
faith!** we can inherit every promise. Faith is moved with godly
fear, and takes heed! Faith obeys and forsakes all, and presses
on to enter the land! Faith looks to Jesus, holds fast its boldness,
and draws nigh to God, and goes forth without the camp. Faith
sees how in Christ God has worked out His will, sees that this
God will just as surely work in us too what is pleasing in His
sight, and conquers every difficulty and every enemy. By faith
we inherit every promise, and dare to sing even now: *To Him be
glory for ever and ever!*

*1. You will find it most profitable to look back over the whole Epistle, and
see whether you have grasped its teaching. And then to say whether you are
making it the one aim of your life to live up fully to its glorious revelation of
the life of God.*

*2. The Holiest of All is the title of our book. I think you see how it ex-
presses the central thought of the Epistle. It is the spiritual life-state into
which Jesus entered, and opened the way for you, and calls you to enter in.
Have you entered? Are you dwelling there? Are you there now daily drinking
in the Holy Spirit of Jesus, yielding to the Father to make you perfectly conformed to the humble, obedient, holy Jesus, your Leader and Forerunner?*

Oh, rest not without a full experience of the heavenly priesthood of Jesus, and of the heavenly sanctuary as your abode.

3. Grace be with you all, beloved readers; all the grace this Epistle has so wondrously revealed; all the day and for all and every need. With all of you, not one excepted—Amen.